THE END OF STRATEGIC STABILITY?

Also from Georgetown University Press

*The Future of Extended Deterrence: The United States,
NATO, and Beyond*
Stéfanie von Hlatky and Andreas Wenger, Editors

North Korea and Nuclear Weapons: Entering the New Era of Deterrence
Sung Chull Kim and Michael D. Cohen, Editors

Nuclear Authority: The IAEA and the Absolute Weapon
Robert L. Brown

*Strategy in the Second Nuclear Age: Power, Ambition,
and the Ultimate Weapon*
Toshi Yoshihara and James R. Holmes, Editors

When Proliferation Causes Peace: The Psychology of Nuclear Crises
Michael D. Cohen

THE END OF STRATEGIC STABILITY?

NUCLEAR WEAPONS AND THE CHALLENGE OF REGIONAL RIVALRIES

LAWRENCE RUBIN AND
ADAM N. STULBERG, EDITORS

GEORGETOWN UNIVERSITY PRESS
Washington, DC

Library of Congress Cataloging-in-Publication Data

Names: Rubin, Lawrence, 1973- editor. | Stulberg, Adam N., 1963– editor.
Title: The End of Strategic Stability? : Nuclear Weapons and the Challenge of
   Regional Rivalries / Lawrence Rubin and Adam N. Stulberg, editors.
Description: Washington, DC : Georgetown University Press, 2018. | Includes
   index.
Identifiers: LCCN 2017053582 (print) | LCCN 2018017535 (ebook) | ISBN
   9781626166042 (ebook) | ISBN 9781626166028 q(hardcover : qalk. paper)
| ISBN 9781626166035 q(pbk.: qalk. paper)
Subjects: LCSH: Nuclear crisis stability. | Nuclear weapons—Government
   policy. | Strategic forces. | Deterrence (Strategy) | Security,
   International. | Military policy.
Classification: LCC U263 (ebook) | LCC U263 .E557 2018 (print) | DDC
   355/.033—dc23
LC record available at https://lccn.loc.gov/2017053582

19 18   9 8 7 6 5 4 3 2   First printing

Printed in the United States of America

Cover design by Pam Pease

CONTENTS

ACKNOWLEDGMENTS

AFTER THE COLD WAR, scholarship and policy analyses seemed to drift away from issues concerning nuclear security. The subsequent September 11, 2001, terrorist attacks and the wars in Afghanistan and Iraq drew US policymakers' attention toward counterterrorism, largely at the expense of investing in expertise in nuclear proliferation. Today, both the academy and policymaking communities find themselves again preoccupied with challenges presented by the nuclear equation.

However, unlike during the first nuclear revolution, more attention now centers on the regional dimension of nuclear strategy and interaction. The nuclear ambitions of Iran and North Korea—coupled with the competing local agendas, stakes, and enduring rivalries among the nuclear possessor states; the strategic considerations vis-à-vis nuclear energy aspirant states; and the diffusion of emerging technologies with strategic effects—have seemingly shifted the center of gravity for nuclear strategy, crisis bargaining, and arms racing from the global US-Soviet/Russian perspective to diverse, asymmetric, multilateral, and cross-domain regional contexts. The contributors to this volume embraced the challenge of this shifting landscape, relaxing conventional wisdom and extending their analyses of national nuclear postures and deterrence, so they could grapple with the complexities and opportunities presented by diverse understandings and interactions among key regional powers.

This volume grew out of and derived intellectual sustenance from the Program on Strategic Stability Evaluation (POSSE), which Adam Stulberg codirected with William C. Potter of the Middlebury Institute of International Studies in Monterey, California. POSSE strove to renew interdisciplinary, international scholarship on issues of strategic stability in an era when nuclear weapons were no longer the main event but nonetheless cast diverse and weighty shadows. This effort stimulated novel, policy-relevant scholarship and nurtured dialogue between the next generation of international scholars from the United States, the Russian Federation, the People's Republic of China, India, Pakistan, France, and Israel. The global network of scholars systematically probed new criteria for strategic stability that could fill knowledge gaps in traditional frameworks in order to address a variety of strategic choices and outcomes, ranging from the escalation of subconventional conflict to the possible elimination of nuclear weapons.

We wish to thank the numerous individuals and organizations that inspired and facilitated our efforts to bring this volume to fruition. The generous and sustained financial support for POSSE provided by the Carnegie Corporation of New York was invaluable, if not prescient. The funding created stimulating and open settings for our contributors to generate, exchange, critique, and refine new ideas; engage with senior and working-level policymakers and diplomats (who often represented rival national perspectives); and forge lasting professional contacts. We thank Stephen J. Del Rosso for his initial support, and we owe deep gratitude to Carl Robichaud for his unwavering and enthusiastic endorsement all along the way. At the Georgia Institute of Technology, Joseph Bankoff, chair of the Sam Nunn School of International Affairs, provided important encouragement and administrative relief, while Marilu Suarez and Maria Hugee wielded deft logistical and budgetary hands to ensure that related workshops in Washington and Monterey, California, got off without a hitch. It is safe to say that the book project simply would have languished without the tireless and unflappable administrative, research, editorial, and logistical prowess of Chris McDermott, POSSE's right-hand man. In addition, several academic colleagues offered guidance and constructive critique of various chapters, and we express our appreciation to Robert Brown, T.V. Paul, William Potter, Nikolai Sokov, Christopher Twomey, and Jon Wolfsthal as well as to two anonymous external reviewers. John Krzyzaniak provided insightful comments and excellent editorial assistance throughout the course of this project. We also wish to acknowledge the input, if not practical correctives, provided by numerous officials at the US Department of State, the Department of Defense, the National Security Council, and the Joint Chiefs of Staff, who actively engaged with and challenged our contributors. Of course, as coeditors, we are deeply appreciative of the commitment to this book project extended by each of the authors, as well as the encouragement and oversight of the publication process by Don Jacobs at Georgetown University Press.

Finally, we owe very special thanks to our life partners, Cara Gilbert and Adi Rubin. Their encouragement, prodding, sympathy, and enduring support gave tangible meaning to the word "stability" that enabled us to cross the finish line. This book is dedicated to them.

Introduction

ADAM N. STULBERG AND
LAWRENCE RUBIN

"LET IT BE AN ARMS RACE. We will outmatch them at every pass and outlast them all," president-elect Donald Trump quipped on the *Morning Joe* MSNBC television show a week after he tweeted about the need to greatly expand the US nuclear arsenal. This followed carping about the pointlessness of manufacturing nuclear weapons that could not be used.[1] Upon election, President Trump submitted a budget that projected an increase in strategic modernization funding by over 20 percent of that proposed by the preceding Obama administration. The Pentagon, in turn, was instructed to undertake a new *Nuclear Posture Review*, framed to ensure US deterrence that is "modern, robust, flexible, resilient, ready, and appropriately tailored"—terms generally associated with enhancing rather than maintaining existing capabilities.[2] These remarks, including open discussions of missile and warhead replacement programs coupled with reduced funding for arms control and dismantlement, roiled national security circles both at home and abroad. The incoming US administration seemed intent on reversing almost four decades of efforts to reduce the nuclear stockpile and avoid loosely considering their use.

However, before his appointment as secretary of defense, General James A. Mattis offered what appeared to be a clarion call for new strategic thinking. In 2015 testimony before the US Senate, Mattis challenged the American national security establishment to think about moving from a triad to a dyad in an effort to reduce the danger of a false alarm response.[3] In contrast to the prevailing views of the current administration, this represents a very different strategic outlook. In short, there is a great deal of confusion about the strategic direction of the contemporary US nuclear arsenal. Although some underscore the need to recapitalize capabilities and fan unpredictability, others opine that such provocative actions and failure to fundamentally restructure the nuclear stockpile will be destabilizing for global peace and security.

Russia's contemporary leaders also send conflicting nuclear signals. President Vladimir Putin flaunted Russia's nuclear prowess during the height of the Crimean crisis in 2014. He warned the United States and its NATO allies that "it is best not to mess with us. . . . I want to remind you that Russia is one of the leading nuclear powers."[4] This statement coincided with Russia's testing and deployment of a ground-launched cruise missile, in violation of the 1987 Intermediate-Range Nuclear Forces Treaty, that put Poland and Lithuania within striking distance of Russia's tactical nuclear force. These actions catalyzed discussions in Moscow about the utility of using low-yield nuclear weapons to terminate a conventional conflict on terms favorable to Russia. Yet, at the same time, Putin expressed willingness to cooperate with the incoming Trump administration. "I hope after you assume the position of the president of the United States of America that we will be able—by acting in a constructive and pragmatic manner—to take real steps to restore the framework of bilateral cooperation in different areas as well as bring our level of collaboration on the international scene to a qualitatively new level."[5] This was followed by an on again / off again agreement during the first half of 2017 to resume high-level talks on strategic stability that vied with reciprocal economic sanctions and other political differences for center stage in efforts to recast the US-Russian relationship.

How can we make sense of the contradictions emanating from atop the nuclear order? Do reciprocal fears of a surprise attack animate thinking and behavior about nuclear use? If nuclear weapons were once pillars of mutual security between the superpowers during the Cold War, what do these contending escalatory and conciliatory gestures say about the foundations of strategic stability today? Is the concept malleable and still meaningful in the post–Cold War era? If so, what will it look like in the next ten to fifteen years?

"Strategic stability" is a common frame of reference for how nuclear weapons affect global peace and security. It turns the destructiveness of nuclear weapons technology into a foundation for coexistence among rival possessor states. Rather than touting surprise and victory as principles of warfare among hostile great powers, the crux of strategic stability rests with reducing the need and incentives for arms racing or delivering a devastating first blow in a crisis. Stability requires that rivals have confidence that each party could achieve its aims through retaliation, and not by exploiting a perceived advantage.

However, historically, strategic stability is not this simple. Throughout the Cold War, US and Soviet nuclear doctrines, military force postures, targeting strategies, and arms control policies often were misaligned—both internally, with respective grand strategies, and externally, with their foreign policies, capabilities, and intelligence estimates. Such disconnects contributed decisively to two crises, in 1962 and 1983, that brought the United States and the Soviet Union to the brink of nuclear war.[6]

These strategic inconsistencies surrounding nuclear weapons are especially conspicuous amid complex and countervailing post–Cold War global trends. On one hand, the collapse of the Soviet Union raised the promise of radical force reductions. Global trade, the spread of technology and information, and enhanced communications continue to flourish—all factors presumed to improve stability. On the other hand, significant numbers of nuclear weapons persist and the quality of possessor state arsenals is steadily improving. Moreover, the landscape of global nuclear politics today is marred by a host of factors—the mounting tensions in US-Russian relations after a period of cooperation on nuclear security; the modernization of China's nuclear arsenal and its assertiveness in the South China Sea; North Korea's ongoing nuclear testing and missile development; the recurrent cross-border attacks and tension between India and Pakistan; and the renewed interest in nuclear energy, especially among aspirant states in the Middle East and Southeast Asia. Symptomatic of the current palpable anxiety, experts at the *Bulletin of the Atomic Scientists* welcomed 2017 by moving the infamous Doomsday Clock forward 30 seconds, to two and a half minutes to midnight, signifying the greatest risk of nuclear war since the height of the Cold War in 1953.[7]

For many international security policy experts and scholars, however, the global nuclear order continues to rest on classic strategies of deterrence and conditions of strategic stability aimed at arresting mutual fears or temptations to launch disarming preemptive nuclear strikes. The proponents claim that during the Cold War, both the US and Soviet strategic communities broadly adhered to core intellectual precepts that could penetrate the fog of confrontation to prevent crises and arms races from spinning out of control. Given the unique and universal destructive power of nuclear weapons, these foundational strategic paradigms can be readily absorbed and adapted across regions and political relationships in the post–Cold War era, under the right conditions.[8] Conversely, the detractors contend that strategic stability offered little as an organizing principle, even during the heyday of the bipolar Cold War. The growing complexity of multilateral and multidimensional relationships among numerous nuclear powers only intensifies the problems. This critique derives sustenance from today's competitive nuclear landscape, which is characterized by the dangerously close encounters between US and Russian military forces in and around Europe and Syria, the mounting anxiety in Beijing about the efficacy of Washington's missile defense systems, ongoing nuclear modernization in India and Pakistan, the potential spread of nuclear weapons latency, and the prominence of asymmetric regional threats.[9] However, for all the intellectual, practical, and technical handwringing, strategic stability persists as the lodestar for assessing changes to force posture, risk of escalation, and prospects for arms control among rival nuclear weapons states. As summed up in a 2016 report by the International Security Advisory Board to the US State Department, the prevention of nuclear war, whether by deliberate decision or unintended escalation, will ultimately hinge on new conceptual frameworks for extending the "characteristics and practices" of strategic stability among many pairs of nuclear-armed states.[10]

The purpose of this book, therefore, is to unpack and examine the contemporary meaning and significance of strategic stability. How well has the concept held up and adapted to new realities? With the strategic terrain in flux, has its relevance indeed decreased? Alternatively, are there factors amid changing contexts that sustain, if not elevate, its pertinence? In short, is the concept of strategic stability an anachronism—a contested intellectual artifact of the unique confluence of nuclear weaponry and the bipolar Cold War paradigm? Or does it offer a prism for making sense of the complex contemporary nuclear and strategic relationships, if not a benchmark for guiding future collective action? If so, to whom, how, and to what strategic effect?

STRATEGIC STABILITY REVISITED IN THE SECOND NUCLEAR AGE

A central theme of this book is that there is no consensus on what the term "strategic stability" means, despite its widespread use. It connotes different things to different actors in different contexts. However, we can gain purchase on this term's traction by understanding where it came from, how it evolved, and where we are with it today.

To be clear, there are two main and generalizable components at the heart of strategic stability. First, strategic stability refers to a condition in which adversaries understand that altering military force posture in response to vulnerability—whether to avoid being emasculated or to preempt one's opponent—would be either futile or foolish.[11] Second, strategic stability reflects the ease with which nuclear-armed adversaries can return to stable relations after a period of escalation. Actors can maintain strategic stability even in a crisis by not responding to a provocative action. The ability to delay a response is bolstered by the actor's confidence in its retaliatory strike. Conversely, instability can be caused by a perception or uncertainty that one side may exploit advantages to steal the initiative, and that the costs incurred by hesitating will be outweighed by the advantages of acting precipitously. Factors that enhance surprise, vulnerability, and damage limitation and that create perceptions or realities of unreliable command and control, accidental launch, or uncontrolled action/reaction may also destabilize. A "delicate" balance illustrates how drivers of stability and instability are related, and how pernicious the predicament can become if disturbed.[12]

These considerations generated exacting criteria that informed Cold War thinking on military force modernization, deterrence, and arms control. They also constituted an important subset of the broader calculus of "crisis stability" that extended beyond the nuclear realm, intermingling with factors related to aggregate power positions and the pathologies of decision making to distort strategic calculations, perceptions, and incentives for escalation in international confrontations.[13]

Despite the elegance of the concept, the underlying assumptions for and practical significance of strategic stability remain contested. The concept has been treated as a broad condition for avoiding war or establishing peace, promoted as a national objective to inform specific strategies, and relied on as a benchmark for assessing alternative ways of achieving foreign policy objectives. Moreover, stability is often conflated with deterrence that pertains to specific national strategies for discouraging an adversary's aggression (typically, through threats of punishment or denial) against core national and allied interests. These distinctions are important. Strategic stability applies to the consequences of reciprocal fears and incentives confronting adversaries, whereas deterrence rests with efforts to shape the calculus of one rival by another. Moreover, the two concepts can work at cross purposes. For example, the introduction of specific technologies—such as long-range, standoff cruise missiles—can bolster deterrence by augmenting the survivability of the bomber leg of the US triad. The same systems, however, can be potentially destabilizing by stoking an adversary's first-strike fears, owing to the greater stealth, precision, and lower yield of the American nuclear bomber force. Accordingly, naysayers take exception to the concept of strategic stability altogether, deeming it to be a danger to effective national deterrence strategies that employ highly accurate and lethal delivery capabilities to discourage nonnuclear aggression.[14]

The meaning of strategic stability also changed over the course of the Cold War. The components of this concept evolved to encompass contending elements of surprise, survivability, mutual vulnerability, and parity.[15] This rendered respective dimensions of strategic stability inconsistent. The goal of first-strike stability, as noted above, fit poorly with limiting damage if deterrence were to fail or with credibly extending deterrence to allies. Efforts to reduce the risk of a massive nuclear attack exacerbated the incentives for adversaries to engage in lower levels of aggression, including attacks on highly valued allies, while obfuscating the risks of crossing redlines between conventional and nuclear operations.[16] In addition, abstract models of strategic stability did not directly translate into Cold War nuclear force planning, targeting, doctrine, or arms control; bureaucratic politics and political considerations may have also affected these policy outcomes.[17]

Compounding this confusion, the US and Soviet strategic communities maintained different understandings of nuclear stability. Neither first-strike stability, nor mutual vulnerability, nor parity sat well with the Soviet High Command, which preferred to blunt the threat of perceived US nuclear coercion and bolster the political utility of its own nuclear arsenal by embracing notions of damage limitation and war fighting. Soviet nuclear superiority was the foundation for long-term stability vis-à-vis otherwise politically hostile relations among conflicting social and class systems.[18]

What little consensus evolved about the meaning and attributes of strategic stability during the Cold War seemingly broke down when it ended. The relative simplicity of the US-Soviet dyad gave way to what is now often referred to as the "second nuclear age." As summed up by Paul Bracken, this era is characterized by "shifting great powers, rising regional powers, and great uncertainty about the shape of world order."[19] The second nuclear age introduces new levels of complexity associated with managing multifaceted arms races, crises, and strategic competition among nuclear near-peers and non-peers, while altering the political and relative power dimensions between the United States and Russia carried over from the earlier era. This varied and asymmetric nuclear geometry challenges the fundamentals on which classic legacy concepts such as strategic stability were predicated, and thus warrants a reassessment.

There are a number of reasons why the second nuclear revolution is different. First, the absence of a systemwide global political rivalry leads many to assume that nuclear weapons are much less relevant now than they were in the past. This thinking presents a dilemma for nuclear crisis management because these weapons are either too blunt or too accessible to wield in the delicate process of controlling incentives for escalation. On one hand, nuclear weapons appear too weakly tied to conflict to impose discipline on crisis behavior. As underscored by scholars such as John Mueller, the value and prominence of nuclear weapons recede "as international status becomes determined by more economic and other nonmilitary factors, and as the world becomes dominated by non-threatening, wealth seeking countries."[20] This condition, for example, fundamentally altered the strategic objectives and relationship between the United States and contemporary Russia, rendering remote the risk of a surprise all-out nuclear first strike conducted by either side. On the other hand, lowered barriers to entry into the nuclear club and expanding plausible use scenarios attendant on the very processes of globalization intensify, if not inflame, enduring rivalries and empower nonstate actors, thus making regional conflicts potentially even more dangerous for peer, near peer, and nonpeer regional actors alike. As new nuclear players face shifting balances of power and security threats from diverse opponents—both outside and within a region—strategic calculations based on nuclear dyads are seemingly anachronistic for restoring equilibrium at the crux of strategic stability.[21]

Second, asymmetry and uncertainty distinguish the contemporary nuclear context from the past. Russia's and China's leaders today seem willing to run military risks to remake regional orders and preserve local spheres of influence in response to perceptions of unconstrained encroachment by the United States and its allies. Professed asymmetries of resolve and distance, coupled with sophisticated military buildups designed to challenge US forward presence, fuel respective nuclear brinkmanship on these critical regional issues.[22] Similarly, because regional nuclear powers possess smaller arsenals that are often engaged in local conflicts and have weaker political institutions, they make different choices about their nuclear postures that, in turn, carry divergent implications for deterrence and conflict.[23] Disparities in posture and management practices—combined with distinct strategic cultures, close proximity, and variation in geographic size among respective rivals—throw into question considerations of the absolute costs and risks of a regional nuclear exchange. These factors can empower some states to mount a devastating first strike, while rendering others incapable of absorbing even a limited nuclear blow. Accordingly, they can make meaningful victory in a nuclear war seem attainable, at least for one side, thus confounding a traditional bedrock of strategic stability. Moreover, the spread of sensitive nuclear technology, matériel, and know-how among regional powers generates additional concerns for instability attendant on latent nuclear force postures. Here, the uncertainty about technical capabilities to acquire and to weaponize fissile material and to operationalize disassembled and unproven systems undermine the credibility of military threats and retaliation needed for effective signaling.[24]

An added complication for strategic stability in the second nuclear age is that regional nuclear powers face threats from multiple directions simultaneously. This gives rise to "strategic trilemmas," whereby the actions taken by one nuclear power to defend itself against a regional rival can provoke responses from an extraregional nuclear power, such as the United States, Russia, or China. Similarly, as evidenced by India's "surgical strike" across the Line of Control with Pakistan in Kashmir in September 2016, regional nuclear powers face mounting domestic pressures to do something in response to attacks by militant groups backed by a regional nuclear rival while still maintaining strategic restraint. Successive war games among planners in India and Pakistan reveal that this can create perverse incentives to inflame a nuclear crisis, including a reticence to practice clear nuclear signaling, moral hazard and overreliance on third-party intervention, and disregard for an adversary's nuclear redlines.[25] The upshot of these overlapping and asymmetrical nuclear bilateral relationships is that "changes in one state's nuclear posture or policy can have a cascading effect on the other nuclear-armed states," thus confusing strategic calculations at both the regional and global levels.[26]

A third challenge in the second nuclear era relates to the cross-domain character of the threats presented by emerging technologies. As displayed since the 1991 Persian Gulf War, a variety of nonnuclear military technologies—such as long-range precision strike systems, missile defenses, antisatellite weapons, cyber weapons, unmanned vehicles, hypersonic glide systems, remote sensing, and additive manufacturing—carry the potential to "replicate, offset, or mitigate" the strategic effects of nuclear weapons.[27] These technologies are being diffused more readily to different customers at unequal rates than they were in previous military revolutions, complicating efforts by Washington to manage extended deterrent relationships. This can increase the risks to US command-and-control assets on land, in air, in space, and in the cyber domain. It can also enhance the preemptive capabilities of regional nuclear, nonnuclear, and nonstate actors in gray-zone and local conflicts. Consequently, the risk of escalation is multifaceted, fueling misperceptions among a variety of rising local and regional actors, and also emboldening revisionists and rogues arguably less motivated by the expected utility calculations at the core of classic calculations of strategic stability.

The absorption of emerging technologies also threatens to expand both windows of opportunity and vulnerability among nuclear rivals. As noted above, the procurement of these technologies by the United States has widened the gap in global power projection capabilities, undermined the basic symmetry of the US-Russian nuclear force posture, and given Washington conventional capabilities to reduce its reliance on nuclear weapons for conducting strategic counterforce operations. However, the very impressiveness of US nonnuclear capabilities elevates incentives for China to modernize its nuclear and conventional capabilities, which in turn risks blurring lines and affecting both countries' decisions about using their nuclear weapons before and during crises. Presented with other dimensions of nonnuclear inferiority, Moscow today seems to place greater reliance than during the Cold War on nuclear first-strike systems and on a posture aimed at escalating regional conflicts in order to "de-escalate" large-scale conventional threats, coupling its nuclear with nonnuclear options to deter encroachment on its vital national interests.

REGIONS REDUX

Nonetheless, common claims about the diminished contemporary salience of strategic stability seem premature. Such assertions are rooted in elements of change, but they ignore key dimensions of continuity between the first and second nuclear epochs. This critique also fails to address the evidence for regional traction, while confusing the concept's declining relevance with differences and novel twists among national and regional approaches to strategic stability.

The benchmark for assessing the ebbing relevance of strategic stability in the second nuclear revolution is problematic. The security environment of the Cold War was more complicated than can be suggested by a uniform focus on the US-Soviet nuclear dyad. Both superpowers engaged in strategic competition that cut across different regional conflicts, which were also marked by asymmetries among local rivals. Amid this complexity—and despite differences in nuclear force structures, postures, and strategies—leaders in Washington and Moscow arrived at the same conclusion: that strategic stability was the only option to ensure respective national security and coexistence. Yet, as they fumbled toward reconciling differences in their respective strategies of deterrence, both were uncomfortable with extending classical elements of strategic stability, especially mutual vulnerability, to regional nuclear states. Instead, both US and Soviet leaders embraced principles of damage limitation and superiority in dealing with China as critical to preserving regional stability. Accordingly, the divorce of strategic stability assessments from considerations of parity or mutual fears of first nuclear strike is not unique to the second nuclear revolution. Cost/benefit calculations related to nuclear strategies in divergent regional contexts have deep roots in the past.[28]

By the same token, the strategic logic for existing nuclear forces predates the second nuclear revolution. All decisions to initiate and possess nuclear weapons programs were made in the context of the global bipolar superpower rivalry. Although the process and fate of each country's nuclear weapons programs varied, crucial decisions to acquire nuclear weapons were made before the end of the Cold War. For example, some countries initiated weapons programs before developing civilian nuclear programs (such as the United States, Russia, the United Kingdom, China, and Israel) while others (such as Brazil, Japan, Germany, South Korea, Egypt, and Taiwan) terminated their nascent weapons programs at different stages. How emerging regional powers thought about nuclear weapons should be deployed also predates the second nuclear era. Evidence from strategic statements and crisis-signaling behavior between India and Pakistan reveals more overlap than is commonly perceived. Accordingly, there is a conspicuous legacy of strategic thinking rooted in different dimensions of the first nuclear era that informs contemporary doctrine, strategy, and behavior among emerging regional nuclear rivals.[29]

Regional strategic dynamics exemplify the legacy of nuclear paradigms from the first nuclear era. As Michael Cohen details, there are notable similarities concerning the impact of nuclear weapons and the extension of the stability/ instability paradox on the war propensities of political leaderships that transcend the first and second nuclear periods. The fear of imminent nuclear escalation has had a sobering effect on contemporary nuclear crisis decision making, fostering "pessimistic risk choices" to temper compellence in South Asia, just as it had on moderating the revisionism of Soviet leaders during the Cuban missile crisis.[30] Others demonstrate empirical support for the link between strategic nuclear stability and a higher propensity for lower-intensity conflicts that extend consistently across different regional contexts, and also the Cold War divide.[31] As recounted by both Sadia Tasleem and Happymon Jacob in, respectively, chapters 3 and 8 of this volume, the Indian and Pakistani leaderships embrace the nuclear lexicon of the first nuclear era to reference their distinct strategies and weapons programs. Whether such terms and related meanings carry the same weight or reflect pathologies in prevailing nuclear paradigms remain open questions, but they serve as important frames of reference that betray the residual of traditional strategic stability considerations.

Of course, conspicuous distinctions persist in defining the principles and practical meaning of strategic stability across regional contexts. The requirements from the Cold War setting do not readily travel to different regional nuclear states, where extant, evolving, and emerging arsenals are not equally capable. For some, the incontestability of the costs of nuclear war may not be assumed. This is due to questions about the reliability or small size of local nuclear arsenals, uncertainty about an adversary's ability to mount a first strike, or even the effectiveness of conventional capabilities. In other contexts, such as China, the incontestability of costs is measured by other considerations. Beijing's conception of strategic stability purportedly rests more on preserving "lean and effective" capabilities, stemming "science surprises," and arresting strategic innovation gaps than on possessing symmetrical force postures, deploying equivalent systems, or pursuing damage limitation.[32] Within the Pakistani-Indian rivalry, as Tasleem and Jacob make clear, there are deeply rooted strategic assumptions and normative restraints against escalation that paradoxically bolster brinkmanship while reinforcing mutual confidence in avoiding a nuclear war.[33] Furthermore, as discussed by Ala' Alrababa'h in chapter 10, for some emerging regional powers, considerations of redlines and strategic stability may rest more with the metrics of a domestic political regime's survival.[34] Irrespective of this wide divergence in assessments, the criteria for stability are defined by the regional actors themselves, with mutual fears and security considerations tailored to prevailing circumstances. Although the conceptual terrain is more complex and localized, strategic stability as an organizing framework is as relevant as ever.

RETHINKING STRATEGIC STABILITY FROM REGIONAL PERSPECTIVES

The goal of this volume is to examine the regional dimensions of strategic stability as understood and practiced by central local actors. The book brings together insights from leading scholars of nuclear and strategic studies from across different regional security communities. The chapters intentionally jettison a one-size-fits-all approach to explore how key nuclear and other regional stakeholders conceive of strategic stability within their respective contexts. The volume identifies the broader implications for national force modernization, crisis behavior, confidence building, and regional security. However, consistent with the traditional understanding of strategic stability, each chapter addresses how such actors strive to preserve vital interests and balance their respective conceptions with the recognition that related choices are interdependent and outcomes necessitate efforts to manage risks of escalation, including those attendant on an inadvertent regional nuclear conflagration.

A series of questions lie at the crux of this inquiry. How do regional players understand the meaning of stability for themselves, and how does this affect their postures toward arms control, arms racing, and crisis behavior? How does the regional nuclear equation—deployed or latent—affect a state's understanding of strategic stability and its deterrence or compellence strategies? How does a state think its regional adversary understands the same concepts? Finally, what remains unknown, and what are the policy implications of these unknowns?

This focus on strategic stability intentionally extends the discussion beyond the utility of a specific national strategy such as deterrence. Because other types of issues may affect deterrence and states' conceptions of stability, each chapter seeks to illuminate how related concepts and strategies shape a state's consideration of its primary security objectives. This can include factors that extend beyond the nuclear realm. In other words, how does a state understand stability and bargaining across domains of interest—cyber and conventional; domains of actors—global, regional, and subnational; and domains of security—interregional, intraregional, and regime-focused. Accordingly, the chapters assess respective conceptions of strategic stability as they pertain to the interests, interactions, and outcomes deemed most salient for contending with conflict (de)escalation by key regional actors. One of the main goals is to identify the conditions under which nuclear weapons are integral to bolstering or undermining regional stability, and the attendant implications for pursuing deep reductions in standing arsenals or latent capabilities.

Given this charge, this volume is distinct from the extant literature in several respects. First, it situates strategic stability at the center of inquiry. Unlike other recent studies of the second nuclear revolution, strategic stability is treated as distinct from specific strategies, such as deterrence, reassurance, and assurance.[35] Although the latter are certainly important, they do not constitute the full range of strategic responses or provide a benchmark for assessing the trade-offs between the pursuit of narrow national objectives and the risks of an escalation of a regional nuclear conflict or arms competition. Similarly, in contrast with other studies that detail national decisions, military force postures, and strategies, this volume problematizes the consequences for regional and national security of the interaction of such choices made by regional rivals and key extraregional states, such as the United States.

Second, because the widely used concept of strategic stability is so fungible, the volume embraces a comparative perspective to identify the salient interests, interactions, and consequences of strategic stability that are implicated across different regional nuclear contexts. Accordingly, it explores the concept's meaning, discourse, policy drivers, and implications as understood by local and regional actors rather than testing definitions of strategic stability or regional security imported explicitly from the US-Soviet/Russian context. At the same time, the chapters seek to tease out similarities and differences between approaches to strategic stability that cut across different national and regional contexts.

Third, the volume goes beyond a nuclear-centric understanding of strategic stability by exploring other types of issues that may affect how a state thinks about strategy and stability. For example, the book complements emerging work in the field by investigating how states perceive and employ cross-domain reassurance, deterrence, and coercion, and how these efforts affect their understandings of managing risks of escalation, both more broadly and against the shadow of deployed and latent nuclear weapons capabilities.[36] By casting the analysis of strategic stability widely, we can begin to explore how nonnuclear, subconventional, nonkinetic, and other all-encompassing concepts of regime security interests can affect regional security.

PLAN OF THE BOOK

The book is divided into three parts. Part I explores how various actors and their adversaries within a particular region interpret strategic stability and deterrence. It begins with a chapter on the United States' views of these concepts across regions, followed by chapters on Russia, Pakistan, Iran, and Israel. These regional cases focus on how broad strategic concepts shape specific postures and outcomes among regional rivals regarding crisis behavior, arms control, and arms racing. The section concludes with a commentary written by Rajesh Basrur that highlights the issues for scholarship on international relations and strategic studies pertaining to the regional dimension of deterrence and strategic stability.

In chapter 1 Evan Montgomery examines the emerging sources of regional instability and related US nuclear policy implications. He identifies two trends intended to temper the growing optimism about nuclear weapons and strategic stability. The first is "the return of geopolitics," whereby US nuclear planning must now contend with regional revisionists, including Russia, China, and Iran. The second major trend includes a new set of challenges posed by "rising powers, rogue nations, and regional rivals" that have emerged in the second nuclear age.

In chapter 2 Andrey Pavlov and Anastasia Malygina provide the flip side of the great power equation from the Russian perspective. The authors examine the roles that nuclear weapons play in Russia's defense doctrine and how interpretations of strategic stability have evolved and differ from those in other countries. Interestingly, Malygina and Pavlov point out that strategic stability was an instrumental concept used for negotiating with the United States. The definition changed over time and applied only to the sphere of nuclear weapons. The authors assert that today, mutual deterrence vis-à-vis the United States is premised on broader concepts of parity and balance that underpin contemporary strategic stability.

Moving to the regional perspective, in chapter 3 Sadia Tasleem elucidates the Pakistani understanding of strategic stability. She explores how terms of reference for strategic stability have been distorted from the US-Soviet/Russian context, which in turn feed into how political and military interactions with

India have affected Pakistani threat perceptions. At base, Tasleem asserts that Pakistan's views are shaped by regional concerns and that the resolution of the Kashmir dispute is central to Islamabad's security interests. She concludes that for strategic stability to persist, the discourse in South Asia needs to be reframed so decision makers can think beyond strategic balance through either mutual restraint or military parity.

In chapter 4 Emily Landau examines the evolution of strategic threat perceptions in the Middle East. Focusing on the nuclear domain, and Iran and Israel more specifically, she argues that regional actors do not comprehend strategic stability in the same manner as the superpowers because many of the basic assumptions, such as transparency, are not interpreted in the same light by regional rivals. Examining two cases—the Arms Control and Regional Security talks, and Iran's pursuit of a nuclear program—Landau argues that Israel's unique policy of nuclear ambiguity—also known as opacity—was a source of stability. This ambiguity, coupled with the perception among Arab states that Israel did not pose an offensive threat, allowed Arab leaders to avoid the painful costs of engaging in a nuclear arms race. This outcome, she claims, contrasts starkly with Iran's nuclear behavior, which has exacerbated threat perceptions by both its Israeli and Arab neighbors due to Tehran's regional policies, which are widely seen as offensive. Opacity, pursued in the context of established and widespread outside interpretations of Tehran's belligerence, confirms other states' fears of its malign intentions.

In chapter 5 Annie Tracy Samuel takes a different approach to one of the issues that Landau sees as a factor of instability in the region: Iran's behavior. Tracy Samuel draws on primary sources to examine how regional actors have helped to shape Iranian conceptions of strategic stability. She asserts that the nuclear element plays very little role in the development of concepts of deterrence and strategic stability. Rather, she explains how Iran's respective conceptualizations have evolved and primarily rest on conventional military capabilities. She argues that Tehran seeks regional cooperation under its leadership to bolster deterrence and reduce the likelihood of war. Strategic stability includes regional security and the prevention of outside influence. Tracy Samuel makes the case that these views have been heavily influenced by Iran's postrevolutionary experience in the Iran-Iraq War. Finally, she reminds us that the Iranian leadership has framed the Joint Comprehensive Plan of Action as consistent with its views of deterrence, thus constituting a mechanism for building cooperation with its neighbors and, potentially, regional stability.

Part II of the volume examines how five regional actors—Russia, China, India, Israel, and Saudi Arabia—understand cross-domain deterrence and how this concept relates to a state's strategic posture and related understanding of strategic stability. This part ends with a commentary by Jeffrey Knopf that highlights the key conceptual challenges, themes, and dimensions to cross-domain interaction within regional contexts. Each chapter focuses on the conceptual underpinnings (technology, offense vs. defense, actor, etc.) of the cross-domain strategies, postures, and behavior that are embraced by a regional actor, and the attendant implications for interaction with a regional rival.

Part II begins with what may turn out to be a harbinger of change for US-Russia relations, if not the global nuclear order. In chapter 6 Dima Adamsky explores how Moscow views the information, or cyber, element of Next Generation War, which has been otherwise misconstrued in the West as "hybrid warfare." He examines how this tool fits into Russian national security policy and the effect of employing this new tool for strategic stability. Synthesizing views from Russian military writing and policy statements, he suggests that the cyber component of Russian military doctrine is a coercive tool for manipulating the adversary's perceptions. He coins the term "cross-domain coercion" to refer to a host of Russia's efforts to deter and compel its adversaries across different nuclear, subnuclear, and informational realms. He concludes that the implications for strategic stability are mixed. On one hand, this Russian operational art expands the continuum of options on the escalation ladder and contributes to strategic stability by incentivizing self-deterrence. On the other hand, an informational campaign can result in crisis instability and inadvertent escalation by obfuscating nuclear, conventional, and informational forms of coercion.

In chapter 7 Tong Zhao draws on primary sources to explain China's concerns about hypersonic weapons, how these concerns affect strategic stability, and the implications for US-China relations. Zhao relates that Chinese experts initially regarded economic, military, diplomatic, and political factors as determinants of strategic stability. Today, however, the Chinese strategic community embraces a concept much closer to the US understanding of mutual vulnerability. This explains why China has pursued nuclear modernization so fervently, even to the extent of eliciting fear in the United States. Furthermore, growing attention to the mutual vulnerability requirement for strategic stability explains why China views the United States' development of hypersonic weapons as destabilizing; hypersonic weapons can undermine the credibility of China's nuclear deterrence. Thus, in response, there seems to be a consensus among Beijing's experts that it should develop its own hypersonic weapons. But Chinese countermeasures are not limited to hypersonic weapons. Experts have proposed revising China's nuclear posture, expanding its nuclear arsenal, and building up its nuclear war-fighting capabilities. Zhao concludes that the emerging competition between China and the United States means that misperceptions about intentions may exacerbate the existing security dilemma to the detriment of strategic stability.

The India-Pakistan case exemplifies the important link between cross-domain deterrence and strategic stability among regional adversaries. In chapter 8 Happymon Jacob suggests that India and Pakistan embrace drastically different conceptions of strategic stability due to their contrasting respective orientations of a status quo power versus a revisionist power. To be sure, he finds that a state's notion of strategic stability contributes to how cross-domain deterrence operates on the ground, and the existence of such cross-domain deterrence has an impact on its notion of strategic stability. Jacob also suggests that to enhance stability in the region, issues related to instability at lower levels of conflict, where it is easier to control escalation, must be addressed. This underscores the utility of talks on nuclear confidence-building measures, strategic concepts, and military doctrines.

Israel, a nuclear weapons state that faces nonnuclear, conventional, and asymmetric threats, is an interesting comparative case for understanding strategic stability. In chapter 9 Ilai Saltzman writes that the term "strategic stability," as traditionally conceived, does not capture what and how Israel thinks about national security. Saltzman claims that Israel relies on using conventional forces to achieve regional stability; the country's possession of nuclear weapons plays little role in this regard. Thus, Israeli policy has pursued two goals: to prevent an all-out conventional war and to prevent another state in the region from acquiring nuclear weapons. Drawing on the Israeli experience, Saltzman advocates a broader conceptualization of strategic stability that goes beyond the nuclear element and includes a variety of domains (conventional and asymmetric), actors (state and nonstate), and forms of power (kinetic and nonkinetic).

The final chapter in part II addresses the case of Saudi Arabia. In many respects, this case is an outlier, because Saudi Arabia has not to date possessed either a nuclear energy or a weapons program. But the kingdom has been implicated as a key aspirant state on both accounts, while contending with conventional and asymmetric regional rivalries, growing distance in its strategic relations with Washington, and transnational ideological threats. In chapter 10 Ala' Alrababa'h captures these dynamics and their implications for regional conflict and cooperation. He claims that Riyadh has shunned a discernible military strategy. Instead, its primary concerns have been bound up with preserving its sovereignty and its regime's stability. Thus, to protect its national security interests, the kingdom has relied on external balancing with the United States, internal balancing, and ideological deterrence. By implication, reduced US involvement in the region, as opposed to strategic reductions, may encour-

age greater Saudi military involvement in the region to fill the vacuum. Furthermore, if Iran develops nuclear weapons, Saudi Arabia may try to develop its
own program—though Alrababa'h believes that Washington will prevent this
from occurring.

Part III of the book contains two views about the policy implications of the
chapter findings and a conclusion to bring the volume together. In chapter 11
Matthew Kroenig's discussion revolves largely around understanding the
implications for US allies. Starting with the premise that a state's national
security interests dominate its pursuit of strategic stability, he recommends
that Washington tailor its approach to strategic stability to match this reality.
He also recommends, in the case of Russia, that the United States strengthen
its deterrence posture and ensure, together with NATO, that there is a credible
response to any limited Russian nuclear threat or action. With regard to
China, he recommends that Washington maintain a military edge to uphold
stability in Asia and thus to reassure its regional allies, including the development of prompt global strike capabilities. Yet Kroenig does see a possibility
for the United States to maintain its strategic advantage and at the same time
allow China to establish a secure second-strike capability. In South Asia, he
recommends that Washington continue to convene Track II diplomacy and
facilitate confidence-building measures in order to arrive at a more stable
nuclear deterrence relationship. Finally, in the Middle East, Kroenig asserts
that even if the Joint Comprehensive Plan of Action remains in place, the
United States' traditional partners fear Tehran, and thus the United States
must do more to reassure its allies that it is committed to defending them from
Iranian influence.

In chapter 12 Adam Mount asserts that twenty-first-century strategic stability will depend on the extent to which Washington is willing to risk restraint to
ensure mutual vulnerability through negotiated agreements. More specifically,
Mount identifies three policy discussions whose outcomes will have a direct
bearing on strategic stability: the US acceptance of mutual vulnerability with
China, the requirements of extended deterrence, and the shape and form of US
nuclear modernization.

The conclusion to the book highlights three important themes that cut
across all its chapters: the contested meaning of strategic stability, the role of
nonstate actors, and the issue of transparency. Ultimately, the challenge will be
how the United States responds to the actions of its adversaries and its allies
with these delicate dynamics in play, especially when it has not committed to a
particular path. However, as this volume highlights, there is a lack of consensus
about the basic terms and about which approach will best ensure strategic
stability.

NOTES

1. Ed Pilkington and Martin Pengelly, "'Let It Be an Arms Race': Donald Trump Appears to Double Down on Nuclear Expansion," *The Guardian*, December 24, 2016, www.theguardian.com/us-news/2016/dec/23/donald-trump-nuclear-weapons-arms-race; and "Donald Trump Won't Take Nuclear Weapons off the Table," on *Hardball with Chris Matthews*, MSNBC, May 30, 2016, www.msnbc.com/hardball/watch/donald-trump-won-t-take-nukes-off-the-table-655471171934.

2. Congressional Budget Office, "Projected Costs of US Nuclear Forces, 2017 to 2026," February 2017, www.cbo.gov/sites/default/files/115th-congress-2017–2018/reports/52401-nuclearcosts.pdf; and White House, *Presidential Memorandum on Rebuilding the US Armed Forces*, January 27, 2017, www.whitehouse.gov/the-press-office/2017/01/27/presidential-memorandum-rebuilding-us-armed-forces.

3. James N. Mattis, "Statement of James N. Mattis before the Armed Services Committee," January 27, 2015, www.armed-services.senate.gov/imo/media/doc/Mattis_01-27-15.pdf.

4. Alexie Anishchuck, "Don't Mess with Russia, Putin Says," Reuters, August 29, 2014, www.reuters.com/article/us-russia-putin-conflict-idUSKBN0GT1D420140829.

5. "Trump Releases Letter from Putin Asking to 'Restore' US-Russia Relationship," *Politico*, December 23, 2016, www.politico.com/story/2016/12/putin-christmas-letter-to-trump-232952.

6. See, e.g., Alexandr Fursenko and Timothy Naftali, *Khrushchev's War: The Inside Story of an American Adversary* (New York: W. W. Norton, 2006); Dmitry Adamsky, "The 1983 Nuclear Crisis: Lessons for Deterrence Theory and Practice," *Journal of Strategic Studies* 36, no. 1 (2013); and Raymond L. Garthoff, *Soviet Leaders and Intelligence: Assessing the American Adversary during the Cold War* (Washington, DC: Georgetown University Press, 2015).

7. Science and Security Board, "It Is Two and a Half Minutes to Midnight: 2017 Doomsday Clock Statement," *Bulletin of the Atomic Scientists*, January 26, 2017, https://thebulletin.org/sites/default/files/Final%202017%20Clock%20Statement.pdf.

8. Frank P. Harvey, "The Future of Strategic Stability and Nuclear Deterrence," *International Journal* 58, no. 2 (Spring 2003): 321–46.

9. Thomas Scheber, "Strategic Stability: Time for a Reality Check," *International Journal*, Autumn 2008, 893–915.

10. International Security Advisory Board of United States Department of State, "Report on the Nature of Multilateral Strategic Stability," April 27, 2016, www.state.gov/documents/organization/257667.pdf.

11. James M. Acton, "Reclaiming Strategic Stability," in *Strategic Stability: Contending Interpretations,* ed. Elbridge A. Colby and Michael S. Gerson (Carlisle, PA: Strategic Studies Institute of US Army War College, 2013), 117–46.

12. Albert Wohlstetter, "The Delicate Balance of Terror," *Foreign Affairs* 37, no. 2 (1959): 8–17.

13. Glenn A. Kent and David E. Thaler, *First-Strike Stability: A Methodology for Evaluating Strategic Forces, R-3765-AF* (Santa Monica, CA: RAND Corporation, 1989).

14. Elbridge Colby, "Defining Strategic Stability: Reconciling Stability and Deterrence," in *Strategic Stability*, ed. Colby and Gerson, 49–50.

15. Michael S. Gerson, "The Origins of Strategic Stability: The United States and the Threat of Surprise Attack," in *Strategic Stability*, ed. Colby and Gerson, 1–46.

16. Colby, "Defining Strategic Stability," 47–84.

17. Desmond Ball and Jeffrey Richelson, eds., *Strategic Nuclear Targeting* (Ithaca, NY: Cornell University Press, 1986).

18. Aleksandr' G. Savel'yev and Nikolay N. Detinov, *The Big Five: Arms Control Decision-Making in the Soviet Union*, trans. Dmitriy Trenin and ed. Gregory Varhall (Westport, CT: Praeger, 1995). See also David A. Yost, *Strategic Stability in the Cold War: Lessons for Continuing Challenges* (Paris: Institut français des relations internationales, 2011).

19. Paul Bracken, *The Second Nuclear Age: Strategy, Danger, and the New Power Politics* (New York: Henry Holt, 2012), 1.

20. John Mueller, "The Escalating Irrelevance of Nuclear Weapons," in *The Absolute Weapon Revisited: Nuclear Arms and the Emerging International Order*, ed. T.V. Paul, Richard J. Harknett, and James J. Wirtz (Ann Arbor: University of Michigan Press, 1998), 73–98.

21. Bracken, *Second Nuclear Age*, 93–126; and C. Dale Walton and Colin S. Gray, "The Geopolitics of Strategic Stability: Looking beyond Cold Warriors and Nuclear Weapons," in *Strategic Stability*, ed. Colby and Gerson, 85–116.

22. Brad Roberts, *The Case for US Nuclear Weapons in the 21st Century* (Stanford, CA: Stanford University Press, 2016). See also discussion in *Strategy in the Second Nuclear Age: Power, Ambition, and the Ultimate Weapon*, ed. Toshi Yoshihara and James R. Holmes (Washington, DC: Georgetown University Press, 2012).

23. Vipin Narang, *Nuclear Strategy in the Modern Era: Regional Powers and International Conflict* (Princeton, NJ: Princeton University Press, 2014).

24. Gaurav Kampani, "New Delhi's Long Nuclear Journey: How Secrecy and Institutional Roadblocks Delayed India's Weaponization," *International Security* 38, no. 4 (Spring 2014): 79–114; and Rupal N. Mehta and Rachel Elizabeth Whitlark, "Unpacking the Iranian Nuclear Deal: Nuclear Latency and US Foreign Policy," *Washington Quarterly* 39, no. 4 (Winter 2017): 45–61.

25. Feroz Hassan Khan, Diana Wueger, Andrew Giesey, and Ryan Morgan, "South Asian Stability Workshop 2.0: A Crisis Simulation Report," Report 2016–001, Project on Advanced Systems and Concepts for Countering Weapons of Mass Destruction, 2016, http://hdl.handle.net/10945/48613.

26. Gregory D. Koblentz, *Strategic Stability in the Second Nuclear Age*, Special Report 71 (New York: Council on Foreign Relations, 2014). See also Linton Brooks and Mira Rapp-Hooper, "Extended Deterrence, Assurance, and Reassurance in the Pacific during the Second Nuclear Age," in *Strategic Asia 2013: Asia in the Second Nuclear Age*, ed. Ashley J. Tellis, Abraham M. Denmark, and Travis Tanner (Washington, DC: National Bureau of Asian Research, 2013); and Robert Einhorn and W. P. S. Sidhu, *The Strategic Chain: Linking Pakistan, India, China, and the United States* (Washington, DC: Brookings Institution, 2017), www.brookings.edu/wp-content/uploads/2017/03/acnpi_201703_strategic_chain.pdf.

27. Koblentz, *Strategic Stability*, 3; and Roberts, *Case for Nuclear Weapons*.

28. Charles L. Glaser and Steve Fetter, "Should the United States Reject MAD? Damage Limitation and US Nuclear Strategy toward China," *International Security* 41, no. 1 (Summer 2016): 49–98. As these authors point out, however, there are now new

conditions of interdependence that may present a less daunting security environment, and China's nuclear and conventional modernization undoubtedly raises real questions about the future feasibility and marginal value of pursuing an enhanced US damage-limiting strategy.

29. Lisa Koch, "Explaining the Path and Pace of Nuclear Weapons Programs" (PhD diss., University of Michigan, 2014); and Todd C. Robinson, "What Do We Mean by Nuclear Proliferation?" *Nonproliferation Review* 22, no. 1 (2015): 53–70. Notable exceptions, however, are likely to be Iran and North Korea.

30. Michael D. Cohen, *When Proliferation Causes Peace: The Psychology of Nuclear Crises* (Washington, DC: Georgetown University Press, 2017).

31. Robert Rauchhaus, "Evaluating the Nuclear Peace Hypothesis: A Quantitative Approach," *Journal of Conflict Resolution* 53, no. 2 (2009): 258–77.

32. Li Bin, "Differences between Chinese and US Nuclear Thinking and Their Origins," in *Understanding Chinese Nuclear Thinking,* ed. Li Bin and Tong Zhao (Washington, DC: Carnegie Endowment for International Peace, 2016), 3–19.

33. Lu Yin, "Reflections on Strategic Stability," in *Understanding Chinese Nuclear Thinking*, ed. Bin and Zhao, 127–48.

34. Toby Dalton, Togzhan Kassenova, and Lauryn Williams, eds., *Perspectives on the Evolving Nuclear Order* (Washington, DC: Carnegie Endowment for International Peace, 2016).

35. Yoshihara and Holmes, *Strategy*; and James Clay Moltz, "Regional Perspectives on Low Nuclear Numbers," *Nonproliferation Review* 20, no. 2 (2013): 195–204.

36. T.V. Paul, Patrick M. Morgan, and James J. Wirtz, eds., *Complex Deterrence: Strategy in the Global Age* (Chicago: University of Chicago Press, 2009); and Jeffrey W. Knopf, ed., *Security Assurances and Nuclear Proliferation* (Stanford, CA: Stanford University Press, 2012). For a similar focus at the conventional level, see Dmitry Adamsky, "From Israel with Deterrence: Strategic Culture, Intra-war Coercion and Brute Force," *Security Studies* 26, no. 1 (2017): 157–84.

PART I

General Approaches to Regional Stability

1

Sources of Instability in the Second Nuclear Age

An American Perspective

EVAN BRADEN MONTGOMERY

FROM THE EARLY DAYS of the Cold War until the rivalry between the United States and the Soviet Union came to an end, the concept of strategic stability was a focal point of debate and an important driver of policy, particularly in the United States. For those who wrestled with this concept, both in theory and in practice, the goal was straightforward: Identify and establish the conditions under which neither side would have incentives to launch a nuclear attack against the other, whether during peacetime or in the midst of a crisis. Although translating this objective into reality was rarely easy, these efforts left a significant mark on US nuclear planning, doctrine, force structure, and command-and-control arrangements. They also generated research on a host of issues, such as the complex relationship between offensive and defensive capabilities.[1]

For the most part, however, concerns about strategic stability have faded into the background during the post–Cold War era, while the enormous intellectual investment made by earlier generations has atrophied.[2] The reasons are hardly surprising. With the collapse of the Soviet Union and the start of the unipolar moment, an entire paradigm of international politics suddenly seemed obsolete. Rather than engaging in a nuclear arms race, Washington and Moscow took unilateral and bilateral steps to draw down the massive arsenals they had built up over the preceding decades. And instead of worrying about nuclear brinkmanship or windows of vulnerability, policymakers in the United States became much more attentive to the possibility of Russian nuclear weapons, material, and expertise falling into the wrong hands, along with attempts by hostile nations and nonstate actors to acquire nuclear weapons by other means.

This situation is starting to change, for two reasons. First, after a temporary lull in traditional forms of interstate competition, a return of geopolitics is at hand.[3] Since the early 1990s, the United States has confronted few serious threats to the regional orders that it helped to establish and continues to sustain. Today, however, revisionist powers are attempting to alter the status quo in various locations and a variety of ways, including Russia's territorial aggrandizement in its near abroad, China's aggressive actions throughout its near seas, and Iran's efforts to extend its influence across its neighborhood. Second, the world is now in the midst of a "second nuclear age," which combines the risks of an earlier era with a new set of challenges.[4] Although the urgency of direct and extended deterrence vis-à-vis a nuclear peer has diminished, this core objective has never gone away. Meanwhile, rising powers, rogue nations, and regional rivals are all expanding and enhancing their nuclear arsenals.

Individually, but especially together, these broad trends in the security environment are eroding (or could erode) strategic stability. Unlike the first nuclear age, however, when threats to stability were almost entirely a product of the US/Soviet rivalry and were frequently global in scope, sources of instability in the second nuclear age have more diverse origins and more local implications. Diagnosing and remedying them will therefore require a regionally differentiated perspective.

In certain areas, for example, nations are developing capabilities to offset their conventional military disadvantages and, as a result, are lowering the barriers to nuclear use. In other areas, nuclear multipolarity has already obtained or is on the horizon, which could make defense planning and crisis diplomacy far more challenging. Elsewhere, countries might seek out and receive nuclear deterrence guarantees from patrons other than the United States, undermining Washington's influence and increasing the prospects for horizontal escalation. Finally, and perhaps most worrisome, these developments are not mutually exclusive. In fact, some regions are already experiencing more than one. The purpose of this chapter, therefore, is to describe these existing and emerging sources of instability and how they might evolve over time. It then sketches out some implications for US grand strategy, alliance relationships, and nuclear forces.[5]

THE PURSUIT OF ESCALATION DOMINANCE

One of the most immediate and worrisome challenges for strategic stability is the pursuit of nuclear capabilities (including weapons and associated concepts of employment) that are eroding the "firebreak" between conventional and nuclear conflict—and are lowering the barriers to nuclear use.[6] In particular, nations such as Russia and Pakistan not only place greater emphasis on their nuclear arsenals as a tool of security policy but also appear to believe they can engage in limited nuclear strikes in some contingencies without provoking a nuclear reprisal.

The underlying logic that has spurred this development is not new. In general, nations that find themselves in unfavorable conventional military positions relative to their adversaries have strong incentives to pursue nuclear weapons if they do not yet possess them, or to depend more on their nuclear arsenals if they already do. During the Cold War, for instance, the United States confronted a daunting situation in Central Europe, where the Soviet Union was able to leverage its manpower, military-industrial capacity, and geographic proximity to field large numbers of conventional ground and air forces, far more than the United States could possibly keep abroad. Consequently, Washington relied on its strategic nuclear arsenal and its forward-based and forward-deployable nonstrategic nuclear weapons to offset this disadvantage, and it never abandoned the right to initiate nuclear use if it were losing a conventional conflict. Moscow, by contrast, claimed that it would not be the first side to employ nuclear weapons, which was not surprising given its conventional military advantage, although the credibility of this pledge was never very high.

Understandably, Washington's calculus shifted in the aftermath of the Cold War, as did Moscow's. Although it has yet to adopt a policy of no first use of nuclear weapons, the United States has been able to lean more heavily on its superior conventional military capabilities for deterrence. According to the Pentagon's 2010 *Nuclear Posture Review* (*NPR*), "The United States has reduced our reliance on nuclear weapons as Cold War nuclear rivalries have eased and as our conventional military forces and missile defense capabilities have strengthened."[7] Perhaps the most tangible indicator of this shift has been the changing size and composition of the US nonstrategic nuclear arsenal, which traditionally coupled the United States to its vulnerable frontline allies and compensated for conventional military disadvantages in key theaters.

In the past, the United States maintained a diverse set of nonstrategic nuclear weapons, from gravity bombs and artillery shells to air defense missiles and antisubmarine rockets. Many of these weapons were also stationed on the territory of US allies in Europe and Northeast Asia, or were kept on aircraft carriers, surface combatants, and attack submarines.[8] But this force structure and posture began to change dramatically during the final years of the Cold War and continued to change throughout the post–Cold War era. In 1987 the United States and the Soviet Union signed the Intermediate-Range Nuclear Forces Treaty, which prohibited both sides from testing or fielding ground-launched, surface-to-surface missiles with ranges between 500 and 5,500 kilometers. Then, in 1991, the United States announced that it would withdraw and destroy all its shorter-range, nuclear-armed missiles and artillery systems that were still based abroad, and it would also remove nonstrategic nuclear weapons from its ships, submarines, and land-based naval aircraft. Later, in the 1994 *NPR*, it determined that aircraft carriers and surface combatants no longer needed the ability to carry nuclear weapons at all. Finally, the 2010 *NPR* announced that the nuclear variant of the Tomahawk Land-Attack Missile would be retired.

Cumulatively, these decisions denuclearized US ground forces entirely, left the Navy without any nonstrategic nuclear weapons, and meant that the United States would need to rely almost exclusively on its strategic arsenal (i.e., the triad of heavy bombers, land-based intercontinental ballistic missiles, and ballistic missile submarines) for both direct and extended nuclear deterrence. At present, the US nonstrategic arsenal consists solely of the Air Force's B61 nuclear gravity bombs.[9] Although Washington is currently extending the life span of these weapons, this effort will also result in a further reduction in the size of the arsenal.[10] Moreover, whereas US and allied forces were once prepared to conduct nuclear operations on short notice, public reports suggest that it would now take far longer to generate that capability.[11]

Russia has been moving in the opposite direction, however. Rather than decrease its reliance on nuclear weapons, it has actually increased its dependence on them in the post–Cold War era, a trend that can be attributed to major changes in the distribution of power.[12] For instance, while its conventional military forces were in sharp decline during the 1990s and the 2000s, the United States was spearheading multiple rounds of NATO expansion, enhancing its ballistic missile defenses, and demonstrating the effectiveness of its conventional precision strike capabilities. Meanwhile, China was experiencing a rapid economic rise and using its wealth to enhance its military power. Under these conditions, Russia's nuclear arsenal was one of the only viable ways to offset its quantitative and qualitative disadvantages along two fronts. Notably, Moscow continues to have many more nonstrategic weapons than does Washington, along with a far more diverse arsenal.[13]

Although Russia's current emphasis on nuclear weapons might seem familiar, there is a significant difference between US dependence on these weapons during the Cold War and Russia's reliance on them today. Simply put, Russia is a revisionist power that seems determined to chip away at the current regional order in Europe and reestablish its influence abroad. Consistent with these motives, it appears to view its nonstrategic nuclear arsenal as a tool of intimidation and coercion rather than just an instrument of deterrence.

In recent years, Moscow has repeatedly rattled its nuclear saber in an effort to unnerve its neighbors. It has also gravitated to the idea that nonstrategic nuclear weapons can be employed effectively to de-escalate a conventional conflict.[14] According to Gen. (Retired) Philip Breedlove, former commander of European Command and Supreme Allied Commander Europe, "The Russians speak about, write about, and train to use tactical nukes as a logical and understood extension of conventional war."[15] From this perspective, the resort to demonstration shots or limited strikes with low-yield weapons would erase any doubts about Moscow's determination to end a clash on favorable terms—and convince an adversary to back down rather than continue to fight with its conventional forces or conduct a nuclear reprisal.

Consider, for instance, two potential scenarios. In the first one, Moscow might attempt to use nuclear threats against NATO's frontline members to undermine its cohesion. That is, Moscow might calculate that other NATO members will remain on the sidelines due to their fears of escalation. In the second scenario, Moscow could be tempted to employ nuclear weapons during a conventional conflict to get the upper hand. By conducting a handful of strikes against key targets, it might improve its position on the battlefield and put the onus on its adversaries to continue climbing the escalation ladder. Either contingency would put NATO in a very difficult position because it does not have many options to respond in kind. US nonstrategic nuclear weapons are few in number and might not be immediately available, while the legacy aircraft tasked with delivering them might not survive against advanced Russian air defenses. Alternatively, the threat to retaliate with US strategic nuclear weapons, which have much higher yields, might not be credible in response to a limited nuclear attack.[16]

Europe is not the only region where this dynamic is at play. An analogous situation is unfolding in South Asia, where the India/Pakistan rivalry now displays strong similarities to the current US-Russian relationship. For instance, India remains the stronger conventional military power, thanks in large part to its greater wealth, territory, and population.[17] Although the acquisition of nuclear weapons by both sides initially appeared to level the playing field between them, proliferation has had more complicated implications. Consistent with the stability/instability paradox, the risks of nuclear war have enabled Pakistan, as the party with revisionist aspirations, to engage in lower-level provocations that impose costs on its rival, from supporting proxy forces to employing its own troops in limited engagements.[18]

This has prompted a dangerous tit-for-tat, one that could erode strategic stability in the region.[19] Due to lengthy mobilization times that undermined their responsiveness and expansive war aims that could have triggered a nuclear reprisal, New Delhi's conventional military forces have so far proven unable to deter Islamabad from pursuing a cost-imposing strategy. To rectify this situation and reestablish deterrence, New Delhi moved toward a new army doctrine, often referred to as "Cold Start," which envisions rapidly deployable combined-arms formations making shallow penetrations into Pakistan—punishing Islamabad for its actions and seizing territory small enough that it would not threaten the integrity of the nation but large enough that it would serve as a valuable bargaining chip.[20]

Not surprisingly, Pakistan has taken steps of its own to deter this type of retaliation. Specifically, Islamabad appears to have developed what Vipin Narang refers to as an "asymmetric escalation" posture, which calls for the limited use of relatively low-yield weapons to slow Indian forces and, perhaps even more important, demonstrate a clear willingness to conduct additional nuclear strikes.[21]

Just as the possibility of Russian limited nuclear use would put NATO in a difficult bind given the alliance's dwindling nuclear options, the prospect of a limited nuclear attack by Pakistan would leave India in a similar situation. To date, India has opted for a nuclear posture of assured and massive retaliation, one that emphasizes absorbing the first blow and launching a devastating reprisal.[22] Yet this threat would not be very credible in the aftermath of a limited attack because it could trigger a massive retaliation by Pakistan. India might then face a difficult all-or-nothing dilemma of its own.

THE EMERGENCE OF MULTIPOLAR NUCLEAR COMPETITIONS

The growing likelihood of limited nuclear use is not the only challenge to strategic stability that the United States needs to worry about; it also needs to assess the implications of multipolar nuclear competitions in a number of regions, something that it did not need to seriously consider in the past.

Traditionally, the concept of strategic stability has been developed, analyzed, and refined almost exclusively in a bipolar context, which reflects the extent to which the US/Soviet rivalry dominated thinking on this issue. Multipolar competitions have the potential to be far more complicated, however, because nations must base their policies, doctrines, and force structure decisions on two or more opponents rather than just one. Shifting coalitions can also quickly upend the existing nuclear balance.[23] Of course, competitions involving several nuclear powers (or more) existed during the Cold War and persist today. For instance, the United States, Britain, and France all possessed nuclear weapons and were aligned against the Warsaw Pact. The United States was also engaged in rivalries with the nuclear-armed Soviet Union and nuclear-armed China, at least until the Sino-Soviet split and the Sino-American rapprochement altered the geopolitical landscape. And now the United States and its allies in Northeast Asia must take into account two nuclear powers, China and North Korea.

In each of these cases, the potential impact of having more than two nuclear-armed competitors was dampened by factors such as alliance relationships and disparities in arsenal size. Thus bipolar dynamics (whether US-Soviet, US-Russian, or US-Chinese) remained the key to identifying the sources of strategic stability and instability. Yet this might not be the case for much longer. Current proliferation trends, along with broader changes that are taking place in the security environment, suggest that genuine multipolar nuclear competitions could become more common.

For instance, a multipolar competition is starting to play out in South Asia, where India, Pakistan, and China all possess nuclear weapons and have arsenals of roughly comparable size. Moreover, each of these nations is engaged in significant modernization efforts: India is close to fielding a strategic triad by adding an undersea leg to its current force structure; Pakistan is expanding its fissile material production capacity and pursuing the limited nuclear options outlined above; and China is developing new delivery systems and upgrading older ones. In this strategic triangle, moves by any one nation could quickly alter calculations on the part of the other two, providing added fuel for a potential arms race. The situation is especially precarious for India given the close ties between Pakistan and China and the need to plan against both rivals.

Another region where a multipolar nuclear competition could emerge is the Middle East.[24] This possibility has been a topic of frequent speculation given Iran's nuclear ambitions. For years, policymakers have warned that a proliferation "cascade" or "chain reaction" would be the likely consequence if Tehran managed to acquire nuclear weapons. According to then-president Barack Obama, a nuclear-armed Iran "would spark an arms race in the world's most unstable region."[25] For instance, Saudi Arabia could perhaps leverage its long-time support for Pakistan, convincing Islamabad that it should provide its benefactor with weapons that would counterbalance an Iranian bomb. Likewise, nations such as Egypt, Turkey, and the United Arab Emirates might go down a similar path for a variety of reasons, from regional power politics to domestic or international prestige. Although these scenarios do not seem very likely in the near term due to the agreement between Iran and the P5+1 (the five permanent members of the United Nations Security Council plus Germany) that has temporarily curbed Tehran's nuclear program, they could become more plausible if this agreement falls apart or after it expires.

Finally, the prospect that additional nuclear powers might emerge in East Asia should not be ignored.[26] South Korea and Japan both have the resources necessary to acquire nuclear weapons if they decide they need them, and the consequences of such a decision would be enormous. If these neighbors were to go nuclear, the region would suddenly be home to five nuclear-armed nations with overlapping rivalries, deep historical tensions, and various contemporary disputes. In fact, this scenario might be more plausible than many suspect, due to North Korea's growing nuclear arsenal and China's growing conventional military power.

During the past decade, North Korea has firmly established itself as the latest addition to the nuclear club, despite repeated efforts by the international community to avoid this outcome. Publicly available estimates suggest that it has perhaps a dozen or more nuclear weapons in its arsenal, the fissile material to make twice as many, and the potential to build fifty or more weapons by the end of the decade.[27] In addition, Pyongyang has continued to expand and improve its inventory of ballistic missiles. According to one Pentagon report, it already "has an ambitious ballistic missile development program and has deployed mobile theater ballistic missiles capable of reaching targets throughout the ROK [Republic of Korea—South Korea], Japan, and the Pacific theater."[28] Even before its recent spate of missile tests, which have demonstrated considerable progress toward fielding an intercontinental ballistic missile, some senior Defense Department officials had suggested that North Korea might have the ability to field nuclear warheads small enough and sturdy enough to be carried by an intercontinental ballistic missile.[29]

The combination of more warheads, more delivery systems, and longer-range weapons would increase the survivability and the reach of North Korea's nuclear arsenal. What does this mean for the possibility of proliferation in the region? To date, South Korea and Japan have both been content to take shelter under the US nuclear umbrella and forgo nuclear weapons of their own. Once North Korea has the ability to absorb a counterforce attack and launch follow-on nuclear strikes, and especially after it has the ability to credibly threaten a nuclear attack against US territory, American allies might begin to have serious doubts about the viability of extended deterrence—especially extended nuclear deterrence. This situation would give them a new incentive to reconsider their views on nuclear weapons.[30]

Along with the nuclear threat from North Korea, Japan has another challenge to worry about: a declining conventional military balance with China. During the past two decades, Beijing has been implementing a significant program of military modernization and reform. As a result, the People's Liberation Army has been able to undermine many of the advantages that Japan and the United States have taken for granted in the past, such as the ability to operate freely throughout China's maritime periphery. Specifically, the People's Liberation Army has moved away from its traditional emphasis on continental defense against rival land powers and embraced counterintervention against opposing sea powers, or what many US analysts refer to as antiaccess / area denial (A2/AD).[31] This entails efforts to defend its eastern air and maritime approaches at progressively greater ranges (and perhaps to carve out a sphere of influence in and around its near seas) by fielding a variety of land-attack, sea-denial, counterair, and counternetwork capabilities.

Thus, China has not only narrowed and perhaps reversed the relative military power gap with Japan; it has also undermined the United States' ability to come to the defense of its ally. Under these conditions, policymakers in Tokyo might eventually conclude that a small nuclear deterrent is the only way to guarantee Japan's security.[32] And, as then–vice president Joe Biden warned Chinese leaders, Tokyo could go nuclear "virtually overnight."[33]

THE END OF THE EXTENDED NUCLEAR DETERRENCE MONOPOLY?

With an extensive network of allies and security partners, the United States has always had unique responsibilities when it comes to extended deterrence. Over the course of decades, it has formed defense pacts with dozens of countries throughout the world and has provided informal security assurances or guarantees to a number of others, many of which still remain in effect. As one recent article explains, "The United States is legally obligated to defend a patchwork of nations that spans five continents, contains 25 percent of the world's population, and accounts for nearly 75 percent of global economic output."[34] This impressive tally does not even include many of Washington's informal alliances, such as its unwritten guarantees to members of the Gulf Cooperation Council.[35]

Since the end of the Cold War, the United States has also been the only nation to unambiguously cover other countries with its nuclear umbrella, not only to prevent attacks against them but also to dissuade them from pursuing nuclear capabilities of their own. An underappreciated consequence of the second nuclear age, however, is that the number of potential security providers is increasing. Washington could therefore find that other nations eventually become willing to accept the risks and reap the benefits that come from offering nuclear guarantees.

One place where this might occur is the Middle East, a region where US commitments are informal, US partners have close ties to other nuclear powers, and US rivals might look for opportunities to extend their influence at Washington's expense. For instance, if Tehran were to violate its nuclear agreement with the P5+1, then its neighbors might look to other external actors for support, especially if they determine that Washington cannot or will not offer more robust commitments to protect them. Alternatively, even if the nuclear deal remains intact, local nations might simply conclude that Washington intends to retrench from the region in order to refocus its attention elsewhere. If so, they might conclude that finding a new ally makes more sense than managing Tehran on their own, and that getting a nuclear guarantee might enhance their security once the nuclear deal expires.

How plausible are these scenarios? As noted above, there has been considerable speculation over the years that Saudi Arabia and Pakistan have some type of arrangement that would help Riyadh acquire nuclear weapons of its own or give it a nuclear-backed security guarantee, if the desert kingdom were under duress.[36] According to one report, "Saudi officials have long believed they have the semblance of a nuclear umbrella provided by Pakistan, a fellow Sunni nation whose own nuclear weapons program was launched decades ago with generous Saudi help."[37] This could become more tangible in a variety of ways, from an announcement by Islamabad that it would employ its nuclear weapons against an aggressor if Riyadh were attacked, to the actual deployment of Pakistani nuclear weapons on Saudi territory. Looking further ahead into the future, Beijing or Moscow might view nuclear guarantees as a way to extend its influence in the region. Security commitments could, for example, give Beijing more sway over the nations that supply much of its oil, and could help to reestablish Moscow's status as a global competitor of Washington.

Regardless of the particular scenario, extended nuclear deterrence commitments by other nations would not only weaken the United States' leverage over its partners in the region but would also raise the likelihood of horizontal escalation as nuclear crises in the Middle East draw in outside powers or as conflicts in other regions spill into the Middle East.

IMPLICATIONS FOR THE UNITED STATES

What does this all mean for policymakers in Washington? The return of geo-politics, the emergence of a second nuclear age, and the sources of instability that might arise from the intersection of these trends will have major implications for the United States—including its role in the world, the shape of its alliances, and the details of its nuclear strategy and force structure.

First and foremost, looming challenges—such as the search for nuclear escalation advantages by revisionist powers, the emergence of multipolar nuclear competitions in different regions, and the possibility of other nations getting into the extended nuclear deterrence business—should reinforce America's role in the world by highlighting the dangers of retrenchment. Put another way, these challenges make it even less likely that the United States will abandon its existing grand strategy of global leadership and engagement in favor of an alternative grand strategy such as offshore balancing.

In general, global leadership and engagement rests on several principles, including the need to preserve the freedom of the commons, to prevent the emergence of hostile hegemons, and to protect overseas allies. Offshore balancing, by contrast, would involve abrogating many US security commitments and significantly reducing the United States' forward military presence in most areas.[38] Although the latter approach has a number of potential drawbacks, one of the biggest is that burden shedding and buck-passing could incentivize former allies to develop their own nuclear weapons (or, failing that, to find other security providers willing to offer nuclear guarantees). In other words, while offshore balancers believe that US allies can often check aggression on their own, doing so against stronger and more capable rivals could require taking steps that would make nuclear crises more likely and nuclear escalation more difficult to manage. Policymakers, therefore, will be reluctant to adopt a strategy that could catalyze or exacerbate the sources of instability described above.

Second, rather than pulling back from its allies, the United States might find that it needs to move closer to them as it tries to dampen or avoid strategic instability. For instance, to enhance deterrence vis-à-vis Russia despite the capability gap that has emerged in Europe, the United States might consider adapting NATO's institutional structure. During the Cold War, the alliance developed two important mechanisms that formalized and underpinned the United States' nuclear umbrella. First, the Nuclear Planning Group allowed any interested NATO member to participate in high-level discussions on nuclear issues, and therefore gave those members a greater voice in US policy.

Second, nuclear-sharing arrangements allowed select NATO members to host US nuclear weapons on their territory and to deliver them with US authorization during a conflict against the Warsaw Pact. Together, these mechanisms kept NATO members like West Germany from pursuing their own nuclear weapons by giving them a more acceptable substitute; assured local nations that the United States would fight on their behalf by giving them more influence over escalation dynamics; and deterred conflict by putting nuclear weapons into the hands of frontline nations that were most at risk from Soviet aggression. Expanding these nuclear-sharing arrangements to include newer NATO members that are the most directly threatened by a resurgent Russia, the most determined to counter Moscow's provocations, the most supportive of NATO's nuclear status, and the most willing to engage in nuclear operations if necessary would send a clear signal that NATO will not cede escalation dominance, and therefore might prevent limited nuclear use by a revisionist rival.[39]

In a similar vein, Washington could decrease the odds of proliferation in East Asia by importing NATO-like mechanisms into the region. Although the United States has explicitly extended its nuclear umbrella to South Korea and Japan, and although it previously stationed nuclear weapons in the area, it has never implemented the type of combined nuclear planning and nuclear sharing institutions that it developed in Europe. If South Korea and Japan begin to seriously consider nuclear acquisition, however, this might need to change. With a clearer window into US nuclear operations and a direct role in these operations, at least under certain conditions, Seoul and Tokyo might be willing to forgo indigenous nuclear weapons programs—an option that would require enormous resources and could lead to a permanent rupture with Washington. As for Washington, moving toward combined nuclear planning and nuclear sharing might be preferable to watching two of its closest allies develop and field independent nuclear weapons. In such a scenario, the United States would have no control over these weapons, including when and how they might be used. Moreover, Japanese and South Korean nuclear arsenals that were untethered to the United States could end up being a major source of instability between these two nations, irrespective of their impact on North Korea and China.

Avoiding instability in the Middle East presents a thornier problem in some respects than either Europe or Asia, simply because the United States' options for assuring its local allies are more limited. For example, it is highly unlikely that Washington would offer public, formal, and binding guarantees to any Gulf Arab nations given the political backlash that would surely follow. And it is even less likely that Washington would store nuclear weapons on the territory of local allies given persistent fears of instability and concerns that they might fall into the wrong hands. The United States could, however, revisit its decision to abandon sea-based, nonstrategic nuclear weapons. By reintroducing tactical nuclear weapons at sea (either by putting nuclear gravity bombs on carriers or, more likely, by placing a future nuclear-tipped cruise missile on surface combatants or submarines), Washington would be able to dedicate part of its nonstrategic arsenal to the defense of nations in the region without having to base nuclear weapons on their territory. This, in turn, might be sufficient to convince them not to seek out other nuclear umbrellas.

Third, these sources of instability and the potential means to mitigate them strengthen the case for reassessing US nuclear strategy and weaken the case for significant nuclear cuts, two issues that are closely intertwined.

For more than two decades, the United States' nuclear strategy has been a recurring topic of debate. These debates have centered on three questions: What principles are enduring, what aspects are obsolete, and what new elements should be introduced? The issues discussed above highlight the importance of these questions and suggest a starting point when it comes to looking for answers. As the security environment continues to change, the United States needs to not only manage the global strategic balance with Russia but also needs to address regional nuclear challenges that differ from one another in their character, scope, and wider implications. This provides an added impetus to develop and implement what the 2010 *Quadrennial Defense Review Report* referred to as "tailored, regional deterrence architectures."[40]

Debates over US nuclear strategy have gone hand-in-hand with calls for deep reductions in the US nuclear arsenal and the eventual elimination of nuclear weapons. At least until recently, these calls were growing louder due to a variety of factors: fears that terrorist groups will acquire a nuclear device, downward pressure on the US defense budget, and the apparent decline of great power competition. In the second nuclear age, however, the United States still has a diverse set of concerns, from deterring conflict with a nuclear peer to assuring allies that face growing threats. This, in turn, suggests that the United States should think twice before making additional cuts to its nuclear arsenal that could create or widen capability gaps with potential rivals, embolden competitors to expand their own arsenals, or encourage allies to get nuclear weapons of their own because security commitments have become less credible. In fact, the United States might actually find itself in need of a larger nuclear arsenal—in particular, a larger nonstrategic nuclear arsenal—because it remains unclear whether a shrinking stockpile will be adequate to deter increasingly serious threats to its allies in Europe, dissuade proliferation on the part of its increasingly vulnerable partners in East Asia, and ensure that Middle Eastern nations remain on its side.

CONCLUSION

Throughout the post–Cold War era, there has been a growing sense of optimism in many circles that nuclear weapons were becoming anachronistic and obsolete—and that the dangers of an earlier era were just an aberration. The two major powers that were responsible for producing the vast majority of the world's nuclear arms were no longer rivals, and one of them no longer even existed. Meanwhile, the United States enjoyed an unprecedented conventional military advantage over any adversary that remained, and therefore was able to rely less and less on its nuclear arsenal to prevent acts of aggression. Over the past several years, however, this optimism has waned.

Tensions in Europe have been worsening as Russia has annexed Crimea, destabilized Ukraine, violated arms control agreements, and engaged in nuclear intimidation. The situation in East Asia is not much better and might even be worse, with China building artificial islands in disputed areas and North Korea continuing to test nuclear weapons and delivery systems. South Asia remains a potential flashpoint, while the nuclear agreement with Iran has reduced the likelihood of proliferation in the Middle East over the near term but left US relations with its regional allies in a delicate state. In short, renewed geopolitical competition and the enduring problem of proliferation have made that earlier sense of optimism seem premature. They have also combined to generate a new (but not necessarily novel) set of challenges for the United States—namely, the prospect of limited nuclear use, the possible spread of nuclear weapons to close allies, and the potential for other allies to seek out nuclear guarantees from those that might be willing and able to provide them.

Although these challenges might pale in comparison with those that Washington faced during the Cold War, they illustrate just how complex the security environment has become and why a more regionally differentiated approach is now needed to understand the sources of strategic instability and identify possible solutions. These challenges will also require a reassessment of the United States' grand strategy, alliance relationships, and nuclear capabilities—and perhaps a reinvigoration of all three.

NOTES

1. Important treatments of these issues include those by Thomas C. Schelling, *The Strategy of Conflict* (Cambridge, MA: Harvard University Press, 1960); Robert Jervis, *The Meaning of the Nuclear Revolution: Statecraft and the Prospect of Armageddon* (Ithaca, NY: Cornell University Press, 1990); and Charles L. Glaser, *Analyzing Strategic Nuclear Policy* (Princeton, NJ: Princeton University Press, 1991). For general overviews of US nuclear capabilities and strategy, and how both evolved throughout the Cold War,

see Fred Kaplan, *The Wizards of Armageddon* (Stanford, CA: Stanford University Press, 1983); Scott D. Sagan, *Moving Targets: Nuclear Strategy and National Security* (Princeton, NJ: Princeton University Press, 1989); and Lawrence Freedman, *The Evolution of Nuclear Strategy*, 3rd ed. (New York: Palgrave Macmillan, 2003).

2. For a notable exception, see the essays in *Strategic Stability: Contending Interpretations*, ed. Elbridge A. Colby and Michael S. Gerson (Carlisle, PA: Strategic Studies Institute of US Army War College, 2013).

3. Walter Russell Mead, "The Return of Geopolitics: The Revenge of Revisionist Powers," *Foreign Affairs* 93, no. 3 (May–June 2014): 69.

4. See, e.g., Colin S. Gray, *The Second Nuclear Age* (Boulder, CO: Lynne Reinner, 1999); Andrew F. Krepinevich, *Meeting the Challenge of a Proliferated World* (Washington, DC: Center for Strategic and Budgetary Assessments, 2010); Paul Bracken, *The Second Nuclear Age: Strategy, Danger, and the New Power Politics* (New York: Times Books, 2012); and Gregory D. Koblentz, *Strategic Stability in the Second Nuclear Age* (Washington, DC: Council on Foreign Relations, 2014).

5. Some of the arguments presented in this chapter draw on Evan Braden Montgomery, *Extended Deterrence in the Second Nuclear Age: Geopolitics, Proliferation, and the Future of US Security Commitments* (Washington, DC: Center for Strategic and Budgetary Assessments, 2016).

6. On the potential blurring of conventional and nuclear operations, see Barry D. Watts, *Nuclear–Conventional Firebreaks and the Nuclear Taboo* (Washington, DC: Center for Strategic and Budgetary Assessments, 2013).

7. Office of the Secretary of Defense, *Nuclear Posture Review Report* (Washington, DC: US Department of Defense, 2010), 5–6.

8. On the size, composition, and location of US nonstrategic nuclear weapons over time, see Stephen I. Schwartz, ed., *Atomic Audit: The Costs and Consequences of US Nuclear Weapons since 1940* (Washington, DC: Brookings Institution Press, 1998); and Robert S. Norris and William M. Arkin, "Where They Were," *Bulletin of the Atomic Scientists* 55, no. 6 (1999).

9. Hans M. Kristensen, *Non-Strategic Nuclear Weapons*, Special Report 3 (Washington, DC: Federation of American Scientists, 2012); Hans M. Kristensen and Robert S. Norris, "Worldwide Deployments of Nuclear Weapons, 2014," *Bulletin of the Atomic Scientists* 70, no. 5 (2014); and Amy F. Woolf, *Nonstrategic Nuclear Weapons* (Washington, DC: Congressional Research Service, 2015).

10. All the Air Force's nonstrategic nuclear weapons are variants of the B61 gravity bomb (the B61–3, B61–4, and B61–10). The current life-extension program will consolidate four variants of the B61 (also including the strategic B61–7) into a single model, which can be carried by short-range fighters and long-range bombers alike. Because the tactical B61–4 will be the basis for the newly renovated weapon, the end result will be a smaller pool of bombs that are expected to fulfill both strategic and nonstrategic missions. See Hans M. Kristensen, "The B61 Life-Extension Program: Increasing NATO Nuclear Capability and Precision Low-Yield Strikes," Federation of American Scientists Issue Brief, June 2011; and Hans M. Kristensen and Robert S. Norris, "The B61 Family of Nuclear Bombs," *Bulletin of the Atomic Scientists* 70, no. 3 (2014).

11. See George Perkovich, Malcolm Chalmers, Steven Pifer, Paul Schulte, and Jaclyn Tandler, *Looking beyond the Chicago Summit: Nuclear Weapons in Europe and the*

Future of NATO (Washington, DC: Carnegie Endowment for International Peace, 2012), 7, 9.

12. Stephen J. Blank, "Russia and Nuclear Weapons," in *Russian Nuclear Weapons: Past, Present, and Future*, ed. Stephen J. Blank (Carlisle, PA: Strategic Studies Institute of US Army War College, 2011), 293. Moscow formally abandoned any pretense that it would not be the first side to resort to nuclear escalation in the early 1990s.

13. Hans M. Kristensen and Robert S. Norris, "Russian Nuclear Forces, 2015," *Bulletin of the Atomic Scientists* 71, no. 3 (2015).

14. Jacob W. Kipp, "Russian Doctrine on Tactical Nuclear Weapons: Contexts, Prisms, and Connections," in *Tactical Nuclear Weapons and NATO*, ed. Tom Nichols, Douglas Stuart, and Jeffrey D. McCausland (Carlisle, PA: Strategic Studies Institute of US Army War College, 2012), 133. See also Roger McDermott, "Putin's Use of the 'Nuclear Card,'" *Eurasia Daily Monitor* 12, no. 122 (June 30, 2015); and Matthew Kroenig, "Facing Reality: Getting NATO Ready for a New Cold War," *Survival* 57, no. 1 (February–March 2015). The extent to which Moscow has actually developed the capabilities, operational concepts, and command-and-control arrangements needed to fully put this type of nuclear strategy into practice remains unclear, however. See Dmitry Adamsky, "Nuclear Incoherence: Deterrence Theory and Non-Strategic Nuclear Weapons in Russia," *Journal of Strategic Studies* 37, no. 1 (2014).

15. Quoted by Alex Lockie, "Former NATO Commander: We Need to Talk to Russia about Nuclear Deescalation," *Business Insider*, June 11, 2016. These concerns appear to be widely held among US officials. See Geoff Dyer, "Obama's Plans for Nuclear Arsenal Raise Fears of New Arms Race," *Financial Times*, March 31, 2016.

16. Keir A. Lieber and Daryl G. Press, "The Nukes We Need: Preserving the American Deterrent," *Foreign Affairs* 88, no. 6 (November–December 2009); and Keir A. Lieber and Daryl G. Press, "The New Era of Nuclear Weapons, Deterrence, and Conflict," *Strategic Studies Quarterly* 7, no. 1 (Spring 2013).

17. The extent of India's conventional military advantage has often been dampened by a number of factors, however, including the need to disperse its resources to manage a variety of internal and external threats, as well as the long timelines required to mobilize its garrisoned forces and maneuver them to the front.

18. This paradox was introduced in Glenn Snyder, "The Balance of Power and the Balance of Terror," in *Balance of Power,* ed. Paul Seabury (San Francisco: Chandler, 1965). On its applicability to South Asia, see Michael Krepon, "The Stability-Instability Paradox, Misperception, and Escalation Control in South Asia," in *Escalation Control and the Nuclear Option in South Asia*, ed. Michael Krepon, Rodney W. Jones, and Ziad Haider (Washington, DC: Henry L. Stimson Center, 2004); and Šumit Ganguly, "Nuclear Stability in South Asia," *International Security* 33, no. 2 (Fall 2008).

19. See Evan Braden Montgomery and Eric S. Edelman, "Rethinking Stability in South Asia: India, Pakistan, and the Competition for Escalation Dominance," *Journal of Strategic Studies* 38, nos. 1–2 (2015).

20. Walter C. Ladwig III, "A Cold Start for Hot Wars? The Indian Army's New Limited War Doctrine," *International Security* 32, no. 3 (Winter 2007–8).

21. Vipin Narang, "Posturing for Peace? Pakistan's Nuclear Postures and South Asian Stability," *International Security* 34, no. 3 (Winter 2009–10); and Vipin Narang, *Nuclear Strategy in the Modern Era: Regional Powers and International Conflict* (Princeton, NJ: Princeton University Press, 2014).

22. Ashley J. Tellis, "India's Emerging Nuclear Doctrine: Exemplifying the Lessons of the Nuclear Revolution," *NBR Analysis*, May 2001.

23. Evan Braden Montgomery, *Rethinking the Road to Zero* (Washington, DC: Center for Strategic and Budgetary Assessments, 2013).

24. See, e.g., Andrew F. Krepinevich, *Critical Mass: Nuclear Proliferation in the Middle East* (Washington, DC: Center for Strategic and Budgetary Assessments, 2013).

25. White House, Office of the Press Secretary, "Remarks by the President on the Iran Nuclear Deal," August 5, 2015, www.whitehouse.gov/the-press-office/2015/08/05/remarks-president-iran-nuclear-deal.

26. For a discussion of this possibility, see the various contributions to the round-table "Approaching Critical Mass: Asia's Multipolar Nuclear Future," *Asia Policy* 19 (January 2015).

27. Joel S. Wit and Sun Young Ahn, *North Korea's Nuclear Futures: Technology and Strategy* (Washington, DC: US-Korea Institute of Paul H. Nitze School for Advanced International Studies at Johns Hopkins University, 2015); and David Albright, *North Korea Plutonium and Weapon-Grade Uranium Inventories* (Washington, DC: Institute for Science and International Security, 2015). A more recent estimate suggests that Pyongyang could actually have more than twenty nuclear weapons, thanks to additional production of weapons-grade uranium. See David Albright and Serena Kelleher-Vergantini, "Plutonium, Tritium, and Highly Enriched Uranium Production at the Yongbyon Nuclear Site," Imagery Brief, Institute for Science and International Security, June 14, 2016.

28. Office of the Secretary of Defense, *Annual Report to Congress: Military and Security Developments Involving the Democratic People's Republic of Korea* (Washington, DC: US Department of Defense, 2014), 10.

29. Aaron Mehta, "US: North Korean Nuclear ICBM Achievable," *Defense News*, April 8, 2015; Elizabeth Shim, "US Commander: North Korea Has Capacity to Miniaturize Nuclear Warheads," *UPI*, October 9, 2015; and Elizabeth Shim, "Pentagon: North Korea Not Yet Capable of Striking US," *UPI*, April 14, 2016.

30. South Korea might have another reason to consider acquiring nuclear weapons—namely, to negate the escalation advantage that has enabled North Korea to engage in lower-level provocations, from sinking ships to shelling islands. In other words, policymakers in Seoul might conclude that nuclear weapons would provide them with greater latitude to retaliate, and therefore might help to deter these provocations.

31. In general, antiaccess capabilities are used to prevent or constrain the deployment of opposing forces into a distant theater of operations, whereas area-denial capabilities are used to restrict their freedom of maneuver once in theater. On these challenges, see Andrew F. Krepinevich, "The Pentagon's Wasting Assets," *Foreign Affairs* 88, no. 4 (July–August 2009); and Evan Braden Montgomery, "Contested Primacy in the Western Pacific: China's Rise and the Future of US Power Projection," *International Security* 38, no. 4 (Spring 2014).

32. Japan's willingness and ability to acquire nuclear weapons are frequently discussed in the security studies literature. See, e.g., Llewelyn Hughes, "Why Japan Will Not Go Nuclear (Yet)," *International Security* 31, no. 4 (Spring 2007); James R. Holmes and Toshi Yoshihara, "Thinking about the Unthinkable: Tokyo's Nuclear Option," in *Strategy in the Second Nuclear Age: Power, Ambition, and the Ultimate Weapon*, ed. Toshi Yoshihara and James R. Holmes (Washington, DC: Georgetown University Press,

2012); and Richard J. Samuels and James L. Schoff, "Japan's Nuclear Hedge: Beyond 'Allergy' and Breakout," in *Strategic Asia 2013–14: Asia in the Second Nuclear Age*, ed. Ashley J. Tellis, Abraham M. Denmark, and Travis Tanner (Seattle: National Bureau of Asian Research, 2013). It is important to also note that South Korean and Japanese calculations will almost certainly influence one another. Given the tensions that still exist between these two neighbors, if one were to go nuclear, the other would face added pressure to follow suit. Mark Fitzpatrick, *Asia's Latent Nuclear Powers: Japan, South Korea and Taiwan* (New York: Routledge / International Institute for Strategic Studies, 2016), 13.

33. "Japan Could Get Nuclear Weapons 'Virtually Overnight,' Biden Tells Xi," *Japan Times*, June 24, 2016.

34. Michael Beckley, "The Myth of Entangling Alliances: Reassessing the Security Risks of US Defense Pacts," *International Security* 39, no. 4 (Spring 2015): 7.

35. For instance, after a high-profile meeting between President Barack Obama and officials of the Gulf Cooperation Council (GCC) nations at Camp David in May 2015, the White House issued a joint statement declaring that the United States was "prepared to work jointly with the GCC states to deter and confront any external threat to any GCC state's territorial integrity that is inconsistent with the UN Charter." See White House, Office of the Press Secretary, "US–Gulf Cooperation Council Camp David Joint Statement," May 14, 2015, www.whitehouse.gov/the-press-office/2015/05 /14/us-gulf-cooperation-council-camp-david-joint-statement.

36. For discussions of this possibility, see *Chain Reaction: Avoiding a Nuclear Arms Race in the Middle East*, Report to the Committee on Foreign Relations of US Senate, 110th Congress, Second Session, February 2008 (Washington, DC: US Government Printing Office, 2008); Eric S. Edelman, Andrew F. Krepinevich, and Evan Braden Montgomery, "The Dangers of a Nuclear Iran: The Limits of Containment," *Foreign Affairs* 90, no. 1 (January–February 2011); and Christopher Clary and Mara Karlin, "The Pak–Saudi Nuke, and How to Stop It," *The American Interest* 7, no. 6 (June 2012).

37. Yaroslav Trofimov, "Saudi Arabia Considers Nuclear Weapons of Offset Iran," *Wall Street Journal*, May 7, 2015.

38. On global leadership and engagement, see Stephen G. Brooks, G. John Ikenberry, and William C. Wohlforth, "Don't Come Home, America: The Case against Retrenchment," *International Security* 37, no. 3 (Winter 2012–13): 7–51; and Evan Braden Montgomery, *Reinforcing the Front Line: US Defense Strategy and the Rise of China* (Washington, DC: Center for Strategic and Budgetary Assessments, 2017). On offshore balancing, see Eugene Gholz, Daryl G. Press, and Harvey M. Sapolsky, "Come Home America: The Strategy of Restraint in the Face of Temptation," *International Security* 21, no. 4 (Spring 1997); Christopher Layne, *The Peace of Illusions: American Grand Strategy from 1940 to the Present* (Ithaca, NY: Cornell University Press, 2006); and Barry R. Posen, *Restraint: A New Foundation for US Grand Strategy* (Ithaca, NY: Cornell University Press, 2014).

39. Brad Roberts, *The Case for Nuclear Weapons in the 21st Century* (Stanford, CA: Stanford University Press, 2016), 194–95.

40. US Department of Defense, *Quadrennial Defense Review Report* (Washington, DC: US Department of Defense, 2010), 14.

2

The Russian Approach to Strategic Stability

Preserving a Classical Formula in a Turbulent World

ANDREY PAVLOV AND ANASTASIA MALYGINA

WHAT ROLE IS ASSIGNED to nuclear weapons in the modern Russian defense doctrine? How does the modern Russian military and political establishment interpret the definition of strategic stability and the factors that endanger it? To what extent do changes in the economic, technological, and political environment affect Russia's understanding of ways to maintain strategic stability? This chapter takes a close look at these questions.

The accepted understanding of "strategic stability" in Russia differs fundamentally from the definitions used by other countries. Examining the history of the formation of this term can reveal the reason for this phenomenon. During the Cold War, the nuclear arms rivalry between the USSR and the United States was an important factor in Soviet foreign policy. The need to continuously adapt the configuration of its nuclear forces and to present a strong position during negotiations forced Russia to create a clear and comprehensive conceptual framework in order to effectively carry out these tasks. The result became the initial conceptualization of strategic stability. Given its rather narrow "instrumental" nature, the concept was applied in the Soviet Union only in the sphere of nuclear weapons.

As a legacy from the Soviet Union, Russia inherited nuclear weapons, the foundations of nuclear strategy, and the interpretation of the term "strategic

41

stability." However, the modern Russian vision of strategic stability is not solely limited to defining the role of nuclear arms. The contemporary Russian conceptualization of strategic stability takes into account new trends in the modern world's political, economic, and technological development. Considerable attention is given to factors such as the development of missile and antiballistic technology, conventional precision weaponry, and space systems. At the same time, nuclear weapons still hold primary importance in modern Russian military strategy. From this perspective, Russia's approach to strategic stability can be seen as an adaptation of the Soviet legacy to the modern world.

After the collapse of the Soviet Union, the Russian concept of strategic stability evolved in several stages and was affected by both internal and external factors. On one hand, the unrealistic hopes of the Russian leadership for equal partnership with the West in the 1990s collided with the reality of a systemic crisis. The weakening economy, along with major problems in the social sector, tested the established logic behind the concept of strategic stability. On the other hand, the expansion of NATO to the East, and especially the operation against Kosovo in 1999, generated an external impulse that directed further development of the Russian concept of strategic stability toward a more traditional understanding.

The first section of the chapter examines the fundamental elements of the concept of strategic stability during Gorbachev's perestroika in the 1990s. It was during this time that Russo-American nuclear arms control cooperation resulted in the formal expression of the concept of strategic stability that existed during the Cold War period in an implicit form. The second section explores the results of a shift from romanticism to pragmatic traditionalism that occurred in the first decade of the 2000s. In the third section, we go into the details of the contemporary agenda of Russian military and political debates. The formula of strategic stability constructed during the Cold War period is relevant to the present time because it is the basis for defining the technical requirements of the Russian modern weaponry systems that are needed to support strategic stability. The core logic of this formula, which remains unchanged, is the absence of incentives for a first nuclear strike. In the fourth section, we look at the range of options available for maintaining strategic stability that are currently being discussed in Russia.

The classical understanding of strategic stability that was formed during the Cold War period did not undergo any fundamental changes during perestroika and the collapse of the USSR, and it provides the analytical foundation for modern Russian defense policy. In today's rapidly changing global environment, the Russian concept of strategic stability retains its conservative nature but also tends to adapt to the rapid changes in technologies and in the international arena. Thus, any future prospects concerning the development of the Russian concept of strategic stability should be considered, depending on how the Russian military and political establishment interprets the factors that undermine strategic stability and the factors that can help to maintain it.

PERESTROIKA AND THE 1990S: ILLUSIONS VERSUS REALITY

The idea of "stability" was often used in the Soviet rhetoric of the Cold War period. Although it was somewhat amorphous in the sociopolitical discourse, and this ambiguity remains to this day, this does not imply that, in military-political and diplomatic circles, this term was loosely defined. On the contrary, during the Cold War, among Soviet officials, the term "strategic stability" contained precise semantic content and was used to define specific military-political circumstances. By the end of the Cold War, Soviet military theoreticians frequently used the term "strategic balance" on par with the concept "strategic stability." These two terms were widely used in the field of nuclear strategy, and both described a situation that allowed for the possibility of mutually assured destruction—MAD. However, the terms were not synonymous. As a multifactorial phenomenon with its own internal dynamics, strategic stability played the role of an important element of national defense and security in the USSR, and later in the Russian Federation as well. The understanding of strategic stability primarily as nuclear parity with the United States allowed the construction of policies in the spheres of the development of strategic weaponry and strategic arms control based on more or less accurate calculations. Scientists at the Academy of Sciences of the USSR and at military think tanks have developed a methodology for assessing the strategic balance through the use of mathematical modeling and systematic analysis.[1]

Mikhail Gorbachev's reform policies, and the resulting process of mutual reduction of nuclear weapons, did not change the interpretation of the term "strategic stability" as it had been established during the Cold War. A joint Soviet-American statement in June 1990 reiterated the original interpretation of the basic formula of strategic stability: "The objectives of these negotiations [for the Strategic Arms Reduction Treaty, START] will be to reduce further the risk of outbreak of war, particularly nuclear war, and to ensure strategic stability, transparency, and predictability through further stabilizing reductions in the strategic arsenals of both countries. This will be achieved by seeking agreements that improve survivability, remove incentives for a nuclear first strike, and implement an appropriate relationship between strategic offenses and defenses."[2]

Thus, the formula of strategic stability in 1990 reflected an understanding that was grounded in the logic of the Cold War. The lack of incentives for a nuclear first strike suggested that neither party would be immune to danger. Even if one party were to strike the first blow, the other party would still have the means to strike back with sufficient force to deal unacceptable damage to the enemy. Given such interplay of the nuclear forces, neither nation would need to choose between striking first and losing everything without an opportunity to retaliate. This formula became the basis for calculating the degree of military capability necessary to maintain strategic stability, and it remains relevant to this day.

The collapse of the Soviet Union, and Russia's inheritance of its status as a nuclear state, took place in several stages. On June 12, 1990, the Russian Soviet Federative Socialist Republic declared state sovereignty. However, Russia, led by Boris Yeltsin, remained in the USSR for almost one and a half years after that. At the time, Russia had its own Ministry of Foreign Affairs, but it did not have a Ministry of Defense, a General Staff, or any structured security agencies. On August 21, 1991, Yeltsin's supporters suppressed a coup attempt aimed at preserving the Soviet Union and removing the Soviet president, Mikhail Gorbachev. Thus began a rapid process of the complete collapse of the Soviet Union. The prominent Russian analyst Roland Timerbaev remarks that, during this transition period, "mechanisms related to foreign and military policy continued to work with the Soviet inertia." On December 8, 1991, Russia, Ukraine, and Belarus signed the Belavezha Accords, legalizing the collapse of the Soviet Union. On December 25, 1991, the first Russian president, Boris Yeltsin, took the "nuclear button" from the first and only Soviet president, Gorbachev.

The aim of Russian policy at the beginning of the 1990s was to preserve strategic stability, which was defined, by default, along the same lines as in the late Soviet period, amid the process of bilateral reductions of strategic offensive weapons. The negotiations on further reductions of strategic armaments that began between the USSR and the United States continued between Russia and the United States. Therefore, it was important for the Russian delegation to know what level of nuclear forces should be considered sufficient and what configuration of nuclear forces would be optimal for maintaining strategic stability. The formula stated in the 1990 joint Soviet-American statement remained the basis for any calculations regarding the level and configuration of nuclear forces.

At the same time, some among the Russian leadership had hopes for the development of a strategic partnership with the United States. As a result, the government made compromises that caused sharp disagreement among the politicians and the military. For example, a number of disputes arose in response to the main provisions of the second Strategic Arms Reduction Treaty (START II), which was signed in 1993. This agreement included an obligation to eliminate all intercontinental ballistic missiles (ICBMs) with multiple warheads and to destroy all heavy ICBMs. Such was a condition was put forth by the United States, and Russia accepted it, even though these missiles formed the basis of its nuclear forces. To carry out this task, Russia would need to radically alter the structure of its nuclear forces, which would prove to be an exceedingly difficult task in light of Russia's ongoing economic crisis.[3]

During Russo-American negotiations, the lack of unified opinions among experts complicated Russia's task of defining its positions on certain issues. The situation in the 1990s was truly controversial. The leadership of the Russian Federation, as well as the leadership of the late Soviet Union, had unreasonably high hopes for a future equilateral partnership with the United States, and believed that the importance of mutual nuclear deterrence would decline in correlation with the implementation of agreements aimed at overcoming the logic of the Cold War confrontation. On January 27, 1992, President Yeltsin sent a message to the UN secretary-general highlighting Russia's goal "to make its weighty contribution to the creation of a single global space of cooperation and security." The letter said: "We are no longer adversaries of the United States and the other NATO countries, and we consider as obsolete a situation in which we aim our nuclear sights at each other. We must by joint effort decisively deliver ourselves from this legacy of the period of confrontation and 'cold war.' "[4]

These sentiments reflect that the concept of "strategic stability" and "strategic balance" were used side by side with the term "strategic partnership" in the Russian political discourse of the 1990s. The notion of "strategic partnership" served as a reference to the expectations of equal cooperation; trust; long-term, mutually beneficial agreements; and equality in decision-making with regard to the configuration of the new world order. After the end of the Cold War, Russia was not ready to engage in a dialogue framed in zero-sum terms. When coming to decisions on strategic issues, Moscow expected Washington to see it as a partner with an equal status.

However, the systemic crisis that engulfed Russia after the collapse of the Soviet Union inevitably affected the situation of the Russian armed forces. In light of this context, the Russian military and certain political elites perceived that the Russian nation's sovereignty and defensive capabilities, as well as its chance to maintain the status of a great power and its ability to influence the configuration of the new emerging world order, were closely linked with the image of Russia as a nuclear superpower. This was the main reason why, during the transition period of the 1990s and early 2000s, the Russian leadership chose to adapt the foundations of nuclear strategy to the new military-political and economic conditions rather than reformulate them completely.

Moreover, NATO's eastward expansion and the response of the West to the disintegration of Yugoslavia were perceived by Russia as a violation of the partnership agreements and an act of infringement on its national interests. The illusions held by the Russian leadership about the possibility of building a strategic partnership with the United States quickly dissipated and were replaced with a more pragmatic approach to foreign relations. The traditional interpretation of strategic stability—which implied Russia's preserving nuclear parity with the United States, and Russia's carrying out the arms reduction process without excessive concessions—became a natural part of the new Russian leadership's pragmatic thought. Even during the period of the government's most "romantic" policy, many influential Russian officers, politicians, and experts continued to believe in the need to maintain strategic balance with the United States. Under the new conditions, their ideas were in demand.

THE 2000S: FROM ROMANTICISM TO PRAGMATIC TRADITIONALISM

Marshal Igor Sergeev—who held the post of chief of the Russian Strategic Missile Forces from 1992 to 1997 and served as the Russian defense minister from 1997 to 2001—consistently advocated for the preservation of the priority role of strategic nuclear forces and for maintaining parity with the United States. His understanding of strategic stability and parity remained traditional and was nearly identical to the one that prevailed during the Cold War.

However, the chief of the General Staff, Gen. Anatoly Kvashnin, had different ideas. He sought to drastically and unilaterally reduce Russian strategic nuclear forces; he believed that deterring the United States did not require maintaining parity in nuclear weapons. This idea was not a result of any newly developed concept of strategic stability. Rather, it was an effort to find resources to restore the combat capability of the degraded Russian ground forces. In the context of Russia's serious economic crisis, this objective could be achieved only by reducing other weapons purchases within the available military budget.

Kvashnin's plan called for a reduction of land-based ICBMs, the elimination of mobile, ground-based ICBMs, and the reassignment of the Strategic Missile Forces to the command of the Air Force. Strategic submarines were to be the main component of the nuclear triad. The plan also included significant overall reductions in the number of nuclear weapons, which was to be carried out unilaterally. According to Sergei Rogov, the director of the Institute for US and Canadian Studies at the Russian Academy of Sciences, if the plan were to be implemented, by 2010 the Russian Federation would have 100 single-warhead

ICBMs, 8 to 10 strategic submarines with 160 to 200 submarine-launched ballistic missiles, and 50 to 60 strategic bombers.[5] Kvashnin practically proposed copying the structure of the US nuclear triad, but at a much lower level. With such drastic measures, he hoped to raise the necessary funds for an intensive development of the weakening conventional forces.

Kvashnin's proposal caused a number of sharp disagreements, with the opinion of the expert community divided and the minister of defense strongly against it. Rogov believed that "Kvashnin's proposal [is] a strategic surrender; the Russian Federation refuses the model of mutual nuclear deterrence on which strategic stability was based for decades."[6] According to Rogov and the other experts who preserved traditional views on strategic stability, the implementation of Kvashnin's plan would enable US nuclear forces to launch a disarming strike on the Russian strategic nuclear forces, completely depriving Russia of its ability to retaliate. Moreover, a unilateral reduction of Russian nuclear forces would nullify the desire of the United States to continue negotiations with Russia on the reduction of offensive weapons.[7]

President Vladimir Putin's first reaction to this initiative was positive. However, the United States' decision in 2001 to withdraw from the Anti–Ballistic Missile (ABM) Treaty and to create a national ballistic missile defense forced him to reassess. Putin was also influenced by Igor Sergeev, his recently appointed adviser on strategic stability issues. Sergeev held a broad interpretation of the concept of "strategic stability," according to which strategic stability is a situation when "neither party has options or interests and intentions for military aggression."[8] Such a situation is achieved through a variety of complex political, economic, military, and other measures, but nuclear balance nevertheless remains paramount.[9]

Marshal Sergeev believed that to accurately calculate the level of unacceptable damage would be a nearly hopeless or at least a highly demanding task, because the assessment would have to take into account too many diverse factors. According to Sergeev, the only reliable criterion was a rough equality of nuclear forces, in terms of parity in the number of weapons and their combat capabilities. He believed that such an interpretation of the concept of "strategic stability" allowed a more or less precise set of criteria for assessing the various actions of Russia and the United States in terms of their influence on any given situation. This had a twofold benefit. First, the actions of one or the other actor could be assessed as catalysts in reinforcing or undermining strategic stability. Second, the bilateral system of strategic arms control gained a relatively structured scale for determining the possible scope and limits of further negotiations on nuclear disarmament.

THE CONTEMPORARY AGENDA

The understanding of strategic stability supported by Sergeev was preserved by later generations as well. The main area of study regarding this problem in the 2010s was an assessment of how different actions, programs, and factors affect strategic stability. There were, however, proposals to revise the interpretation of the term and fill it with new meanings. In 2012, retired major general Vladimir Dvorkin wrote that "the relict concept of mutual nuclear deterrence of Russia and the United States not only lacks reason after the end of confrontation between the two world systems but also serves as a major obstacle to wholesome cooperation in many spheres of security."[10] Rather than focusing on strategic stability, he proposed addressing issues of global, transregional, and regional stability.

However, even critics such as General Dvorkin acknowledged that the traditional interpretation of strategic stability had become so deeply rooted among the Russian Federation's military-political leaders that attempting to change it would be pointless.[11] Evidently, the idea of mutual strategic deterrence for Russia and the United States remains a key element of modern Russian strategic thinking. Though there is debate about the extent to which certain conventional weapons affect deterrence, nuclear weapons still predominate in the calculus.

Collectively, then, five factors have been preserved from Soviet military-strategic thought that affect strategic stability and remain key variables in the contemporary formula, and the remainder of this section examines them in detail:

- Ballistic missile defense (BMD) systems;
- Conventional precision-guided munitions (PGM);
- Space-based weapons;
- Antisubmarine warfare; and
- The nuclear arsenals of the other nuclear countries, besides Russia and the United States.[12]

The progress in antisubmarine warfare today is rather limited, so, on contemporary agendas, the other four factors are regarded as the most important.

Ballistic Missile Defense

Problems associated with BMD always were the focus of Russo-American relations. In fact, in the early 2000s, some Russian experts wrote that "the preservation of the ABM Treaty is the foremost priority of the security policy of the Russian Federation, more important than even the continuation of nuclear arms reductions and the 'follow-through' regarding the question of the implementation of START II."[13] During this period, official declarations from Moscow equated the strengthening of strategic stability with the preservation the ABM Treaty in a static, unchanging state.

This interpretation of the meaning of the ABM Treaty was tied to the preservation of traditional conceptions of strategic stability. In 1972, the Soviet Union and the United States agreed to abandon their plans for the creation of a national missile defense system and to restrict their regional systems to one per nation. This was done precisely because expert opinions indicated that these systems could undermine strategic stability. The nations believed that a high level of security might provoke one of the parties to strike the other first in the event of a bilateral crisis. The preservation of past perceptions with regard to the basic principles of strategic stability in the new era also led to an unchanged approach to the ABM Treaty.

After the United States' withdrawal from the ABM Treaty, the development (and subsequent deployment) of US missile defense systems was seen in Russia as a key factor negatively affecting strategic stability. The problem became particularly acute when the Americans announced their intention to place a third position for missile interceptors in Europe. Regardless of the statements made by the US claiming that the system was designed to protect against the threats originating from the ballistic programs of North Korea and Iran, senior Russian political and military leaders believed that the Americans were building a system against nonexistent threats, and therefore they suspected that it could be directed against Russia in order to tilt the strategic balance in favor of the United States.

The ability of the most advanced elements of BMD to intercept ballistic targets was seen as a probable threat to the Russian potential for nuclear retaliation. In the 2000s, Russia's nuclear forces were constantly shrinking because of the disposal of old strategic missiles that had become outdated. In addition, the country was unable to maintain its previous level of armaments because it could not replace older missiles with an appropriate number of new ones. The obvious conclusion resulting from such reasoning has been a belief, consistently echoed by President Putin, that the US BMD system undermines strategic stability.

During the negotiations concerning New START in 2009–10, Russia attempted to include strategic defensive arms—namely, the elements of the US BMD—into the sphere of subjects susceptible to restrictions. President Barack Obama's decision in the summer of 2009 to review the plans regarding the deployment of missile defense elements in Europe greatly contributed to the ultimate agreement, while Russian diplomatic efforts yielded relatively modest success. The only achievement of Russian negotiators was the inclusion of a provision in the introductory part of the agreement that recognized "the existence of an interrelationship between strategic offensive arms and strategic defensive arms, that this interrelationship will become more important as strategic nuclear arms are reduced, and that current strategic defensive arms do not undermine the viability and effectiveness of the strategic offensive arms of the Parties."[14] This excerpt was later officially used by Moscow as a starting point for dialogue with the United States. Specifically, Russian officials have repeatedly declared that Russia might withdraw from the treaty if the United States chooses to strengthen its BMD system to a level that would emasculate strategic stability.

At a time when Russia and the United States were negotiating New START, the US BMD deployment plan was only at the first stage of implementation. The deployment of a limited number of systems capable of intercepting Russian ICBMs was not able to seriously alter the strategic balance. The biggest concern of the Russian military was the fact that the US political leadership had not entirely given up on the deployment of BMD elements near Russia's border. According to the Russian military, future deployment of antimissile interceptors in Romania and Poland, along with the creation of bases for ships equipped with antimissile systems in these and other European countries, may have changed the situation. The US plans concerning the creation of a global BMD system are still regularly reviewed. If such a decision were made, the creation of a structure that bases BMDs in Europe would allow the US to quickly increase the combat capabilities of missile defense systems.

Soon after the commencement of START 2010, President Dmitry Medvedev announced in November 2011 that Russia may withdraw from New START in response to the deployment of missile defense elements in Europe.[15] This was premised on a broad military assessment of the detrimental consequences for Russia's strategic deterrence endorsed by the High Command. As detailed by the chief of the General Staff, Nikolay Makarov, the Russian military would adopt an appropriate plan of action to preserve strategic stability that would include

1. Entry into service of the new radar in the Kaliningrad region to improve control over launches of American missiles and antimissile interceptors.
2. Strengthening the defenses of strategic nuclear sites: the deployment of additional air and missile defense capabilities, the use of special measures for camouflage, and the restriction of information regarding the status and activities of the strategic nuclear forces.

3. Equipment of ICBMs and submarine-launched ballistic missiles (SLBMs) with new advanced warheads and BMD penetration aids.
4. Adoption of measures to disrupt the functionality of various BMD system elements in different ways—from electronic jamming to physical destruction.
5. Deployment of new strike weapons in the south and northwest of Russia for the possible destruction of BMD components.
6. Refusal to enact further plans aimed at disarmament and arms control, including the withdrawal from START.

Although Moscow's official position remains unchanged, and fundamentally represents the static position of the Russian leadership in the second half of the 1990s, Russian experts have been engaging in a dynamic debate with a rich variety of arguments and analyses. The famous Russian experts involved in the creation of the book *Anti–Ballistic Missile Defense: Confrontation or Cooperation?* believe that the prospective US missile defense system in Europe will not be able to seriously affect the capability of Russian strategic nuclear forces to retaliate in the event of a hypothetical conflict, and thus is not able to undermine strategic stability.[16] Their conclusions are based on detailed analyses and comparisons of the technical characteristics of Russian strategic systems with elements of the US missile defense.

The experts' calculations show that the interceptor missiles stationed in Europe will be able to threaten only a small fraction of the Russian warheads that pass over Scandinavia, given the fact that Russian strategic missiles are equipped with means of overcoming missile defense systems. Moreover, the majority of Russian warheads launched from the Russian territory pass over the Arctic. Taking into account the time it takes to detect the launch and to make the decisions to intercept targets, a comparison of the interceptors' and the warheads' flight rates shows the impossibility of destroying the Russian warheads.

Experts of the leading Russian think tank, the Institute for US and Canadian Studies of the Russian Academy of Sciences, reached the same conclusion in their report titled *Ten Years without START: The Problem of Anti–Ballistic Missile Defense in Russian-American Relations*. At the same time, these experts do not deny the danger of the United States making a decision to further develop this system after the enactment of the modern missile defense deployment plan. A potential threat in the long term could be posed not only by an increase in different means of interception but also by the creation of entirely new tools and in particular by the deployment of strike missile defense elements in space.[17]

For politicians, one possible indication that such plans may develop is the United States' rejection of the proposal to create a joint missile defense system with the participation of Russia. Russia also repeatedly offered to sign a formal agreement that would include the technical parameters of the future US missile defense system. An official consolidation of these parameters would provide Russia with a guarantee that any future missile defense system would not be aimed at undermining Russia's nuclear deterrence potential. The United States' refusal to discuss this option was seen as a sign of its hidden intentions to use the development of a missile defense system to exert political pressure on Russia in the future. Such perceptions were reinforced by the initial deployments of the US BMD system in Romania, which coincided with the ongoing Ukraine crisis.

Conventional Precision-Guided Munitions

Another question that is being actively discussed in political and expert circles is the assessment of how the development of existing and future PGMs undermines strategic stability. These systems, which are already available in the United States, are among the most advanced weapons systems in existence. US military strategists highly value the capabilities of these high-precision systems, and predict that they will primarily be used not for deterrence but for combat in a wide range of potential and existing conflicts. In addition, one must also take note of the fact that long-range, high-precision weapons systems affect strategic stability in its traditional nuclear understanding, because they could theoretically be used in the initial counterforce strike to reduce Russia's retaliation potential. Concerning this outcome, the opinions of the Russian analysts differ in their degrees of objectivity. An authority on this issue, Yevgeny Miasnikov, believes that the importance of US precision weapons for strategic stability should not be overstated, because their application in a hypothetical disarming strike against Russian nuclear forces cannot be unexpected and sufficiently fast, and their predicted effect decreases with the development of Russian mobile ICBMs. However, he also believes that "in the medium term, PGMs are a bigger threat for the survival of Russian strategic offensive weapons than BMD. This is because a breakthrough in the development of missile defense that would increase their effectiveness against ICBMs is not likely, and because the United States already has a large number of high-precision weapons that are continuously improved and multiplied."[18]

Today, the debate concerns itself with the prospective influence of the US Conventional Prompt Global Strike (CPGS) program on strategic stability. CPGS involves both the creation of new systems, such as the hypersonic X-51 system, and a possible use of existing ones, such as ICBMs and SLBMs armed with conventional warheads. In 2015, CPGS was still in the research-and-development stage, so neither NATO nor Russia was clear about exactly what type and quantity the US would deploy. In addition, although the use of ICBMs and SLBMs armed with conventional warheads is now no longer part of any US plans, Russia still considers the possibility of the US incorporating them in the future.

This uncertainty regarding the United States' plans for CPGS was perceived by Russian experts as a potential threat, and one that Moscow takes very seriously. In order to ensure strategic stability, Russia raised the issue of CPGS during the negotiations on strategic offensive arms, but that only partially solved the problem. In START 2010, nonnuclear ICBMs and SLBMs were recognized as nondeployed and were included among the restrictions. However, the development of high-precision weapons, which prove most worrisome for Russia, were not limited by any agreements whatsoever. In July 2013, the deputy prime minister, Dmitry Rogozin, stated that "under existing US estimates," the US high-precision weapons can destroy 80 to 90 percent of Russia's nuclear potential.[19] The studies that form the basis for this statement are unclear, and there is no evidence that such estimates were made by US experts. Nevertheless, Rogozin's claim carries a symbolic meaning, showing that Russia's political leadership is seriously concerned about the destabilizing potential of the American precision weapons.

Some experts point out that the American development of BMD systems, together with an increase in PGM weapons, may mutually reinforce one another to generate a cumulative destabilizing effect. Although acknowledging that these programs have no significant effect on strategic stability today, due to the relatively small quantities of available weapons, Russian experts still discuss the future development of these systems. The most radical opinion is one that considers the BMD system and PGM as elements of a general coordinated plan aimed to undermine Russia's nuclear deterrence potential. Here, the reduction of strategic nuclear forces is also part of this plot, which is the reason why the United States continues to offer reductions of offensive strategic weapons and actively seeks to discuss the reduction of the superior quantity of tactical (nonstrategic) nuclear weapons owned by the Russians.[20] The reduction of Russian tactical weapons, in their view, would weaken the "strategic deterrence at the regional level."[21] It is this particular future imbalance that Russian experts believe may become a potential threat caused by the Americans' intending to reduce strategic offensive arms while increasing nonnuclear weapons without any limits.

Space-Based Weapons

The possibility of the militarization of outer space is another problem that worries Russian experts. However, the types of weapons that can be placed in space and the impact of such initiatives remain unclear.

Space-based weaponry is understood as combat space systems that serve to destroy objects in and from outer space. Parity in space capabilities is considered to be critical for strategic stability. According to a report published by the Center of Political-Military Studies, an ABM system with elements deployed in space or effective antisatellite systems have destabilizing potential. The superiority of one party in space may create preconditions for its victory in any war or conflict. Disruption-of-space intelligence, surveillance, target acquisition, and reconnaissance systems may lead to the inability to control the situation on the battlefield. The inability to send commands to reconnaissance and strike complexes will in turn cause the loss of the ability to destroy attacking strategic bombers, submarines on duty, and mobile, ground-launched missile systems. The report argues that Russia maintains equality with the US in the range of space capabilities but falls behind the US with regard to the quality of the systems.[22]

Russia has consistently pushed for a number of initiatives in various international discussions in order to develop a legally binding restriction on the placement of weapons in outer space and also to prevent the transformation of outer space into a sphere of armed confrontation. Russian diplomats have argued for the idea of focusing on prohibition of these actions and their consequences rather than the means by which such actions can be implemented. None of the Russian efforts and initiatives have been able to gain the necessary support. The fact that Washington evades discussing any concrete steps toward preventing the further weaponization of outer space sparks serious concerns in Moscow. Many representatives of the Russian expert community believe that the lack of international legal mechanisms to prevent hostile actions of the involved parties with respect to aircraft deployed into orbit is a potential threat to the survival of Russian strategic nuclear forces and also creates a way for the United States to achieve hegemony in space.

The ambiguity of American BMD plans, in combination with a stalemate in space-based arms control negotiations, creates uncertainty that forces Russian experts to consider worst-case scenarios. Russian experts express their concerns that in the future, technically advanced antisatellite and orbit-based BMD systems may be deployed in outer space. If the US did deploy such systems, Russia would need to enforce the nuclear component of its strategic deterrence and develop more technically sophisticated antisatellite systems. In that scenario, the US would then most likely increase the number and capacity of its strategic offensive arms and BMD systems. According to Russian experts, this would lead to an arms race and would undermine "crisis stability."[23] A space-based arms race would be destabilizing, potentially leading to "horizontal nuclear proliferation and a breakup of the nuclear nonproliferation regime."[24]

A member of the Russian Institute for Strategic Studies, Vadim Kozin, characterized US actions as a process of implementation of a far-reaching plan to "gradually establish in space a powerful potential of information- and intelligence-gathering tools and space strike weapons."[25] The lack of clarity persisting in the US plans regarding research and development in this area calls for increased alertness and is interpreted by experts as a potential challenge to Russia's military security. The Center for Military-Political Studies at the Russian Foreign Ministry issued a report on the problem of preventing the militarization of outer space. The report states:

> Russian security and defense capabilities directly depend on the capacity and condition of strategic warning mechanisms aimed at identifying preparations for aggression, the beginning of a nuclear attack, as well as the quality of comprehensive, all-encompassing support of the space security forces, the Army and the Navy in peacetime and wartime. The military/strategic balance in the world and the prevention of large-scale conventional and nuclear wars today is guaranteed by Russia's ability to deliver an effective nuclear missile strike to the aggressor.

The authors suggest that if Russia cannot achieve parity in its conventional weapons with the United States, its main focus should be on maintaining its armed forces "at a level that impedes the ability to achieve the domination of the adversary in several areas of combat: in the air and space, and at sea and on land," while "any space assets are seen as strategic components, the parity of which is critical to the preservation of a military-strategic balance."[26] The report proposes introducing the concept of "space parity" and considering it as part of the military/strategic balance. Notably, the Center of Military-Political Studies mentions that the United States and China are potential rivals of Russia because these countries are actively involved in space exploration and may claim dominance in space. This was reinforced by an analysis by a leading civilian military expert and former deputy ministry of defense, Andrei Kokoshin, who highlighted the risks to strategic stability presented by US and Chinese space-based and antisatellite systems due to their direct threats to the ground- and space-based components of Russia's early warning systems.[27]

Other Nuclear Powers

A relatively new idea is a proposal to expand the scope and perspective of strategic stability to a triangular framework of Russia–US–China.[28] A well-known expert, Alexander Khramchikhin, wrote about the Chinese threat in 2013, when he published a book on the problems of the balance of forces and the increased military-political potential of China.[29] He believes that Russia should pay more attention to China's growing power, which, combined with the internal social and economic problems faced by this country, can become a source of military danger for Russia. Given that a conflict with the US is unlikely, Khramchikhin urges the Russian government to instead contain China. However, given the recent deterioration of US-Russian relations and the Russian leadership's declared intent to "turn to the East," his ideas are not currently supported. Certain military-strategic decisions can be regarded as an attempt to strengthen deterrence in the East, although this is never openly stated. Yet a "strategic partnership" with China does not raise concerns on an official level. Thus a shift of focus in the perception of strategic stability is currently off the agenda.

Still, the factoring of other nuclear powers into consideration has roots in the Cold War. Although maintaining stable deterrence with the United States was paramount, strategic stability had a European dimension as well. The Soviet Union considered the system of nuclear deterrence in the European theater an important element of the overall strategic balance. During the negotiations on strategic arms limitations in the 1970s, the Soviet side tried to include both US forward-based systems and nuclear weapons of US allies as topics on the agenda. The US consistently rejected the inclusion of these systems in the sphere of limitations. Unable to symmetrically expand its forward-based systems near the US border, the Soviet Union began to build up its nonstrategic nuclear potential in the European part of the country. NATO responded with a decision to deploy American missiles in Europe. The Soviets, in turn, reacted with an even greater buildup of forces.

In the early 1980s, the conflict regarding intermediate-range missiles deployed in Europe was one of the main sources of growing tension between the US and the Soviet Union. At the beginning of perestroika, the Treaty on the Elimination of Intermediate-Range and Shorter-Range Missiles (INF Treaty, 1987) solved this problem and served as the starting point for the bilateral nuclear arms reduction process.

In sum, the United States' development of BMD and PGMs, along with the lack of a solution to the problem of space militarization, undermines strategic stability from Moscow's perspective and therefore makes further agreements on the reduction of strategic offensive arms (e.g., START) unlikely. The Russian deputy defense minister, Anatoly Antonov, who headed his country's delegation at the negotiations on strategic offensive arms in 2009–10, summarizes this view:

> Russia cannot ignore the fact that, of the many factors that predetermine the maintenance of military security, Americans strive to stabilize only strategic nuclear weapons, while decisions regarding [problems] where the advantage is on the side of the United States are drown out. On this basis, the prospect of further reductions of strategic offensive arms is very problematic. Under these conditions, further reductions in strategic offensive arms in Russia and the US will serve not to strengthen strategic stability, but rather the opposite—to undermine it.[30]

PROSPECTS FOR MAINTAINING STRATEGIC STABILITY: THE EVOLUTION OR ADAPTATION OF THE CONCEPT

What is the suggested course of action for maintaining strategic stability that would meet the interests of the Russian Federation? The first and most obvious option is to build up strategic nuclear forces. But the implementation of this option is constrained by certain international, legal, economic, and technological obstacles. The main limit is established by New START, which assumes that by 2018, Russia and the US should have no more than 700 deployed ballistic missiles and heavy bombers, and 800 deployed and nondeployed launchers with 1,550 warheads on them.[31] Russian officials have repeatedly stated that in case of further deployment of US BMD systems and PGM systems, Russia may withdraw from New START. However, whether it will do so is highly questionable because Russian nuclear arms reductions have continued regardless of whether they were required by any agreements.

The basis of the Russian strategic nuclear forces remains the missile complexes included in the Strategic Missile Forces, but many of these have served their time and are out of date.[32] In 2015, according to expert assessments, Russian strategic forces had approximately 305 ICBMs—180 of which were old SS-19 (RS-18) ICBMs with 6 warheads each, and SS-18 (RS-20V) ICBMs with 10 warheads each—and also had single-warhead SS-25 Sickle (RS-12M "Topol") missiles, numbering about 850. The newest missiles were produced in 1992.[33] The shelf life of these missiles was repeatedly extended, with some systems reaching an impressive figure of thirty years. For example, in 2014 the shelf life of the missile complex SS-18 (RS-20V) was extended to twenty-seven years, and, for the first time, this procedure was performed without a test launch.[34] Extending missile shelf life involves a number of difficulties, so the outdated systems are phased out, resulting in a gradual and steady decline of Russia's nuclear forces. The year 2020 will see the expiration of a large number of the older missiles. It is fairly likely that the shelf life of a number of the most recent missiles of the older generation can be extended, but only for the duration of the period required to produce the same amount of new missiles necessary for the full replacement of the obsolete systems. An increase in the number of deployed strategic submarines is just as unlikely. New submarines are being built, but they are intended to replace the ones that already exist. By the early 2020s, there should be a total of 8 new ballistic missile submarines, meaning that once the new boats enter into service, the old ones will be decommissioned.

Still, new systems are being actively designed and manufactured. In December 2008, the commander of the Strategic Missile Forces, Gen. Nikolay Solovtsov, announced that Russian specialists were developing a new liquid-fuel missile, the characteristics of which will not yield to a complex SS-18 Satan (RS-20).[35] In December 2009, the commander of Russian strategic forces, Gen. Andrey Shvaychenko, announced plans to create a new Russian heavy liquid-fuel missile by the end of 2016.[36] Subsequently, the missile became known under the name "Sarmat" (RS-28). In June 2014, the director of the Center for Public Policy Research, Col. Vladimir Yevseyev, suggested that the complex Sarmat developed by the Makeyev Design Bureau should be deployed in 2018–20.[37] In addition to the ongoing creation of the missile complex Sarmat, there is also another missile in production: a solid-fuel ICBM with multiple, independently targetable reentry vehicles, SS-27 Mod 2 (RS-24 "Yars"). Another new mobile missile, "Rubezh" (RS-26), has been in the testing phase since 2011, and in 2013 the military began the development of a new rail-based system to be armed with RS-24 Yars.[38] The missile systems for submarines are currently being upgraded along with the others. The year 2007 was marked by the activation of an upgraded version of the liquid-fuel missiles manufactured from the mid-1980s to the mid-1990s: the ballistic missile named RSM-54 "Sineva," which is able to carry from 4 to 10 warheads. In 2014, the Russian command adopted the R-29RMU2 "Layner" missile.[39] The year 2012 was the first year for the serial production of the ballistic missile for strategic submarines named SS-NX-32 (RSM-56 "Bulava").

The basic priorities of the Russian nuclear forces are reflected in the State Armament Program 2020. Details of the plan for comprehensive modernization of the Russian armed forces have been refined in a number of Putin's speeches. In particular, in February 2012 he said that over the next ten years the army would receive more than 400 new ballistic missiles, that 8 new submarines would come into operation, and that the existing fleet of strategic bombers would be maintained and modernized.

Some experts have expressed doubts about the feasibility of completing certain drafted plans within the designated time frame.[40] However, even if the program is successfully implemented in the coming years, Russia's strategic nuclear forces will be subjected to reduction. Additionally, the development of strategic nuclear forces fully complies with the new framework of START, and although experts are considering several different options for its further development, none of these require exceeding the limitations of START 2010 in order to ensure the effectiveness of nuclear deterrence.[41] The restrictions of the new treaty provide Russia with sufficient opportunities to nimbly and flexibly respond to changes in the military-political sphere and allow the development of a wide range of advanced nuclear weaponry without violating the limits.

Moreover, according to numerous statements made by Russian politicians, military officials, and diplomats, the new Russian nuclear weaponry is fitted with advanced systems for overcoming both existing and predicted forms of BMD. In the context of the available technological, economic, and international legal restrictions, Russia has chosen to work on developing an asymmetric response to US actions, while the aim to maintain strategic stability in the traditional sense remains unchanged.

Although existing bilateral arms control agreements are not being seriously questioned, future prospects for arms reductions in the current political circumstances seem rather bleak. Russia does not have much motivation to engage in discourse on further reductions of strategic offensive arms or to discuss the prospects for limitations on nonstrategic nuclear weapons. Some of the most radical experts periodically return to the discussion of withdrawal from the INF Treaty, but it seems that this idea is not yet being taken seriously in political circles, and Moscow has not issued any official statements on it. For example, Anatoly Antonov believes that withdrawal from the INF Treaty could have negative consequences both for Russia and for the entire international arms control regime.[42] At the same time, the possibility of terminating the agreement cannot be completely ruled out as a result of one party's actions. With increasing intensity, Russia and the United States accuse each other of violating the agreement. Both states believe that the other is preparing to secure advantages by means of such a violation, and the possibility of one side losing its patience certainly exists.

Another option for strengthening strategic stability is the possibility of combining nuclear and nonnuclear weapons systems. The problem of nonnuclear deterrence has been a relevant topic of discussion among Russian experts for quite some time. The well-known Russian expert Andrei Kokoshin, who held the post of deputy defense minister (1992–1997), wrote that he had raised the issue of the strategic importance of conventional forces even then. Today, he still continues to advocate for the expansion of the scope of Russia's nonnuclear deterrence system: "Any forceful threat to use a high-precision, long-range delivery vehicle with a conventional warhead could become the basis of the prenuclear deterrence system that amplifies the nuclear deterrence system. In this regard, a potential aggressor must bear in mind that it may expect not just a strike on its military assets and forces, which are deployed and directly targeted at Russia, but on a number of other assets."[43]

He believes that in the case of aggression directed at Russia, conventional weapons may play a role of "the last warning" before the initiation of the use of nuclear weapons. The threat of sufficiently powerful nonnuclear attacks on major military targets, followed by attacks on civilian targets, would expand the range of available responses to various types of threats. Kokoshin believes that conventional means of strategic deterrence have the potential to become one of the elements of a new strategic triad, along with nuclear weapons and offensive and defensive cyber weapons.[44]

For a long time, ideas concerning nonnuclear deterrence were discussed only by experts and did not find support in official doctrinal documents. Among the tasks of the armed forces in peacetime, the Military Doctrine of 2010 contained "strategic deterrence, including the prevention of armed conflicts," and its 2014 edition added a bracketed phrase, "nuclear and non-nuclear," to the concept of strategic deterrence. This fact indicates that these ideas were eventually accepted at the highest level as well but so far have not been developed further.

At the same time, the idea of nonnuclear deterrence is heavily criticized by those who support the preservation of the traditional approach to strategic stability, which is built on the basis of nuclear deterrence. These objections are expressed primarily by military officials. The authors of an article in the journal *Military Thought*, published by the Ministry of Defense, believe that the "discourse on 'strategic nonnuclear deterrence' is at the very least inappropriate. Moreover, it is dangerous because it leads to a destructive transformation of Russian nuclear deterrence into nonnuclear [deterrence]."[45]

The main characteristics of such weapons should feature long-range and high accuracy, in conjunction with the high firepower of each missile. Such characteristics are present in the sea-based, long-range cruise missiles that are in service at the moment and in those that are under development. Another possible option is the conventional tactical missile SS-26 Stone ("Iskander"), which has a range of up to 500 kilometers. Moscow has repeatedly stated that this relatively new advanced system can be used to neutralize the elements of Washington's missile defense system in Europe.[46] In principle, this missile can also carry nuclear warheads, but this is never specified.

Several of the most advanced types of defensive conventional weapons also carry strategic significance. The development of air and space defenses is one of the most important priorities for modern Russia. In 2015 the Russian government decided to establish the Aerospace Forces, with Aerospace Defence as a part. Moreover, the newest antiaircraft systems, the S-400s, which are now coming into service, have the capability to intercept some cruise and medium-range ballistic missiles. According to official estimates, the S-500 system will have even greater capabilities for intercepting missiles of various types.[47] These systems can also be used to protect the positions of strategic nuclear forces in order to increase their survivability in the event of an enemy's counterforce strike. In this way, the threat posed by the use of high-precision nonnuclear weapons in the first disarming strike can be partially neutralized. Meanwhile, Russia has no plans to create a national missile defense system with capabilities that are comparable to those of the US system.

CONCLUSION

The concept of strategic stability is a core principle of Russian military strategy. Russo-American nuclear deterrence represents the foundation of Russia's nuclear strategy. Since the Cold War, multifactorial changes in the domestic and international realms have created a situation in which Russia has begun to treat nuclear weapons as the major rather than the sole instrument for maintaining strategic stability. In this way, Russia has tried to follow traditional principles in a rapidly changing world.

The commitment to the concept of mutual strategic deterrence has become deeply rooted in modern Russian strategic culture. Russia seeks to maintain strategic parity with the United States in a way that meets Russia's national interests. The military and political leaders of modern Russia believe that there is no alternative to mutual nuclear deterrence. They are confident that mutual nuclear deterrence continuously proves its efficiency in maintaining global security and stability. Furthermore, the modern Russian leadership sees no domestic or international imperatives to change established fundamental beliefs and behaviors.

The few opponents who criticize the traditionalist approach of the Russian government do not suggest any substitutes for the formula of strategic stability that was established during the Cold War. Their publications do not include any criteria or methodology for assessing defense programs or arms control agreements. Meanwhile, the concept of strategic stability remains narrow and instrumental. All Russian experts, including the opponents of preserving the concept of strategic parity, use the same traditional paradigm to study the factors that influence strategic stability. There are no innovative ideas concerning strategic stability that could serve as a solid basis for a public debate on the modernization of the core principles of Russian foreign and defense strategy.

Strategic stability is currently interpreted by the Putin administration in the same manner as the military and political establishments understood it during the presidency of Boris Yeltsin. Mutual deterrence in relations with the United States, based on the strategic balance and parity in the available options, remains the guarantee of strategic stability to this day.

Russia's nuclear arsenal is still a guarantor of its sovereignty and influence in international affairs. On one hand, it is important for Russia to maintain its status as an equal partner in dialogues with the United States. On the other hand, Moscow recognizes that for economic and technological reasons, it cannot maintain strategic parity with the United States in the field of conventional arms. The country's leadership recognizes that strategic stability is a multifaceted phenomenon. The multivector development of conventional weapons and the rapid development of informational and digital technologies are seen as factors with the ability to upset the strategic balance, but thus far the Russian leadership has not shown willingness to fundamentally revise the existing concept. The traditional interpretation, based on strategic balance and limited to the basic framework of bilateral relations between Russia and the United States, remains adequate and functional precisely because it provides sufficiently clear criteria for evaluating the parties' actions that can serve as a guide, both for the formulation of certain priorities for the modernization of conventional and nuclear weapons and also for navigating political issues concerning arms control. In light of the evolving conflict between Russia and NATO, the traditional foundation of strategic stability is becoming stronger. The growth of mutual suspicion and mistrust is not conducive to a joint search for new solutions. Rather, it makes the possibility of one side refusing to strive for the preservation of equality with a potential enemy even more impossible.

NOTES

1. В. И. Геловани, А. А. Пионтковский, *Эволюция концепций стратегической стабильности: Ядерное оружие в XX и XXI веке* (V. I. Gelovani and A. A. Piontkovskii, *The Evolution of the Concept of Strategic Stability in the 20–21st Centuries*) (Moscow: LKI, 2008).

2. "Soviet–United States Joint Statement on Future Negotiations on Nuclear and Space Arms and Further Enhancing Strategic Stability," June 1, 1990.

3. Анатолий Антонов, Контроль над вооружениями: История, состояние, перспективы (Anatoly Antonov, *Arms Control: History, State of Affairs, Perspectives*) (Moscow: Rosspen, 2012), 35.

4. Message dated January 27, 1992, from the President of the Russian Federation, B. N. Yeltsin, to the UN Secretary-General, A/47/77-S/23486.

5. Сергей Рогов, "Стратегическая капитуляция" (Sergei Rogov, "Strategic Capitulation"), *Nezavisimaja gazeta*, July 26, 2000, www.ng.ru/world/2000-07-26/1_strateg .html.

6. Ibid.

7. Сергей Рогов, "Ставка на ядерный щит" (Sergei Rogov, "Stake on Nuclear Shield"), *Nezavisimoje vojennoje obozrenije*, August 8, 2000, http://nvo.ng.ru/forces /2000-08-04/1_stavka.html.

8. Игорь Сергеев, "Без первого удара: Проблемы стратегической стабильности—История и современность" (Igor Sergeev, "Without the First Strike: Problems of Strategic Stability—History and Present"), *Rossiiskaja gazeta*, November 13, 2001, https:// rg.ru/Anons/arc_2001/1113/hit.shtm.

9. Ibid.

10. Владимир Дворкин, "Что способно разрушить стратегическую стабильность" (Vladimir Dvorkin, "What May Destroy Strategic Stability"), *Nezavisimoje vojennoje obozrenije*, August 17, 2012, http://nvo.ng.ru/concepts/2012-08-17/1_terror.html.

11. Владимир Дворкин, "Постстратегическая стабильность и дестабилизирующие факторы" (Vladimir Dvorkin, "Poststrategic Stability and Destabilizing Factors"), *Nezavisimoje vojennoje obozrenije*, February 22, 2013, http://nvo.ng.ru/concepts /2013-02-22/1_models.html.

12. Dvorkin, "What May Destroy Strategic Stability."

13. В. А. Орлов, Р. М. Тимербаев, А. В. Хлопков, Проблемы ядерного нераспространения в российско-американских отношениях: История, возможности и перспективы дальнейшего взаимодействия (V. A. Orlov, R. M. Timerbajev, and A. V. Khlopkov, *The Problems of Nuclear Nonproliferation in Russo-American Relations: History, Possibilities, and Perspectives of Further Interaction*) (Moscow: PIR-Center, 2001), 169.

14. Treaty between the United States of America and the Russian Federation on Measures for the Further Reduction and Limitation of Strategic Offensive Arms (START), 2010.

15. Dmitry Medvedev, "The Statement of the President of Russian Federation concerning the Situation Connected with the NATO Missile Defense System in Europe," November 23, 2011.

16. В. Пырьев, В. Дворкин, "Программа США/НАТО и стратегическая стабильность" (V. Pyriev and V. Dvorkin, "Program USA/NATO and Strategic Stability"), in *Противоракетная оборона: Противостояние или сотрудничество? (Anti–Ballistic Missile Defense: Confrontation or Cooperation?*), ed. A. Arbatov and V. Dvorkin (Moscow: Rosspen, 2012), 191–92.

17. Десять лет без договора по ПРО: Проблема противоракет- ной обороны в российско-американских отношениях (*Ten Years without START: The Problem of Anti–Ballistic Missile Defense in Russian-American Relations*), Academic Report of the Institute for US and Canadian Studies of the Russian Academy of Sciences (Moscow: Spetskniga, 2012).

18. Евгений Мясников, "Контрсиловой потенциал высокоточного оружия" (Evgenii Miasnikov, "Counterforce Potential of Precision-Guided Munitions"), in

Ядерное распространение: Новые технологии, вооружения и договоры (*Nuclear Proliferation: New Technologies, Weapons, and Treaties*), ed. A. Arbatov and V. Dvorkin (Moscow: Rosspen, 2009), 122–23; Евгений Мясников "Высокоточное обычное оружие" (Yevgeny Miasnikov, "Precision-Guided Conventional Weapons"), in *Ядерная перезагрузка: Сокращение и нераспространение вооружений* (*Nuclear Reset: Arms Reduction and Nonproliferation*), ed. A. Arbatov and V. Dvorkin (Moscow: Rosspen, 2011), 421.

19. "Dmitry Rogozin's Speech at the Press Conference at *Rossiiskaja gazeta*," *Rossiiskaja gazeta*, June 26, 2013, https://rg.ru/2013/06/28/doklad.html.

20. В. М. Буренок, Ю. А. Печатнов, "Стратегическая стабильность: Заблуждения и перспективы" (V. M. Burenok and A. Y. Petchatnov, "Strategic Stability: Delusions and Perspectives"), *Nezavisimoje vojennoje obozrenije*, March 7, 2014, http://nvo.ng.ru/concepts/2014-03-07/1_stabilnost.html.

21. Ibid.

22. И. Н. Голованев, В. А. Меньшиков, "Военно-космическая деятельность в современных геополитических условиях: Предотвращение милитаризации космического пространства" (I. N. Golovanev and V. A. Menshikov, "Military Space Activity in Modern Geopolitical Circumstances: Prevention of the Militarization of Outer Space"), Center of Political-Military Studies, www.eurasian-defence.ru/?q=node/33705.

23. А. Г. Арбатов, В. З. Дворкин, А. А. Пикаев, С. К. Ознобищев, *Стратегическая стабильность после холодной войны* (A. G. Arbatov, V. Z. Dvorkin, A. A. Pikayev, and S. K. Oznobischev, *Strategic Stability after the Cold War*) (Moscow: IMEMO RAN, 2010), 25.

24. Ibid., 35.

25. Владимир Козин, "Проблема предотвращения размещения оружия в космосе: Сравнительный анализ позиций США и России" (Vladimir Kozin, "The Problem of Prevention of Weapons Deployment in Outer Space: Comparative Analysis of USA and Russia's Positions"), *Problemy natsionalnoi strategii* 2, no. 11 (2012): 77.

26. Golovanev and Menshikov, "Military Space Activity."

27. Andrei Kokoshin, "Ensuring Strategic Stability in the Past and Present: Theoretical and Applied Questions," Belfer Center for Science and International Affairs, Harvard Kennedy School, June 3, 2011, 57, www.belfercenter.org/sites/default/files/legacy/files/Ensuring%20 Strategic%20S tability%20by%20A.%20Kokoshin.pdf.

28. A. Arbatov and V. Dvorkin, *The Great Strategic Triangle* (Moscow: Carnegie Moscow Center, 2013), http://carnegie.ru/2013/04/01/great-strategic-triangle-pub-51362.

29. Александр Храмчихин, *Дракон проснулся?* (Alexandr Khramtchikhin, *Is the Dragon Awake?*) (Moscow: Kliutch-S, 2013).

30. Antonov, *Arms Control*, 65.

31. New START Treaty, 2010.

32. Виктор Баранец, "Командующий РВСН генерал-лейтенант Сергей Каракаев: 'Владимир Владимирович был прав—мы можем уничтожить США быстрее, чем за полчаса'" (Victor Baranets, "Commander of Russian Strategic Missile Forces General Sergei Karakaev: 'Vladimir Vladimirovich Was Right—We Can Destroy the US More Quickly Than in Half an Hour'"), *Komsomolskaja Pravda*, December 16, 2011, www.kp.ru/daily/25805/2785953/.

33. Стратегическое ядерное вооружение России: "Ракетные комплексы" (Strategic Nuclear Armament of Russia: "Missile Complexes"), russianforces.org/rus/missiles/.

34. Владимир Мухин, "'Сатана' послужит России еще пять лет" (V. Mukhin, "'Satan' Will Serve Russia Five Years More"), *Nezavisimaja gazeta*, June 23, 2014, www.ng.ru/armies/2014–06–23/1_satan.html.

35. NEWSru.com, "В России разрабатывается новая тяжелая стратегическая ракета, подобная 'Сатане'" ("A New Heavy Strategic Missile Similar to 'Satan' Is Being Developed in Russia"), www.newsru.com/russia/19dec2008/raketa.html#close.

36. Лента.ру, "Россия создаст замену 'Сатане'" (Lenta.ru, "Russia Will Develop Replacement for 'Satan'"), https://lenta.ru/news/2009/12/16/antisatan/.

37. Mukhin, "'Satan' Will Serve Russia."

38. Российское информационное агентство, "Россия воссоздает боевые железно-дорожные ракетные комплексы" (Russian Information Agency, "Russia Is Reconstructing Combat Railway Missile System"), https://ria.ru/defense_safety/20130423/934029183.html#13667004582993&message=resize&relto=register&action=addClass&value=registration.

39. Интерфакс, "'Лайнер' пойдет в тираж" (Interfax, "'Layner' Will Propagate"), www.interfax.ru/russia/210987.

40. E.g., Юрий Федоров, "Государственная программа вооружений—2020: Власть и промышленность" (Yuri Fedorov, "State Program of Armament—2020: Government and Industry"), *Indeks bezopasnosti* 19, no. 2 (2013): 41–59.

41. E.g., Владимир Евсеев, "России нет смысла выходить из Договора о СНВ: Это никак не повлияло бы на решения американцев" (Vladimir Evsejev, "Russia Has No Sense to Withdraw from START: This Would by No Means Influence the Americans' Decision"), *Nezavisimoje vojennoje obozrenije*, February 21, 2014, http://nvo.ng.ru/realty/2014–02–21/1_snv.html.

42. Antonov, *Arms Control*, 68.

43. Kokoshin, *Ensuring Strategic Stability.*

44. Андрей Кокошин, "Стратегическое ядерное и неядерное сдерживание: Приоритеты современной эпохи" (Andrei Kokoshin, "Strategic Nuclear and Nonnuclear Deterrence: Priorities of the Modern Epoch"), *Vestnik rossiiskoi akademii nauk* 3, no. 84 (2014): 204, doi: 10.7868/S0869587314030086.

45. Владимир Полегаев, Владислав Алферов, "О неядерном сдерживании, его роли и месте в системе стратегического сдерживания" (Vladimir Polegajev and Vladislav Alferov, "On Nonnuclear Deterrence, Its Role and Place in the System of Strategic Deterrence"), *Vojennaja Mysl* 7 (2015).

46. Dmitry Medvedev, "The Statement of the President of Russian Federation concerning the Situation Connected with the NATO Missile Defense System in Europe," November 23, 2011; Николай Макаров, "О взглядах Министерства обороны Российской Федерации на проблемы противоракетной обороны" (Nikolai Makarov, "On the Views of the Ministry of Defense of Russian Federation on the Problems of Ballistic Missile Defense"), Speech at the Conference on ABM Held by the Ministry of Defense of Russian Federation, Moscow, May 3, 2012, http://stat.mil.ru/conference_of_pro/news/more.htm?id=11108 033@egNews.

47. Сергей Разыграев, "Роль войск ПВО в новом облике вооруженных сил РФ" (Sergei Razygrajev, "The Role of Anti–Ballistic Missile Defense Forces in the New Configuration of the Armed Forces of the Russian Federation"), Radio Ekho Moskvi, September 26, 2009, http://echo.msk.ru/programs/voensovet/622283-echo/.

3

Pakistan's View
of Strategic Stability

A Struggle between Theory and Practice

SADIA TASLEEM

"STRATEGIC STABILITY" is an acquired term in Pakistan's security discourse. Having tested its nuclear weapons almost two decades ago, it is only gradually developing its view of nuclear realities. Pakistan's view of strategic stability is narrowly shaped by regional concerns. At the strategic level, stability requires resolution of the Kashmir problem. At the operational level, Pakistani decision makers believe that stability will be attainable only by making one of two choices: Either India and Pakistan mutually agree to pursue a "strategic restraint regime," which would require a cap not only on nuclear weapons and missiles but also on conventional military capabilities; or Pakistan maintains a rough military parity—nuclear plus conventional—with India, both in quantitative and qualitative terms.

Given the existing stalemate over Kashmir, along with the unlikelihood of India agreeing to Pakistan's proposal for a strategic restraint regime (because of its concerns vis-à-vis China), Pakistan is increasingly defining stability from the perspective of maintaining a balance of nuclear forces vis-à-vis India. This is evident from Pakistan's efforts to diversify the number and types of its weapons and delivery systems. Also, it is rapidly increasing its fissile material stockpile.[1] It has started testing multiple independently targetable reentry vehicles and other medium- and short-range ballistic missiles. It also is reportedly

66

building a missile with sea-based, second-strike capability.[2] At the doctrinal level, it is gradually moving toward what may appear to be a war-fighting doctrine based on an asymmetric escalation posture.[3]

The concept of strategic stability, as originally developed in Western discourse during the Cold War, was largely framed in a bilateral context and considered the maintenance of a strategic balance—in the earlier phase, by engaging in an arms race, and later, through mutual restraint—to be essential for stability. This chapter argues that, contrary to the indigenously developed discourse on strategic stability during the Cold War, in South Asia the discussion regarding strategic stability was largely a product of international concerns regarding the likelihood of a preemptive nuclear war. Therefore, the early sensitization toward strategic stability even preceded operational nuclear deterrence. But after the operationalization of nuclear deterrence, the bilateral focus of the framework of strategic stability for maintaining a balance proved inappropriate for the qualitatively different quadrilateral dynamics of rivalries—involving Pakistan, India, China, and the US—marked by power asymmetries in South Asia. It created unnecessary pressures for weaker states to pursue arms competition vis-à-vis stronger rivals in an effort to maintain a balance. A similar operational understanding of strategic stability—rooted in a bilateral framework and the necessity to maintain a balance—has pushed Pakistan from the pursuit of minimum deterrence to full-spectrum deterrence, in view of the perceived growth of India's military potential, which itself is a consequence of India's threat perception vis-à-vis China.

This chapter attempts to explain Pakistan's view of strategic stability and to underscore the conceptual challenge of using strategic stability as a framework for analysis. For this purpose, it briefly traces the evolution of the concept of strategic stability in South Asia over the past few decades and highlights the challenge of applying a Cold War framework to a nuclear South Asia. It then explains Pakistan's view of strategic stability in light of the current political and military trajectories of India and Pakistan, which largely shape Pakistan's threat perceptions. It further explains the role of nuclear weapons in Pakistan's strategic calculus and sheds light on the questions about Pakistan's view of the credibility of its nuclear posture for deterrence purposes. Finally, the chapter analyzes the implications of Pakistan's ongoing military modernization efforts and evolving force posture, which it views as essentially stabilizing.

The chapter suggests that old terminologies such as "strategic stability," even if they are convenient to use, may create unnecessary incentives for a destabilizing arms competition among rival states. This could only be avoided by pursuing one of two options. The first option would be for Pakistan, India, China, and the US to develop mutually agreed-on criteria for assessing stabilizing technologies and weapons systems, and to make commitments to refrain from introducing destabilizing technologies. This idea, however, has serious limitations and therefore may not be practical. The second option these five states could choose in order to avoid the pitfalls of a destabilizing arms competition would be to frame their discourse in a language that takes into account the challenges faced by smaller and weaker states in the context of contemporary security dynamics. This could be accomplished by encouraging the development of an indigenous lexicon reflecting how India and Pakistan problematize their security issues pertaining to nuclear weapons—a lexicon not overshadowed by Cold War definitions and biases.

THE EVOLUTION OF "STRATEGIC STABILITY" IN SOUTH ASIA

Tracing the evolution of the idea of strategic stability in South Asian discourse reveals unique trends. The first signs of recognition of the prospects of instability in South Asia appeared in the 1980s, soon after India and Pakistan started making noticeable headway in their nuclear weapons programs. In the wake of India's Punjab crisis in 1984, Pakistanis, with the help of an American warning, suspected a preventive strike by the Indian Air Force against Pakistan's nuclear facility at Kahuta.[4] Pakistan put its forces and defense systems at Kahuta on alert. The crisis dissipated without any advance movement by the Indian Air Force.

Once this crisis was over, then–Indian prime minister Rajiv Gandhi—under the repeated calls from the Reagan administration to stabilize relations, and with advice from K. Subrahmanyam, the then–director-general of the Institute of Defense Studies and Analysis in New Delhi[5]—proposed to Pakistan the idea of signing a bilateral agreement with India not to attack each other's nuclear infrastructure.[6] Pakistan's president, General Zia-ul-Haq, agreed. However, the agreement was not signed until 1988[7]—one year after another major crisis, called Brasstacks—and was not ratified until the end of 1990, one year after still another military crisis, called the Compound Crisis.[8] From that time onward, Pakistan and India, realizing the potential risk, exchanged lists containing the coordinates of each other's nuclear-related facilities.[9] This step was at best a nuclear confidence-building measure, and an indicator of the efforts being made by policymakers in India and Pakistan to reduce the likelihood of a preventive war.

Changes in the global security environment after the end of the Cold War brought new concerns regarding threats of a further proliferation of nuclear weapons in relatively less stable and less developed parts of the world. Fear of nuclear use, either accidental or deliberate, the management of nuclear weapons, technical challenges related to safety and security, and the overwhelming fear of the possibility of terrorists getting access to these weapons had begun to occupy an important place on the agenda of the US Clinton administration.[10]

Strategic stability became the recommended path for the new nuclear-armed states, but with a focus on maintaining a balance by pursuing "restraint." As a result, the Clinton administration not only began to sensitize the governments in Islamabad and New Delhi regarding the need to work toward achieving strategic stability, but also helped them frame the requirements for stability in a nuclear South Asia.[11] To begin with, the US government urged both India and Pakistan to adopt a minimum deterrence policy. This would entail agreeing to impose a limit on the types of ballistic missiles, not to mount warheads on rockets, and not to deploy missiles near each other's borders. The US government also pressed the two sides to sign the Comprehensive Nuclear-Test-Ban Treaty and to enter into negotiations over the Fissile Material Cutoff Treaty, as well as adopt stringent nuclear- and missile-related export control measures and resume a dialogue with each other to resolve the root causes of their conflict.[12]

At about the same time, the United Nations Security Council had already passed Resolution 1172, which urged both India and Pakistan to adopt responsible behavior.[13] Under US sanctions and fear of international isolation, it was hard for India and Pakistan to completely dismiss the proposals advanced by the Clinton administration. At the time of the nuclear tests, the notion of "existential deterrence," based on restraint, was considered effective in both India and Pakistan.[14]

Therefore, both India and Pakistan agreed to follow through on some of the ideas proposed by the US administration. For instance, both countries announced their commitment to the idea of minimum deterrence.[15] Though neither state was ready to sign the Comprehensive Nuclear-Test-Ban Treaty or the Fissile Material Cutoff Treaty, both announced unilateral moratoriums against further testing of nuclear weapons.[16] Both states also made unilateral commitments to keep their weapons de-mated, off alert, and nondeployed.[17]

The leaders of both India and Pakistan dismissed international concerns about the dangers of nuclear war in South Asia.[18] Observers outside the region, however, were divided on the impact of nuclearization on peace and stability in South Asia. Some seasoned scholars in the US predicted that nuclear weapons would make South Asia more stable.[19] Others raised concerns about the ability of South Asian nations to deal with the complex technological challenges of nuclear weapons.[20]

Inside South Asia, however, euphoria kept growing—particularly when the political leaders on both sides agreed to resume dialogue with each other. As a result, Indian prime minister Atal Bihari Vajpayee, hailing from the hard-line right-wing Bharatiya Janata Party, visited Lahore and signed the Lahore Declaration with Pakistani premier Nawaz Sharif. The text of this declaration provided every reason to celebrate the ushering-in of a new era of peace in the region.[21] If the spirit of the Lahore Declaration had not been quashed by the Kargil Crisis, which began in May 1999, this could have easily been an unprecedented case of strategic sensibility and a foundation for strategic stability in the years ahead.

The Kargil Crisis was the outcome of a series of controversial moves planned by a core group of senior army officers under the command of the then–army chief general Pervez Musharraf. Pakistan's Northern Light Infantry troops moved in to the Indian side of the Line of Control in the Kargil area and captured forward positions on the crests, ridgelines, and mountaintops. Once the Indian government detected the Northern Light Infantry's ingress, it ordered its army to respond. A tactical operation soon brought India and Pakistan to the verge of a full-scale war. The Kargil Crisis revealed that Pakistan had not internalized the need to avoid confrontation under the nuclear overhang. An externally stimulated process of sensitization to vulnerability did not prove sustainable.

Kargil made South Asia once again the center of international attention. President Bill Clinton called Kashmir the world's most immediate nuclear flashpoint.[22] Scholars revisited old ideas of strategic stability in the light of this new case study. These ideas included survivability issues, a balance of forces, command and control, preventive war, risk reduction, crisis management, arms control, and confidence-building measures. The results were diverse. Some argued that the Kargil Crisis had exposed a serious fault line in nuclear South Asia that meant the threat of war and therefore that escalation had not disappeared from the nuclear subcontinent.[23] Others argued that the very fact that the Kargil Crisis remained limited and that India, despite having to fight under difficult circumstances, did not open hostilities across the international border meant that a large-scale war was no longer possible in South Asia.[24] Some also debated if the Kargil Crisis was a classic manifestation of Glenn Snyder's stability/instability paradox, a proposition suggesting that stability at the higher end of a conflict spectrum instigates instability at the lower end.[25] Later, the debate was further advanced by the introduction of a new framework built on what is called the stability-instability paradox, where a weaker revisionist state exploits the likelihood of the use of nuclear weapons in favor of changing the status quo by engaging the stronger side in a subconventional war.[26]

Regardless of the arguments of proliferation optimists and pessimists, one thing became obvious against the backdrop of Kargil: South Asia would need to struggle through its own periods of instability and learn how to manage both nuclear weapons and nuclear crises. The decade after Kargil uncovered new phases of optimism and skepticism, and major disappointments. During the last sixteen years, India and Pakistan have faced two serious crises, along with a nearly four-year-long peace process that garnered hopes but remained inconclusive because of numerous domestic and regional factors. All these years have affected the nature of the debate on strategic stability in South Asia, leading to an increased focus on strengthening nuclear deterrence capabilities.

Strategic Stability: Differences between Cold War Europe and Nuclear South Asia

As mentioned above, strategic stability is not an indigenous concept for South Asia, but a framework and policy objective recommended by the US. This section highlights the distinctions between the nuclear realities of Cold War Europe and contemporary South Asia. The aim is to explain why a conversation framed in the language of strategic stability may not be appropriate for the dynamics of nuclear deterrence in South Asia.

To begin with, South Asia is completely different from the Western world in its sociocultural context. Both Indian and Pakistani strategic culture embrace uncertainty, unlike in the United States, where science has driven the country to the path of reducing uncertainty as much as possible. Moreover, what is considered irrational in the West is often glamorized and romanticized in the popular cultures of India and Pakistan. As a matter of fact, when Pakistan conducted nuclear tests—knowing full well both the diplomatic and military consequences of its decision—Pakistan's prime minister, Nawaz Sharif, recited a verse from the national poet, Allama Muhammad Iqbal:

> Transliteration: *Bay khatar quod parha aatish-e-Namrood mein Ishq.*
> *Aql hai mehv-e-tamashai-lab-e-baam abhee.*
> Translation: Love plunged into Nimrud's fire without hesitation.
> Reason is on the rooftop, just contemplating the scene.[27]

So, through a sociocultural lens, stability, certainty, and crisis prevention are not priorities in India and Pakistan. However, it is important to mention here that India's and Pakistan's approaches to dealing with nuclear weapons have been somewhat detached from their cultural ethos. Given the fact that nuclear technology was "adopted" or "imitated" from the West, the absence of relevant knowledge was filled in with the ideas borrowed from the West, inducing caution as a result. Still, though the presence of nuclear weapons might have introduced some degree of concern or caution, it cannot fundamentally alter the thinking and strategic outlook of the political and military elites who largely shape the discourse on nuclear issues.

A second crucial factor that makes the conceptual space in South Asia entirely different from that of the Cold War is the belief system about nuclear weapons. Although the US and USSR engaged in proxy wars, they did not attack each other's core interests in a way that could invite a risk of nuclear escalation. By contrast, India and Pakistan firmly believe that nuclear weapons, by virtue of their presence, render large-scale war impossible; and thus they assume that they have some space under the nuclear overhang to explore and exploit. For instance, both states are engaged in a proxy war not only in Afghanistan but also in each other's territories, in addition to the one in Kashmir. Pakistan apparently continues to decouple militancy from military conflict, whereas India continues to refer to punitive strikes as a viable response to any future act of terrorism on Indian territory. Both states perceive their positions as legitimate, uncompromising, and achievable. These characteristics make stability in South Asia more precarious than during the Cold War.

Moreover, external pressure deeply framed the early discussions about strategic stability in South Asia. Some measures to encourage stability, like the nonattack agreement on each other's nuclear facilities and proposals for restraint regimes, were taken even before the testing of the atomic bomb, and certainly long before the ensuing prospects of a nuclear competition emerged. Consequently, the incentive to work toward stability as a higher objective was not internalized.

A third factor is the relative balance of power. Whereas the US and the USSR were equals, Pakistan and India do not share parity, given the huge differences in their landmasses, populations, power structures, military capabilities, and economic growth potential. As the smaller member of this asymmetric relationship, Pakistan is trying to establish some sort of nuclear balance with India to protect itself against India's perceived hegemonic ambitions and conventional military superiority. This makes the case of South Asia qualitatively different from the Cold War.

Fourth, the US and the USSR largely defined the global nuclear order during the Cold War. The new nuclear-armed states in the post–Cold War era have been less instrumental in controlling a variety of variables that could have implications for peace and stability in their respective regions. These factors include, but are not limited to, geopolitics, the arms trade, access to modern technologies, and the growing power of nonstate actors. Although the influence of external actors—particularly the US—has helped strengthen stability by facilitating the prevention of crisis escalation in the region, the role of the US has also been called destabilizing by India and Pakistan vis-à-vis the issues related to political alliances, arms aid and trade, and the transfer of sensitive technologies.

Fifth and finally, the pattern of hostilities in South Asia is deeply intricate. Pakistan and India have made several attempts in the past to reconcile their problems in a bilateral framework, but a crucial element that complicates the debate on strategic stability is the quadrilateral dynamics of political rivalry:[28] Pakistan feels threatened by Indian military developments; India looks at China with suspicion; and China observes the US with caution. Also, the strategic partnership between Pakistan and China further accentuates Indian concerns. Strategic stability, which in the West has largely developed within a bilateral framework, fails to explain or address the tenuousness of this situation.

Regardless of all these issues, however, strategic stability still comes up in statements by the political leaders of India and Pakistan, and it remains an issue of discussion in South Asia. Given the challenges identified above, this study isolates the case of Pakistan and explains what strategic stability means to Pakistani thinkers and policymakers.

WHITHER STRATEGIC STABILITY: IS THERE A PAKISTANI VIEW?

Pakistan claims to be committed to achieving strategic stability in South Asia. Pakistan's National Command Authority, in its statement released on September 9, 2015, reiterated its position: "Pakistan seeks peace and strategic stability in South Asia as the cornerstone of its policy and considers conflict resolution as the means to achieve its end."[29] But what does this mean?

Strategic stability, as explained above, is an acquired term in Pakistan's discourse. It is difficult to find a precise equivalent of this term in Pakistan's national language, Urdu. This reveals only a small part of the challenge of analyzing the country's perspective on strategic stability. And because this term is "foreign," an indigenous criterion for stability has also been very difficult to develop. So far, the most comprehensive attempt to explicitly define a purely Pakistani idea of strategic stability has been made by a serving military officer in Pakistan's Strategic Plans Division, Brig. Gen. Zahir Kazmi. He notes, "For South Asia, strategic stability would be a situation between South Asian nuclear powers, in which Pakistan has the confidence that India is serious in resolving the territorial disputes and that Indian strategic partnerships with the developed world are not at the cost of Pakistan's security. Likewise, India's confidence in Pakistan's willingness to resolve bilateral disputes without alleged indirect strategy."[30]

This definition identifies two issues as central to strategic stability from Pakistan's perspective. First, India must demonstrate its willingness to resolve the territorial disputes with Pakistan as a precondition for strategic stability; second, by referring to the impact of Indian strategic partnerships for Pakistan's security, it implicitly alludes to Pakistan's concerns regarding a military balance in the region (which are discussed in detail in the writings of other Pakistani authors). Pakistan's strategic elites feel convinced that India's conventional military superiority has placed India in an advantageous position. As a result, policymakers in Pakistan look at the nuclear-plus-conventional military balance as central to stability between India and Pakistan, and they do so not only in terms of current capabilities but also in terms of capabilities that India might acquire in subsequent decades.

Given the fact that Pakistan's evolving view of strategic stability in the region appears embedded both in the need to change the status quo over Kashmir and in military developments in the region, how does Pakistan assess the prospects for stability, and what is Pakistan doing for its part? This can be addressed only by having in mind a clear view of where Pakistan and India stand today.

Pakistan and India have followed different trajectories since conducting nuclear tests in May 1998. Pakistan ventured into Kargil soon after the overt nuclearization of the region. This had a huge impact on how the nuclear Pakistan would be viewed by India and the rest of the world in the years ahead. Despite the fact that Pakistan soon became a frontline ally of the US in the war on terrorism, the Kargil misadventure continues to mar perceptions of Pakistan's nuclear behavior.[31]

These perceptions were compounded by India's concerns and the subsequent international campaign against Pakistan over three other issues: first, for sponsoring terrorism in Indian-held Kashmir and also on its mainland;[32] second, for allegedly facilitating the attack on the Indian Parliament in December 2001; and third, for A. Q. Khan's involvement in illicit international nuclear proliferation.[33] Besides, Pakistan's relations with the United States also underwent serious challenges due to a lack of trust and disagreements over the two nations' approaches to dealing with the Taliban.[34]

Meanwhile, Pakistan also had to battle many other challenges, including a declining economy; major natural disasters, including an earthquake in 2005 and recurring floods; suicide bombings in its major cities; a separatist movement in its largest province, Baluchistan; the unpopularity of the war on terrorism; and military operations against its own citizens in places like Swat, South Waziristan, North Waziristan, and, currently, in its major urban centers. Pakistan's relations with Afghanistan have remained unstable, accentuating Pakistan's fear of India encircling it.[35] Along the way, Pakistan has also needed to cope with its political transition from a military dictatorship to civilian rule.

Meanwhile, it has received much negative media attention for several reasons, including its nuclear program and its nuclear policies.[36]

Conversely, India has remained relatively stable. India's economic power, political clout, and military capabilities have constantly kept increasing. At the international level, particularly in the United States, India is viewed as an emerging power and as the largest democracy in the world.[37] India's relations with the US have improved remarkably. Moreover, India's landmark achievement has been the conclusion of a nuclear cooperation agreement with the US.[38] This has opened up the possibility of India's purchasing advanced nuclear technology from other states under the Nuclear Suppliers Group waiver granted in India's favor. As a result, India has also concluded agreements with Russia, France, the United Kingdom, South Korea, the Czech Republic, Canada, Australia, Argentina, Kazakhstan, Japan, Mongolia, and Namibia.[39]

Pakistan looks at these developments as not only discriminatory and unfair but also as potentially destabilizing because they may, in Pakistan's view, tremendously increase the already growing power asymmetry between India and Pakistan.[40] This perception is accentuated by Pakistan's fear that India is being aided by the US to emerge as a major power—which, by implication, could result in India being dismissive of Pakistan's concerns. This could lower the likelihood of India's participating in a dialogue on resolving territorial disputes on equal terms.[41]

Pakistan's Evolving Threat Perception

The above-mentioned trends are shaping Pakistan's view of a threat scenario that has been deeply compounded during the last decade. This, in turn, has altered Pakistan's view of its military requirements to strengthen deterrence and improve the prospects for stability in the region.

To begin with, Pakistan does not find itself in a position to change the status quo. It perceives an increasing danger from India's military rise that could prove potentially destabilizing. Several peculiar features of India's growing military potential have generated much discussion in Pakistan:

1. India's conventional military modernization, which may at some point give India the ability to strike Pakistan's strategic targets without the use of nuclear weapons;[42]
2. India's ballistic missile defense program, which, in Pakistan's view, would provide India with a false sense of security, resulting in a temptation to undertake aggression against Pakistan;[43]

3. India's proactive military operation strategy, which could give India the ability to desecrate Pakistan's territorial sovereignty; and
4. India's ability to increase its fissile material stockpile, which could help it establish nuclear superiority.[44]

Pakistani military planners (and some commentators) naturally argue that India can and will gain these feared capabilities quickly and will effectively mobilize them. Past Indian performance suggests that these assessments may be exaggerated. Still, perceptions matter, and worst-case thinking is common in security establishments.

From the Pakistani military's standpoint, if and when India acquires these capabilities, Pakistan would be confronted with one or more of three possible consequences. First, India could undertake active military aggression against Pakistan (under its proactive military operations). Second, India could dismiss Pakistan's demands for negotiation to resolve the Kashmir dispute and other issues.[45] And third, India could gain overall hegemony, which eventually would compel Pakistan to concede space to India.[46] Each of these alternatives, in Pakistan's view, would increase the likelihood of war, which could even result in the use of nuclear weapons.

While Pakistan's diplomatic choices are being exhausted, its economic future remains uncertain, shrinking its ability to make heavy investments in conventional armaments. The country's military leadership finds itself trapped in a situation where nuclear weapons are considered the only equalizers that could help it neutralize India's growing military power and deter Indian aggression while creating conditions conducive for India and Pakistan to sit down at the negotiating table to resolve the Kashmir dispute. Consequently, nuclear weapons will continue to have a central role in Pakistan's security calculus.

Nuclear Weapons in Pakistan's Strategic Calculations

Pakistan's view of nuclear weapons and their possible role has evolved significantly during the last several decades. Nuclear weapons, which were once considered a panacea for many ills, are now considered essentially an effective tool for deterrence only, and probably a complementary tool for bargaining. Faith in the ability of nuclear weapons to ensure deterrence has reached an unprecedented level.

Pakistani decision makers, for instance, strongly believe that nuclear weapons have been a force for stability in South Asia. They often cite the absence of a major war since 1971 as evidence of the success of nuclear deterrence—with recessed, existential, and now asymmetric escalation / assured retaliation postures. Nuclear deterrence is hailed by Pakistani military officers, politicians, and a large number of defense analysts for ensuring that all major crises—including Brasstacks, the Compound Crisis in 1990, the Kargil Crisis, the Military Standoff in 2001–2, and the Mumbai attacks in 2008—did not turn into full-scale wars.[47]

The cognitive dissonance, however, manifests itself in striking ways. For instance, Pakistanis often suggest that Pakistan's military capability deterred India from operationalizing proactive military operations in the wake of the Mumbai Crisis in 2008. However, Pakistan later tested its Nasr short-range ballistic missile, claiming that this would help it plug the gap between strategic and operational deterrence.[48] It is continuously diversifying its warheads and delivery means. And it appears to be gradually moving away from its long-held commitment to pursue minimum credible deterrence and toward what it calls full-spectrum deterrence.[49] For instance, Pakistan has officially stated that its short-range ballistic missiles are meant to plug the credibility gap created by India's infamous Cold Start doctrine, which is allegedly meant to exploit the space below Pakistan's strategic deterrence. Moreover, the testing of the Nasr missiles—and also of Ababeel, a missile capable of deploying multiple independently targetable reentry vehicles, and of Shaheen III, a medium-range ballistic missile meant to reach India's strategic bases in the Nicobar and Andaman Islands—indicates a possible shift from a countervalue targeting strategy to what Pakistan calls a combination of a countervalue and counterforce-targeting strategy.[50]

Pakistani officials tend to assume that, given their limitations, they could choose either deterrence stability or crisis stability and arms race stability. They assume that a struggle to keep the nuclear threshold high vis-à-vis the superior conventional force of India may help them increase crisis stability, but only at the cost of deterrence stability, which is not an option for Pakistan. From Pakistan's perspective, a limited war initiated by India that may not justify the use of strategic weapons would become a potential source of escalation. Therefore, Pakistan justifies lowering the nuclear threshold by evoking the threat to use battlefield weapons. But Pakistani officials fail to address the escalatory potential of short-range ballistic missiles in case short-range ballistic missiles fail to deter aggression.

Policymakers in Pakistan appear convinced that nuclear deterrence will hold in times of crisis; if it fails, Pakistan might consider using nuclear weapons to deny victory to the enemy, as opposed to winning the war.[51] Pakistan's defense minister, Khawaja Asif, reiterated his country's position on the use of nuclear weapons in a televised interview. Speaking of nuclear weapons, he said, "We should pray that such an option never arises; but if we need to use them for our survival, we will."[52] Pakistan's former army chief, Pervez Musharraf, also made a similar claim: "We do not want to use nuclear capability, but if our existence comes under threat, who do we have these nuclear weapons for?"[53]

On Credibility

Given the fact that Pakistan is heavily focused on maintaining deterrence stability vis-à-vis India, the question of credibility becomes central to Pakistan's strategic calculations. The discussion of the credibility of deterrence in Pakistan is mostly based on the Cold War literature suggesting that possession of capability and communication of intent are crucial for establishing credibility.[54] Pakistan's nuclear behavior clearly reflects its heavy emphasis on developing capabilities and communicating its resolve to use nuclear weapons. It measures Indian perceptions of its credibility by analyzing how clearly its message has been communicated.

Only a year after the nuclear tests in 1998, Pakistani policymakers who had announced a commitment to minimum deterrence began to add the element of credibility as an essential condition for deterrence—an idea that made the requirements for effective deterrence dynamic and flexible, as opposed to quantifiable.[55] In Pakistan's view, the requirements for credible deterrence would entail taking India's military developments into consideration. As a result, Pakistan has been investing in modernizing and diversifying its nuclear arsenal.

Pakistan is believed to have developed cruise missiles to neutralize India's ballistic missile defense systems. Likewise, Pakistan claims to have tested its short-range ballistic missile that is designed to plug the credibility gap caused by disproportionality between India's low-cost, proactive military operations and Pakistan's high-cost, strategic deterrence.[56] Pakistan's strategic elites feel convinced that the introduction of its short-range ballistic missiles has strengthened the credibility of its nuclear deterrence.

From the Indian perspective, it appears that the nuclear factor has altered India's choices.[57] However, most Indian scholars argue that Pakistan's threat to use tactical weapons does not enjoy credibility in Indian decision-making circles.[58] It is argued that Pakistan's use of battlefield nuclear weapons would be tantamount to "destroying Pakistan to deter India" by causing heavy civilian casualties in Pakistan's territory bordering India.[59] Writing about Pakistan's short-range ballistic missiles, Praveen Swami, a noted Indian journalist, claimed that Pakistan's "nuclear weapons may not deter Indian retaliation—and may not succeed in ending a conventional war, should one begin."[60]

Another important issue related to credibility is Pakistan's "no to a no-first-use posture," which means that Pakistan, in case of need, can resort to a first strike.[61] The size of Pakistan's arsenal and the fact that nuclear warheads and missiles are stored separately raises questions about the credibility of Pakistan's threat of nuclear retaliation. Pakistan's notion of nuclear retaliation is grounded in the idea of mutual suicide, as opposed to a struggle for victory in war. It is this posture of "irrationality" that in Pakistan's view adds to the credibility of its threat. Furthermore, Pakistan has tacitly communicated its model of readiness, which would help it respond effectively, even in a short time.[62]

Moreover, Pakistan has been relying heavily on nuclear signaling, mainly conveyed by statements as well as actions such as missile testing, both during peacetime and crises.[63] Pakistani discourse keeps referring to the statements made by Indian military officials and political leaders alluding to their restraint due to the presence of nuclear weapons. However, there is not much discussion about particular incidents when India planned to attack Pakistan, regardless of the nuclear deterrence.

Pakistan appears to be confident about the credibility of its nuclear deterrence.[64] It considers the absence of a large-scale war with India during the last three decades as a testimony to the credibility of its deterrence. This assumption, however, has not been thoroughly investigated. Although Pakistan's deterrence may have altered India's behavior, it is hard to prove if the change in India's behavior serves Pakistan's purpose.

CAN PAKISTAN'S PURSUIT OF STABILITY
PROVE DESTABILIZING?

Pakistan's increasing fissile material stockpile, the testing of its short-range Nasr and medium-range Shaheen III missiles, the building of its naval strategic command, and its changing force postures have all drawn international attention and spurred concerns regarding the future of stability in South Asia. Nevertheless, Pakistan's leaders appear confident about the ability of their country's nuclear weapons to deter war.[65] Although it is difficult to ascertain whether ongoing nuclear trajectories would make South Asia more or less stable, it is nonetheless important to identify the potential for some of these developments to cause instability.

Historically, the leaders of India and Pakistan have resorted to saber rattling during each crisis between the two countries.[66] In the case of Pakistan, nuclear signaling also became part of the process, often at an early stage. However, there has been an unflinching faith in the credibility of Pakistan's nuclear deterrence to prevent war. A serious challenge might emerge in the future if India decides to launch a proactive military operation inside Pakistani territory, particularly one using air power. In such a scenario, the confrontation might escalate. In the past crises between India and Pakistan, the US has played an effective role in defusing tensions between the two sides.[67] However, due to the changing political realities in South Asia, the United States' willingness or ability to play an active role at the early stage of a crisis remains uncertain.[68] Although Pakistan has a sizable conventional force to defend its territory, an actual military attack by India on its territory would not only suggest the breakdown of nuclear deterrence but also increase uncertainty about the future of stability in South Asia.

Will Pakistan use nuclear weapons in case of war? Although Pakistan has a sufficiently well-equipped and well-trained military force, Islamabad would be faced with serious challenges in case of war due to its weak economy, shortage of energy, and limited foreign exchange reserves. Sustaining defense over a prolonged period could become challenging. Under such circumstances, Pakistan's military might find itself in a trap, in which its options would be to either use nuclear weapons or risk the credibility of its nuclear deterrence. This might increase pressure to resort to the use of tactical weapons, which could result in further escalation.

In addition, issues such as the future of Kashmir remain uncertain. Pakistan fears India's growing dismissiveness, but so far it has not faced complete neglect. If a time arrives when Indian political and military leaders begin to completely ignore Pakistan, and contain their responses to militancy within India's own territory, Pakistan will be faced with little room, in its view, to have negotiations over Kashmir. Under such circumstances, Pakistan might choose to maintain some of its threats and capabilities in order to compel India not to ignore it. As a result, both sides might fall into a vicious cycle of finding ways to neutralize each other's threats, making the region unstable.

CONCLUSION

The policies aimed at achieving strategic stability in South Asia have been externally suggested and stimulated. Such policies preceded the presence of active, operational nuclear deterrence and, therefore, the internalization of dangers of nuclear war and the necessity to avert it. Also, Pakistan's view of strategic stability has evolved from a balance by means of a minimum deterrence to a balance with full-spectrum deterrence.

However, will Pakistan's maintaining a strategic balance by pursuing an arms buildup and establishing full-spectrum deterrence help it strengthen strategic stability? Pakistan's view of strategic stability is narrowly shaped by regional concerns and preferences, not international factors. At the political level, Pakistan defines strategic stability in the context of peaceful resolution of the Kashmir dispute. At the operational level, however, it defines stability in terms of a strategic balance vis-à-vis India that may help it deter war. It does not plan to attain victory in a nuclear war.

In view of these goals, an operational approach requiring an arms buildup to maintain a strategic balance may prove no more effective than minimal deterrence. One does not find any direct correlation between a strategic balance and dispute resolution. Likewise, it is hard to establish whether deterrence or denial of victory requires a huge and diverse arsenal. However, Pakistan continues to view a strategic balance as essential for strategic stability. This approach is clouded by the existential bias carried by the term "strategic stability," given that it evolved as a framework for analysis during the Cold War.

Such frameworks often sabotage the debate from the core issues and cloud judgment regarding the practical utility of nuclear weapons in view of a state's key policy objectives. In the case of Pakistan, for instance, there have hardly been any in-depth studies exploring the actual potential of a strategic balance to help Pakistan achieve its political or military objectives vis-à-vis India.

For all the international actors interested in stability in South Asia, this chapter suggests that the idea of developing an indigenous lexicon reflecting how the new nuclear-armed states problematize their security issues should be promoted and encouraged. Anachronistic terminologies and frameworks—carried forward from the Cold War era—consider maintenance of the nuclear balance as a precondition for stability. But such an approach is a recipe for arms race instability in a world that is characterized by nuclear-armed rivalries in quadrilateral equations.

Only a discourse focused on an informed appraisal of the utility and limits of nuclear weapons for the achievement of foreign policy objectives, including but not confined to security, would help contain incentives for a destabilizing arms competition. As this chapter suggests, Pakistan's military and political leaders may endorse nuclear restraint only if such a discourse on nuclear issues grows indigenously, taking into account Pakistan's peculiar circumstances.

NOTES

1. "Fourth Plutonium Production Reactor in Pakistan Appears Operational," IPFM Blog, January 19, 2015, http://fissilematerials.org/blog/2015/01/fourth_plutonium _producti.html.

2. For details of Pakistan's nuclear weapons and missile-related developments, see "Chapter Six: Asia," *Military Balance* 114, no. 1 (2014): 220–21; and "A Conversation

with Gen. Khalid Kidwai," Carnegie International Nuclear Policy Conference 2015, March 23, 2015, http://carnegieendowment.org/files/03-230315carnegieKIDWAI.pdf.

3. Vipin Narang, *Nuclear Strategy in the Modern Era: Regional Powers and International Conflict* (Princeton, NJ: Princeton University Press, 2014), 55–93.

4. Šumit Ganguly and Devin T. Hagerty, *Fearful Symmetry: India-Pakistan Crises in the Shadow of Nuclear Weapons* (New Delhi: Oxford University Press, 2005), 44–61.

5. George Perkovich, *India's Nuclear Bomb: The Impact on Global Proliferation* (New Delhi: Oxford University Press, 2000), 276–77.

6. C. Raja Mohan and Peter R. Lavoy, "Avoiding Nuclear War," in *Crisis Prevention, Confidence Building, and Reconciliation in South Asia*, ed. Michael Krepon and Amit Sevak (Washington, DC: Henry L. Stimson Center, 1995), 28.

7. None of the historical accounts on Pakistan's nuclear program, policies, and crisis provide sufficient details about the nonattack agreement. It could be assumed that the changing dynamics of the domestic political landscape in both countries, along with mounting tensions due to misperceptions regarding military exercises, may have caused the delay. It is interesting to note that the agreement was reached during Zia's regime, signed during Benazir Bhutto's government, and ratified during Nawaz Sharif's rule.

8. For the text of the treaty, see "Agreement between India and Pakistan on the Prohibition of Attack against Nuclear Installations and Facilities (India-Pakistan Non-Attack Agreement)," signed by India and Pakistan on December 31, 1998, available from Nuclear Threat Initiative, www.nti.org/media/pdfs/aptindpak.pdf.

9. Kamran Yousaf, "Pakistan, India Exchange Lists of Nuclear Installations, Prisoners," *Express Tribune*, January 1, 2015, http://tribune.com.pk/story/815634/pakistan-india-exchange-lists-of-nuclear-installations-prisoners-2/.

10. Clinton White House Archives, "Leading the Way in Nonproliferation," http://clinton5.nara.gov/WH/EOP/NSC/html/nsc-16.html.

11. Strobe Talbott, *Engaging India: Diplomacy, Democracy, and the Bomb* (New Delhi: Penguin Books, 2004), 90–111.

12. Ibid.

13. United Nations Security Council Resolution 1172, June 6, 1998, available from Ministry of Foreign Affairs of Japan, www.mofa.go.jp/mofaj/gaiko/naruhodo/data/pdf/data6-1.pdf.

14. For a detailed analysis, see Devin T. Hagerty, "Opaque Proliferation, Existential Deterrence, and Nuclear Weapon Stability," in *The Consequences of Nuclear Proliferation: Lessons from South Asia*, by Devin T. Hagerty (Cambridge, MA: Harvard University Press, 1998), 39–62.

15. For Pakistan's earlier position, see Abdul Sattar, Zulfiqar Ali Khan, and Agha Shahi, "Securing Nuclear Peace," *The News*, October 5, 1999. For India's commitments, see "India's Draft Nuclear Doctrine," Arms Control Association, July 1, 1999, www.armscontrol.org/act/1999_07-08/ffja99.

16. For Pakistan, see "Pakistan Announces Unilateral Moratorium on Nuclear Testing," Federation of American Scientists, June 11, 1998, http://fas.org/news/pakistan/1998/06/980611-gop2.html; for India, see "Speech by the Prime Minister Atal Bihari Vajpayee at the United Nations General Assembly," September 24, 1998, available from Acronym Institute, www.acronym.org.uk/spsep98.htm.

17. For details about how Pakistani decision makers made these choices, see Feroz Hassan Khan, *Eating Grass: The Making of the Pakistani Bomb* (Stanford, CA: Stanford University Press, 2013), 287–301.

18. See "Joint Statement: India-Pakistan Expert-Level Talks on Nuclear CBMs," Ministry of External Affairs of India, June 20, 2004, available from Nuclear Threat Initiative, www.nti.org/media/pdfs/26_ea_india.pdf?=1316627913; and Shamshad Ahmed, "The Nuclear Subcontinent," *Foreign Affairs*, July–August 1999, 125.

19. Hagerty, *Consequences*; David J. Karl, "Proliferation Pessimism and Emerging Nuclear Powers," *International Security* 21, no. 3 (Winter 1996–97): 87–119; John J. Mearsheimer, "Here We Go Again," *New York Times*, May 17, 1998; and Kenneth N. Waltz, "More May Be Better," in *The Spread of Nuclear Weapons: A Debate*, ed. Scott D. Sagan and Kenneth N. Waltz (New York: W. W. Norton, 1995), 1–45.

20. Scott. D. Sagan, "The Perils of Proliferation in South Asia," July 19, 2001, http://web.stanford.edu/class/polisci243b/readings/sagan.pdf; and Clayton P. Bowen and Daniel Wolven, "Command and Control Challenges in South Asia," *Nonproliferation Review* 6, no. 3 (1999): 25–35.

21. See "Lahore Declaration," signed by India and Pakistan on February 21, 1999, available from Nuclear Threat Initiative, www.nti.org/media/pdfs/aptlahore.pdf.

22. See Jonathan Marcus, "Analysis: The World's Most Dangerous Place?" BBC News, March 23, 2000, http://news.bbc.co.uk/2/hi/south_asia/687021.stm; and "President Clinton's Visit to South Asia," Acronym Institute, March 2000, www.acronym.org .uk/spvisit.htm.

23. M. V. Ramana and Zia Mian, "The Nuclear Confrontation in South Asia," Stockholm International Peace Research Institute, 2003, 197–98, www.princeton.edu /sgs/publications/articles/SIPRI-03-Ramana-Mian.pdf.

24. See Šumit Ganguly's arguments in *India, Pakistan, and the Bomb: Debating Nuclear Stability in South Asia*, by Šumit Ganguly and S. Paul Kapur (New York: Columbia University Press, 2010). Officials from India and Pakistan called nuclear weapons a factor of stability in their Joint Statement issued in June 2004; see "Joint Statement: India-Pakistan Expert-Level Talks on Nuclear CBMs."

25. Rajesh Kumar, "Revisiting the Kashmir Insurgency, Kargil, and the Twin Peak Crisis: Was the Stability/Instability Paradox at Play?" *Journal of Political Science* 3, no. 1 (Fall 2008), http://connection.ebscohost.com/c/articles/35612707/revisiting-kashmir -insurgency-kargil-twin-peak-crisis-was-stability-instability-paradox-at; Anuj Panday, "The Stability-Instability Paradox: The Case of the Kargil War," *Penn State Journal of International Affairs*, Fall 2011, https://psujia.files.wordpress.com/2012/04/the-stability -instability-paradox-the-case-of-the-kargil-war.pdf; Michael Krepon, "The Stability-Instability Paradox, Misperception, and Escalation Control in South Asia," in *Escalation Control and the Nuclear Option in South Asia*, ed. Michael Krepon, Rodney W. Jones, and Ziad Haider (Washington, DC: Henry L. Stimson Center, 2004); Rajesh Rajagopalan, "What Stability-Instability Paradox? Subnational Conflicts and the Nuclear Risk in South Asia," SASSI Research Paper 4, February 2006, www.files.ethz .ch/isn/99913/RP%20No%2004.pdf; Adil Sultan, "South Asian Stability-Instability Paradox: Another Perspective," *IPRI Journal* 14, no. 1 (Winter 2014): 21–37, www.ipri pak.org/wp-content/uploads/2014/04/Article-no.-2-dr.-Adil.pdf; and Varun Sahni, "The Stability-Instability Paradox: A Less Than Perfect Explanation," in *The India-Pakistan Nuclear Relationship*, ed. E. Sridharan (New Delhi: Routledge, 2007), 185–207.

26. Paul Kapur, *Dangerous Deterrent: Nuclear Weapons Proliferation and Conflict in South Asia* (Stanford, CA: Stanford University Press, 2007).

27. Nawaz Sharif's Address to the Nation, May 28, 1998.

28. Gregory D. Koblentz, *Strategic Stability in the Second Nuclear Age*, Special Report 71 (New York: Council on Foreign Relations, 2014), 3, www.cfr.org/sites/default/files/pdf/2014/11/Second%20Nuclear%20Age_CSR71.pdf.

29. Inter-Services Public Relations, Press Release, Pakistan, September 9, 2015, www.ispr.gov.pk/front/main.asp?o=t-press_release&id=3026#pr_link3026. For a similar statement by Pakistan's Foreign Office, see "Pakistan Remains Actively Engaged in Nuclear Stability: FO," *Daily Times*, October 7, 2015, www.dailytimes.com.pk/national/07-Oct-2015/pakistan-remains-actively-engaged-on-nuclear-stability-fo.

30. Zahir Kazmi, "Tactical Nuclear Weapons, Deterrence and Strategic Stability," Institute of Regional Studies, Islamabad, www.irs.org.pk/strategic/spso12.doc.

31. A communiqué articulated the G-8's position on the resolution of the Kargil Crisis on June 21, 1999. Also see Ashley J. Tellis, C. Christine Fair, and Jamison Jo Medy, "The Significance of the Kargil Crisis," in *Limited Conflicts under the Nuclear Umbrella: Indian and Pakistani Lessons from the Kargil Crisis* (Santa Monica, CA: RAND Corporation, 2001), 8–13, www.rand.org/content/dam/rand/pubs/monograph_reports/MR1450/MR1450.ch2.pdf; and Amir Mir, "Pakistan: Kargil Conspiracy Still Unravelling," Inter Press Service News, June 5, 2008, www.ipsnews.net/2008/06/pakistan-kargil-conspiracy-still-unravelling/.

32. Atal Bihari Vajpayee's speech at the UN, quoted by Rajan Roy, "India's Prime Minister Denies Wanting War, Blames Pakistan for Fueling Terrorism," *St. Augustine Record*, September 14, 2002, http://staugustine.com/stories/091402/wor_985706.shtml#.VhEn4-yqqko; "India Blames Pakistan for Terror," BBC News, September 30, 2002, http://news.bbc.co.uk/2/hi/south_asia/2287009.stm; Randeep Ramesh, "Indian PM Accuses Pakistan Agencies of Supporting Mumbai Terror Attacks," *The Guardian*, January 6, 2009, www.theguardian.com/world/2009/jan/06/mumbai-attacks-india; and "Modi Blames Pakistan for Spreading Terrorism in India," *Dawn*, January 8, 2015, www.dawn.com/news/1186931.

33. Bruno Tertrais, "Khan's Nuclear Exports: Was There a State Strategy?" in *Pakistan's Nuclear Future: Worries beyond War*, ed. Henry D. Sokolski (Carlisle, PA: Strategic Studies Institute of US Army War College, 2008), 13–58, http://npolicy.org/books/Pakistans_Nuclear_Worries/Full_Book.pdf; and Ahmed Rashid, "NATO's Top Brass Accuse Pakistan over Taliban Aid," *Daily Telegraph*, October 6, 2006.

34. Bruce Riedel, *Deadly Embrace: Pakistan, America, and the Future of the Global Jihad* (Washington, DC: Brookings Institution Press, 2011).

35. "Afghan Leader Calls on Pakistan to Stop Attacks," *New York Times*, September 28, 2015, www.nytimes.com/aponline/2015/09/28/world/middleeast/ap-un-united-nations-summit-the-latest.html?_r=0; Brajesh Upadhyay, "Pakistani Fears over India Afghan Role 'Not Groundless,'" BBC News, August 7, 2013, www.bbc.com/news/world-asia-india-23598521; and Munir Akram, "Afghanistan, Is Hope Real?" *Dawn*, March 29, 2015, www.dawn.com/news/1172504.

36. See, e.g., Seymour M. Hersh, "Defending the Arsenal: In an Unstable Pakistan, Can Nuclear Warheads Be Kept Safe?" *The New Yorker*, November 16, 2009, www.newyorker.com/magazine/2009/11/16/defending-the-arsenal; Jeffrey Goldberg and Marc Ambinder, "Ally from Hell," *The Atlantic*, December 2011, www.theatlantic.com

/magazine/archive/2011/12/the-ally-from-hell/308730/; Mark Urban, "Saudi Nuclear Weapons 'on Order' from Pakistan," BBC News, November 6, 2013, www.bbc.com /news/world-middle-east-24823846; Heather Saul, "ISIS Claims It Could Buy Its First Nuclear Weapon from Pakistan within a Year," *Independent*, May 23, 2015, www .independent.co.uk/news/world/middle-east/isis-claims-it-could-buy-its-first-nuclear -weapon-from-pakistan-within-12-months-10270525.html; and Jeffrey Goldberg and Marc Ambinder, "The Pentagon's Secret Plans to Secure Pakistan's Nuclear Arsenal," *National Journal*, November 9, 2011.

37. "US to Help Make India a 'Major World Power,'" *China Daily*, March 26, 2005, www.chinadaily.com.cn/english/doc/2005-03/26/content_428361.htm. Also see "Speech of President Bill Clinton to the Joint Session of Indian Parliament on March 22, 2000," www.indianembassy.org/indusrel/clinton_india/vajpayee_parliament_march_22 _2000.htm; Condoleezza Rice, "Our Opportunity with India," *Washington Post*, March 13, 2006, www.washingtonpost.com/wp-dyn/content/article/2006/03/12/AR20060312 00978.html; "Obama to Modi: India Can Emerge as a Major World Power," *India Today*, September 30, 2014, http://indiatoday.intoday.in/story/live-narendra-modi-us -president-barack-obama-washington/1/393552.html; and Narendra Modi and Barack Obama, "A Renewed US-India Partnership for the 21st Century," *Washington Post*, September 30, 2014, www.washingtonpost.com/opinions/narendra-modi-and-barack -obama-a-us-india-partnership-for-the-21st-century/2014/09/29/dac66812-4824-11e4 -891d-713f052086a0_story.html.

38. Pallava Bagla, "Best Moment for Me as PM Was When We Signed Nuclear Deal with US: PM," NDTV, January 3, 2014, www.ndtv.com/india-news/best-moment -for-me-as-pm-was-when-we-signed-nuclear-deal-with-us-pm-546693.

39. "Nuclear Power in India," World Nuclear Association, updated June 2017, www.world-nuclear.org/info/Country-Profiles/Countries-G-N/India/.

40. Pakistan's former interior minister, Rehman Malik, called the granting of an NSG waiver to India discriminatory. For details, see Rasheed Khalid, "Waiver to India by NSG a Discrimination," *The News*, March 23, 2011, www.thenews.com.pk/Todays -News-6-37691-Waiver-to-India-by-NSG-a-discrimination; Mateen Haider, "Indo-US Nuclear Deal Will Negatively Impact South Asia: Sartaj Aziz," *Dawn*, January 28, 2015, www.dawn.com/news/1159804; and Pakistan Ministry of Foreign Affairs, Press Release, "Statement of the Adviser," January 27, 2015, www.mediapoint.pk/press-release-mofa -on-us-india-statements-27-jan/.

41. Narang, *Nuclear Strategy*.

42. Baqir Sajjad Syed, "Minimum N-Deterrence Will Be Maintained: FO," *Dawn*, May 21, 2009; Air Commodore Khalid Banuri communication to the Congressional Research Service cited by Paul K. Kerr and Mary Beth Nikitin, *Pakistan's Nuclear Weapons: Proliferation and Security Issues* (Washington, DC: Congressional Research Service, 2012), 8; and Ali Sarwar Naqvi, "Seventeen Years of Deterrence," *The News*, May 28, 2015, www.thenews.com.pk/Todays-News-9-320560-Seventeen-years-of-deterrence. Also see the proceedings of a roundtable session titled "Arms Control Prospects in South Asia," Center for International Strategic Studies Pakistan, September 13, 2012, www .ciss.org.pk/pages_inner.php?page_id=38; Malik Qasim Mustafa, "Pakistan's Military Security and Conventional Balance of Power," *Strategic Studies* 29, no. 1 (Spring 2009): 36; "Countries Should Commit to No-First-Use Policy," *Express Tribune*, May 16, 2014; Mansoor Ahmed, "Security Doctrines, Technologies and Escalation Ladders: A

Pakistani Perspective," paper presented at US-Pakistan Strategic Partnership: A Track II Dialogue, Phuket, Thailand, September 18–19, 2011; Zafar Nawaz Jaspal, "Perilous Indian Military Buildup," *Weekly Pulse* 2 (November 2012); and Zulfqar Khan, *India Pakistan Nuclear Rivalry: Perceptions, Misperceptions, and Mutual Deterrence* (Islamabad: Islamabad Policy Research Institute, 2005).

43. "Pakistan Considers India's Ballistic Missile System as Destabilizing: FO," *The Nation,* May 9, 2015, http://nation.com.pk/islamabad/09-May-2013/pakistan-con siders-indias-ballistic-missile-system-as-destabilizing-development-fo; Zafar Nawaz Jaspal, "The Introduction of Ballistic Missile Defense in South Asia: Implications on Strategic Stability," Nuclear Learning in South Asia: The Next Decade, June 2014, 127–28 .www.nps.edu/documents/104111744/106151936/11+Nuclear+Learning_Jaspal .pdf/150ce371-2c21-42ae-a684-2c0f480cef6b.

44. "The South Asian Nuclear Balance: An Interview with Pakistani Ambassador to the CD Zamir Akram," Arms Control Association, www.armscontrol.org/act/2011 _12/Interview_With_Pakistani_Ambassador_to_the_CD_Zamir_Akram.

45. This point is mentioned quite often in the roundtable discussions by senior Pakistani officials from the Foreign Office and other relevant institutions.

46. For a detailed analysis of the Pakistani army's perception of India, see Christine C. Fair, *Fighting to the End: The Pakistan Army's Way of War* (Karachi: Oxford University Press, 2014); Also see Inter-Services Public Relations Press Release, "16th NCA Meeting," January 13, 2010, www.ispr.gov.pk/front/main.asp?o=t-press_release&id=1110#pr _link1110.

47. These claims about the success of nuclear deterrence in preventing war are repeatedly made by policymakers as well as scholars at seminars, conferences, and even university classrooms.

48. Inter-Services Public Relations, press release, April 19, 2011, www.ispr.gov .pk/front/main.asp?o=t-press_release&id=1721. Also see Adil Sultan, "Pakistan's Emerging Nuclear Posture: Impact of Drivers and Technology on Nuclear Doctrine," Institute of Strategic Studies, Islamabad, www.issi.org.pk/publication-files/1340000 409_86108059.pdf.

49. For details on the shift from minimum credible full-spectrum deterrence to full-spectrum credible minimum deterrence, see these official press releases: Inter-Services Public Relations, press release, December 14, 2010, www.ispr.gov.pk/front/main.asp?o=t-press_release&id=1608#pr_link1608; and Inter-Services Public Relations, "Statement Issued at the Test Firing of Hatf IX," November 5, 2013, www.ispr.gov.pk/front/main.asp ?o=t-press_release&date=2013/11/5. Also see Inter-Services Public Relations, September 26, 2014, www.ispr.gov.pk/front/main.asp?o=t-press_release&date=2014/9/26. Inter-Services Public Relations, press releases issued November 13, 2014, and November 17, 2014, used the term "full-spectrum minimum credible deterrence." See Inter-Services Public Relations, press release, November 13, 2014, www.ispr.gov.pk/front/main.asp?o=t-press _release&date=2014/11/13; and Inter-Services Public Relations, press release, November 17, 2014, www.ispr.gov.pk/front/main.asp?o=t-press_release&date=2014/11/17.

50. "Conversation with Gen. Khalid Kidwai." Also concluded from a private conversation with a senior Strategic Plans Division official.

51. Christopher Clary, "What Might an India-Pakistan War Look Like?" *MIT Center for International Studies Newsletter,* Spring 2012, http://web.mit.edu/cis/precis /2012spring/india_pakistan.html#.VszGa3197IU. Also see Michael Krepon, "Pakistan's

Nuclear Strategy and Deterrence Stability," Spearhead Research, 2012, http://spear headresearch.org/SR_CMS/wp-content/uploads/2012/12/Pakistan_Nuclear_Strategy _and_Deterrence_Stability.pdf.

52. "Option to Use Nuclear Weapons Always Available: Asif," *Geo News*, July 6, 2015, www.geo.tv/latest/4351-option-to-use-nuclear-weapons-always-available-asif.

53. "We Didn't Build Nuclear Weapons to Fire on Shab-e-Baraat, Says Musharraf," *Times of India*, July 11, 2015, http://timesofindia.indiatimes.com/world/pakistan/We -didnt-build-nukes-to-fire-on-Shab-e-Baraat-Musharraf-says/articleshow/47628510 .cms.

54. "Nuclear deterrence is only credible if you clearly communicate that this is our capability, this is our national resolve, and this is how we will retaliate if we are attacked," said Maria Sultan in "Nuclear Deterrence Conference: Countries Should Commit to No-First-Use-Policy," *Express Tribune*, May 16, 2014, http://tribune.com .pk/story/709038/nuclear-deterrence-conference-countries-should-commit-to-no -first-use-policy/.

55. It is important to note here that Pakistan does not have a declared nuclear use doctrine. Therefore, the statements made by key officials from the Foreign Office or the Strategic Plans Division are the only sources that provide insight into Pakistan's doctrinal thinking. Most of the thinking on Pakistan's articulation of minimum deterrence and its variants is referred back to the following sources. See Foreign Minister Abdul Sattar's address at the National Defence University, Islamabad, May 24, 2000; and Abdul Sattar's address at the Institute of Strategic Studies, Islamabad, November 1999. For an analysis, see Sadia Tasleem, "Towards an Indo-Pak Lexicon—II: Credible Minimum Deterrence," Institute of Peace and Conflict Studies, February 11, 2011, www .ipcs.org/article/nuclear/towards-an-indo-pak-nuclear-lexicon-ii-credible-minimum -deterrence-3330.html.

56. To gain a better understanding, see the detailed discussion by a serving Strategic Plans Division official, Air Commodore Adil Sultan, "Pakistan's Emerging Nuclear Posture: Impact of Drivers and Technology on Nuclear Doctrine," *Strategic Studies* (June 2014): 161–63, www.issi.org.pk/wp-content/uploads/2014/06/1340000409_8610 8059.pdf.

57. Email interviews conducted by the author with several Indian scholars verify this claim.

58. See Arun Vishwanathan, "Nuclear Signals in South Asia," *Bulletin of the Atomic Scientists*, September 8, 2013, http://thebulletin.org/nuclear-signals-south-asia; and email interviews conducted by the author with several Indian scholars, which verify the claim.

59. J. Sankaran, "Destroying Pakistan to Deter India? The Problem with Pakistan's Battlefield Nukes," *Bulletin of the Atomic Scientists*, July 1, 2014, http://thebulletin .org/2014/july/destroying-pakistan-deter-india-problem-pakistans-battlefield -nukes7287.

60. Praveen Swami, "Pakistan's Nuclear Weapons May Not Deter Indian Retaliation, but Destruction Mutual," *Indian Express*, October 28, 2015, http://indianexpress .com/article/opinion/columns/pakistans-nuclear-weapons-may-not-deter-indian -retaliation-but-destruction-mutual/.

61. Pakistan has not declared a formal nuclear doctrine. However, a close reading of Pakistan's doctrinal thinking suggests that while Pakistan retains the option of using

nuclear weapons against a conventional military strike, it may or may not do so during an actual military conflict. Pakistan does not proclaim a "first-use" policy akin to the policies pursued by the US and Russia that require a high degree of readiness, even during peacetime.

62. Narang, *Nuclear Strategy*, 85.

63. Moeed Yusuf, "US as Interlocutor in Nuclear Crises: Deriving Future Policy Implications from a Study of the 2001–2002 India-Pakistan Standoff," Center for Strategic and International Studies, October 1, 2009, http://csis.org/images/stories/poni /110921_Yusuf.pdf; and Arun Vishwanathan, "Nuclear Signals in South Asia," *Bulletin of the Atomic Scientists*, September 8, 2013, http://thebulletin.org/nuclear-signals-south -asia.

64. "Conversation with Gen. Khalid Kidwai."

65. See General Khalid Kidwai, quoted in "Pakistan Needs Short-Range 'Tactical' Nuclear Weapons to Deter India," *Express Tribune*, March 24, 2015, http://tribune .com.pk/story/858106/pakistan-needs-short-range-tactical-nuclear-weapons-to-deter -india/; and Sartaj Aziz, *Between Dreams and Realities: Some Milestones in Pakistan's History* (Karachi: Oxford University Press, 2009), 408.

66. P. R. Chari, "Nuclear Signalling in South Asia: Revisiting A. Q. Khan's 1987 Threat," Carnegie Endowment for International Peace, November 14, 2013, http://car negieendowment.org/2013/11/14/nuclear-signaling-in-south-asia-revisiting-a.q .-khan-s-1987-threat; "Saber-Rattling: New Indian Chief Issues Warning to Pakistan," *Express Tribune*, August 2, 2014, http://tribune.com.pk/story/743257/sabre-rattling -new-indian-chief-issues-warning-to-pakistan/; and Saeed Shah and Jonathan S. Landay, "Could Saber-Rattling Lead to War between India and Pakistan?" McClatchy Newspapers, December 26, 2008, www.mcclatchydc.com/news/nation-world/world /article24517933.html.

67. Pervaiz Iqbal Cheema, P. R. Chari, and Stephen Cohen, *Four Crises and a Peace Process* (Washington, DC: Brookings Institution Press, 2007). See also Poly Nayak and Michael Krepon, "The Unfinished Crisis: US Crisis Management after the 2008 Mumbai Attacks," Henry L. Stimson Center, February 2012, www.stimson.org/images /uploads/research-pdfs/Mumbai-Final_1.pdf.

68. In some circles in Pakistan, it is increasingly assumed that the US may want to let India make some gains by undertaking punitive action against Pakistan. In the US, however, some scholars argue that the US might lose its ability to intervene early in a future crisis because of the changing dynamics of its relations with the nuclear-armed South Asian rivals. See Nayak and Krepon, "Unfinished Crisis."

4

Strategic Stability in the Middle East

Through the Transparency Lens

EMILY B. LANDAU

THIS CHAPTER EXAMINES the evolution of strategic perceptions in the Middle East, based on the manner in which ambitions and capabilities related to weapons of mass destruction (WMD)—with a particular focus on the nuclear realm—have unfolded in the strategic thinking of states in this region. The history of the Middle East confirms that the role and significance of nuclear capabilities and deterrence is very much a function of the particular context within which they emerge and evolve. This context includes the specific state motivations and patterns of behavior that underlie nuclear and other WMD developments, as well as the matrix of interstate relations that defines the relevant regional political landscape.

Much of what has transpired in the Middle East, some of which is fleshed out in this chapter, tends to go against some of the basic assumptions about the role and impact of nuclear weapons according to the classic neorealist and deterrence theory developed during the Cold War. Notions of strategic balancing and stability, assumptions of state motivations for acquiring nuclear weapons, and the means of delivering credible nuclear deterrent threats have all developed differently in this region as compared with the global level.[1]

Specifically, one of the more interesting challenges to conventional thinking regards the role and impact of transparency in the nuclear realm, which is the focus of this chapter. Transparency with respect to nuclear capabilities is generally considered necessary for establishing nuclear deterrence (for the credible delivery of nuclear threats) as well as conducive to the establishment of strategic stability. Regarding the latter, the arms control theory that developed in the Cold War years was geared to stabilizing the superpower mutual-deterrent relationship.[2] A core concept developed in that context was that of confidence-building measures (CBMs), or confidence-and-security-building measures (CSBMs), including the notion of transparency.[3] The assumption regarding transparency—as a CSBM—is that when states know what they are up against in the nuclear realm, this fosters a measure of confidence regarding the likely intentions of the other side as well as a basis for communication that can further clarify intentions and minimize misunderstandings—all geared to enhancing stability. Conversely, when there is uncertainty about nuclear capabilities, this is assumed to breed fears of the unknown and possible worst-case scenarios, thereby increasing risks of strategic miscalculation and a crisis.[4]

The first challenge to this conception of the role and effects of transparency is encapsulated in Israel's policy of ambiguity. As is discussed at length below, Israel's policy, which lacks transparency, goes against conventional thinking on both counts; it did not preclude Israel from establishing credible nuclear deterrence against existential threats, and it demonstrated that stability is not undermined, and can even be enhanced, in an environment that lacks transparency with regard to nuclear capabilities.

Against the backdrop of Israel's unique policy of ambiguity, this chapter then proceeds to examine two case studies—regional actors' perceptions of Israel during the Arms Control and Regional Security (ACRS) talks, and regional actors' perceptions of Iran beginning in 2003—in order to further tease out the complexities that characterize the Middle East in this regard. Both cases involve a state that is not transparent in the nuclear realm, and yet the lack of transparency plays out very differently in each case in terms of the implications for strategic stability. The differences are a function of attributes of the state—namely, its policies and behavior—rather than the question of openness as such. Moreover, in Israel's case, the rules of the game that were established over the years through its behavior on the ground proved more important than a priori biases against Israel based on identity. In the case of Iran, a possible closer affinity with Arab states on the basis of religious identity (Islam) did not give Iran the benefit of the doubt regarding its questionable capabilities—again, this can be attributed to Iran's regional policies and behavior.

EMPIRICAL ANALYSIS: FROM ISRAEL'S POLICY OF AMBIGUITY TO IRAN'S NUCLEAR AMBITIONS

This chapter's analysis begins with an in-depth look at Israel's policy of nuclear ambiguity, laying important groundwork for explaining the features and ramifications of the unique nuclear model that was established in the late 1960s and continues to the present day. It focuses on Israel's motivation in the nuclear realm, the nature of the deterrence that it established, and how the country's nuclear posture affected strategic thinking and perceptions in the region. For years, Israel was the major point of reference for the development of strategic thinking in the Middle East, and an understanding of Israel's policy is an essential basis for examining the two case studies.[5]

The first case study is the ACRS talks of the early 1990s, which provides a test case for assessing regional perceptions about WMD in general and Israel's assumed nuclear weapons capability in particular.[6] These talks—part of the multilateral track of the Madrid peace process that was initiated in the wake of the 1991 Gulf War—were the first opportunity for most of the states in the region to broach the topic of arms control outside the framework of international forums and the Nuclear Non-Proliferation Treaty (NPT). As was the case with all five working groups that made up the multilateral track, ACRS was a broad-based regional dialogue that included Israel. In the ACRS working group, strategic perceptions were on the agenda for discussion, revealing how states were thinking about the role and impact of WMD. This case study enables an examination of Israel's ambiguous posture "in action"—how much of a constraint it actually presented to the discussion in the working group, which was focused specifically on building mutual confidence through different types of CSBMs.[7]

Since the turn of the millennium, the regional picture has become much more complex, as reflected in a number of significant events and developments: the 2003 US war against Iraq, which was aimed at destroying WMD in that country; the September 2007 bombing of a North Korean–style nuclear facility under construction in Syria; Assad's actual use of chemical weapons against his own population in August 2013; and Egypt's ongoing and focused diplomatic campaign against Israel in the nuclear realm, which rose to prominence in the 2010–15 period, following an NPT mandate that regional states work to convene a conference on a WMD-free zone in the Middle East.[8] Additionally, from 2003 to 2015 there was an ongoing international diplomatic effort to stop Iran's military nuclear plans, via a negotiated deal. This process culminated in July 2015, with the Joint Comprehensive Plan of Action (JCPOA), colloquially known as the "Iran deal."[9] The ACRS talks provide a baseline for assessing how perceptions continued to evolve among the key regional actors in light of these developments.

The second case study centers on Iran's nuclear ambitions and the international efforts over the course of twelve years—carried out at different times and in different frameworks by the EU-3 (France, Germany, and the United Kingdom—the three leading members of the European Union), the members of the UN Security Council, the International Atomic Energy Agency (IAEA), the Obama administration, and the P5+1 (the five permanent members of the UN Security Council plus Germany)—to negotiate an agreement with Iran that would bring it back into the fold of its NPT commitments. The goal of the P5+1 negotiators in the 2013–15 period was to achieve a final and comprehensive agreement that would ensure that Iran backed away from its military nuclear ambitions and would never be able to obtain a nuclear weapon.[10] But the long-term process culminated with a deal that does not on its own prevent Iran from achieving a military nuclear capability, particularly because many of the deal's stipulations expire after ten to fifteen years.[11]

For the purpose of this chapter, what is important is how the negotiations and the JCPOA itself have been perceived across the Middle East, especially as regards the lack of transparency from Iran in the military (nuclear) realm. With a lack of information about nuclear capabilities being a feature of both Israel's and Iran's nuclear programs, an analysis of this case helps flesh out where the differences between the two states lie. Israel's defensive orientation in the nuclear realm—borne out by over forty-five years of responsible behavior as an assumed nuclear state—comes into sharper relief when juxtaposed with Iran's offensive agenda, which is closely linked to the latter state's hegemonic aspirations in the region and beyond.[12] Comparing and contrasting the two cases—the different goals of these two states in the nuclear realm as well as their record of behavior in this regard—helps explain the different regional reactions and perceptions that have emerged. Again, the role and meaning of nuclear capabilities are very much a function of the specific context within which they are integrated, and the meaning they assume for different states.

One might argue that the most important difference between Israel and Iran is the fact that Israel is normally assumed to have acquired nuclear weapons, whereas Iran has not yet crossed the nuclear threshold. It is this very assumption that this chapter seeks to challenge. Because nuclear weapons take on meaning *in context*, the fact that one state is considered to be a nuclear state while the other is still striving to reach this goal is not the relevant independent factor that explains perceived strategic stability in the Middle East. Perceptions in the region are influenced by the fact that Iran is moving toward its goal, and states have demonstrated that they are reacting mainly to the motivations and patterns of behavior of both Israel and Iran, along with the specific matrix of interstate relations and rules of the game that each state has established with regard to its assumed (Israel) or aspired-for (Iran) nuclear weapons.

Moreover, in the event that it becomes a nuclear state, there is good reason to believe that Iran will not play by the rules of the game developed in the US-Soviet superpower context. Iran's nuclear weapons capability will most likely be useful primarily as a cover for enhancing its regional aggression. Nuclear weapons will provide Iran with a measure of invulnerability to counterattack, or to coercive measures that extraregional powers might consider in response to Iran's own (conventional) moves. Thus, it will likely enhance Iran's adventurism in the Middle East, in line with the current regime's hegemonic aspirations. This benefit of nuclear weapons for Iran will apply across the region, with serious implications also for Israel, but will be outside the specific (potential) Israel-Iran bilateral nuclear dynamic. If, for example, Iran were to contemplate taking over Bahrain after becoming a nuclear state, this would not foment escalation with Israel; however, external powers would be extremely reluctant to take any action in response, as was the case in 1991, when the United States and its coalition did react with massive military force to Saddam Hussein's takeover of Kuwait.

Although this chapter is geared primarily to empirical analysis, it seeks conceptual insights as well. A primary goal at the conceptual level is to highlight for scholars, who have been strongly influenced by neorealist and classic nuclear deterrence thinking grounded in the US-Soviet experience of the Cold War, that their assumptions are context-dependent. In other words, theorizing about nuclear weapons and their strategic impact is influenced by that particular context; as such, the different regional realities that prevail in the Middle East should encourage scholars to rethink assumptions about how nuclear issues play out among states. As noted, the primary puzzle examined here goes to the role of transparency as an enhancer of strategic stability.

At the policy level, implications can be drawn in relation to the Iranian nuclear crisis: understanding how the threat that Iran poses is actually perceived, and on that basis looking at opportunities within the region for perhaps carving out new and innovative strategies of cooperation to confront the ongoing threat of a nuclearizing Iran.

ISRAEL'S UNIQUE POLICY OF NUCLEAR AMBIGUITY

An essential starting point for understanding the regional landscape in the Middle East and assessing strategic perceptions is an appraisal of the unique model that Israel established through its policy of ambiguity in the nuclear realm. The model of "nuclear ambiguity" was born of an understanding forged in late 1969 between US president Nixon and Israeli prime minister Meir, and has been strictly maintained by Israel for over forty-five years.[13] The meaning of this policy—often misconstrued as a simple exercise in secrecy—is essential for assessing the evolution of strategic perceptions in the Middle East, and its implications are far-reaching.[14] As such, it is important to lay out in broad strokes the prominent features of Israel's policy and Egypt's reaction to it.

Over the years since the 1969 meeting, Israel's policy has developed into a strategy with a life and logic of its own. What it came to mean for Israel and the region—certainly by the early 1990s, when ACRS was initiated—goes well beyond a guessing game of whether Israel does or does not have a military nuclear capability. Although Israel's policy no doubt hinges on maintaining secrecy in the nuclear realm, it is not fundamentally about keeping a secret. Rather, the essence of Israel's policy of ambiguity is to maintain a low profile in the nuclear realm.[15] This low profile—no nuclear threats or posturing, no nuclear tests—has become the hallmark or "seal of approval" for the purely defensive nature of Israel's nuclear policy, which has also been recognized by states in the region.[16] The few official Israeli comments that have been made over the years in reference to its policy only serve to underscore that Israel views this as a last resort capability—an insurance policy in the event that Israel were to face a threat of annihilation.[17]

The benefits of this policy for Israel are well known. After Israel's assumed nuclear capability became common knowledge in the international community, Israel's ambiguous public posture afforded it an effective means for deterrence against existential threats. Over the decades, the threats have been quite concrete at times. Israel's ambiguous public posture ensured that there would be no pressure from the United States for Israel to join the NPT or open its facilities to inspections.

A comprehensive study of Arab states' perceptions of Israel's nuclear posture reveals that, despite Israel's policy of ambiguity, its neighbors nevertheless perceive it to be a nuclear state. Moreover, according to Arab sources, they have very clear ideas about the nature of Israel's deterrence—namely, to ward off an existential threat to the country. Although these sources do not spell out precise redlines that they believe could spark a nuclear response if crossed, they do break down three main features of what is considered an "existential threat": a breach of the "green line"; a multitude of Israeli casualties in general and civilian casualties in particular; and a large-scale wearing-down of Israeli conventional forces during warfare. And though Israel's deterrence is perceived to be most credible vis-à-vis an existential threat, there are additional scenarios that might provoke a nuclear response. In decreasing order of credibility, these are a massive nonconventional strike on cities and/or densely populated areas; a war of attrition with many casualties; and the use of nonconventional weapons against military targets.[18] As such, Israel's nuclear policy underscores that in order to communicate a credible nuclear deterrent threat, the deterring state does not necessarily need to be explicit in its rhetoric; indeed, it can even be purposely ambiguous.

Another intriguing consequence of Israel's policy is that not only Israel has reaped benefits. Indeed, throughout the years, it became apparent that Israel's policy of ambiguity encouraged a measure of stability for the region as a whole. The implied threat of Israeli nuclear retaliation to an existential threat signaled to other states that they should not even consider posing one. At the same time, it also projected to these states that as far as Israel was concerned, any war short of an existential one would remain conventional and relatively limited. As such, the rules of the game in the nuclear realm were established through Israel's behavior over the years, even through the veil of ambiguity, and with it the mutual expectations that foster and enhance stability.[19]

Israel's policy of ambiguity also made it easier for Egypt and the other Arab states to resist developing their own nuclear capability. It was not that there was an absence of calls in the Arab media for specific states—or the Arab world as a collective—to build an "Arab bomb" in response to Israel, but the idea did not gain traction at policy levels.[20] Moreover, the major debate was held in Egypt, and was much less pronounced in the other Arab states.[21] As is discussed further below, those countries in the region that did proceed down the military nuclear route, in direct violation of their NPT commitments—namely, Iraq, Iran, Syria, and Libya—were not reacting to Israel but rather were responding to other domestic and regional challenges.[22]

Egypt from the start was staunchly opposed to Israel's assumed nuclear capability, and in the early 1960s it took initial steps to match Israel (limited to the ballistic missile realm).[23] However, as the years went by, Egypt was able to put these plans to rest—not least because Israel never explicitly threatened Egypt in the nuclear realm. In fact, while Egypt remained openly and very vocally opposed to the situation, it seems that it also concluded that until Israel's assumed nuclear weapons were dismantled, a policy of ambiguity probably better served Egypt's interests as well. President Anwar El Sadat implied as much in the mid-1970s when he said that if Israel issued a nuclear threat, it would force Egypt to respond.[24]

By the late 1970s—when Sadat signed a peace agreement with Israel without making it contingent on Israel's joining the NPT—Egypt had evidently already made the decision to redirect its efforts to neutralize Israel's nuclear capability to the international/diplomatic arena.[25] Egypt has been staunchly adamant since the early 1980s in seeking to convince strong international actors to adhere to a broad-based initiative to force Israel's hand in the nuclear realm. Specifically, Egypt has sought to pressure Israel in different international forums to join the NPT, which would necessarily entail disclosing and dismantling whatever nuclear capability it has. At the 2010 NPT Review Conference, Egypt gained important ground in this regard when the idea for holding a conference on a WMD-free zone (WMDFZ) in the Middle East by the close of 2012 was adopted in the conference's final document. However, agreement among the relevant parties for holding the conference was not secured by that date, nor by the 2015 Review Conference, despite intense efforts on the part of the conference facilitator. The issue has been taken off the NPT agenda, at least until the next Review Conference in 2020.[26]

Significantly, however, Egypt's ongoing diplomatic campaign against Israel in the nuclear realm has not had an adverse effect on the peace process between the two countries. Egypt has steadfastly upheld the peace agreement—even in the face of challenges over the years, such as the 1982 Lebanon War. And more recently, in the heat of the five-year struggle over if and when to hold a WMDFZ regional conference, Egypt has at the same time significantly stepped up its bilateral security cooperation with Israel, especially in the face of security threats emanating from the Sinai.[27] Egypt's perceptions of Israel, against the backdrop of the two states' bilateral relations, are clearly more complex than what a superficial assessment might reveal, and the ACRS talks are probably the best indication of this.

ACRS: STRATEGIC PERCEPTIONS UNFOLD IN A REGIONAL DYNAMIC

The complexity of Egypt's attitude toward Israel's strategic capabilities was apparent from the start. In the early 1960s, when suspicions regarding Israel's nuclear intentions became public, Egypt and Israel were bitter enemies. Egypt no doubt felt directly threatened by what it perceived as Israel's emerging nuclear capability, and it took steps to answer in kind, with an accelerated ballistic missile program assisted by German scientists.[28] Moreover, Egyptian president Nasser stated his intent to lead a collective response to the new challenge posed by Israel on behalf of Egypt and the Arab states. The response in the 1965–66 period had two components: developing a nuclear bomb and—the more conspicuous aspect of Egypt's public response—carrying out a preventive war to stop Israel's nuclear program.[29]

However, several years later, by the late 1960s, the situation had changed quite dramatically: Egypt's missile program had been thwarted, it had suffered defeat in the 1967 war, and Israel was presumed to have crossed the nuclear threshold sometime toward the close of the decade.[30] Egypt carried out a surprise attack against Israel on Yom Kippur in 1973, in an attempt to recapture the Sinai Peninsula, which Israel had conquered in the Six-Day War. Its failure to achieve this goal through warfare encouraged Egypt to pursue diplomacy, and by the mid-1970s, Egypt and Israel had embarked on a process of confidence building regarding Sinai that culminated in the 1979 peace agreement.[31] It was in this period that President Sadat hinted that as long as Israel had a nuclear weapons capability, he would prefer for Israel not to talk about it— granting implicit support to Israel's policy of ambiguity. Signing a peace agreement with Israel in 1979 without neutralizing the latter's assumed nuclear capability was a strong message that Egypt did not view this as a direct security threat; nor was it going to allow the nuclear issue to interfere with the realization of more salient Egyptian interests, such as the return of Sinai.

In the ACRS talks of the early 1990s, the significance of Egypt's regional agenda came to the fore in a manner that had not been seen before. It became clear during this multilateral process that the broader regional picture in the Middle East was affecting Egypt's calculations vis-à-vis Israel, and not a perceived security threat related to Israel's assumed nuclear capability. The Israel/Egypt dyad was no doubt prominent in the talks, because the two states were often engaged in bilateral discussions over the nuclear issue.[32] Indeed, from Egypt's perspective, while Israel was no longer an enemy, Egypt nevertheless had no interest in Israel's maintaining regional prominence by means of its ongoing strategic superiority (or "strategic edge"), the apex of which was its assumed nuclear capability. As such, to the degree that Egypt was focused on Israel directly, it was in order to "cut it down to size"—to make Israel look more like a "normal" state in the region, in tune with its geographic size and population.[33] But it was not about eliminating a nuclear threat.

The salient dynamic for Egypt that emerged was the regional one.[34] The bilateral Egypt-Israel dialogue was integrated into the web of multilateral interactions that constituted Arab politics, and in the early 1990s, this regional framework had very important implications for Egypt. ACRS was initiated at a particularly vulnerable time for Egypt in regional terms, just as it was taking its first steps back into the fold of Arab politics after being ostracized for ten years for its "crime" of forging a peace agreement with Israel. With its regional concerns high on the agenda, Egypt's interests vis-à-vis Israel became closely tied to its regional perspective. Egypt was concerned about cutting Israel down to size, not because of a potential Israeli threat to Egypt but rather because of the implications for Egypt's leadership role among the Arab states.

Egypt wanted to reassert its leadership role in all the new regional dialogues that took place under the auspices of the multilateral track of the Madrid peace process, as well as the regionwide economic conferences that were initiated at about the same time.[35] The additional challenge of these new regional forums was the inclusion of Israel and the new opportunities for direct dialogue between Israel and many of the other Arab participants. Trying to take charge at a vulnerable time, and with the added complication of Israel's participation, Egypt became ever more focused on taking the lead in carving out the Arab approach to ACRS and neutralizing the potential interference of dialogues that Israel might conduct with other Arab states, beyond Egypt's control.[36]

From Israel's perspective, due to the historic peace agreement of 1979, Egypt was the regional neighbor that raised the least concern in security terms. Clearly, by the early 1990s Egypt was not a state that Israel was concerned about in terms of posing an existential threat, and therefore Egypt was outside Israel's purview as far as its nuclear policy was concerned. But Israel had other potential challenges to consider, and its nuclear policy was always regional in scope. Israel had to consider threats that might develop in the future. Taking into account the history of Israel since 1948, this was not an unwarranted approach. So while Egypt tried to convince Israel during the talks that its nuclear deterrent was no longer needed because Israel had finally been accepted as a fait accompli by the Arab states, Israel was looking very nervously toward Iran, which had just recently restarted its military nuclear program.[37]

In sum, regional politics was a central factor in the calculations of both Egypt and Israel, but factored into their calculations in a very different manner, in line with their basic interests and identities. Although the dynamic seemed to be very much bilateral on the surface, with each state reacting to the other, each state's true focus was elsewhere. Israel directed its strategic posture and calculations to possible existential threats that could emerge from different directions, and the threat on the horizon for Israel in this period was most likely Iran.[38] For its part, Egypt was also not chiefly concerned with Israel as such. Rather, its strategic perceptions took on meaning primarily in the context of its geopolitical interests, the most important one being its regional leadership role within the Arab world. This dynamic underscores that for Egypt, the most vocal Arab state in the ACRS talks, the concerns it raised within the talks were not focused on a security threat that emanated from Israel's assumed nuclear capability. Raising this issue served other interests that Egypt sought to address.

What about the perceptions of the other regional participants in the talks? Most were not too concerned with Israel's nuclear capability, certainly not in concrete security terms. Research into perceptions of Israel's nuclear posture in Arab states across the region reveals a huge disparity between the relatively large volume of discussion (official statements, speeches, and interviews as well as media reports and commentary) in Egypt as opposed to what was published in all the other states combined.[39] Moreover, many of the other Arab states began to view the ACRS talks quite favorably; they were very willing participants in the discussions on CSBMs, and they identified an unprecedented opportunity to explore issues of common concern with Israel, including fighting terrorism.[40]

The case of Jordan deserves particular attention in this regard. Jordan was one of the three states (together with Israel and Egypt) that came into the talks with a well-prepared agenda, and in Jordan's case this centered on the creation of the Conference on Security and Cooperation in the Middle East (CSCME), along the lines of the Conference on Security and Cooperation in Europe (CSCE). As such, Jordan was particularly interested in the different CSBMs being discussed, and it took the lead in the group that focused on establishing Regional Security Centers in three countries: Tunisia, Qatar, and (the main one) Jordan. Jordan was so enthusiastic about this idea that the Jordanians insisted on holding what turned out to be a final meeting on the topic in Amman in September 1995, when Egypt had already made its growing dissatisfaction with the talks well known. Needless to say, Egypt was not pleased, and it ended up casting a dissenting vote on setting up the centers, blocking the necessary consensus for their establishment.[41] Moreover, Jordan sparked Egyptian displeasure throughout the talks whenever it assumed the role of mediator between Egypt and Israel, to help settle disputes between the two states over the nuclear issue, as mediation grants power and influence.[42] Significantly, the talks also helped prepare important ground for the Israel-Jordan peace agreement of late 1994, with some of the text in the agreement lifted straight from the ACRS framework.[43]

These dynamics were very problematic from Egypt's perspective. Overall, the more Arab states showed interest in the CBMs being discussed in the working groups, putting out feelers to Israel, the more uncomfortable Egypt became with the process in regional terms. Traditionally, when Egypt presented and/or backed an initiative, the other Arab states were expected to fall in line, in recognition of Egypt's leadership role. In ACRS, not only were they not falling in line, but they were also "breaking ranks" by taking on independent initiatives and roles, as Jordan demonstrated in particular. For Egypt, the talks were treading on too much uncharted territory, and things were moving too rapidly, complicating Egypt's task of reasserting its regional role. So, ironically, the more progress that was made regarding confidence building, the more frustrated

Egypt became as far as regaining regional control, and the more determined it became to bring the talks to a close, which happened in December 1995.[44]

REGIONAL RESPONSES TO IRAN'S OFFENSIVE NUCLEAR ATTRIBUTES

Iran's military nuclear ambitions have added a new and dangerous element to the strategic mix in the Middle East. Arab states as well as Israel have been nervously following the advances it has made with its nuclear program, along with the implications for its regional standing and influence. Although Israel had been following Iran's nuclear program starting in the 1990s, it came on to the international radar full force only in 2002, with the revelations regarding two nuclear facilities—Natanz and Arak—that Iran had not declared to the IAEA, in violation of its safeguard agreements with the agency. International efforts to confront Iran's ambitions began in 2003, when the EU-3 initiated talks; the three European states hoped to thwart Iran's plans to work on the nuclear fuel cycle in the earliest stage.[45] The initiation of these negotiations—which continued in different formats until 2015—indicated that a second "nuclear player" had been injected into the Middle East strategic arena, and strategic perceptions in the region began to evolve.

While Israel began openly voicing its concerns about Iran's nuclear activities from the start of the negotiations, the Arab states have tended to be much more low key, even over the past decade. Still, during the Mubarak years, Egypt voiced its fears about Iran's nuclear advances, especially in light of Iran's hegemonic ambitions.[46] More recently, since 2010, Saudi Arabia has been more vocal since the WikiLeaks release of secret cables recounting King Abdullah's repeated requests for the US to attack Iran's nuclear facilities in order to "cut off the head of the snake."[47] Since then, especially during the latter months of the P5+1–Iran negotiations, Saudi Arabia has also clarified that whatever capabilities Iran was allowed, Saudi Arabia would want as well.[48]

If one were to assess the Iranian nuclear program without appreciating how Israel's nuclear policy had come to be perceived in the Middle East, the history of interstate relations in the region including the experience of ACRS, and the reactions of other actors in the Middle East to Iran's nuclear program, one might assume that Iran's nuclear moves were an accepted regional response to Israel's assumed capability—a capability that other regional players had ostensibly been trying to balance for years. Indeed, disregarding history and regional politics, one might be tempted to conclude, as Kenneth Waltz did in an article published in *Foreign Affairs* in 2012, that an Iranian nuclear capability would finally establish the stability that the region had been craving ever since Israel "went nuclear" over four decades earlier. According to this reading, which draws on the global Cold War experience and thinking, an Iranian nuclear capability should be a welcome development for regional actors.[49]

But this has hardly been the case. First, Israel's nuclear policy did not create instability in the region. Although there was talk (especially in the initial years, more often than not in media commentary) about creating an Arab response to Israel, there was no indication—certainly since the early 1970s—of any real urgency at policymaking levels to balance the assumed nuclear state. Moreover, as expectations and rules of the game with regard to Israel's ambiguous nuclear policy became increasingly entrenched in regional perceptions and practices, stability was actually enhanced.

Significantly, other states in the region that took steps in the nuclear realm were not focused on Israel. Though difficult to determine definitively, Iraq went down the nuclear route in the 1970s and 1980s for reasons of prestige, in order to gain prominence within the Arab world, and for regime survival within the Persian Gulf setting; it was not primarily about balancing Israel.[50] Libya also demonstrated interest in nuclear development in the 1970s for reasons of prestige and its standing in the Arab world.[51] When Iran restarted its military nuclear program in the middle to late 1980s as a direct reaction to Iraq, with which it was engaged in years-long warfare, the centrality of the Iran-Iraq bilateral dynamic was further underscored. As far as Egypt was concerned, it not only scrapped plans from the early 1960s to perhaps respond to Israel in kind, but also later signed a peace agreement with Israel under the assumption that it had a nuclear weapons capability.

It is important to recognize that states in the Middle East have their different and crosscutting interests and relationships, and they are not all singularly focused on Israel as their primary adversary or as a burning source of instability. Today, actors in the Middle East are keenly aware that the violence and instability that is ripping through the region—as in Syria, Iraq, and Yemen—has absolutely nothing to do with Israel's nuclear posture; most is not related to Israel at all.

Beyond the impact of Israel's nuclear policy and regional politics over the decades, reactions in the Middle East to Iran's nuclear ambitions have not been positive, which can be attributed to Iran itself. In particular, two main features of Iran's nuclear ambitions have caused them to trigger threat perceptions in a number of states in the Middle East. The first goes to Iran's current motivation for pursuing a military nuclear capability, and the second to its record of deceit in the nuclear realm.[52]

Iran's neighbors in the region believe that its primary motivation to pursue a military nuclear capability is in the context of its regional hegemonic aspirations; specifically, to deter coercive action by strong international actors in response to any aggressive moves that Iran might contemplate in the Middle East.[53] Iran's hegemonic aspirations are no secret—they are written about and discussed openly, and a nuclear capability can be a strong asset for Iran in this regard.[54] There is little evidence to support a reading whereby Iran is defensively oriented in the nuclear realm; nor do its nuclear ambitions seem to be about ensuring its security. A case could be made that Iran would not have faced threats of possible military force over the past decade if it had not been pursuing a military nuclear capability in the first place, or threatening others in the region both directly and via proxies. The danger that Iran poses in the nuclear realm is something that resonates strongly with the status quo Arab states, as noted above. With open criticism a rarity, the fact that Saudi Arabia issued a few clear statements is an indication of the level of concern. Such statements are out of the norm for this country.

The second issue—Iran's strategic deception in the nuclear realm—is most likely a factor that affects Israel's strategic perceptions more than those of other states in the Middle East. For Israel, Iran's deceit joins the deceit that was also practiced by Iraq, Libya, and Syria in the nuclear realm—and is another indication of the dismal record of states in the region that joined the NPT and then cheated on their commitment not to work on a military nuclear capability.[55] Nevertheless, Iran's record is the greatest concern not only because it has gone on for decades but also because Iran has a vast nuclear infrastructure that it might use to develop nuclear weapons down the line. Significantly, Iran's deception was not cleared up over the course of the P5+1–Iran negotiations, or in the framework of the nuclear deal itself. The inquiry into Iran's past weaponization activities—dubbed the "possible military dimensions" of its program by the IAEA—was delayed, and ultimately left outside the framework of the JCPOA.[56] The final report was released by IAEA director-general Yukiya Amano on December 2, 2015, and the results—even on the basis of what Amano noted was only partial cooperation on the part of Iran—were significant: Iran had been working on a military nuclear program in a coordinated manner up to 2003, and in a less coordinated manner until at least 2009.[57] However, in the face of this assessment, the IAEA Board of Governors nevertheless closed the file in its final report on the possible military dimensions that was released two weeks later.[58] This decision to close the file—despite the assessment that Iran had been working on a military program, in violation of its commitment according to the NPT not to do so—has enabled Iran to continue with its misleading narrative of having "done no wrong" in the nuclear realm, a platform for which there are already indications that Iran will continue to abuse for its purposes.[59]

Many states in the Middle East are unsatisfied with the JCPOA and remain unconvinced that Iran's nuclear and/or regional ambitions have been put to rest. As such, Iran's lack of transparency reverberates in a manner that breeds both suspicions that Iran is purposely hiding capabilities and intentions that it flatly denies exist, and fears that Iran could continue in this direction in a manner that would enable it to use its nuclear program to support hostile action in the region. The result is that the lack of transparency in the Iran case serves to undermine stability in the Middle East.

DISCUSSION

Coming full circle to the puzzle raised at the outset with regard to the effect of transparency on perceptions of strategic stability, the analysis in this chapter reveals a decades-long regional story that cannot easily be reduced to a focus on transparency as a defining factor for states when they assess existing and emerging nuclear capabilities. Indeed, Israel pursued a purposeful policy of ambiguity, and Iran is hiding the truth about its work on a military nuclear program. But the relevant issues that have an impact on regional perceptions go to the identity, motivations, and behavior of the two states in question—namely, who they are, what their motivations are in the nuclear realm and how they have been conducting their nuclear affairs, why Israel has insisted on ambiguity, and why Iran has been deceiving the international community. It is the answers to these questions—much more than whether all facts regarding their nuclear options are transparent—that feed perceptions of confidence and stability, or threat.

This chapter has focused heavily on Egyptian perceptions of Israel's nuclear posture—not because Egypt is the only state that matters but because it has been the most prominent voice from among the Arab states over the years. From the 1960s onward, the media debate in Egypt on this topic was by far the richest in terms of content and frequency. What we have seen in this debate is a dynamic perception of Israel that has developed in tune with regional developments and Israel's behavior. Egypt started out projecting fear regarding Israel's nuclear option, but by the early 1970s it was viewing the situation differently—though not happy with the capability attributed to Israel, Egypt was not fearful for its security. There were further developments in Egypt's approach over the years, but the key to their explanation is Egyptian interests vis-à-vis regional politics, and not Israel as such.

ACRS

In ACRS, Egypt was hoping that its arms control agenda that focused on Israel would help it gain support from, and leadership among, the Arab states. Toward the end of the talks, in an almost desperate attempt to convince the other Arab states to come on board Egypt's agenda and cease cooperation with CSBMs, Egypt began playing up the Israeli nuclear threat in a process of securitization. So, if at the start of the process the Egyptians emphasized that Israel's assumed nuclear capability must be dealt with because Israel could not be treated as an exception, by the end of the talks, there were references to the proximity of Dimona to Cairo, hinting at the possibility of a more direct nuclear threat.[60] However, once ACRS was taken off the agenda in December 1995, there was a sharp decline in Egyptian references to Israel and the nuclear realm, and Egypt turned exclusively to the NPT framework, where it hoped to push forward its agenda for the creation of a WMDFZ in the Middle East. In more recent years (2010–15), Egypt's "Israel nuclear" agenda has become much harder to explain, because it is increasingly at odds with the intensification of Egyptian-Israeli bilateral security relations. One can only speculate on the motivation—but it seems to be fueled in large part by the internal bureaucratic interests of the Egyptian Foreign Ministry, which has traditionally led this campaign in Egypt.

Egyptian leaders and officials over the years would often note that they were speaking not only for Egypt but also for the entire Arab world. However, the ACRS talks demonstrated that other states in the region were voicing their opinions, and they were not necessarily identical to those of Egypt. So while Egypt was increasingly playing up the nuclear issue in the talks, Israel's nuclear profile was not hindering progress on CSBMs in the arms control working group. It has been argued elsewhere that Israel's policy of ambiguity precludes effective discussion of regional arms control in the Middle East.[61] However, that depends on how arms control is defined, and the logic that is adopted. If the logic is that weapons systems must be addressed and dismantled in the first stage, then the argument is valid. But ACRS followed a different logic—the idea was to begin regional arms control discussions with a focus on lowering tensions among the states, and building confidence in military intentions.[62]

As such, not only did the ACRS talks incorporate the CSBM logic of tension reduction in interstate relations, but this was the major focus of the talks. However, though at the global superpower level, confidence building was and is closely linked to nuclear transparency, in the Middle East the work that needed to be done as far as building confidence and trust was far beneath the nuclear threshold. Transparency was a component of the CSBMs that was discussed, but relating to the conventional realm—exchange of military information and prenotification of military exercises—not WMD. It is noteworthy that in the course of the talks, and building on attitudes to transparency taken from the superpower experience, Egypt did advocate that Israel reveal what it had in the nuclear realm, as a first step for building confidence. But because of the progress being made in the CSBM discussions, the idea did not resonate with the organizers or with the other participants.[63]

Iran

The Iran case study demonstrated that Middle Eastern states' perceptions of Iran's military nuclear activities derived from their perceptions of Iran itself—its motivations and behavior. For Saudi Arabia and Egypt in particular, the concern focused primarily on Iran's hegemonic aspirations, and the implications of a nuclear capability in this framework. For Israel, there was an added measure of urgency—especially for Prime Minister Netanyahu—when leaders referred to the emerging Iranian threat as "existential." Moreover, for Israel, Iran's record of deception was highlighted—the inability to trust arrangements with Iran because Iran had a proven record of cheating on its nuclear commitments.

The difference between the Israel and Iran cases in regional perceptions is underscored by the fact that Iran's nuclear advances have sparked concerns that are expressed in terms of the need to respond to Iran in kind. The statements issued by Saudi Arabia are the most clear-cut, but the challenge also finds expression in the fact that in 2006, six states in the Middle East suddenly expressed their desire to the IAEA to advance civilian nuclear programs. Although this could be explained by renewed interest in nuclear energy at the time, an established path for NPT member states that strive for a military nuclear capability is to use a civilian program as cover for a military one.[64] Additionally, there has been growing interest in the region—especially in the Gulf states—to secure more advanced defensive capabilities from the US in order to counter threats from Iran in the wake of the P5+1–Iran deal.[65]

CONCLUSIONS

Israel's policy of ambiguity in the nuclear realm created a unique model of nuclear deterrence that has had a profound impact on how strategic perceptions have evolved in the Middle East. This is something that is reflected in the attitudes and behavior of Middle East states, if not openly expressed in their rhetoric. It helps explain the perhaps counterintuitive collective silence from different regional quarters following Israel's September 2007 attack on the nuclear facility under construction in Syria.[66] With all the enmity toward Israel at the rhetorical level, the regional players nevertheless recognized that Syria is not Israel, and nuclear capabilities do not have the same significance in the hands of every state. So though Israel is an adversary, it is not a danger in the nuclear realm, unless a state poses an existential threat to Israel. Conversely, nuclear weapons in the hands of Bashar al-Assad—or Ayatollah Ali Khamenei— would likely create a very different challenge, and could pose a concrete threat to other states, whether directly or in terms of regional prominence. So it was accepted, perhaps even applauded in some quarters, when Israel took action to stem the nascent Syrian threat.[67]

Strategic perceptions develop in context, and in the Middle East, broad regional political dynamics must be part of any analysis of strategic stability. Even though Israel and Egypt were prominent in ACRS, and analysts tend to focus on the nuclear dimension in that regard, the explanation for Egypt's attitude in the talks goes to regional politics. Similarly, though analyses of Iran's nuclear ambitions often tend to focus exclusively on Israel, the reality is that Iran is also clearly affecting additional actors.

Perceptions of stability or the lack thereof have been influenced more by the behavior and motivations of the state in question, the nature of interstate relationships, and the rules of the game established over the years than by WMD as such. This also goes for the issue of transparency and openness with regard to capabilities. Israel's long-term policy of ambiguity—underpinning the purely defensive nature of its assumed nuclear capability—helped establish certain rules of the game in the Middle East at the strategic level that the other players have come to accept, albeit grudgingly. When expectations prove reliable over the long term, stability follows. New potential contenders in the nuclear realm—first and foremost Iran—are challenging stability in dangerous ways. The record of Iran as far as deceiving the international community about its intentions and activities, and its aggressive regional profile, portend a more dangerous Middle East, and we are seeing regional states respond accordingly. This new reality could drive additional states in the Middle East to develop their own military nuclear capabilities.[68] It could also foster new opportunities for cooperation and coordination among the Arab states and Israel—states that have a similar assessment of what does and does not pose a concrete threat to their security in the nuclear realm.

NOTES

1. See Kenneth N. Waltz, "Nuclear Myths and Political Realities," *American Political Science Review* 84, no. 3 (September 1990): 730–45; and Alexander L. George

and Richard Smoke, "Deterrence and Foreign Policy," *World Politics* 41, no. 2 (January 1989): 170–82.

2. See, e.g., Thomas C. Schelling and Morton H. Halperin, *Strategy and Arms Control* (New York: Twentieth Century Fund, 1961); and Jeffrey A. Larsen, "An Introduction to Arms Control," in *Arms Control: Cooperative Security in a Changing Environment,* ed. Jeffrey A. Larsen (Boulder, CO: Lynne Rienner, 2002), 1–15. For a recent formulation of the US arms control approach, see Frank A. Rose, "Nuclear Arms Control and Disarmament Approaches in a Changed Security Environment," *US Department of State Archives,* September 30, 2015, https://2009–2017.state.gov/t/avc/rls/2015/247623.htm.

3. Since the establishment of the US-Soviet hotline after the Cuban missile crisis, CBMs have been part of US-Soviet and US-Russian arms control. For background material on the concepts of CBMs and CSBMs, see Jonathan Alford, ed., *The Future of Arms Control: Part III; Confidence-Building Measures* in *The Adephi Papers* 19, no. 149 (London: International Institute for Strategic Studies, 1979); Johan Jorgen Holst, "Confidence-Building Measures: A Conceptual Framework," *Survival* 25, no. 1 (January–February 1983): 2–15; and UN Department for Disarmament Affairs, "Confidence and Security Building Measures: From Europe to Other Regions," in *Disarmament: Topical Papers No. 7* (New York: United Nations, 1991).

4. See Alan Platt, *Arms Control and Confidence Building in the Middle East* (Washington, DC: US Institute of Peace Press, 1992).

5. Ariel Levite and Emily B. Landau, *Israel's Nuclear Image: Arab Perceptions of Israel's Nuclear Posture* (in Hebrew) (Tel Aviv: Papyrus, 1994). This was the case even though other states were active in the WMD realm—with chemical weapons programs, and some moving in the direction of nuclear weapons development—Iraq in particular.

6. For a comprehensive analysis, see Emily B. Landau, *Arms Control in the Middle East: Cooperative Security Dialogue and Regional Constraints* (Brighton: Sussex Academic Press, 2006). For a very concise account (including reference to additional sources on the talks), see Emily B. Landau, "ACRS: What Worked, What Didn't, and What Could Be Relevant for the Region Today," *Disarmament Forum* 2 (2008): 13–20, www.unidir.org/files/publications/pdfs/arms-control-in-the-middle-east-en-327.pdf.

7. Ibid. The four categories of CSBMs discussed in ACRS related to the maritime realm, prenotification of military exercises and exchange of military information, a regional communications network, and regional security centers.

8. On these developments, see the following sources on the Iraq War: George W. Bush, "Transcript: George Bush's Speech on Iraq," *The Guardian,* October 7, 2002, www.theguardian.com/world/2002/oct/07/usa.iraq; and George W. Bush, "President Bush's Address on the Iraq Invasion," *Wall Street Journal,* March 18, 2013, http://blogs.wsj.com/dispatch/2013/03/18/full-text-of-president-george-w-bushs-speech-march-19–2003/. On the attack in Syria, see Daveed Gartenstein-Ross and Joshua D. Goodman, "The Attack on Syria's al-Kibar Nuclear Facility," *inFocus Quarterly,* Spring 2009, www.jewishpolicycenter.org/826/the-attack-on-syrias-al-kibar-nuclear-facility. On the use of chemical weapons in Syria, see "Timeline of Syrian Chemical Weapons Activity, 2012–2015," Arms Control Association, August 19, 2014, www.armscontrol.org/factsheets/Timeline-of-Syrian-Chemical-Weapons-Activity. And on Egypt's diplomatic campaign, see Emily B. Landau, "Egypt, Israel, and the WMDFZ Conference for the Middle East: Setting the Record Straight," *Israel Journal of Foreign Affairs* 8, no. 1 (2013),

www.inss.org.il/uploadImages/systemFiles/Emily%20-%20Egypt,%20Israel,%20 and%20the%20WMDFZ%20Conference.pdf.

9. "Full Text of the Iran Nuclear Deal," *Washington Post*, July 14, 2015. http:// apps.washingtonpost.com/g/documents/world/full-text-of-the-iran-nuclear-deal/1651/.

10. On a visit to Israel in February 2014, US negotiator Wendy Sherman said there was only one measure of success for a comprehensive agreement, "and that is if an agreement means that Iran will never obtain a nuclear weapon"; "Final Nuclear Deal with Iran by July, Top US Negotiator Says," *Times of Israel*, February 22, 2014.

11. See, e.g., Emily B. Landau, "The Iran Nuclear Deal: Bitter Fruits of a Failed Nonproliferation Policy," *The Tower*, September 28, 2015, www.thetower.org/2378-the -iran-nuclear-deal-bitter-fruits-of-a-failed-nonproliferation-strategy/.

12. See Gerald M. Steinberg, "The Evolution of Israeli Military Strategy: Asymmetry, Vulnerability, Pre-emption and Deterrence," in *Israel Studies: An Anthology*, ed. Mitchell Bard (2011), www.jewishvirtuallibrary.org/israel-studies-an-anthology-israeli -military-strategy. Also see "Iranian Hegemony," Reut Insitute, 2007, http://reut-institute .org/Publication.aspx?PublicationId=1405.

13. Avner Cohen, *Israel and the Bomb* (New York: Columbia University Press, 1998), 336–37.

14. For an article that focuses on secrecy, see Douglas Birch and R. Jeffrey Smith, "Israel's Worst Kept Secret," *The Atlantic*, September 16, 2014, www.theatlantic.com /international/archive/2014/09/israel-nuclear-weapons-secret-united-states/380237/.

15. See Emily B. Landau, "Being Clear about Ambiguity," *Haaretz*, May 13, 2010; and Emily B. Landau, "2012 Middle East WMDFZ Conference: Israel's Calculations and Concerns," in *Preparing for a Constructive 2012 Conference on the Middle East Weapons of Mass Destruction Free Zone*, ed. W. P. S. Sidhu and Bruce Jones, with Colette Jaycox (New York: Center on International Cooperation at New York University, 2012), 22–31.

16. Levite and Landau, *Israel's Nuclear Image*, 156–67. This study shows that Arab states have regarded Israel's nuclear deterrence as credible in relation to a threat to its existence.

17. Louis Rene Beres, "A Survival Imperative: Israel's Nuclear Weapons and Strategy," *Jerusalem Post*, February 26, 2014, www.jpost.com/Experts/A-survival -imperative-Israels-nuclear-weapons-and-strategy-343613.

18. See Landau and Levite, *Israel's Nuclear Image*, 166. This includes a summary of the threat scenarios and the degree that Israel's nuclear deterrent is credible for the different scenarios.

19. On the concept of rules of the game, see Raymond Cohen, "Rules of the Game in International Politics," *International Studies Quarterly* 24, no. 1 (March 1980): 129–50, www.jstor.org/stable/2600131?seq=1#page_scan_tab_contents; and as applied to the Middle East, see Daniel Sobelman, "New Rules of the Game: Israel and Hizbollah after the Withdrawal from Lebanon," JCSS Memorandum 69, January 2004, www.inss .org.il/uploadimages/Import/(FILE)1190276456.pdf.

20. See Joseph Longa, "Then and Now: Arab Reactions to the Israeli and Iranian Nuclear Programs," in *A Collection of Papers from the 2009 Nuclear Scholars Initiative* (Washington, DC: Center for Strategic and International Studies, 2009), http://csis.org /images/stories/poni/110921_Longa.pdf.

21. Levite and Landau, *Israel's Nuclear Image*. Egypt often speaks in the name of all Arab states—this is part of its leadership agenda—but throughout the years, it has become apparent that the other states are not necessarily on board Egypt's campaigns to the degree that Egypt claims them to be.

22. Shai Feldman distinguishes between public rhetoric that tends to focus on Israel, and the fact that the nuclear policies of Arab states and Iran have often actually been motivated by developments in each other's capabilities: Shai Feldman, *Nuclear Weapons and Arms Control in the Middle East* (Cambridge, MA: MIT Press, 1997). For domestic factors and considerations underlying weapons development, see Etel Solingen, *Nuclear Logics: Contrasting Paths in East Asia and the Middle East* (Princeton, NJ: Princeton University Press, 2007). See also Emily B. Landau, "When Neorealism Meets the Middle East: Iran's Pursuit of Nuclear Weapons in (Regional) Context," *Strategic Assessment* 15, no. 3 (October 2012): 30–31, www.inss.org.il/uploadImages/systemFiles/adkan15_3c ENG3%20(2)_Landau.pdf.

23. Nuclear Threat Initiative, "Egypt: Missile," January 2015, www.nti.org/country -profiles/egypt/delivery-systems/.

24. Levite and Landau, *Israel's Nuclear Image*, 77–78.

25. This dovetailed with Egypt's decision to shift its global orientation from the Soviet Union to the United States, a major advocate of nuclear nonproliferation. For an analysis of Egypt's decision to remain nonnuclear, see Robert J. Einhorn, "Egypt: Frustrated but Still on a Non-Nuclear Course," in *The Nuclear Tipping Point: Why States Reconsider Their Nuclear Choices*, ed. Kurt M. Campbell, Robert J. Einhorn, and Mitchell B. Reiss (Washington, DC: Brookings Institution Press, 2004), 43–82.

26. Emily B. Landau and Shimon Stein, "2015 NPT RevCon: WMDFZ Conference off the Table, for Now," *INSS Insight* 705, June 3, 2015.

27. Ben Caspit, "Israel-Egypt Anti-Terrorism Cooperation at Zenith," *Al-Monitor*, May 23, 2014, www.al-monitor.com/pulse/originals/2014/05/israel-egypt-security-coop eration-netanyahu-livni-nuclear.html.

28. Nuclear Threat Initiative, "Egypt."

29. For analysis of statements by Nasser and Muhammed Hasanyn Haykal (a journalist who served as Nasser's spokesman) in the 1965–66 period, see Ariel Levite and Emily B. Landau, "Arab Perceptions of Israel's Nuclear Posture, 1960–1967," *Israel Studies* 1, no. 1 (Spring 1996): 34–45.

30. Cohen, *Israel;* and Levite and Landau, *Israel's Nuclear Image*.

31. On the common aversion to war after 1973 that enabled a move to negotiations, see Janice Gross Stein, "A Common Aversion to War: Regime Creation by Egypt and Israel as a Strategy of Conflict Management," in *Conflict Management in the Middle East*, ed. G. Ben-Dor and D. Dewitt (Lexington, MA: Lexington Books, 1987). For more on the Egypt-Israel confidence-building process of the 1970s, see Brian S. Mandell, "Anatomy of a Confidence-Building Regime: Egyptian-Israeli Security Cooperation, 1973–1979," *International Journal* 45 (Spring 1990): 202–23. See also Emily Landau, "The Role of Public Declarations in Egyptian-Israeli Relations," in *Declaratory Diplomacy: Rhetorical Initiatives and Confidence Building*, ed. Michael Krepon, Jenny S. Drezzin, and Michael Newbill (Washington, DC: Henry L. Stimson Center, 1999), 53–86, www.stimson.org/images/uploads/research-pdfs/declan dau.pdf.

32. See, e.g., Bruce Jentleson, *The Middle East Arms Control and Regional Security Talks: Progress, Problems, and Prospects*, IGCC Policy Paper 26 (San Diego: Institute on Global Conflict and Cooperation at the University of California, San Diego, 1996). The general nature of the bilateral discussion is well known; but the ACRS talks were closed, and therefore more detail regarding the precise content cannot be provided.

33. Landau, *Arms Control*, 146–52.

34. Ibid., 120–59.

35. The first economic conference was held in late 1994, in Casablanca: "MENA Summits and Conferences," European Institute for Research on Mediterranean and Euro-Arab Cooperation, www.medea.be/en/countries/arab-world-general/mena-summits -and-conferences/.

36. See Landau, *Arms Control*, 120–59; and Dalia Dassa Kaye, *Beyond the Handshake: Multilateral Cooperation in the Arab-Israeli Peace Process, 1991–1996* (New York: Columbia University Press, 2001), 99–109.

37. Scott Peterson, "Imminent Iran Nuclear Threat? A Timeline of Warnings since 1979," *Christian Science Monitor*, November 8, 2011, www.csmonitor.com/World /Middle-East/2011/1108/Imminent-Iran-nuclear-threat-A-timeline-of-warnings -since-1979/Earliest-warnings-1979-84.

38. In the 1990s, Israel was clearly focused on Iran, not Iraq, as the prime threat— this was just after the 1991 war and Iraq's defeat. If there has been debate on this question (Iran or Iraq), it relates to the 2002–3 period. In a lecture at the Institute for National Security Studies on December 1, 2015, Uzi Arad said that there were Israeli officials who tried to convince the Americans that the correct target in 2003 was indeed Iran, not Iraq.

39. Levite and Landau, *Israel's Nuclear Image*, 71–96.

40. Emily Landau, "Egypt and Israel in ACRS: Bilateral Concerns in a Regional Arms Control Process," JCSS Memorandum 59, June 2001, 45–50.

41. Landau, *Egypt and Israel in ACRS*, 19.

42. See Omer Shapira, "Exploring the Concept of Power in Mediation: Mediators' Sources of Power and Influence Tactics," *Ohio State Journal on Dispute Resolution* 535 (2009): 24.

43. Landau, *Arms Control*, 44–47, 53–54, 61–70.

44. Ibid., 120–59. The decision to put the talks on hold indefinitely in late 1995 was made by the US—the Americans feared that the growing disagreement between Egypt and Israel on the nuclear front might have an adverse effect on the peace agreement between the two states.

45. Emily B. Landau, *Decade of Diplomacy: Negotiations with Iran and North Korea and the Future of Nuclear Nonproliferation*, INSS Memorandum 115 (Tel Aviv: Institute for National Security Studies, 2012).

46. For an analysis and prominent quotations, see Amos Yadlin and Avner Golov, "A Nuclear Iran: The Spur to a Regional Arms Race?" *Strategic Assessment* 15, no. 3 (October 2012): 7–26, www.inss.org.il/uploadImages/systemFiles/adkan15_3cENG3 %20(2)_Yadlin%20and%20Golov.pdf. See also Keinan Ben Ezra, "The Iranian Nuclear Program: The Egyptian View," in *Arms Control Dilemmas: Focus on the Middle East*, ed. Emily B. Landau and Anat Kurz, INSS Memorandum 122 (Tel Aviv: Institute for National Security Studies, 2012), 61–71.

47. Ross Colvin, "'Cut off Head of Snake,' Saudis Told US on Iran," Reuters, November 29, 2010, www.reuters.com/article/us-wikileaks-iran-saudis-idUSTRE6AS0 2B20101129.

48. Yoel Guzansky, "Whatever Iran Gets in Nuclear Talks, Saudi Arabia Wants as Well," *Jerusalem Post*, March 30, 2015.

49. Kenneth N. Waltz, "Why Iran Should Get the Bomb: Nuclear Balancing Would Mean Stability," *Foreign Affairs* 91, no. 4 (July–August 2012). For a response to Waltz's argument, see Landau, "When Neorealism Meets the Middle East."

50. For the mix of Iraqi motivations, see Ibrahim al-Marashi, "Saddam's Iraq and Weapons of Mass Destruction: Iraq as a Case Study of a Middle Eastern Proliferant," *Middle East Review of International Affairs* 8, no. 3 (September 2004).

51. See Malfrid Braut-Hegghammer, "Libya's Nuclear Intentions: Ambition and Ambivalence," *Strategic Insight* 8, no. 2 (April 2009).

52. Iran's "deceit" refers to the evidence that it worked on a military nuclear program, which Iran flatly denies. The element of deceit has been strongly underscored by the IAEA report on Iran's possible military dimensions, released in early December 2015; see, e.g., William Tobey, "Iran Lied about Its Nuclear Program—What Is the United States Going to Do about It?" *Foreign Policy*, December 2015.

53. With regard to Iranian nuclear motivations, all assessments—including the one included here—cannot be grounded in "hard facts" because Iran denies that it ever worked on a military nuclear capability. Assessments are based on a strategic analysis of Iran's situation and interests. So, e.g., in the 1980s, when embroiled in a war with Iraq, a country itself developing nuclear weapons, and that used chemical weapons against Iran, there is good reason to attribute Iran's reactivation of its program to these factors. Later on, other motivations were attributed to Iran by regional players, mainly connected to its regional hegemonic aspirations.

54. Soner Cagaptay, James F. Jeffrey, and Mehdi Khalaji, "Iran Won't Give Up on Its Revolution," *New York Times*, April 26, 2015, www.washingtoninstitute.org/policy -analysis/view/iran-wont-give-up-on-its-revolution. On how Iran viewed NATO's attack on Libya, in terms of the implications of WMD possession when facing potential attack, see Emanuele Ottolenghi, "Iran Looks On as the West Wrestles with Contradictions over Libya Intervention," *Commentator*, April 5, 2011, www.thecommentator.com /article/38/iran_looks_on_as_the_west_wrestles_with_contradictions_over_libya _intervention.

55. See Shaul Chorev's statement to the 56th General Conference of the IAEA, September 2012, http://iaec.gov.il/About/SpeakerPosts/Documents/IAEA%20statement %20Sep2012.pdf.

56. According to an anonymous US official who was engaged with the issue in October 2015, the Iran Deal would be implemented regardless of the content of the IAEA's final report, which at that time was due to be issued only two months later; see Patrick Goodenough, "Iran Nuclear Deal Formally Begins; IAEA Probe into Iran's Wea- ponization Activities Doesn't Matter," CNS News, October 18, 2015.

57. See "Final Assessment on Past and Present Outstanding Issues regarding Iran's Nuclear Program," IAEA Report GOV/2015/68, December 2, 2015, http://isis -online.org/uploads/isis-reports/documents/IAEA_PMD_Assessment_2Dec2015.pdf; and David Albright, Andrea Stricker, and Serena Kelleher-Vergantini, "Analysis of the

IAEA's Report on the Possible Military Dimensions of Iran's Nuclear Program," ISIS Report, December 8, 2015, www.isisnucleariran.org/assets/pdf/ISIS_Analysis_of_the _IAEA_PMD_Report_December_8_2015_Final.pdf.

58. See Emily B. Landau and Ephraim Asculai, "The IAEA Investigation into Iran's Nuclear Past: Why Was the PMD File Closed?" *INSS Insight* 780, December 21, 2015, www.inss.org.il/index.aspx?id=4538&articleid=11144.

59. Foreign Minister Zarif's interview with *The Guardian* in late July 2015 is an example. For an analysis of the interview, see Shimon Stein and Emily B. Landau, "Iran's Nuclear Fairytale Continued," *The National Interest*, August 18, 2015. The final report of the IAEA clarifies that Iran did work on a military nuclear program in a coordinated effort up to 2003, and that some activities continued up until 2009. The report, while exposing Iran's deceit, is nonetheless inconclusive on important issues, and its impact remains to be seen. See Emily B. Landau, "Analysis: Ignoring Iran's Past Deceptions Dooms Nuclear Deal," *The Tower*, December 3, 2015.

60. Landau, *Arms Control*, 67. On the concept of securitization, see Barry Buzan, Ole Waever, and Jaap de Wilde, *Security: A New Framework for Analysis* (Boulder, CO: Lynne Rienner, 1998).

61. Avner Cohen and Marvin Miller, "Bringing Israel's Bomb out of the Basement: Has Nuclear Ambiguity Outlived Its Shelf Life?" *Foreign Affairs*, September–October 2010.

62. In the opening session of ACRS, held in Moscow in January 1992, then–US secretary of state James Baker set forth the logic of the talks as an exercise in confidence building. See Landau, *Arms Control*, 39.

63. Moreover, it could be argued that for Israel to "open up" would more likely have been perceived as a threatening, rather than reassuring, step.

64. See Emily B. Landau, "New Nuclear Programs in the Middle East: What Do They Mean?" *INSS Insight* 3 (December 11, 2006); and Yoel Guzansky and Gallia Lindenstrauss, "Nuclear Mirage? Assessing Civilian Nuclear Programs across the Middle East," Foreign Policy Research Institute, July 13, 2012, www.fpri.org/article/2012/07/nuclear-mirage-assessing-civilian-nuclear-programs-across-the-middle-east/.

65. See Jay Solomon and Carol E. Lee, "Gulf States Want US Assurances and Weapons in Exchange for Supporting Iran Nuclear Deal," *Wall Street Journal*, May 2, 2015. www.wsj.com/articles/gulf-states-want-u-s-assurances-and-weapons-in-exchange-for-supporting-iran-pact-1430585002.

66. The story behind Israel's attack has been related by Elliott Abrams, then the deputy national security adviser in charge of the Middle East portfolio; see Elliott Abrams, "Bombing the Syrian Reactor: The Untold Story," *Commentary*, February 1, 2013, www.commentarymagazine.com/articles/bombing-the-syrian-reactor-the-untold-story/.

67. This message was communicated to the author in private conversations.

68. Yadlin and Golov, "Nuclear Iran."

5

Beyond Strategic Stability

Deterrence, Regional Balance, and Iranian National Security

ANNIE TRACY SAMUEL

THIS CHAPTER EXAMINES the Islamic Republic of Iran's conception of strategic stability in order to shed light on how the perspectives of regional actors are shaping post–Cold War understandings of this concept. The Middle East and the Persian Gulf subregion were, in some senses, far removed from the main nuclear theater of the Cold War. Therefore, it should not be surprising that the classical definition of strategic stability is not readily applicable to Iran, especially in the decades since the end of the Cold War. Nonetheless, there are elements of strategic stability that provide a useful analytical framework for understanding Iranian security strategies, which in turn provide insight into the evolution and relevance of this concept in the contemporary world.

Iran represents an interesting and challenging case study for examining a traditionally nuclear-based concept such as strategic stability. Since its rise to power in 1979, the Islamic Republic has had an ambivalent attitude toward nuclear weapons, and it has pursued a nuclear capability with varying levels of determination at different points in time. However, Iran has at no point possessed an operable nuclear weapons capability; nor has it really come close. Therefore, nuclear weapons have only a hypothetical role in Iran's security doctrine, whereas its actual security doctrine is based, quite naturally, on its actual capabilities, which do not include nuclear weapons. Further complicating the examination is the implementation of the Joint Comprehensive Plan of Action (JCPOA) regarding Iran's nuclear program, which was concluded by Iran and the P5+1 (the five permanent members of the UN Security Council plus Germany) in July 2015. Although supporters have said that the JCPOA will greatly reduce the chances of Iran acquiring nuclear weapons, detractors have argued that the agreement does not do enough to guarantee this outcome.

In an effort to take on this challenge, this chapter focuses first on the actual rather than the hypothetical, and examines those aspects of strategic stability that are most relevant for understanding Iran's security strategies. I argue that deterrence is the most relevant strategic stability concept for understanding Iran. For Iran, deterrence is understood in traditional terms, as measures that a state adopts in order to prevent or discourage another state (or states) from pursuing threatening and aggressive policies, war being foremost among them, and is based on conventional military capabilities. Additionally, Iran sees regional cooperation and promoting itself as a regional leader as related to deterrence, in that both goals will decrease the likelihood of war. Thus, in contrast to the nuclear-based deterrence that is central to strategic stability, deterrence for Iran is not about achieving parity or a stalemate with a nuclear adversary. This is not to say that deterrence and strategic stability should be seen as synonymous, either for Iran or more broadly, but rather that deterrence is a critical aspect of strategic stability for Iran, as it is generally.

Indeed, though "deterrence" (*bāzdārandigī*) is a term that Iranian leaders and analysts use with great frequency, "strategic stability" (*sabāt-i istrātazhīk*) is not a commonly cited term. The somewhat related concept that Iranian leaders do use is "regional stability," which is based, like deterrence, on regional cooperation as well as on the termination of outside interference in the Middle East. Examining Iran's understanding of regional stability also provides an opportunity to assess how Iran views its competitors, foremost among them the United States.

In addition to the core concepts of deterrence and regional stability, the chapter highlights a number of features of Iran's security doctrine that are useful for understanding its relationship with strategic stability. Most important, the chapter argues for the significance of the Iran-Iraq War (1980–88) in understanding the development of Iran's conception of deterrence and the importance the country attaches to it, particularly given Iran's determination to prevent a military attack of the kind it experienced in that war. It also examines the links between domestic and foreign policy, and the roles of asymmetric strategies, strategic culture, and a cross-domain perspective throughout the discussion.

The chapter's concluding section addresses Iranian perceptions of weapons of mass destruction (WMD), especially as they relate to deterrence and regional stability. Even though a nuclear capability could not be part of Iran's existing, operational security strategy, assessing Iran's view of WMD is important for understanding the country's nuclear program and the implications of the JCPOA.

THEORETICAL BACKGROUND

Much of the analysis of Iran in the English-language literatures on international relations and international security has focused on drawing inferences about Iran's behavior as a nuclear state and, in the context of deterrence, on how a nuclear-armed Iran might be deterred. However, nuclear weapons play no clear role in Iran's security strategy because it does not possess nuclear weapons at this time. Though much has been written about Iranian policy and security strategy, scholars have not considered these subjects in the framework of strategic stability. They also have tended to rely on English-language and secondary sources, though there are many sources written by Iranian officials and scholars in Persian that pertain to the relevant subjects.[1] Accordingly, the existing scholarship does not shed sufficient light on how Iran seeks to protect its national security and deter threats, which is what this chapter seeks to address.

The concept of national security is of great importance for Iran, in part because Iranian leaders and analysts view national security as the all-encompassing basis of national activity. According to a report from Iran's Majlis (Parliament) Research Center, "Security is the basis and foundation of every action of political, economic, and social development, and if there is not security, none of the elements of development can grow or flourish."[2] Threats to national security are similarly broadly defined as including military, political, economic, social, and environmental elements.[3] The importance of national security is also bolstered by Iran's tendency to conflate "external" and "internal" threats and by its fear that threats to the regime are foreign in origin. In contrast to states that enjoy a high degree of legitimacy and internal stability, and that are therefore primarily concerned with its external dimension, national security for states like Iran must serve the country and regime alike, and must therefore protect against threats stemming from crises of "legitimacy," "identity," and popular "participation."[4] As is discussed below, Iran's conceptions of deterrence and regional stability reflect this broad understanding of national security and are thus similarly comprehensive in their strategies and intended outcomes.

Iran's understanding of deterrence, particularly in theory, is very similar to the definition of deterrence widely accepted in the United States and in the English-language international relations literature. This common understanding is not surprising considering that American social scientists have contributed much to the literature on the concept and that Iranian analysts usually base their discussions of deterrence on this literature.[5] For example, a Majlis Research Center report on deterrence theory defines deterrence as "persuading an opponent that the costs or risks of a policy are likely greater than its benefits."[6] An article in the Iranian academic publication *Journal of Defense Policy* by an Iranian professor of political science provides a similar definition, adding that "the strategy of deterrence is not a strategy for war making, but a strategy for protecting an existing position."[7]

Like their counterparts elsewhere in the world and the contributors to the present volume, Iranian analysts have been considering the changing nature of deterrence in the post–Cold War world.[8] Though they do not employ the term, their discussion concerns deterrence in the context of strategic stability. The Majlis report referenced above, for example, argues that the theory of nuclear deterrence is closely connected to the Cold War and to the presence of two nuclear superpowers. Accordingly, it suggests that deterrence in its traditional conception will likely be less effective in a world characterized by nuclear multipolarity, and that deterrence strategy should be refined to reflect present conditions.[9]

An additional factor shaping Iran's understanding of strategic stability is its perception of its adversaries, foremost among them the United States and Israel. Though the provocative comments of some may seem to suggest otherwise, Iranian leaders and analysts have made concerted efforts to assess the perspectives and policies of other countries, and have often tried to do so rationally and dispassionately. In the case of the United States, Iranian sources reveal careful consideration of American politics and political institutions, how the political climate in the United States affects Washington's approach toward other countries, and how the disunity and divisiveness endemic to American politics often result in an inconsistent foreign policy. Furthermore, and in contrast to what analysts have often assumed, Iran does not have a hard-and-fast view of its allies and enemies, and it thus sees relations between countries as a function of variable conditions and policies.[10]

IRAN AND STRATEGIC STABILITY: DETERMINANTS AND CHANGES OVER TIME

Iran's view of strategic stability provides fertile ground for ongoing efforts to reconsider the definition of this concept and to revise the central role it allots to nuclear weapons. As noted above, "strategic stability" is not a term that Iranian officials employ—at least not publicly. However, an assessment of Iranian statements, sources, and policies reveals that two concepts related to strategic stability—deterrence and regional stability—play a central role in Iranian security discourse. The goal of both deterrence and regional stability is the prevention of an armed conflict in the Middle East, particularly a conflict that would directly threaten Iran's security and territory. Accordingly, applying the idea of strategic stability to Iran requires broadening the term and refocusing on the element of nonnuclear deterrence.

In this regard, Iran's understanding of and strategies for promoting strategic stability have remained fairly consistent, from the time of the Iranian monarchy under Mohammad Reza Shah Pahlavi to the present under the Islamic Republic.[11] For both regimes, strategic stability has centered on strong deterrence (itself broadly defined), on regional cooperation, and on promoting Iran's role as an effective regional leader. Though this overall conception of strategic stability has been characterized by long-term continuity, there have been a number of changes in emphasis and orientation. For example, both the monarchy and the Islamic Republic emphasized Iran's vital role in the region and the importance of establishing regional autonomy. However, whereas the shah asserted his leadership by playing the role of policeman of the Persian Gulf and often saw his interests as aligning with those of the United States and the West, the Islamic Republic has more emphatically resisted outside interference in the Middle East, seeing the United States as a major source of regional instability, and has sought to assert its leadership by expanding its cooperation with other countries in the region.[12] Further, though both regimes suffered from legitimacy deficits and domestic opposition, the Islamic Republic has more often fixated on the external sources thereof and has accordingly viewed security policy with an eye toward domestic ends.

The most important event that has shaped the Islamic Republic of Iran's security doctrine is the Iran-Iraq War, which was waged from 1980 to 1988. Though several factors contributed to the outbreak of hostilities, the results and reverberations of the Iranian Revolution formed the war's most significant catalysts. Iran's postrevolutionary government was based on the centrality of Islam in public life, and its leader, Ayatollah Ruhollah Khomeini, vowed to fight for the revival of Shi'ism and for the freedom of the oppressed throughout the world.[13] Saddam Hussein—then the president of Iraq, who presided over a Sunni-dominated, secular government ruling a Shi'i majority—saw the policies of the new Islamic Republic of Iran as a threat to his power.[14]

At the same time, Iran appeared to be in a vulnerable position, as violent conflicts over the nature of the Islamic Republic persisted into its second year. Hussein decided to take the opportunity to launch what he hoped would be a quick military operation to defeat the Revolution and safeguard his rule and, while he was at it, to seize the oil-rich territory in western Iran and assert his leadership of the Arab world.[15] With these considerations in mind, and after a year of steadily worsening relations, Iraqi forces invaded Iran and initiated an aerial assault on Iranian bases on September 22, 1980, marking the beginning of the Iran-Iraq War.

What Hussein intended to be a swift and easy strike to check the revolutionary state was quickly transformed into a brutal and drawn-out conflict that instead revitalized the flagging Revolution. After a string of victories allowed Iraqi forces to advance into Iran until the beginning of 1981, Iranian forces halted the march and retook most of their territory over the course of the next year. Iran then took the fight into Iraq in the summer of 1982 but was unable to gain much ground. As the war stalled, it also broadened, entangling the rest of the Middle East and both superpowers, and it spread from the land to a tanker war in the Persian Gulf and several series of aerial attacks on civilian areas. The war continued largely as a bloody stalemate until the summer of 1988. It ended on August 20, 1988, when the cease-fire terms of United Nations Security Council Resolution 598 came into force. The end of the war restored the status quo ante, with both regimes still in power and without territorial adjustments. Neither side emerged as the clear victor, but the war had a profound impact on both countries.

The significance of the war, both for Iran as a whole and for its conception of security in particular, is difficult to overstate. A 2001 publication on the Iran-Iraq War produced by Iran's Islamic Revolutionary Guards Corps asserts that the Iran-Iraq War, "because of its vast impact and outcomes, will affect every issue of internal and foreign policy of the Islamic Republic of Iran for at least the next several decades."[16] The vast amount of research on the war published by Iranian governmental and other institutions, the very high frequency with which Iranian leaders refer to the war and its ongoing significance, and the fact that strategic lessons derived from the war inform military and defensive planning in Iran all provide further evidence of the war's importance.[17] Finally, the epithets Iranians use to describe the war—the Sacred Defense (*Difā'-i Muqaddas*) and the Imposed War (*Jang-i Tahmīlī*)—further reveal how they understand the conflict and the nature of its significance.

Quite naturally, the area in which the Iran-Iraq War has had a particularly direct and substantial effect is Iran's security doctrine. The lessons that Iran has taken from its experience in the war and has subsequently adopted as national security strategies also provide insight into how it defines strategic stability. Two of the most important of these strategies are (1) an effort to prevent Iran's international isolation and (2) independent and aggressive deterrence.[18] The goals of both these strategies are the two strategic stability concepts applicable to Iran, deterrence and regional stability.

OUT OF ISOLATION

The outbreak of the Iran-Iraq War and the extensive support that states both within and outside the region provided to Iraq helped Iran understand that its 1979 Islamic Revolution and its policies in the immediate postrevolutionary period were received in the opposite way from what the new leaders had hoped. Instead of inspiring similar Islamic movements and convincing other countries to follow its lead, the Revolution turned Iran into the primary threat to regional stability in the eyes of many of its neighbors. The extent to which Iran was seen as the instigator of instability was made perfectly clear when Iraq invaded and carried on an eight-year-long war against Iran, and did so with substantial support and in the name of protecting the Middle East from the Iranian menace. As a result of this experience, Iran has worked to portray itself as a state committed to maintaining stability and as eager to work with other states in the region to achieve this goal.

According to Iranian sources, the Islamic Republic's isolation during the Iran-Iraq War was one of the conflict's defining features—one that had a significant impact on the war's course and outcome. In fact, in Iran the war is often defined not as a conflict only between Iran and Iraq but as one that Iran fought against a powerful multinational cohort.[19] A primary reason for Iran's solitude was the Islamic Revolution, which many countries feared would threaten their strategic, political, and economic interests.[20] This fear was in part the result of the declared positions of the new Iranian regime, which "clearly announced its opposition to the domination of the two great powers," and which inherently presented a challenge to the status quo.[21]

This experience of isolation in the war has guided the way Iranian leaders have sought to prevent the growth of hostility toward their country in the subsequent decades. In their view, Iraq effectively used widespread opposition to the Revolution to gain allies and material support for its aims, confident that its "vindictive opposition to Iran" bolstered its popularity.[22] Iraq's strategy in this regard resembles more recent efforts by countries such as Saudi Arabia and Israel to heighten enmity toward Iran in order to perpetuate Iran's status as an outcast and to prevent the nuclear deal from changing this status.[23]

Iran's isolation during the war made its ability to prosecute the conflict much more difficult.[24] In addition to Iran's general lack of allies and Iraq's plethora of them, what significantly hindered Iran's war-fighting capabilities was its inability to secure needed supplies of weapons and other matériel.[25] As is discussed in the next section, its lack of both allies and weapons has shaped Iran's postwar defensive doctrine of independent deterrence. Though the imbalance between the belligerents characterized the length of the war, it was particularly significant during the conflict's second half, when its seeming interminableness, combined with the perceived threat of Iran, prompted more active intervention to try to end it and preclude an Iranian victory.[26] Indeed, the heightened and direct involvement of third parties in the war in support of Iraq is one of the main reasons cited by Iranian sources as forcing the war's termination.[27]

The fact that Iran was the object of such widespread enmity throughout the war constituted an important lesson for its leaders, which they have subsequently adopted as a strategy for promoting national security. Though it does not often appear as such to outside observers, and though Iranian officials rarely discuss policies in these terms, in practice the strategy of preventing Iran's isolation has entailed a recognition that its own policies and rhetoric during the war contributed significantly to its beleaguerment.[28] The result of this recognition, which is an explicit part of Iranian policy, has been Iran's effort to portray itself as an important member of the region and the international community, one that can contribute to regional cooperation and stability.

This effort began before the war ended, in Iran's "diplomatic opening [*gushāyish-i dīplumāsī*]" during the spring and summer of 1985. Led by then–Majlis speaker Akbar Hashemi Rafsanjani, this opening was intended to improve Iran's relations with other countries through a softening of rhetoric and the active cultivation of ties with world leaders. According to an Iranian study of the initiative, it "was designed to overcome Iran's relative isolation and indicated a kind of reconciliation with international norms and responsibility in the global family" through "dialogue with the international community."[29]

Iran's promotion of its role in regional and global affairs is currently a central and explicit part of its security strategy. In more recent years, this can be seen in the policies of Iran's Fifth Development Plan, which was inaugurated in 2011. According to official documents outlining the plan, Iran's goals in the realm of political, defensive, and security affairs centered on "promoting the status, position, value, and role of the Islamic Republic of Iran in the region and international system in order to strengthen [its] national security and advance [its] national interests." The Iranian government put special emphasis on several goals: "strengthening constructive relations" and "bilateral, regional, and international cooperation," with a focus on "neighboring," "Muslim," and "nonhostile" countries; reforming international structures, especially the United Nations, and "organizing joint efforts to establish new economic, political, and cultural regional and world systems, with the goal of securing justice, peace, and security"; and "efforts to free the region from the military presence of foreigners."[30]

Previous statements of Iran's general policies and development plans have set out very similar goals of promoting the country's role in regional and international affairs and strengthening its constructive relations with other countries, with the ultimate aim of preserving peace and stability. As is suggested by some of these provisions, Iran's leaders maintain that the current structure of the international system enables a few major powers to control the entire world, to the disadvantage of smaller countries or those with visions of the international order that challenge the existing configuration. This, according to Iranian leaders, also forms an important source of strategic instability in the world generally, and especially in the Middle East. Accordingly, to promote regional stability, Iranian security policy seeks to confront and reform the problematic and inequitable structures of the international order and to replace them with institutions that will allow countries like Iran to have greater influence in the world system.[31]

In an article published by the prominent Center for Strategic Research, the Iranian scholar and former politician Mahmud Va'izi cites these issues when explaining why the Middle East has long been so insecure and unstable. "In the past half century," he writes, "numerous security arrangements have been established in the region, each of which failed because of the inattention to some of the important constituents of the Middle East." For security and stability to have a fighting chance, he claims, "the planning and implementation of a security pattern for the Middle East must take into consideration the native structure of the region, including multilateral and regional cooperation among the countries of the Middle East, and [must] especially emphasize the effective role of the regional powers and their interaction with one another in providing security." Though Iran has long opposed the presence of foreign military forces in the region as contrary to its interests and as a source of instability, Va'izi acknowledges that "the success of any plan for securing the Middle East depends greatly on coordination and greater interaction among the regional and extraregional powers." Finally, the article argues that "as a regional power, the Islamic Republic of Iran has an important position in establishing security in the Middle East and can play a critical role in constructive interaction with other countries of the region in establishing stability and solving long-term crises."[32]

This concept of "constructive interaction [*ta'āmul-i sāzandih*]" further reveals the ways Iran seeks to promote strategic stability and its own security. According to Iranian sources, constructive interaction is part of Iran's grand strategy, and it consists of expanding effective and meaningful cooperation with other countries. Particular areas of focus include the establishment and strengthening of economic partnerships, of healthy diplomatic relationships, and of regional initiatives to deal with crises.[33]

The particular formulation of the concept of constructive interaction also likely reflects the way Iran is trying to market its policies to both foreign and domestic audiences. For other countries, this phraseology serves to affirm Iran's congenial intentions and to emphasize the mutually beneficial nature of its proposed interactions. This message is being directed especially toward countries that have viewed Iran as hostile and have thus seen interaction with it as deleterious rather than constructive. To Iranian domestic audiences, a policy of constructive interaction signals that, in cooperating with other countries, Iran will not compromise its rights or principles. In April 2015, for example, President Hassan Rouhani defended his policy of engaging in negotiations over Iran's nuclear program by arguing that "the nuclear negotiations are the first step in establishing constructive interaction with the world, because, in today's world, progress, development, stability, and security in the region and world are not possible without cooperation and coordination."[34]

An examination of Iranian foreign policy documents reveals a notable divergence between the stated goals of this policy and how Iran's relations with other countries have developed in practice. The picture of Iran that emerges from the documents alone is of a country earnestly pursuing cooperation, seeking to "avoid tension," and working particularly to improve relations with its Arab and Muslim neighbors.[35] There is also a recognition, noted above, that the Islamic Republic of Iran initially contributed to tensions and its own isolation—one document lists as a goal "presenting a clear picture of the Islamic Revolution and explaining the political, cultural, and economic achievements and experiences of the Islamic Republic."[36] In practice, however, Iran has continued to have a very difficult time convincing other countries of its benevolent intentions, and it has not refrained from the sort of rhetoric and action that tend to provoke animosity.[37] Fear of Iranian influence in the region has continued to rise, especially since the conclusion of the JCPOA, while the widespread instability in the wake of the Arab Spring has given states like Iran and Saudi Arabia the chance to wage a hot war for regional supremacy.

Clearly cognizant of these challenges, Iranian leaders have continued to highlight the importance of regional cooperation and Iranian leadership as the JCPOA's implementation has progressed. In June 2015, Iranian foreign minister Mohammad Javad Zarif asserted that "the issues and conflicts of the Middle East must be resolved without outside interference and by the states and peoples of these countries."[38] Zarif subsequently wrote an article that appeared in several Arab publications, in which he "requested détente between Iran and the Arab countries of the Persian Gulf" and proposed the "establishment of a regional dialogue forum in the Middle East."[39] One of the areas in which Iran has fought to take part is the campaign against Sunni-inspired terrorism. During a ceremony marking the beginning of Sacred Defense Week (the annual commemoration marking the beginning of the Iran-Iraq War) at the end of September 2015, President Rouhani stated that Iran was "the best defense against terror in the Middle East," pointing to "Iran's role in fighting Da'esh [Islamic State of Iraq and Syria] in Syria and Iraq."[40]

In some cases, this self-promotion is accompanied by attempts to portray other countries or groups as the main threats to regional stability. Though this strategy does not rest on an innate enmity toward other countries, and thus does not in theory contradict Iran's declared policy of constructive interaction, in practice denouncing the actions of other countries impedes cooperation and vitiates Iran's perceived commitment thereto. At the same time, shifting the focus away from Iran is particularly important because of Iran's inherent discreteness as the Shi'i and Persian state in the majority Sunni and Arab Middle East. Iran's minority status has consistently made it hard for it to gain both allies and a sustainable plan for integrating itself into the wider Middle East. Within the region, Israel and Saudi Arabia have most often been the targets of this strategy. In October 2015, Foreign Minister Zarif castigated Saudi Arabia for attempting to "eliminate Iran from the region." He claimed that the Saudi efforts had "caused bloodshed and fomented conflict," and that they therefore "must be stopped."[41] Iranian analysts have also blamed those two countries, working in cooperation with US weapons manufacturers, for fueling an arms race in the region.[42]

The United States has frequently been portrayed as the primary threat to regional stability. In the view of Iranian leaders, US interference in the Middle East has had significant negative effects: It has exacerbated rivalries among the countries of the region and created or deepened divisions between them; increased the prevalence of armed conflict and radical extremism (especially of the Sunni variety, which is extremely threatening to Shi'i Iran); enabled Israel to act with impunity; and promoted the view of Iran as a menace to peace while seeking to exclude it from playing a role in regional and international affairs.[43] In recent decades the United States has worked very effectively to isolate Iran and to portray it as a major threat to stability in the Middle East, specifically because of the fears surrounding its nuclear program.[44] The expectation that the implementation of the JCPOA will result in at least some rolling back of those efforts and will make it easier for Iran to play a role in regional affairs therefore provides Iranian leaders with a compelling reason to uphold the deal's terms.

INDEPENDENT AND AGGRESSIVE DETERRENCE

The second, and equally important, lesson that Iranian leaders took from the Iran-Iraq War was that they must ensure that such a conflict does not occur again. A publication produced by the Islamic Revolutionary Guards Corps (IRGC) and overseen by the IRGC's wartime commander, Mohsen Rezaee, emphasized this point:

> Considering the substantial impact that Iraq's war against Iran had on the country, it is necessary to address this war from various dimensions, especially to acquire experience in order to adopt appropriate measures in critical situations to prevent or lessen the damages that competitors of the Islamic Republic of Iran might impose on the country. Among these experiences, the outcomes were that in this period national security and the preservation of territorial integrity were in such a difficult position that the regime's decision makers and the people have likewise become determined to deter neighbors and great powers from invading Iran's territory.[45]

Indeed, the defining features of this war (at least from Iran's perspective)—an all-out attack on its territory, its almost complete lack of allies, its inability to fulfill its weapons and other matériel needs, its experience as the victim of chemical weapons attacks, and its ability to mobilize its population to prosecute the war—have since become the defining considerations shaping Iran's security policy. In terms of this policy, these features have been manifested as the determination to prevent such an attack from happening again, particularly through robust conventional deterrence; the concerted effort to form regional alliances and to minimize enmity against Iran; the development of indigenous defense industries and capabilities, enabling Iran to be as self-reliant as possible; the denunciation of WMD and the support for a WMD-free zone in the Middle East; and strategies for maintaining popular support for the regime, at least to the extent that such support will prove sufficient to mobilize people to fight in Iran's defense. In this sense, the focus on deterrence operates alongside the quest to prevent Iran's isolation, and with the understanding that allies may be persistently hard to come by, despite its efforts.

Iranian leaders see the country's nearly complete lack of deterrent power as one of the most important factors enabling the outbreak of the Iran-Iraq War.[46] The Islamic Republic was completely unable to deter the Iraqi invasion, as evidenced by its occurrence, and was largely unable to defend itself from that attack, as evidenced by Iraq's initial successes. Simply put, Iran was wholly unprepared to confront Iraq's "full-scale" and "widespread" invasion,[47] and

Iran's "military forces did not have the necessary readiness to answer Iraq's military aggression."[48] As a result, in certain areas the Iraqi army was able to occupy large pieces of territory with relative ease.[49]

One of the most important sources of Iran's deterrence and defensive failures was the ongoing revolutionary transition and the incomplete establishment of a postrevolutionary order.[50] As part of these processes, Iran had taken aim at many of the defining structures of the monarchical regime, including its armed forces, which at the time of the Iraqi invasion remained in a dilapidated state. Further, neither those regular armed forces nor the newly established IRGC had experience fighting a conventional war, and were accordingly not very skilled at doing so.[51] Though Iran had acquired an impressive arsenal of American-made weapons before the Revolution, its armed forces lacked the training to utilize them efficiently.[52] Further adding to the country's vulnerability were the other ongoing weaknesses associated with the Revolution, including the inchoate and divided government, the state's inability to control all parts of the country, and the opposition movements that were fighting political and military battles against the new regime.[53] Iranian sources cite the blatant nature of these susceptibilities as providing Iraq with a powerful impetus to undertake the invasion.[54]

Over the course of the war's eight years, most of these weaknesses were ameliorated. The depletion of Iran's arsenal and the inability to replenish it, however, continued.[55] Iran struggled to procure weapons and matériel, in part as a result of widespread global and regional antipathy toward it. The perpetuation of the war, and specifically Iran's refusal to accept a cease-fire, led to more active efforts to deny Iran weapons.[56] These efforts included Operation Staunch, the Reagan administration's program to prevent Iran from accessing military matériel, which caused severe problems for Iran on the battlefield.[57] In contrast to Iran, Iraq had an abundant supply network. As Iranian sources often say, this allowed Hussein to be "armed to the teeth [*tā dandān musallah*],"[58] which gave rise to an "egregious discrepancy" between the combatants.[59]

In contrast to much of the existing literature on Iran's prosecution of the Iran-Iraq War, which asserts that the Islamic Republic devalued firepower and chose instead to rely on the faith and commitment of its forces, Iranian sources explicitly and repeatedly affirm the tremendous importance of firepower in this war specifically, and in national security generally.[60] One Iranian study of the war states that "one of the main factors determining the fate of wars is the amount and kind of arms in the possession of the two parties in the war," one that is not diminished by also relying on other factors like morale.[61] A clear indication of the importance that Iran attached to firepower can be found in the lengths to which the country was willing to go to get it, which even included working with the Revolution's traditional enemy, the United States, as part of the infamous Iran-Contra Affair.[62]

In the years since the war, Iranian leaders have developed a strategy of deterrence that very much reflects the weaknesses they experienced during the conflict. Accordingly, Iran views effective deterrence in very broad terms, as involving efforts to create not only a strong military and arsenal but also a strong and unified society that will be ready and willing to come to the nation's defense. In other words, Iran's approach to deterrence is based both on a cross-domain perspective (broadly defined) and on fostering a particular strategic culture.

Of top priority since the war has been ensuring that Iran possesses a quantity and quality of armaments more equal to those of its enemies. Maintaining such destructive power would prevent most enemies from attacking in the first place and would make an attack costly for any state that chose to initiate one. Iranian military leaders often emphasize that their defensive capabilities have increased "drastically" since the war in order to warn potential adversaries that they will not be able to invade Iran as easily as Iraq did in 1980.[63] On Iran's Fars News, almost every English-language article about the country's defensive capabilities notes that Iran launched an indigenous and independent arms development program during the "Iraqi imposed war on Iran to compensate for a US weapons embargo."[64] The announcement and unveiling of new domestically developed missiles and the staging of military exercises often coincide with anniversaries of important battles of the war, further indicating the close connections between the war and Iran's current security strategies.[65]

The linkage between strong deterrence and a full and advanced conventional arsenal is one that Iranian leaders, analysts, and media make explicitly and often. An article published on the website of the Majlis News Agency in 2013, for example, claimed in its headline that "New Defensive Achievements Indicate Iran's Rapid Progress in the Field of Deterrence." The achievements were particularly important because of the attempts by the United States and other countries to prevent Iran's defensive development through sanctions, which again signals the importance of independence in Iran's deterrence strategy.[66] Similarly, a June 2015 news article characterized Iran's development of longer-range ballistic missiles as a step toward "establishing deterrence for the country."[67]

One of the most consistent features of Iran's statements regarding arms-based deterrence is the insistence that the country's military advancements are intended only for defensive, not aggressive, purposes. In the 2013 article mentioned above, a member of the Majlis is quoted as emphasizing that "the increase in Iran's defensive capability is only to defend the interests of the regime and the country, and creates no danger for [other] countries," which is a position that Iranian "officials have repeatedly announced." He also stated that Iran would work with other states to ensure the security of the region, which demonstrates the critical connection between deterrence and regional stability and cooperation.[68]

Iranian security analysts have put forward similar positions. In a 2010 article published in the journal *Islamic Republic of Iran Diplomacy*, Rahman Qahremanpour, a disarmament researcher at Iran's Center for Strategic Research, wrote that "Iran's strategy is defensive. . . . The Islamic Republic will not have any plans to attack another country. The recent weapons manufactured by Iran's defense industries are clear proof of that strategy. Politically, unveiling new weapons systems and launching military maneuvers are deterrents by their nature. They are in fact intended to send a message to opponents—that in terms of military power, Iran is prepared to make any country regret adventurism toward it."[69] Qahremanpour also connected deterrence to regional stability, saying that "the Islamic Republic has proven that its preferred regional strategy is détente and building trust. Iran's target is not the regional states, and no neighboring countries are regarded as threats in Iran's military doctrine."[70]

Conventional weapons capabilities are one part of Iran's comprehensive strategy of deterrence.[71] Iranian leaders and analysts most often define this strategy in a particular manner, one that reflects both its breadth and the nature of the threats Iran faces. Iran's military strategy is based on "multilateral defensive deterrence [*bāzdārandigī-i difā'-i hamah jānbih*]," which combines "symmetric and asymmetric deterrence [*bāzdārandigī-i mutaqārin va ghayr mutaqārin*]."[72] The strategy aims to defend Iran against a range of military threats, including traditional symmetric threats from Israel and the United States and asymmetric threats from terrorist groups operating along Iran's borders.[73] Though, in certain analyses, the military threats from Israel and the United States are described as symmetric, other sources point to the importance of using asymmetric strategies in deterring or combating an Israeli or US military attack. Indeed, the key features of asymmetric warfare—combat between parties with substantially differing power and resources, and the weaker party's search for tactics to make up for that discrepancy—are central parts of the military power dynamic between Iran and either Israel or the United States. While attempting to reduce the asymmetry between itself and its adversaries, Iranian leaders have also recognized the military superiority of Israel and the United States, and they have accordingly focused on building asymmetric deterrence and capabilities.[74]

An important aspect of Iran's asymmetric deterrence doctrine is "indirect regional deterrence [*bāzdārandigī-i ghayr mustaqīm-i mintaqah'āy*]," which refers to Iran's support for, and alliances with, various armed groups in the region—foremost among them Hezbollah.[75] Such groups play an important role in Iran's deterrence strategy by serving as a military extension of Iranian power, one that is strategically positioned along the borders of what Iran views as an opponent and military threat. In addition to making Israel more insecure and reducing its ability to open a direct front with Iran, Hezbollah gives Iran greater "strategic depth" and increases its deterrence power by standing ready to retaliate for an attack on Iran.[76] The support that the IRGC's Quds Force gives to armed groups in Iraq, Lebanon, Syria, and elsewhere can be understood as part of this effort. Iran's reliance on such "networked defensive and indirect regional deterrence systems," according to Iranian analysts, is the result of "the lack of strategic symmetry between the opposing interventionist powers and Iran," which means that reliance on "a system of direct and mutual deterrence could be risky."[77] Iran's support for armed groups outside Iran, including some that are engaged in insurgent uprisings and terrorism, represents a kind of asymmetric security dilemma. These measures that Iran views as critical to enhancing its deterrent capabilities are regarded by other states as aggressive and as broadly increasing instability and insecurity.

In addition to the "active [*'āmil*]" deterrence described above, Iran also makes use of "passive [*ghayr 'āmil*]" deterrence or defense in combating threats. Passive defense, according to a Majlis Research Center report, includes "any unarmed preventative measures that cause a reduction in the vulnerability" of Iran's people, resources, information, strategic facilities, or infrastructure.[78] One group of measures for promoting passive defense relates to material and technological preparedness to confront an enemy attack—"increasing the armed forces' retaliatory power and [ability to] respond in kind";[79] ensuring "suitable concealment" of defense systems and armaments;[80] strengthening the security of communications and infrastructure;[81] and continual pursuit of technological advancement in all areas.[82] Another group of passive defense measures concerns maintaining unity and coordination among various levels and institutions of government, especially in the case of a crisis or war.[83] To do so, Iranian policy documents have called for establishing a "comprehensive system of defensive crisis management";[84] for strengthening "ideological-psychological solidarity" among government officials;[85] for consolidating the country's air defense systems;[86] and for enlisting the full range of the country's forces and resources in combating threats.[87]

A final element of passive deterrence concerns the role of the Iranian people in defending the country. This is particularly important because of a threat that has increasingly concerned Iranian leaders and that they have worked to deter—a threat they term "soft war" (*jang-i narm*), which can be understood as the use of soft power against another state in an aggressive manner. For Iran, soft power is conceived primarily as the promotion of certain cultural and political values to achieve particular ends, and Iranian leaders view its aggressive use as a serious threat.[88] Instead of a direct military attack on Iran, which would entail greater costs, Iran's leaders assert that its enemies have adopted a strategy of waging a soft war against the regime in order to erode its bases of support, undermine its legitimacy, and bring it down from within.[89] To combat both soft and hard threats, they stress that the widest possible extent of popular participation in national defense is necessary. Popular participation in this sense is both general and specific: It refers both to connecting as many people as possible to the regime by trying to align their views with those of the regime in a way that will make it more likely for them to play an active role in the nation's defense; and to the paramilitary Basij forces, which function as an organized base of support for the regime.[90]

As the foregoing discussion indicates, Iran's current conceptions of deterrence and strategic stability are based profoundly on a cross-domain perspective, and reflect particularly Iran's experience in the Iran-Iraq War. Indeed, this war is currently the most important experience influencing Iran's strategic culture, especially because the generation that fought in the war is now at the helm of Iran's security and political establishments. In addition to the military aspects of effective defense and deterrence, Iranian leaders place a high value on nonmilitary factors in promoting the same. This, too, is something they came to appreciate firsthand during the Iran-Iraq War, when they actively sought to mobilize a wide variety of military, political, social, and economic war-fighting tools.[91]

One of the most important aspects of this broader deterrence strategy is cultivating unity among the Iranian population, which Iranian leaders view as essential to effective defense. As discussed above, the disunity in Iran following the overthrow of the monarchy undermined the Islamic Republic's ability to deter and defend itself from the Iraqi invasion.[92] "From Iraq's perspective," asserts one Iranian source on the war, "the internal conditions in Iran were stricken by dissolution and disintegration," which in turn created "an obstacle to united [and] popular" resistance to the invasion.[93] The lesson Iranian leaders have drawn from this experience is that a unified population, political stability, and popular support for the Islamic Republic are essential to deterrence and defense. A country that is at war with itself both politically and militarily, that is intensely and deeply divided, will naturally be too occupied with the battles within to prepare effectively to confront external aggression.[94] Yet such aggression, once it comes, can often provide embattled leaders with precisely the antidote they need to assuage those internal lacerations, because few things can bring people together like a common foreign enemy.

Indeed, since its establishment, the Islamic Republic has ruled over a society that is deeply fractured along numerous political and social lines, and is composed of many conflicting opinions of the regime and the Revolution that brought it to power, which have persistently threatened to crack wide open and devour the system. The emergence of a threat from a foreign power like Iraq or the United States, however, has had the effect of palliating those divisions, as Iranian sources document.[95] Accordingly, it is important to appreciate the close and complex connection between regime and national security for the Islamic Republic of Iran, especially when it comes to the importance of internal unity and the role of outside enmity. On one hand, Iranian leaders see unified popular support as essential both to the regime's stability and legitimacy and to the security of the Iranian nation; yet, on the other hand, the presence of outside enmity is often what generates such unified popular support.

An additional aspect of maintaining the commitment and unity of the Iranian population, and one that can work either in conjunction with or independent of external enmity, is what can be broadly termed the ideology based on the Islamic Republic's founding principles. Those principles include independence, revolution, Islam, action, and opposition to "oppressive" forces. Over the course of the past decades, Iranian leaders have found this ideology to be a powerful tool, both in framing the country's positions and in mobilizing its people to defend the regime, which is one reason why they so often invoke its main principles. Furthermore, and as discussed above, Iran's leaders view public support as essential to the country's security because of its role in buttressing Iran's ability to defend itself, in part as a tool in asymmetric combat.[96] As the 2003 US invasion of Iraq and the 1980 Iraqi invasion of Iran demonstrated, believing that a regime lacks popular support can easily bolster a decision to wage war, which is one reason why Iran has concluded that popular support is critical to deterrence as well as to defense.[97]

CONCLUSION: VIEWS OF A NUCLEAR CAPABILITY AND IMPLICATIONS FOR THE JCPOA

Because Iran has at no time possessed an operational nuclear capability, nuclear weapons have not formed part of its conception of deterrence. However, an examination of certain aspects of Iran's views of nuclear and other WMD is informative for understanding its views of strategic stability and of the JCPOA. Here again, the Iran-Iraq War is essential.[98] During that conflict, Iraq deployed chemical weapons against Iranian forces with devastating effect, leaving Iran with distinct and contradictory conclusions about their utility. On one hand, Iranians intimately understand the heinousness of WMD and thus maintain a lasting revulsion and rejection of their use. On the other hand, Iranian officials regard Iraq's deployment of chemical weapons as having been very effective, in that it gave Iraq an important advantage on the battlefield, deterred Iran from launching attacks, and ultimately helped convince Tehran to end the war.

Iran's experience with WMD and the contradictory conclusions drawn from it help explain the country's vacillation regarding the possession of both chemical and nuclear weapons. Although Iran's understanding of the deterrent and practical utility of these weapons has led it to pursue their possession, its repugnance toward them has helped to undermine these efforts.[99] Though it is not possible to determine the extent to which the latter has deterred Iran from proliferating, Iranian leaders have asserted that the country's exposure to chemical weapons during the Iran-Iraq War has contributed to its reluctance to develop an unconventional arsenal. Furthermore, according to Iranian leaders, the negotiation of the JCPOA indicates that the latter conviction has won out.[100]

An additional factor that has pushed Iran away from proliferating is the stated consensus among Iranian leaders and analysts that weaponization would decrease rather than increase security and stability. The way that contention is framed points again to the importance of regional stability and the extent to which Iran sees its own security as being dependent on the regional environment. Indeed, Iranian analysts employ the same reasoning against weaponization as those who are most fearful of this outcome, which is that it would set off a nuclear arms race in the Persian Gulf and perhaps the wider Middle East.[101] Furthermore, the mere possession of a small nuclear arsenal may have negligible benefits, making weaponization a bad trade-off for Iran in terms of security.[102] Iran's policy of promoting a nuclear-free weapons zone in the Middle East reflects this reasoning.[103]

Another important lesson regarding WMD that was reinforced during the Iran-Iraq War was that international institutions and the nonproliferation regime are instruments of the great powers, and are therefore inherently inequitable. Despite Iranian efforts, the international community largely failed to condemn Iraq's use of chemical weapons and other indiscriminate means and methods of warfare, which, Iran claims, greatly facilitated their continued use.[104] Israel's closeted nuclear capability has similarly skirted active condemnation, while Iran's nuclear activities have provoked the opposite, leading to military threats, sanctions, and isolation. For Iranian leaders, such inconsistency corrupts the nonproliferation regime as a whole, as does its domination by the world's major nuclear powers.[105]

Iran's long-held stance of refusing to acquiesce to demands for it to halt its nuclear program reflects the conviction that doing so would place Iran at the mercy of an inequitable international order, and would entail giving up not just a nuclear program but also its security and ideological foundations. Thus, Iran's ability to independently advance its nuclear technology places its leaders in a position of relative power, and reinforces the principles of self-reliance and self-sufficiency that form the core of the country's military and defensive posture. Although independent advancement in any field is something Iranian leaders pursue and prize, their accomplishments in nuclear technology are particularly significant because they represent Iran's success in breaking what they see as the unjust, fiercely held monopoly of the world's major powers and their allies on nuclear technology, from which Iran has been excluded.[106] Iran's focus on self-reliance, however, does not mean that it is opposed to assistance in maintaining and growing a civilian nuclear program, or that cooperation with other countries is intrinsically a bad thing. As the implementation of the JCPOA has demonstrated and Iranian leaders have reiterated, successful and cooperative nonproliferation measures must not disregard Iran's narrative of self-reliance and must not be seen as being "imposed" on Iran in the same manner as were sanctions and the Iran-Iraq War. When handled in the right way, such measures ultimately weaken the rationale and distrust that have heretofore informed that stance. This dynamic was summed up well by the renowned Iranian writer and intellectual Akbar Ganji, who wrote, "[Supreme Leader Ayatollah Ali] Khamenei does not want Iran to be at open conflict with the West, nor does he want it to be a supplicant to the United States. He is signaling that rapprochement is possible, but not at the price of abandoning Iran's resistance to Western hegemony."[107]

The way Iranian leaders have framed the JCPOA reflects this amalgamated position—combining independence, noncapitulation, and cooperation—and the agreement's success in furthering deterrence and inclusive regional stability. In remarks made during Iran's Defensive Industry Day in June 2015, President Rouhani emphasized the mutual interdependence of these elements. A country must have "'power, independence, and stability'" in order to "'pursue real peace,'" Rouhani said, adding that these criteria of national strength can be maintained even when negotiating with opposing parties. He also defined deterrence as something that "cannot be obtained with . . . military power alone," but as something that also requires "cultural, political, defensive, and economic power."[108]

In addition to aligning with Iran's strategy of deterrence, Iranian leaders and analysts have also framed the JCPOA as promoting regional stability and greater cooperation between Iran and the other countries of the Middle East. Though that has not been the case thus far, and though tensions between Iran and a number of its Sunni Arab neighbors have not decreased, Iran has continued to make the case that the JCPOA is good for the region.[109] According to Foreign Minister Zarif, "'the Vienna agreement is a necessary beginning for the region, and is not only not a detriment to any of our neighbors, but is an achievement for the whole region, because an unnecessary and twenty-year-old strain that threatened our region has ended.'"[110] In this regard, it is important to note that since the mid-1980s, Iran's paramount national security goals have been to protect itself from and prevent armed conflict in the Middle East, and to break out of its isolation by reintegrating itself into the regional and international communities, especially after understanding that the source of this isolation was the view of Iran as the major threat to regional stability. Accordingly, if the JCPOA can help achieve these goals, then Iran has a compelling reason to comply with its terms and to ensure its success.[111]

NOTES

1. Vipin Narang, "Nuclear Strategies of Emerging Nuclear Powers: North Korea and Iran," *Washington Quarterly* 38, no. 1 (2015); Austin Long, "Proliferation and Strategic Stability in the Middle East," in *Strategic Stability: Contending Interpretations*, ed. Elbridge A. Colby and Michael S. Gerson (Carlisle, PA: Strategic Studies Institute of US Army War College, 2013); Shahram Chubin, "Extended Deterrence and Iran," *Strategic Insights*, 2009; and Andrew Parasiliti, "Iran: Diplomacy and Deterrence," *Survival* 51, no. 5 (2009).

2. "Iran's National Security in Theory and Practice" (in Persian), Majlis Research Center, Tehran, 1999, 1.

3. Ibid., 2–3, 8.

4. Ibid.

5. Works cited in Iranian articles include those by James Dougherty, Robert Pfaltzgraff, John Baylis, Ken Booth, John Garnett, Phil Williams, and John M. Collins. "Nuclear Deterrence and Security Concerns of Iran" (in Persian), Aftab News (Tehran), May 8, 2006; "Deterrence Theory (Macro Theories of Conflict)" (in Persian), Majlis Research Center, Tehran, 1997.

6. "Deterrence Theory (Macro Theories of Conflict)," 2.

7. Ali Baqari Daulat Abadi, "The Role of Deterrence in the Military Strategy of Iran" (in Persian), *Journal of Defense Policy* 22, no. 85 (2013): 38.

8. Narang, "Nuclear Strategies," 1.

9. "Deterrence Theory (Macro Theories of Conflict)," 2, 15.

10. These points can be seen in Iranian assessments of the Iran-Iraq War, especially in those published by the IRGC's Center for War Studies and Research (all in Persian and published in Tehran): *Chronology of the Iran-Iraq War 1* (1997), 16, 183–84, 190, 619; *Chronology of the Iran-Iraq War 2* (1999), 29–31; *Chronology of the Iran-Iraq War 4* (1993), 20; *Chronology of the Iran-Iraq War 5* (1994), 19; *Chronology of the Iran-Iraq War 7* (2006), 20–26, 117–18, 207–8, 237–39, 255, 299–304, 341–42; *Chronology of the Iran-Iraq War 33* (2000), 22–23; *Chronology of the Iran-Iraq War 37* (2004), 69, 77–82, 86, 337–38; and *Survey of the Iran-Iraq War 1* (1998), 20.

11. For more on the Iranian Revolution, see David Menashri, *Iran: A Decade of War and Revolution* (New York: Holmes & Meier, 1990); Ervand Abrahamian, *Khomeinism* (Berkeley: University of California Press, 1993); and Mohsen Milani, *The Making of Iran's Islamic Revolution*, 2nd ed. (Boulder, CO: Westview Press, 1988, 1994).

12. For more on Iranian foreign policy over time, see R. K. Ramazani, *The Foreign Policy of Iran* (Charlottesville: University of Virginia Press, 1966); Shireen T. Hunter, *Iran and the World: Continuity in a Revolutionary Decade* (Bloomington: Indiana University Press, 1990); K. L. Afrasiabi, *After Khomeini: New Directions in Iran's Foreign Policy* (Boulder, CO: Westview Press, 1994); and Christin Marschall, *Iran's Persian Gulf Policy: From Khomeini to Khatami* (London: RoutledgeCurzon, 2003).

13. Richard N. Schofield, *Evolution of the Shatt al-'Arab Boundary Dispute*, Menas Studies in Continuity and Change in the Middle East and North Africa (Cambridge: Middle East and North African Studies Press, 1986); Efraim Karsh, "Military Power and Foreign Policy Goals: The Iran-Iraq War Revisited," *International Affairs* 64, no. 1 (1987–88); and Efraim Karsh, "Geopolitical Determinism: The Origins of the Iran-Iraq War," *Middle East Journal* 44, no. 2 (1980).

14. In 1980 Shi'is made up about 60 percent of the Iraqi population, though this number could be anywhere between 55 to 65 percent. Helen Chapin Metz, ed., *Iraq: A Country Study* (Washington, DC: US Government Printing Office for Library of Congress, 1988), 87–93; Hanna Batatu, *The Old Social Classes and the Revolutionary Movements of Iraq* (Princeton, NJ: Princeton University Press, 1978), 13–50; and Yitzhak Nakash, *The Shi'is of Iraq* (Princeton, NJ: Princeton University Press, 1994), 13–47.

15. For more on Iraq's decision to go to war, see F. Gregory Gause III, "Iraq's Decisions to Go to War, 1980 and 1990," *Middle East Journal* 56, no. 1 (2002); and Kevin M. Woods, David D. Palkki, and Mark E. Stout, *The Saddam Tapes* (Cambridge: Cambridge University Press, 2011).

16. *Analysis of the Iran-Iraq War 1* (in Persian) (Tehran: Center for War Studies and Research, 2001), 15.

17. Ibid., 14–17; *The Sepah Pasdaran's First Naval Operations in the Persian Gulf* (in Persian) (Tehran: Center for War Studies and Research, 1996), 17–18; *Chronology of the Iran-Iraq War 1*, 15; *Chronology of the Iran-Iraq War 4*, 590; *Battles East of the Karun according to Commanders' Narrative* (in Persian) (Tehran: Center for War Studies and Research, 2000), 13.

18. For more on how Iran's experiences in the war have shaped its nuclear policies and have affected the JCPOA process, see Ariane Tabatabai and Annie Tracy Samuel, "What the Iran-Iraq War Tells Us about the Future of the Iran Nuclear Deal," *International Security* 42, no. 1 (2017).

19. *Chronology of the Iran-Iraq War 1*, 14; *Chronology of the Iran-Iraq War 4*, 608; *Chronology of the Iran-Iraq War 51* (in Persian) (Tehran: Center for War Studies and Research, 2008), 36; "Iran Has Become an Extra-Regional Power," Mehr News via Payvand, September 24, 2007; "War against Iran Saddam's Greatest Crime," Mehr News, July 4, 2004; "Liberation of Khorramshahr Marked Iran's Military Superiority in Region," Mehr News, May 22, 2007; "Commander Reports 40 Armed Confrontations between Iran, US in Persian Gulf," Fars News, October 7, 2011; "Untolds of the Karbala 5 Operation" (in Persian), Islamic Republic News Agency, January 13, 2011.

20. *Chronology of the Iran-Iraq War 1*, 17, 595; and *Analysis of the Iran-Iraq War 1*, 31.

21. *Analysis of the Iran-Iraq War 1*, 25; and *Survey of the Iran-Iraq War 1*, 20.

22. *Chronology of the Iran-Iraq War 4*, 17, 20–22, 28; *Chronology of the Iran-Iraq War 2*, 31–32; *Chronology of the Iran-Iraq War 1*, 15, 638; *Chronology of the Iran-Iraq War 7*, 1010–11; *Analysis of the Iran-Iraq War 1*, 31; and *Chronology of the Iran-Iraq War 33*, 23.

23. "The Complete Transcript of Netanyahu's Address to Congress," *Washington Post*, March 3, 2015; Carol E. Lee, Jay Solomon, and Joe Lauria, "Netanyahu Rebukes UN over Iran Accord," *Wall Street Journal*, October 1, 2015; "Why Saudi Arabia and Israel Oppose Iran Nuclear Deal," Al Jazeera, April 14, 2015; and Frederic Wehrey, Theodore W. Karasik, Alireza Nader, Jeremy Ghez, Lydia Hansell, and Robert A. Guffey, *Saudi-Iranian Relations since the Fall of Saddam* (Santa Monica, CA: RAND Corporation, 2009).

24. *Chronology of the Iran-Iraq War 51*, 36.

25. *Chronology of the Iran-Iraq War 37*, 19, 68, 263, 284; *Chronology of the Iran-Iraq War 47* (in Persian) (Tehran: Center for War Studies and Research, 2002), 30–31, 499–501; *Chronology of the Iran-Iraq War 51*, 36; and *Survey of the Iran-Iraq War 1*, 149–50.

26. *Chronology of the Iran-Iraq War 50* (in Persian) (Tehran: Center for War Studies and Research, 1999), 3–4, 9–10; *Chronology of the Iran-Iraq War 51*, 35–36. Also see *Chronology of the Iran-Iraq War 47*, 28, 36–37; *Chronology of the Iran-Iraq War 52* (in Persian) (Tehran: Center for War Studies and Research, 2003), 28; and *Passage of Two Years of War* (in Persian) (Tehran: IRGC Political Department, 1982), 38–39.

27. *Chronology of the Iran-Iraq War 50*, 3.

28. *Chronology of the Iran-Iraq War 37*, 18–19, 43–45, 52–56.

29. Ibid.

30. "Law 11551: General Policies of the Fifth Economic, Social, and Cultural Development Plan of the Islamic Republic of Iran" (in Persian), Approved January 10, 2009, Laws and Regulations Portal of the Islamic Republic of Iran.

31. "General Policies of the System in the Forthcoming Period" (in Persian), Approved November 3, 2003, Majlis Research Center.

32. Mahmud Va'izi, "Iran in the New Balance of Power in the Middle East" (in Persian), Expediency Council, Center for Strategic Research, Tehran, July 6, 2007.

33. Ibid.; Mahmud Kitabi and Ahmad Rastinih, "The Doctrine of Constructive Interaction in Iran's Foreign Policy and the New Geopolitics of Iraq" (in Persian), *Journal of Political and International Research* 1, no. 3 (2009); Mahmud Va'izi, "The Strategy of Constructive Interaction and the Requirements of Development-Oriented Foreign Policy" (in Persian), Expediency Council, Center for Strategic Research, September 8, 2008; Mahmud Va'izi, "Constructive Interaction in Foreign Policy and the Development of Iran's Oil Industry" (in Persian), Expediency Council, Center for Strategic Research, February 9, 2008; "Constructive Interaction between Iran and Turkey" (in Persian), Islamic Republic News Agency, August 10, 2015; and "Iran Has Supported Constructive Interaction in Order to Establish Peace and Stability" (in Persian), Young Journalists Club, February 17, 2016.

34. "President's Television Interview" (in Persian), President.ir, April 3, 2015. Also see "Rouhani about the Deal: Constructive Interaction with the World Is Correct" (in Persian), RFI, January 17, 2016; "[Rouhani:] Only with Constructive and Friendly Interaction Can We Confront the Problems of the World" (in Persian), Hamshahri,

February 10, 2016; and "[Nuclear] Deal Created Needed Space for Constructive Interaction with the World" (in Persian), Dolat, February 15, 2016.

35. "Iran's National Security," 6; and "General Policies of the System."

36. "General Policies of the System."

37. For more on this, see chapter 4 by Emily Landau in the present volume.

38. "Zarif: Middle East Conflicts Must Be Resolved without Foreign Intervention" (in Persian), Iran Khabar, June 6, 2015.

39. "Zarif Requests the Establishment of a Regional Dialogue Forum in the Middle East" (in Persian), Radio Farda, August 3, 2015.

40. "Review of Rouhani's Remarks in World Media: Iran Is the Best Defense against Terror in the Middle East" (in Persian), Islamic Republic News Agency, September 22, 2015.

41. "Zarif: Stop Saudi Arabia's Effort to Eliminate Iran from the Region" (in Persian), BBC Persian, October 17, 2015.

42. Rahman Qahremanpour, "Iran's Deterrence Strategy," *Islamic Republic of Iran Diplomacy*, August 25, 2010.

43. "Iran's National Security," 7.

44. Ibid., 8.

45. *Analysis of the Iran-Iraq War 1*, 12.

46. *Survey of the Iran-Iraq War 1*, 28; *Guide Atlas 1* (in Persian) (Tehran: Center for War Studies and Research, 2002), 7, 14; *Guide Atlas 2* (Tehran: Center for War Studies and Research, 2001), 33, 39; and *Chronology of the Iran-Iraq War 4*, 31–34.

47. *Chronology of the Iran-Iraq War 4*, 20.

48. *Analysis of the Iran-Iraq War 1*, 100; *Survey of the Iran-Iraq War 1*, 28; *Guide Atlas 1*, 14; *Guide Atlas 2*, 39; and *Chronology of the Iran-Iraq War 4*, 32–34.

49. *Chronology of the Iran-Iraq War 4*, 31.

50. *Chronology of the Iran-Iraq War 1*, 27–28; *Chronology of the Iran-Iraq War 4*, 29; and *Chronology of the Iran-Iraq War 7*, 19–20.

51. *Guide Atlas 1*, 14–15; and *Guide Atlas 2*, 78.

52. *Analysis of the Iran-Iraq War 1*, 97–98.

53. *Guide Atlas 2*, 33; *Chronology of the Iran-Iraq War 4*, 30–32; and *Analysis of the Iran-Iraq War 1*, 100.

54. *Chronology of the Iran-Iraq War 1*, 15, 17; *Chronology of the Iran-Iraq War 4*, 17, 22–23; *Analysis of the Iran-Iraq War 1*, 31; and *Battles East of the Karun*, 19.

55. *Chronology of the Iran-Iraq War 43* (Tehran: Center for War Studies and Research, 1999), 23–24; *Chronology of the Iran-Iraq War 51*, 48; *Chronology of the Iran-Iraq War 52*, 27–28; and *Chronology of the Iran-Iraq War 37*, 69.

56. *Chronology of the Iran-Iraq War 43*, 23–24; *Chronology of the Iran-Iraq War 51*, 48; and *Chronology of the Iran-Iraq War 52*, 27–28.

57. *Chronology of the Iran-Iraq War 37*, 69; and *Chronology of the Iran-Iraq War 51*, 48.

58. See, e.g., "Which Countries Armed Saddam to the Teeth?" (in Persian), Parsine, October 12, 2013; "Governor of Eastern Azerbaijan Emphasizes Utilizing the Management Style of the Sacred Defense," Ministry of the Interior, September 26, 2015; "Saddam Hussein's Set of Assets Was Destroyed with the Conquest of Khurramshahr," Islamic Consultative Assembly News Agency, May 22, 2011. Even the Persian-language Wikipedia page on Saddam includes this language.

59. *Chronology of the Iran-Iraq War 33*, 21, 37; *Chronology of the Iran-Iraq War 43*, 24, 29; *Chronology of the Iran-Iraq War 47*, 32, 421; and *Chronology of the Iran-Iraq War 51*, 42, 48–49.

60. Shahram Chubin, "The Last Phase of the Iran-Iraq War: From Stalemate to Ceasefire," *Third World Quarterly* 11, no. 2 (1989): 3–4; and Dilip Hiro, *The Longest War: The Iran-Iraq Military Conflict* (London: Grafton, 1989), 95–96, 106.

61. *Chronology of the Iran-Iraq War 47*, 30; and *Survey of the Iran-Iraq War 1*, 149–50.

62. *Chronology of the Iran-Iraq War 37*, 69, 80, 318–19; *Chronology of the Iran-Iraq War 43*, 15; *Chronology of the Iran-Iraq War 47*, 30–31, 499–501; Peter Kornbluh and Malcolm Byrne, *The Iran-Contra Scandal: The Declassified History* (Washington, DC: National Security Archive, 1993).

63. "IRGC Warns to Retaliate against West's Cargo Inspection," Fars News, June 24, 2010; and "Bush Trying to Foment Discord in Mideast: IRGC Commander," *Tehran Times*, January 28, 2008.

64. E.g., "Deputy DM: Iran to Provide Armed Forces with Most Advanced Weapons," Fars News, August 3, 2015; "Iran Displays Latest Air Force Capabilities in Army Day Parades," Fars News, April 18, 2015; "Presidential Advisor: Iran Gaining Great Defense Achievements under Sanctions," Fars News, February 23, 2015; and "Commander: IRGC to Double Range of Anti-Warship Missiles," Fars News, May 13, 2014.

65. Two of the most active periods are in late May, to commemorate the liberation of Khurramshahr, and in late September, to mark the beginning of the war. See, e.g., "Special Beginning to Sacred Defense Week Programs with Armed Forces' Parade[s] All over the Country," *Ettelaat*, September 22, 2015; "Opening of Air Force Air Exhibition during Sacred Defense Week," Iranian Labour News Agency, September 21, 2015; "Iran's Guard Corps Receive Mass-Produced Missiles," Islamic Society of North America, May 22, 2011; and "IRGC Stages War Games in Tehran," Fars News, May 25, 2009.

66. "New Defensive Achievements Indicate Iran's Rapid Progress in the Field of Deterrence" (in Persian), Islamic Consultative Assembly News Agency, February 6, 2013.

67. "Iran Has ICBM Capability" (in Persian), Mashregh, June 14, 2015.

68. "New Defensive Achievements." President Rouhani and other officials have reiterated this position in more recent years as well. "Review of Rouhani's Remarks in World Media."

69. Qahremanpour, "Iran's Deterrence Strategy"; and Aliriza Gulshani and Muhsin Baqiri, "The Place of Lebanese Hezbollah in the Islamic Republic of Iran's Deterrence Strategy" (in Persian), *Journal of Political and International Research* 4, no. 11 (2012): 135.

70. Qahremanpour, "Iran's Deterrence Strategy."

71. Daulat Abadi, "Role of Deterrence," 38.

72. Gulshani and Baqiri, "Place of Lebanese Hezbollah," 135; Qahremanpour, "Iran's Deterrence Strategy"; and Daulat Abadi, "Role of Deterrence," 41–42.

73. Ibid.; and "Iran's National Security," 7–8.

74. "8 Deterrence Capabilities of the Islamic Republic of Iran" (in Persian), Afkar News, October 11, 2014; Manuchihr Rizavandi, "America vs. Iran: Tactical Change, Strategic Stability" (in Persian), *Kayhan*, November 9, 2008; and "Iran's Deterrent

Power Has Obstructed America's Ability to Move in the Persian Gulf" (in Persian), Young Journalists Club, September 22, 2015.

75. Gulshani and Baqiri, "Place of Lebanese Hezbollah," 124.

76. Ibid., 123–24; and "8 Deterrence Capabilities."

77. Gulshani and Baqiri, "Place of Lebanese Hezbollah," 136.

78. "The Role and Position of Passive Defense in the Islamic Republic of Iran's Security Diplomacy" (in Persian), Majlis Research Center, Tehran, 2009, 3–4; and "Law 11551."

79. "Role and Position of Passive Defense," 1.

80. Ibid.

81. Ibid., 2–3; Daulat Abadi, "Role of Deterrence," 42; and "Law 11551."

82. "A Short Discussion about National Defense Strategy" (in Persian), Majlis Research Center, Tehran, 1997, 1–2; "Law 11551"; and "General Policies of the System."

83. "Role and Position of Passive Defense," 3–4; Daulat Abadi, "Role of Deterrence," 42; "Short Discussion about National Defense Strategy," 3; and "Law 11551."

84. "Role and Position of Passive Defense," 3.

85. Ibid.

86. Daulat Abadi, "Role of Deterrence," 42.

87. "Short Discussion about National Defense Strategy," 3.

88. Husayn Harsij, Mujtaba Tuysirkani, and Layla Ja'fari, "Iran's Soft Power Geopolitics" (in Persian), *Political Science Research Journal* 4, no. 2 (2009); Asghar Iftikhari and Muhammad Janipur, "The Bases of the Soft Power of Iran's Islamic Revolution" (in Persian), *Islamic Revolution Research Journal* 3, no. 9 (2014); Sayyid Husayn Hijazi, "The Soft Power Capabilities of the Islamic Republic of Iran in Confronting America's Soft Threats" (in Persian), *Report of the President*, 2008, 26–27; Mahmud Kitabi, Inayatullah Yazdani, and Mas'ud Riza'i, "Soft Power and America's Hegemonic Strategy" (in Persian), *Political Knowledge* 8, no. 16 (2012); and "America's Strategic Steps for Influence in Iran" (in Persian), *Khamenei.ir*, September 19, 2015.

89. Daulat Abadi, "Role of Deterrence," 38; "Soft Power, Soft Technology, and Its Effects and Applications in the Defense Sector" (in Persian), Majlis Research Center, Tehran, 2007, 1–3.

90. "Role and Position of Passive Defense," 1–2; Daulat Abadi, "Role of Deterrence," 42–43; "Short Discussion about National Defense Strategy," 1; "Law 11551"; and "General Policies of the System."

91. *Chronology of the Iran-Iraq War 51*, 628.

92. *Chronology of the Iran-Iraq War 1*, 27–28; *Chronology of the Iran-Iraq War 4*, 28–29; *Chronology of the Iran-Iraq War 7*, 19–20, 52; *Guide Atlas 1*, 9, 29, 44; *Survey of the Iran-Iraq War 1*, 56, 61–62, 67, 71–72, 167–68; and *Analysis of the Iran-Iraq War 1*, 100.

93. *Chronology of the Iran-Iraq War 4*, 17, 22–23.

94. *Chronology of the Iran-Iraq War 5*, 19–20.

95. Examples include Iraq's hostility and subsequent invasion, the United States' rupturing of relations with Iran, and the larger-scale entrance of the United States into the war in the Persian Gulf. *Chronology of the Iran-Iraq War 7*, 37–41, 454–56, 571–78, 586–87, 616–18, 632–33, 647–51, 681–82; and *Survey of the Iran-Iraq War 1*, 58.

96. *Chronology of the Iran-Iraq War 5*, 21–22; *Survey of the Iran-Iraq War 1*, 56; *Passage of Two Years of War*, 21–22; *Chronology of the Iran-Iraq War 51*, 43, 608–9, 629; *Chronology of the Iran-Iraq War 37*, 96; *Khurramshahr in the Long War* (in Persian) (Tehran: Center for War Studies and Research, 1998), 15; and *Chronology of the Iran-Iraq War 33*, 23, 39.

97. *Survey of the Iran-Iraq War 1*, 52.

98. For more, see Tabatabai and Tracy Samuel, "What the Iran-Iraq War Tells Us."

99. IAEA Board of Governors, "Final Assessment on Past and Present Outstanding Issues regarding Iran's Nuclear Programme," GOV/2015/68, December 2, 2015; Dan Reiter, "Preventive Attacks against Nuclear Programs and the 'Success' at Osirak," *Nonproliferation Review* 12, no. 2 (2005); "Iran's Chemical and Biological Programmes," in *Iran's Nuclear, Chemical and Biological Capabilities* (London: International Institute for Strategic Studies, 2011); and Gregory F. Giles, "The Islamic Republic of Iran and Unconventional Weapons," in *Planning the Unthinkable*, ed. Peter R. Lavoy, Scott D. Sagan, and James J. Wirtz (Ithaca, NY: Cornell University Press, 2000).

100. "Hashemi Rafsanjani: Combat Chemical and Biological Weapons with Action, Not Speeches," Jaras, June 28, 2010; Mike Wallace, "Interview with Ali-Akbar Hashemi Rafsanjani," *60 Minutes*, CBS, March 8, 1997; "Emphasis on the Prohibition on the Use of Weapons of Mass Destruction," Fars News, February 4, 2016; "The Agency [IAEA] Never Confirmed Iran's Inclination to Build Nuclear Weapons" (in Persian), Iranian Labour News Agency, November 9, 2015; "A Historical Review of Iran's Non-Use of Weapons of Mass Destruction" (in Persian), Khamenei.ir, November 8, 2014; "Arms Control and Proliferation Profile: Iran," Arms Control Association, October 2015; "[Rouhani:] Iran's Defensive Strategy Is Deterrence" (in Persian), President.ir, August 24, 2014; and "Full Text of the President's Speech at the Country's Annual Defensive Industry Day Ceremony" (in Persian), President.ir, August 22, 2015.

101. "Nuclear Deterrence and Security Concerns of Iran."

102. Vipin Narang, *Nuclear Strategy in the Modern Era* (Princeton, NJ: Princeton University Press, 2014), 11; and Narang, "Nuclear Strategies," 88–89.

103. Alireza Nader, "Iran and a Nuclear-Weapon-Free Middle East," *Arms Control Today* (2011); and Narang, *Nuclear Strategy in the Modern Era*, 1.

104. *Genocide in Iraq: The Anfal Campaign against the Kurds* (New York: Human Rights Watch, 1993); *Chronology of the Iran-Iraq War 37*, 26, 91–92; *Chronology of the Iran-Iraq War 47*, 25; and *Chronology of the Iran-Iraq War 51*, 39–41.

105. "Statement in the Sixteenth NAM Summit" (in Persian), Khamenei.ir, September 30, 2012.

106. "The Stance of the Supreme Leader of the Revolution on Sanctions and the Islamic Republic of Iran's Nuclear Diplomacy" (in Persian), Majlis Research Center, Tehran, 2012, 8–11.

107. Akbar Ganji, "Frenemies Forever: The Real Meaning of Iran's 'Heroic Flexibility,'" *Foreign Affairs*, September 24, 2013.

108. "Full Text of the President's Speech."

109. "Post-JCPOA Iran Will Change Middle East Equations in Its Interest" (in Persian), Islamic Society of North America, November 30, 2015. For additional analysis of this issue, see Alireza Nader, "The Days after a Deal with Iran: Continuity and Change in Iranian Foreign Policy," *RAND Perspective*, 2014; Dalia Dassa Kaye and Jeffrey

Martini, "The Days after a Deal with Iran: Regional Responses to a Final Nuclear Agreement," *RAND Perspective*, 2014; and Farideh Farhi, "The Middle East after the Iran Nuclear Deal," Council on Foreign Relations, September 7, 2015.

110. "Zarif Requests the Establishment of a Regional Dialogue Forum."

111. Kayhan Barzegar, "The Nuclear Agreement and the Issue of 'Strategic Stability' in Iran's Regional Policy" (in Persian), Tabnak, March 25, 2015; and Emile Nakhleh, "Nuclear Deal: How Iran Could Enhance Regional Stability," LobeLog, October 7, 2015.

Conclusion to Part I

Regional Approaches to Strategic Stability

RAJESH BASRUR

A QUARTER CENTURY since the end of the Cold War, we are in a position to see our world with a sense of perspective. The terms "post–Cold War era" and "second nuclear age" are frequently used to distinguish the two periods. Instead of one world-embracing conflict between continent-sized ideological adversaries, we now speak of a multiplicity of smaller "cold war" confrontations in the arc between Ukraine and North Korea. Remarking on what he sees as the contrast between the two eras, Thomas Schelling has remarked: "Now the world is so much changed, so much more complicated, so multivariate, so unpredictable, involving so many nations and cultures and languages in nuclear relationships, many of them asymmetric, that it is difficult to know how many meanings there are for 'strategic stability,' or how many different kinds of such stability there may be among so many different international relationships."[1]

Schelling does not say so, but he implies that the more complex world we inhabit today is more difficult to manage and less amenable to stability, not only because of uncertainties posed by changes in the number of players/actors and their different systems and postures, but also because of the challenges wrought by the different meanings and types of stability. Others are more forthright in expressing the view that our times are intrinsically more unstable.[2] The chapters in part I are designed to clarify the extent to which change

141

has occurred, both in basic concepts and in strategic behavior. They enable us to make better judgments as to what strategic stability means today and what we may need to do in order to enhance it. A fundamental point they bring out is that the changes visible in the post–Cold War era apply not just to numbers and force posture but also to differences in basic relationships among the relevant players.

In some obvious ways, the present is more stable than the past. First, some of today's major nuclear-strategic dyads—the United States and Russia, the United States and China, and India and China—may be involved in strategic competition, but they are also engaged in high levels of economic cooperation, which gives them all strong incentives to pursue stable relationships. Second, several contemporary nuclear powers—China, India, Israel, and Pakistan—do not deploy their nuclear weapons on high alert, but keep them in a low-profile, nondeployed state. Third, and consequently, though there have been crises in the present era—notably between India and Pakistan—these have not involved nuclear threats aimed at exercising compellence. Finally, the pace and levels of arms racing have been much less intense than they were during the Cold War.

At the same time, the present age has its own instabilities. First, there are multiple points of tension that are not directly related to one another—currently, Ukraine, Kashmir, the South China Sea and East China Sea, the 38th Parallel—and that cannot be resolved by one overarching negotiation process. Second, the problem is made more complex by a cascading process of arms competition and consequent tension. The US-China arms dynamic has a bearing on the China-India one, which in turn has an impact on the India-Pakistan one (Tasleem, chapter 3; see also Montgomery, chapter 1). Triangular nuclear-strategic politics might also be around the corner with respect to North Korea, South Korea, and Japan (Montgomery). Third, the US propensity to intervene for the sake of stability is sometimes exploited by the initiation of crises to invite such intervention on behalf of one side or the other—a phenomenon visible in the India-Pakistan crises of 1999 (initiated by Pakistan) and 2001–2 (initiated by India). Fourth, new technologies—such as ballistic missile defense, space technology, precision-guided munitions, and cyber technology—have the potential to destabilize relationships by disrupting existing national security arrangements. Fifth, as competition heats up and plays out in regional systems, we might see new manifestations of extended deterrence, with China, Pakistan, and Russia jockeying for position in the Middle East (Montgomery). And sixth, terrorist groups have acquired capabilities that enable them to play an autonomous and unpredictable role in stirring up trouble between nuclear-armed states.

Do Cold War–era concepts relating to strategic stability still apply in what appears to be a significantly altered strategic landscape? There are certainly some changes in the way we think about strategic stability. During the Cold War, the US-Soviet notion of strategic stability rested on a combination of roughly balanced nuclear forces and mutual vulnerability. Today, the picture is more complex. The stability of the US-China relationship is not founded on a proximate balance or the quest for one. The same goes for the US-Russia and India-China relationships (on the former, see chapter 2, by Pavlov and Malygina). The India-Pakistan relationship (Tasleem) is somewhat different because Pakistan is clearly pursuing a balancing strategy. Israel has no nuclear-armed competitor; hence, its focus is on conventional superiority, combined with a covert nuclear capability (Landau, chapter 4), though Iran does not possess nuclear capability and relies on conventional and asymmetric/subconventional deterrence to deter attacks on it (Tracy Samuel, chapter 5). As a result, in grappling with the difficult question of how to ensure strategic stability—where no state has an incentive to go to nuclear or conventional war—we need to think of approaches and mechanisms that apply to each different type of relationship.

Following the end of the Cold War, analysts, particularly from the West, turned from a balance-based understanding of strategic stability to a restraint-based one. To be sure, nuclear restraint was always a part of the Cold War lexicon. It produced sustained efforts at arms control, risk reduction, and, in later years, disarmament. Restraint became predominant in the post–Cold War period, with a push for disarmament, but has gradually subsided because there is no pressure of risk to incentivize it. The view with respect to Asian states (China excepted) remains embedded in the proliferation perspective, and hence the efforts of Western analysts continue to be preoccupied with nonproliferation, nuclear risk reduction, and restraint. Ironically, as some of the chapters in part I demonstrate, states that were until recently focusing on nuclear restraint (disarmament, minimalist doctrine) have been steadily moving toward some form of balancing by means of varying processes of nuclear modernization. Much of the community of strategic thinkers seems to have missed the significance of this shift and the consequent need to grapple with the balancing problem, which has its roots in professional thinking during the Cold War era.

The old definition of strategic stability needs rethinking. The focus on mutual second-strike capability—both sides should have "invulnerable" nuclear weapons for a relationship to be stable—does not correspond to historical reality, which is that all states have avoided nuclear war regardless of the nuclear balance. A broader definition, which finds resonance in the preceding chapters, is one that views strategic stability as resting on incentives not to resort to a major war, whether conventional or nuclear, including by unauthorized means. More difficult—and this is something that today's strategic landscape has in common with the Cold War era—is the problem of dissatisfied states and their propensity to alter the status quo, as in Ukraine or in Kashmir. General strategic stability is not always everyone's cup of tea. Crisis stability is therefore the key concept here, and, as the preceding chapters show, there are plenty of reasons in the form of potential crisis points to focus on stabilization at the political level. The lack of fit between different approaches to deterrence can be problematic—for example, both Iran and Israel focus primarily on conventional weapons for deterrence, but Iran incorporates an asymmetric strategy as an instrument of deterrence, which is not acceptable to Israel and other states, while many of the region's states, not least Iran, are not comfortable with Israel's nuclear monopoly.

Arms race stability remains a concern, but less so than during the Cold War, because there is no runaway competition in this sphere today. One aspect deserving mention is that the standard understanding of stability based on transparency does not quite apply everywhere. On the contrary, it is arguable that states like India and Pakistan are comfortable with opacity (Tasleem) or that Israel's neighbors have come to terms with its covert nuclear capability (Landau). In contrast to the latter, the regional response to the rising possibility of Iran's acquisition of covert nuclear capability has been strikingly negative, which may reflect the underlying perception that Israel is viewed as a status quo power and Iran as a revisionist one.

In sum, the predominant concepts of the Cold War era appear to have lost much of their salience. The balance of power between nuclear states is less important than strategic orientation in terms of the status quo or change in determining stability. The coexistence of multiple dyads, in which at least one of the players is dissatisfied with the status quo—US-Russia, US-China, India-Pakistan—makes for a much more complex setting than before. Moreover, the old preoccupation with elaborate calculations of balances between weapons systems plays a significant part in contemporary strategic politics. Also, the notion that transparency is the bedrock of strategic stability is passé. As mentioned above, several players maintain opaque capabilities and postures; these are not the source of deep anxieties among adversaries. And finally, old nomenclatures for weapons systems do not necessarily apply. During the Cold War, short-range weapons were by definition nonstrategic; this is not the case when the capital cities of nuclear powers can be struck within a very few minutes, as with India, Pakistan, South Korea, North Korea, and Japan.

The relationship between conventional and nuclear forces varies considerably. During the early phase of the Cold War, there was a peculiar "balance" produced by asymmetry—the nuclear monopoly of the United States was ranged against the Soviet Union's conventional advantage in Europe. Gradually, parity emerged on both counts. Today's dyads exhibit wide differences that are unlikely to be bridged in the near future. The US is much stronger (notwithstanding Moscow's upgrading efforts) in both respects than Russia, China, and North Korea. China likewise possesses far greater capabilities than India in both nuclear and conventional capability. In the Pakistan-India relationship, there is both nuclear parity and a simultaneous conventional imbalance. Finally, in contrast to the Cold War era, several of today's competitive nuclear dyads have strong built-in incentives to cooperate. Back then, there was little economic interaction between the United States and the Soviet Union and China and, except during the 1950s, between the Soviet Union and China. Today, there is a high degree of economic exchange among the major nuclear dyads—US-China, US-Russia, and India-China—and hence there are stronger incentives to curb their rivalries. These substantial differences make it hard, therefore, to draw lessons for stability from the Cold War or to adopt approaches that were then in vogue. This underscores the value of the preceding chapters.

There is much to chew on here. Perhaps much more remains to be sampled if we are to arrive at more useful understandings of how states think about strategic stability and how they act on it. Nuclear stabilization in the present age is a work in progress, and this volume marks an important step on the way forward.

NOTES

1. Thomas C. Schelling, foreword to *Strategic Stability: Contending Interpretations,* ed. Elbridge A. Colby and Michael S. Gerson (Carlisle, PA: Strategic Studies Institute of US Army War College, 2013), vii.

2. See, e.g., Paul Bracken, *Fire in the East: The Rise of Asian Military Power and the Second Nuclear Age* (New York: HarperCollins, 1999); Colin S. Gray, *The Second Nuclear Age* (Boulder, CO: Lynne Rienner, 1999); and Christopher P. Twomey, "Introduction: Dangerous Dynamism in Asia's Nuclear Future," *Asia Policy* 19 (January 2015): 2–4.

PART II
Cross-Domain Deterrence and Strategic Stability

6

Strategic Stability and Cross-Domain Coercion

The Russian Approach to Information (Cyber) Warfare

DMITRY "DIMA" ADAMSKY

THIS CHAPTER EXPLORES the information (cyber) component of the Russian "New Generation War" (NGW), and examines implications for strategic stability that result from the Russian employment of this tool of national security policy. Western experts often dub the Russian approach "hybrid warfare" (HW), implying that Moscow incorporates nonmilitary, information, cyber, nuclear, conventional, and subconventional tools of strategic influence in an orchestrated campaign. Ironically, the Russian strategic community envisions its NGW, which it wages across several domains, as a response to what it sees as a Western "hybrid campaign" against Russia.[1] Regardless of the label, the current version of Russia's operational art constitutes an intriguing innovation that occupies a major place in Russian national security policy, and as such has direct implications for strategic stability at the regional and global levels.

The information (cyber) component of the Russian NGW is not a brute force strategy but a coercion campaign that aims to manipulate the adversary's perception, to maneuver its decision-making process, and to influence its strategic behavior. As such, the concept of cross-domain coercion, the most recent evolution in the Russian art of strategy and one of the main instruments of national security policy, directly relates to the concept of strategic stability. In contrast to more traditional warfare, where one could more easily differentiate between offense and defense, the current Russian approach aims to shape the strategic environment, whether in an active or reactive mode. Thus, even if not expressed directly and in these very terms, the implied definition and approach to strategic stability are broad, holistic, and synthetic. The Russian approach addresses threats and challenges at many levels, not just by deterring or countering them but also by shaping the environment across several domains to evaporate the threat.

The chapter aims to describe the new phenomenon in the Russian art of strategy and also to explore how this innovation affects the state of strategic stability. Specifically, it aims to highlight which aspects of NGW may undermine strategic stability and which features may strengthen it.

The chapter advances a threefold argument. First, it explains that the current Russian cross-domain coercion campaign is an integrated whole of non-nuclear, informational, and nuclear types of influence, both military and nonmilitary. Each component is an inseparable part of Russian operational art, cannot be analyzed as a stand-alone issue, and thus can only be understood holistically in the context of one coercion campaign or operation. Second, NGW's essence is a holistic informational (cyber) operation, waged simultaneously on the digital-technological and on the cognitive-psychological fronts, that skillfully merges military and nonmilitary capabilities across nuclear, conventional, and subconventional domains. Third and finally, depending on circumstances, various aspects of this national security tool may undermine strategic stability, while others may strengthen it. The centrality of NGW in the Russian approach is likely to stay intact for the observable future.

The chapter consists of three sections. The first one traces the evolution of NGW. The second section focuses on the main element of NGW—informational (cyber) struggle. And the third section discusses the role of the latter in orchestrating a cross-domain coercion campaign. The conclusion summarizes the findings and outlines ramifications for strategic stability.

A clarification about terms is necessary. Russian thinking on the subject is constantly evolving, sometimes lacking doctrinal codification and an official lexicon. Thus, though a significant corpus of ideas on the subject informs current Russian military theory and policy, Russian and Western experts use different terms to refer to different types of coercion. This chapter sticks to the Russian terminology as much as possible. However, to make possible systematic analysis, it introduces the terms "regional nuclear deterrence" and "cross-domain coercion" as heuristic expressions representing the clouds of ideas circulating in the Russian professional community. The chapter indicates when it is using a Russian term or a Western one, or when it introduces its own term, to describe a phenomenon under scrutiny. Thus, "cross-domain coercion," the term that this chapter introduces, refers to the host of Russian efforts both to deter and to compel adversaries by orchestrating soft and hard instruments of power across various domains, regionally and globally. As such, the term connects the chapter to the main discussion—exploration of how various actors understand strategic stability and the ramifications their main tools of national security have for it.

A disclaimer about the analysis is also necessary. Labeling the Russian approach in a given geographical or historical context as being purely "offensive" or "defensive" does not seem to contribute to a better understanding of the Russian art of strategy and its implications for strategic stability. Such qualifications are subjective, relative, and often politicized. Moreover, both approaches, especially in Russian strategic culture, often coexist and are indistinguishable. This is an important historical-normative debate, but it is beyond the scope of this chapter. This chapter seeks to contribute to the discussion by representing reality as it is seen from Moscow, even if this analytical disposition, and Russian perception, may seem counterintuitive, confusing, and contradictory. This particularly relates to the usage of the term "cross-domain coercion," and also to sections of the chapter that discuss Russian threat perception and countermeasures to perceived challenges.

RUSSIAN NEW GENERATION WAR
VERSUS WESTERN HYBRID WARFARE

This section first provides terminological clarification for emerging Russian operational art. It then goes on to discuss the New Generation Warfare, including its innovativeness.

Terminological Clarification

As experts continue to explore the theory and practice of emerging Russian operational art, terminology matters. For the matter of such effort, utilizing Western terms and concepts to define the Russian approach to warfare may result in mirror imaging, with subsequent inaccuracy in the diagnosis and prognosis of Russian modus operandi. Applying the Western conceptual HW framework to explain Russian operational art—without examining Russian references to this term, divorcing it from the Russian ideational context, and without contrasting it with what Russians say to one another about themselves—may lead to misperceptions. Utilizing the HW terminological apparatus that dominates professional discourse to analyze a distinct Russian NGW concept seems like such a misrepresentation. Experts dealing with the subject have already spotted this analytical mistake of imposing a Western way of thinking about conducting warfare on the Russian version of operational art.[2] This mirror imaging may attribute nonexisting qualities to the Russian approach and overlook its essentials. Whatever the reason for this terminological-conceptual inaccuracy, a brief clarification is necessary to decrease the risk of further misperceptions.

With few exceptions, Western experts utilize the term "hybrid warfare" to describe current Russian military theory and practice.[3] This categorization is, to say the least, inaccurate. Current Russian thinking about the waging of war is different from HW, even if similar in some regards. Russian sources do not define their approach as HW, and they use this term usually in conjunction with the Western waging of war, which they try to counteract. Until recently, HW was not at all part of the official Russian lexicon. Before the 2014 events in Ukraine, the term featured in professional discourse either in reference to US threat perception or to categorize one of the recent trends in US warfare.[4] Since 2014, it has often been used to refer to the Western standoff with Russia.

The term "HW" became widespread in the Western professional lexicon starting in the middle to late 2000s, as the US defense establishment and its allies have been co-exploring emerging forms of warfare. Initially, the empirical context that stimulated this knowledge development hardly had any Russian connection. Although some experts, after the 2008 Georgia War, qualified the Russian modus operandi as HW, Israeli and Western combat experiences against nonstate and state actors in the Middle East served as the main sources of empirical evidence and intellectual inspiration for the HW conceptualization. The subsequent discourse framed HW either as a simultaneous employment of conventional, subconventional, and possibly nonconventional warfare for the sake of political objectives or as a blurring of the political and jihadi identities of the actors.[5] As such, the use of the term in reference to the Russian strategy was misguided because it ignored the Russian NGW conceptualization (which was then nonexistent) and totally neglected the intellectual sources of the Russian approach to warfare, which indeed traditionally compounded several forms of military, clandestine, and special operations. Thus, despite some resonance between the two, Russian NGW and Western HW are essentially different constructs.

New Generation Warfare

Over the last several years, Russian experts have been energetically conceptualizing the changing character of war. This activity, aimed at analyzing the emerging military regime and at distilling relevant military innovations, has been an old Soviet-Russian military tradition. Expressed either in revolution in military affairs (RMA) terminology or in the classification of generations of warfare, it provides an analytical framework, methodological apparatus, and professional jargon for designing a military transformation. Leading up to the 2014 doctrine, Russian understanding of the changing character of war matured into a corpus of ideas under the rubric "NGW" (*voina novogo pokoleniia*), or "Gerasimov Doctrine"—two terms used interchangeably here and elsewhere. Based on the lessons learned from recent conflicts, mainly US campaigns and the defense transformation of the last decade, this is the latest Russian attempt to forecast the evolution of information technology (IT)–RMA into a new era.[6] This corpus of ideas, circulating in the Russian strategic community, shapes its military practice.

With some variance, Russian primary sources frame the strategic thought and operational art debate along similar lines; first, they offer an overview of the current military regime. This outline of trends characterizing the current evolution of warfare is neither a reference to "Western" nor to "Russian" ways of war, but equally relates to both, as the mechanization of warfare in the 1920s or nuclear revolution in the 1950s did. Then, the text refers to how this new type of military conflict applies to Russia and discusses how Russia should react. These three themes coexist in the NGW discussion, which is thus equally about the military threat from the West and about the Russian response.

The essence of NGW is reflected in the statements of the Russian chief of the General Staff and in the Military Doctrine. Here, NGW is an amalgamation of hard and nonkinetic power, across various domains, through a skillful application of coordinated military, diplomatic, and economic tools. The ratio of non-military to military measures is 4 to 1, with these forms of nonmilitary strategic competition being under the aegis of the military. Regime changes brought by the Color Revolutions, and especially by the Arab Spring (and recent events in Ukraine), are seen, within the NGW theory, as a type of warfare capitalizing on indirect action, informational campaigns, private military organizations, special operation forces, and domestic protest potential, backed by the most sophisticated conventional and nuclear military capabilities.[7]

Under the changing character of warfare, these phases and new forms of struggle predominate:[8] (1) commencement of military action without war declaration or preparatory deployment; (2) highly maneuverable stand-off combat actions conducted by combined-arms forces; (3) degradation of the adversary's military-economic potential by swift destruction of military and state critical infrastructure; (4) massive employment of precision-guided munitions (PGMs), special operations, unmanned weapon systems, weapons based on new physical principles, and the involvement of a "military-civilian component" (armed civilians) in combat activities; (5) simultaneous strikes on enemy forces and other targets in the entire territorial depth; (6) simultaneous military action in all physical domains and in the informational space; (7) employment of asymmetric and indirect methods; and (8) management of troops and means in a unified informational sphere.[9]

In an ideal type of NGW campaign, there are seven key components. First, the "informational-psychological struggle" takes a leading role, as the moral-psychological-cognitive-informational suppression of the adversary's decision makers and operators assures conditions for achieving victory. Second, asymmetrical and indirect actions of a political, economic, informational, and technological nature neutralize the adversary's military superiority. Indirect strategy in its current technological form is primarily about using an informational struggle to neutralize the adversary without, or with a minimal, employment of military force, mainly through informational superiority. Third, the complex of nonmilitary actions degrades the abilities of the adversary to compel or to employ force and produces a negative image in world public opinion that eventually dissuades the adversary from initiating aggression. Fourth, the side initiating NGW employs a massive deception and disinformation campaign to conceal the time, scope, scale, and the character of the attack.[10] Fifth, subversion-reconnaissance activities, conducted by special operations and covered by informational operations, precede the kinetic phase of the campaign. Sixth, the kinetic phase starts with space-aerial dominance aimed at destroying the critical assets of the civilian industrial-technological infrastructure and of the centers of state and military management so that the state will be forced to capitulate. Operating under no-fly zones, private military companies and armed opposition groups prepare an operational setup for the invasion. Seventh, by the phase of the territorial occupation, most of the campaign's goals have been achieved, as the ability and will of the adversary to resist have been broken and evaporated.[11]

The Innovativeness of the NGW

Two unique innovations stand out in this exposition offered by Russian military theoreticians. The first is the orchestration of the military and nonmilitary measures ratio aimed at minimizing kinetic engagements and the addition of the informational domain to the space-aerial, naval, and terrestrial ones.[12] Achievement of the NGW campaign's strategic goals depends on establishing informational superiority over the adversary and then waging the campaign's decisive battles on the informational front. Thus, the early (soft) phases of the NGW campaign are more decisive than the final (kinetic) ones.

The second innovation of Russian military thought is an emphasis on asymmetrical and indirect approaches; however, one should not overstate the uniqueness of this approach. Along with HW discourse, another inaccuracy of the Western analysis is to present the Russian emphasis on increasing the role of indirect-asymmetrical actions as innovative Russian practice imported from the West. The Russian quest for asymmetry is neither fundamentally novel nor purely Western. Russian experts are following Western professional discourse and are familiar with its conceptual apparatus; however, it would be inaccurate to argue that Russians are importing Western terminology or giving it a new meaning. For at least half a decade preceding the recent Military Doctrine, the Russian General Staff was systematically exploring the role of asymmetry in modern warfare, learning lessons from historical evidence worldwide, following Western discourse on the subject, and generating insights for the benefits of the military's theory and practice.[13]

Though informed to a certain degree by the Western debate, the concepts of "asymmetry" and "indirect approach" have much deeper, idiosyncratic roots in Russian military tradition. Cunning, indirectness, operational ingenuity, and addressing weaknesses and avoiding strengths are expressed in Russian professional terminology as military stratagem (*voennaia khitrost'*) and have been, in the Tsarist, Soviet, and Russian traditions, one of the central components of military art that complements, multiplies, or substitutes for the use of force to achieve strategic results in military operations.[14] According to Gareev, "Deceit of the adversary and cunning stratagem, dissemination of disinformation, and other, the most sophisticated, malice [*kovarnye*] means of struggle," have historically been integral parts of the military profession.[15]

The previous burst of asymmetry conceptualization in Russian military thought traces back to the 1980s, when Soviet experts sought effective, asymmetrical countermeasures to the US Strategic Defense Initiative. One of its architects, and one of the leading Russian defense intellectuals, Andrei Kokoshin, has been popularizing the term "asymmetrical approach" in professional discourse since the 1990s.[16] Thus, long before the publication of the 2014 doctrine, asymmetry and an indirect approach were incorporated into the jargon of the military brass and political leadership in discussing the correlation of forces and countermeasures with the West.[17]

The Russian theory of victory is asymmetrical at its core because it is a competitive strategy of playing one's strengths to the opponent's weaknesses. However, the Russian approach is also symmetrical from the Russian perspective—the nature of the threat shapes the nature of the response. Moscow saw the United States waging a new type of (hybrid) warfare elsewhere, felt threatened, sought adequate countermeasures, and is now erecting a firewall against what it sees as the soft and hard Western power aimed at Russia in an integrated HW campaign. Because the boundaries between internal and external threats are blurred and the threat is perceived as a cohesive whole, the military is expected to address it in a holistic manner. The rising importance of pressuring adversaries without the military results in an unorthodox multidimensional merging of soft and hard power, operating nonmilitary activities in conjunction with military, covert and overt operations, special forces, mercenaries, and internal opposition to achieve strategic outcomes.[18] NGW is less about traditional military or economic destruction and is more about affecting the opponent's will and manipulating his strategic choices through perception. Consequently, the role of *informational struggle* looms unprecedentedly large in current Russian military theory and practice.

INFORMATIONAL STRUGGLE: LEITMOTIF OF NEW GENERATION WARFARE

Because, according to NGW, the main battlefield is consciousness, perception, and the strategic calculus of the adversary, the main operational tool is informational struggle, aimed at imposing one's strategic will on the other side. Perception, consequently, becomes the campaign's strategic center of gravity. It is difficult to overemphasize the role that Russian official doctrine attributes to the defensive and offensive aspects of informational struggle in modern conflicts. In NGW, it is impossible to prevail without achieving informational superiority over the adversary.[19] "Strategic operation of the theater of informational struggle," aimed at achieving this superiority, blurs war and peace, front and rear, levels of war (tactical, operational, and strategic), forms of warfare (offense and defense), and forms of coercion (deterrence and compellence).[20] Moscow assumes that this trend equally relates to everyone, and it perceives informational struggle as a way of striking back against what it sees as US information warfare. These abuses of soft power serve as instruments of interference in the internal affairs of sovereign countries, and they have intensified, according to Moscow, against the backdrop of the changing character of war. The emerging corpus of ideas on informational struggle aims to counteract what Russian experts see as the indirect approach, soft power, and technologies of "managed chaos," one of the main tools of Western HW.[21]

Informational struggle, in the Russian interpretation, comprises both technological and psychological components designed to manipulate the adversary's picture of reality, misinform it, and eventually interfere with the decision-making processes of individuals, organizations, governments, and societies to influence their consciousness. Sometimes referred to as "reflexive control," it forces the adversary to act according to a false picture of reality in a predictable way, which is favorable to the initiator of the informational strike and seemingly independent and benign to the target.[22] Moral-psychological suppression and manipulation of social consciousness aims to cease resisting (*otkaz ot soprotivleniia*), even supporting the attacker, due to the disillusionment and discontent with the government and the disorganization of the state and military management functions.[23] The end result is a desired strategic behavior.

Despite the puzzlement of several intelligence communities with Moscow's innovative "cyberwarfare," the Russian approach demonstrates remarkable historical continuity. Russian conceptualization of informational (cyber) struggle, in the NGW framework, is an outgrowth of three corpora of professional knowledge. The first source of influence is a Soviet Military-Technical Revolution / RMA thesis from the 1980s that envisioned military organizations of the postindustrial era as reconnaissance-strike complexes. Accordingly, one can defeat the adversary not by kinetic destruction but by disrupting decision-making processes within its system of systems, through an electronic warfare strike on command, control, communications, computer, intelligence, surveillance, and reconnaissance systems. This became a source for the "digital-technological" impetus of the Russian approach. Second, because informational influence is aimed primarily at an adversary's decision making, the Russian approach is informed by the tradition of "active measures" and *maskirovka*— one of the main virtues of the Soviet-Russian intelligence and military art—a repertoire of denial, deception, disinformation, propaganda, camouflage, and concealment. It aims to manipulate the adversary's picture of reality and to produce favorable operational conditions for promoting one's strategic goals. This became a basis for the cognitive-psychological motive. Finally, a unique Soviet definition given to the science of cybernetics (*kibernetika*) left its imprint. Seen as a discipline in the intersection of exact, social, and natural sciences, Soviet scientific society defined cybernetics as science exploring the nature of creation, storage, transformation, utilization, and management of information and knowledge, in complex systems, machines, contiguous living organisms, or societies. In a nutshell, it is a discipline dealing with decision-making management of the highest order.[24]

From the start, the Soviet-Russian definition of cybernetics included digital-technological and cognitive-psychological spheres. Consequently, current Russian doctrine and policy perceive cyberspace as an integral part of the broader informational space. Russian official terminology differentiates between *informational space*, all spheres where societal perception is shaped; *information*, content shaping perception and decision making; and *informational infrastructure*, technological media that gives digital and analog expression to the first two components. Russian national security theory and practice address these three as one integrated whole and emphasize perception (*soznanie*) as the center of gravity of any type of activity in the informational theater of operations, whether it is offense, defense, or coercion.[25] Informational struggle/warfare (*bor'ba/protivoborstvo, voina*), reflecting the field's dual nature, includes electronic warfare, computer network operations, psychological operations, and *maskirovka* activities that enable an integrated informational strike (*informatsionnyi udar*) on the adversary's decision making. The digital-technological and cognitive-psychological components of this informational strike are synthetically interconnected and mutually complementing. Seeing informational struggle as a tool of strategic coercion, Russia defines informational sovereignty as digital-cognitive independence and envisions international regulation of informational (cyber) space in a much broader sense than the West. Initially, the term "cyber" mainly referred to the adversarial, Western, digital attacks on Russian informational infrastructure. Incrementally, it acquired a broader meaning in Russian professional discourse, but it is still an integral subcomponent of informational struggle.[26]

Informational struggle is not a codified concept of operations. However, the contours of this widely used tool are straightforwardly identifiable. Three main characteristics predominate.

First, Russia's approach to informational struggle is *holistic* (*kompleksnyi podhod*); that is, it merges digital-technological and cognitive-psychological attacks. Although digital sabotage aims to disorganize, disrupt, and destroy a state's managerial capacity, psychological subversion aims to deceive the victim, discredit the leadership, and disorient and demoralize the population and the armed forces.

Second, informational struggle is *unified* (*edinstvo usilii*), in that it synchronizes informational struggle warfare with kinetic and nonkinetic military means and with effects from other sources of power; and it is *unified*, in terms of co-opting and coordinating a spectrum of government and nongovernment actors—military, paramilitary, and nonmilitary.

Third and finally, the informational campaign is an *uninterrupted* (*bezpriryvnost'*) strategic effort. It is waged during both "peacetime" and wartime, simultaneously in the adversary's domestic as well as international media domains, and in all spheres of new media. Battles on several fronts—informational, psychological, and digital-technological—enable the creation of managed stability/instability across all theaters of operations.[27]

In addition to these unique but largely known characteristics, the main source of the novelty and distinctiveness of informational struggle is the role that it plays in current Russian operational art. Informational struggle warfare is a leitmotif of the Russian version of NGW as it knits together all operational efforts, serving as a kind of DNA that choreographs coercion activities across nonmilitary and military (nuclear and nonnuclear) domains. Its role of systemic integrator is expressed both verbally and graphically in Gerasimov's programmatic speech.

This unique role of informational struggle is a fundamental difference of the Russian approach from the Western HW model. First, in the Western HW theory, the notion of information struggle is not as central as in the Russian version. Second, as opposed to HW, Gerasimov's doctrine emphasizes only to a minimal extent the use of kinetic force and aims to achieve campaign goals. Against the backdrop of hard power minimalization, perception becomes the center of gravity and informational struggle becomes the main tool of victory. Seizing territory or achieving the desired outcome with minimal fatalities is different from the Western view of HW that seeks victory by nondefeat.[28] Finally, the informational strike is about breaking the internal coherence of the enemy system—and not about its integral annihilation. Gerasimov's doctrine indeed presumes the use of force, but it is primarily the strategy of influence, not of brute force. Consequently, the issue of cross-domain coercion dominates it.

INFORMATIONAL STRUGGLE AND THE CROSS-DOMAIN COERCION CAMPAIGN

Constantly evolving Russian thinking about coercion recently supplemented the *regional nuclear deterrence* concept with two additional variations on the theme: *nonnuclear* and *informational* deterrence.[29] An amalgamation of these three models into a unified program manifests the most up-to-date Russian version of cross-domain coercion. Informational struggle plays a pivotal role in it.

Nonnuclear Deterrence

Since the mid-2000s, Russian defense intellectuals, in conjunction with staff members working on nuclear deterrence, have been popularizing a prenuclear deterrence theory.[30] A prelude to nuclear use, the concept suggests improving deterrence credibility by increasing escalation ladder levels.[31] It was based on a threat of launching long-range conventional PGMs against targets inside and outside the theater of operations. Selective damage to the military and civilian infrastructure should signal the last warning before a limited low-yield nuclear use.[32] However, given the slow procurement of advanced capabilities, Russian experts at the time envisioned "prenuclear deterrence" only as a distant prospect and did not see any nonnuclear alternative to deterring conventional aggression.[33]

In the 2010 doctrine, "nonnuclear deterrence" received a passing reference. It was defined as the armed forces' peacetime mission and stated that the Russian Federation presumes the usage of "high precision weapons" to prevent military conflicts as part of the "strategic deterrence activities of a forceful character" (*strategicheskoe silovoe sderzhivanie*).[34] The latter has two ends—prevention of war (in peacetime) and de-escalation of conflict (in wartime), supported by forceful (military) and nonmilitary means (political-diplomatic, legal, economic, informational-psychological, and spiritual-moral). Back then, however, Russia lacked a unified system of strategic deterrence (codified theory, methodological apparatus, and procedures supporting it) as well as a coordinating organ orchestrating it across all domains. The General Staff identified the creation of such a unified system, based on the complex measures of military and nonmilitary character, as the most important national security task.[35]

During the years leading up to the publication of the 2014 doctrine, a great leap forward toward this cross-domain deterrence was evident. Annual military exercises since 2011 have demonstrated the growing role given to advanced conventional munitions relative to the previous decade, when the nuclear arsenal's role in the theater of operations steadily grew, reaching a peak in the Zapad 2009 and Vostok 2010 exercises. Assuming that modern nonnuclear means of war (PGMs, ballistic and cruise missiles, and informational capabilities) can generate battlefield and deterrence effects compatible with nuclear weapons, Russian experts, more than before, emphasized deterrence as a function of nonnuclear, hard, and soft instruments of power.[36] Leading up to (and after) the events in Ukraine, an assumption emerged in the Russian strategic community that the relevance of strategic nuclear deterrence is limited to a very narrow set of scenarios, unless it is skillfully synthesized with other forms of strategic coercion.[37] The 2014 doctrine, according to a senior expert at the Russian Institute of Strategic Research, manifests this assumption by emphasizing nonnuclear forceful deterrence based on military, political, diplomatic, technical, and economic means, with informational warfare being its main component.[38]

The 2014 doctrine codified these ideas circulating in the Russian expert community. Nonnuclear deterrence (*neiadernoe sderzhivanie*), a complex system "of foreign policy, military and nonmilitary measures aimed at preventing aggression by nonnuclear means," is the doctrine's main innovation. Nonnuclear deterrence does not substitute for, but instead complements, its nuclear analogue as part of the "forceful measures" of strategic deterrence system—a complex of interconnected measures of forceful (nuclear and nonnuclear) and nonforceful character. Nonnuclear deterrence may come in the form of force demonstration to prevent escalation, or even limited use of force as a radical measure of coercion (*krainiia mera vozdeistviia*) aimed at de-escalating hostilities.[39]

Nonnuclear deterrence attributes a special role to the targeting of the adversary's nonmilitary assets and to activating nonmilitary players. Threats of financial and economic disruptions, along with those of energy sources, should be activated in conjunction with the military component of coercion, such as special operation forces and strategic strike systems.[40] Threatening the adversary's assets with massive strikes of advanced nonnuclear PGMs, coupled with a host of activities by the sabotage-reconnaissance groups (*diversionno-razvedovatel'nye gruppy*), signals resolve and capability and communicates the scale of unacceptable political, economic, social, and technological damage that will be imposed on the adversary unless it changes its strategic behavior and avoids military engagement. According to Gerasimov, this intimidation by force (*ustrashenie siloi*), as a method of asymmetrical-indirect action, combines political isolation, economic sanctions, naval and aerial blockades, employment of internal opposition, military interventions under the pretext of the peacemaking and humanitarian missions, and activation of special operations in conjunction with the information (cyber) campaign.[41]

The current Russian "nonnuclear deterrence" modus operandi rests on relatively solid conceptual foundations. Several years before the current doctrine was promulgated, the General Staff's work on an indirect approach in modern warfare recommended incorporating "asymmetrical activities" (*assimetrichnye deistviia*) into Russian national security practice.[42] Back then, the General Staff's experts utilized the term "asymmetrical measures" in a manner that corresponds with the current definition of "nonnuclear deterrence," yet without referring to it in such way. To them, the sophistication of modern weaponry and the threat of military operations' catastrophic consequences force actors to employ the nonmilitary means of strategy. Although, in the past, the "strategy of brute force" dominated military affairs, and the "indirect approach" had a secondary role, the situation has now been reversed. By employing asymmetrical means, the "weak player" can inflict serious damage on the "stronger" one, and even impose its political will, without a traditional, decisive battlefield victory. Success in such a campaign is not a function of the correlation of forces but of a skillful orchestration of military and nonmilitary (political, psychological, ideological, and informational) means. Today, the ability to master an "indirect approach" manifests operational art par excellence, and its culmination is to employ a variety of means, primarily informational dominance, to neutralize the enemy without the use of force.

An "asymmetrical approach" employs "a complex of forms, means, and ways unequal [*netozhdestvenye*] to those of the adversary" that prevents military confrontation or mitigates its consequences. "Asymmetrical actions in the military field may include *measures causing apprehension of the adversary* with regards to intentions and responses of [the Russian Federation]; *demonstrating resolve and capabilities* of the [federation's] groups of forces to repulse the invasion with unacceptable consequences for the aggressor; military actions aimed to deter potential aggressor by assured destruction of the most vulnerable military and other strategically important and dangerous objects, that convince him that aggression is doomed to fail."[43] To deter and prevent aggression against the federation, the experts call for the employment of "asymmetrical measures, of a systemic and complex nature" that incorporate political, diplomatic, informational, economical, military, and other efforts.[44]

Deterring "unacceptable consequences," according to the General Staff experts, "can be a result of defensive (direct) actions, and a function of asymmetrical measures," compensating for the adversary's military superiority by "inflicting unacceptable damage in other spheres of national security."[45] "Combining defensive actions aimed at repulsing aggression and asymmetrical ones . . . creates important preconditions to compel (*prinuzhdenie*) the adversary to cease military activities on the conditions favorable for the Russian Federation. This approach becomes especially relevant since the European economy and infrastructure include a high number of vital objects," sensitive to unacceptable damage.[46] Keeping the competitors' territories under the threat of nonnuclear and nuclear strikes is considered by some Russian experts as the most effective way to generate a deterrence effect.[47]

The coercion mechanism is straightforward. An adversary's understanding that the result of his initiating of military activities cannot lead to victory or achievement of designated goals, but will result in ecological and social-political catastrophe, is an effective deterring factor. Thus, "possible aggression prevention and repulsion should combine direct (symmetrical) actions . . . with the realization of asymmetrical measures that essentially aim at inflicting unacceptable damage in other (nonmilitary) spheres of security."[48] This influencing of the adversary's calculus and behavior by threat, even if it involves the limited use of force, is a strategy of coercion (*sderzhivanie, prinuzhdenie, silovoe vozdeistvie*) par excellence. To ensure credibility of this coercion strategy in the NGW framework, "informational deterrence" enters at the center of the stage.

Informational Deterrence

Since ancient times, information has enabled the deception, surprise, and intimidation (deterrence) of the adversary; but, according to the General Staff's experts, this effect rarely went beyond the tactical realm. Today, however, under the sophistication of means of informational influence, the "indirect approach" and "informational struggle" may solve the campaign's strategic goals and significantly downgrade the adversary's determination to resist.[49] Consequently, informational struggle is perceived as one of the primary tools of nonnuclear deterrence. The idea of *strategic influence*, and not of massive brute force, became the essence of NGW and is the leitmotif of the campaign's planning. A host of ways and means on all fronts is employed to achieve this effect. The term "informational deterrence" (*informatsionnoe sderzhivanie*) is not mentioned in the doctrine but is widespread in the professional discourse. According to Russian experts, this type of coercion may, under the changing character of war, assure strategic stability and shape the adversary's strategic calculus both before and during the hostilities.[50]

In the Russian discourse, the term "informational deterrence" emerged initially to refer to US discourse on cyberdeterrence. Informational (cyber) struggle is perceived as one of the most cost-effective tools of nonnuclear coercion due to its ability to produce strategic effects without massive kinetic devastation. The appeal is in its ability to produce a host of significant strategic effects below the level of unacceptable damage, compatible with one that in the nuclear realm would invite nuclear retaliation.[51] As such, informational deterrence is a crisis management tool aimed at the adversary's leadership and population that can prevent military aggression without the direct employment of military force.[52] "Psychological intimidation" can credibly deter the aggressor for a long period, and in some cases even completely dissuade him from his aggression. Thus, informational deterrence can evaporate aggression and prevent the forceful stage of the conflict altogether.[53] Russian thinking about informational deterrence is genuinely cross-domain, as it aims to prevent not only informational (cyber) aggression but also behavior in other fields of activity, including kinetic conventional operations. Informational pressure (*informatsionnoe davlenie*) on the adversary, its armed forces, the state apparatus, citizens, and world public opinion is aimed at producing favorable conditions for strategic coercion. Exemplifying this point, Russian experts refer to the US informational campaign as preparing conditions for regime change across the Middle East during the Arab Spring.[54]

Informational deterrence incorporates digital-technological and cognitive-psychological forms of influence "through the threat of massive special influence on the informational resources of the potential adversary."[55] Distinct from and broader than its nuclear or conventional analogues, informational deterrence is a new form of strategic influence based on a complex of interrelated political, diplomatic, informational, economic, military, and other means of deterring, reducing, and preventing threats and aggression by the threat of unacceptable consequences. Preventive political-diplomatic activity, through effective informational struggle aimed at preventing and resolving conflict situations, becomes the primary tool of strategic deterrence. Ideally, effective strategic deterrence should enable the attainment of political goals without resorting to conventional military, let alone nuclear means, although their constant readiness and inclusion into the deterrence program are required.[56]

If nonmilitary actions of informational deterrence are deemed ineffective, the state should switch to employing means of "forceful deterrence" (*silovoe sderzhivanie*) aimed at assuring the potential aggressor that the costs of aggression will outweigh the expected benefits. To "insinuate" this to a potential aggressor, the Russian strategic community should "demonstrate readiness" to deploy groupings of forces in the expected area of aggression; "ultimately announce about an immediate use by the Russian side of its nuclear weapons, in case of threat to sovereignty and territorial integrity of the state"; "announce an unlimited use of PGMs to destroy" critical civilian nuclear-electronic, chemical, and hydroelectric energy infrastructure; and substitute and combine all the above "to employ a special informational operation to deceive the enemy with regards to Russian readiness to repulse aggression."[57]

Cross-Domain Coercion

The Western term *cross-domain coercion* is probably the best description of the Russian art of orchestrating *nonnuclear*, *informational*, and *nuclear* influence within a unified program. This art, not yet doctrinally outlined, has manifested itself during the recent standoff in Ukraine and seems rather straightforward. Informational struggle choreographs all threats and moves across conventional and nuclear, and military and nonmilitary, domains to produce the most optimal correlation of trends and forces. It is a coercion "master of ceremonies"; with nuclear manipulations, it constructs a cordon sanitaire that enables immune maneuvering space (*strategicheskii prostor*), a sphere of the possible, within which other forms of influence can achieve tangible results with or without the use of force. Ideally, the image of unacceptable consequences produced by this cross-domain coercion should paralyze Western assertiveness and responsiveness. Uninterrupted informational deterrence waged on all possible fronts against all possible audiences, augmented by nuclear signaling, and supplemented by the intrawar coercion constitutes an integrated cross-domain campaign. The main rationale for this enterprise is to de-escalate, or dissuade the adversary from aggression, and impose Russia's will with minimal violence.

CONCLUSION

Russian informational struggle that orchestrates a cross-domain coercion campaign is a unique military innovation. What are its ramifications for international security and strategic stability? What are the big and useful questions relevant to decision makers that arise from the exposition of the phenomenon under scrutiny? Several issues loom large.

First is the question of how this innovation applies to strategic stability. On one hand, this Russian tool of operational art expands the continuum of options on the escalation ladder while minimizing the scale of kinetic operations. As such, it seemingly contributes to strategic stability. Russia can promote its national security goals without escalating to a major war, mainly by shaping and manipulating the strategic behavior of its adversaries. From the international legal point of view, such a repertoire of coercive actions may fall short of constituting an act of war. In addition, if one actor escalates on the digital-technological dimension above a particular level of damage, the operational outcome, due to the interconnectivity of the global contemporary world, may have self-detrimental or fratricidal effects. Thus, concern with the cascading effects of damage may contribute to a higher level of self-deterrence.

On the other hand, because an informational campaign links together nuclear, conventional, and informational forms of coercion, it can result in inadvertent escalation and crisis instability. The risk of second-order consequences and inadvertent escalation looms large because at this stage Russian practitioners do not possess a method to assess battlefield damage emanating from an informational strike. Moreover, activation of the nongovernment and proxy actors for the sake of informational and cross-domain coercion empowers a large number of additional strategic actors and hampers strategic signaling and its interpretation. The second-order consequences for the large number of actors may result in misperceptions and miscommunication. In addition, this may stimulate cybernetic arms races, and, given the current state of international legislation in this field, it is difficult to imagine the establishment of effective verification procedures, as were designed in the nuclear realm. Finally, due to the emerging beliefs about the superiority of offense over defense in the cyber realm, coupled with short windows of decision making, actors may be predisposed toward authority predelegation and even automatic modes of reaction—some sort of "cyber doomsday machines." This would not only increase the chances for the outbreak of hostilities but also make escalation to the noninformational, kinetic forms of warfare more likely.

Second, what would be the nature of the disruptive innovation in the field of informational struggle? Informational struggle as part of cross-domain coercion is undoubtedly a unique military innovation. However, it appears to be more of an evolutionary than a revolutionary one because it reflects more continuity than change. Its main novelty is not in its essence but in the potential scale of its application and in its constant conceptual evolution and permanent sophistication. Surprise, if experienced by Western intelligence communities from the Russian art of cross-domain coercion driven by NGW (in Crimea, Ukraine, and recently in the Middle East) was most likely the result of a failure of imagination and a poverty of expertise and comprehension rather than Russian disruptive innovation indistinguishable in advance. It should be noted, however, that in all three cases Moscow demonstrated an aptitude for organizational and conceptual learning and improvisation that is rather unorthodox in post-Soviet Russian military practice.

Presumably, at least until recently, the Russian strategic community lacked a clear division of labor in the sphere of NGW in general, and within informational struggle in particular. It seems as if the lack of regulations does not constrain, but instead stimulates, Russian military theory development and operational creativity (*operativnoe tvorchestvo*) in the theaters of operations. Being in the midst of conceptual learning, and with multiple actors competing for resources and responsibilities, the Russian strategic community sees a manifestation of the coexistence of institutional incoherence and relative operational effectiveness. Although the military exercises of the last couple of years indeed have emphasized nonnuclear forms of warfare—and military reform since 2008 has focused on improving NGW; on command, control, communications, computers, intelligence, surveillance, and reconnaissance systems; and on electronic warfare capabilities—the impressive performance in Crimea was not based on exercises simulating Gerasimov's doctrine. They were more of an improvisation than a preplanned strategic-operational design along NGW lines. The Russian strategic community is in the midst of learning lessons, transforming its doctrine, and conceptualizing a new theory of victory. Warfare in Eastern Ukraine is just one of the cases from which Russian experts are learning lessons for the conceptualization of NGW, in keeping with Gerasimov's call in 2013 to explore new forms of struggle, to come up with military innovations, and to shape the armed forces accordingly.

Finally, how will state learning and the diffusion of knowledge affect strategic stability? The current Russian campaign in the Middle East offers the Russian defense establishment a subsequent laboratory for further refining the Russian art of strategy and informational struggle as part of cross-domain coercion. As the contours of the Russian campaign design in Syria are slowly emerging, one may assume that it may also draw from the NGW concept, at least in some aspects. Some of the features of the Russian operation seem to correspond to the characteristics outlined in this chapter. In terms of threat perception, Moscow perceived the situation in Syria as the result of a US effort, albeit one that failed to conduct HW against the incumbent regime along the lines of the Libyan scenario. Moscow's démarche, although driven by the interplay of several factors, was a countermeasure to such a perceived US effort but was shaped along similar operational lines.[58] Sophisticated orchestration of hard and soft power across military, diplomatic, and public domains has already been evident. Intensive informational measures and diplomatic campaigns were synchronized with the military buildup, which enabled the generation of tangible operational results through sophisticated reflexive control.[59]

As such, the campaign's design, at least at the initial stage, seems to reflect the NGW guideline of a 4:1 ratio of nonmilitary to military activities. Synchronized air strikes and informational strikes, ground operations, the use of PGMs, and long-range precision strikes are unprecedented for Russia, and they confirm the feasibility of conventional coercion outlined in this chapter. Also, this impressive demonstration of performance counterbalances the skepticism of Russian commentators, who have argued in recent years that prenuclear deterrence is not a feasible option for the Russian military, because it lacks sufficient IT-RMA era capabilities and thus cannot function as a reconnaissance-strike complex.

If the Russian campaign design continues to capitalize on indirect action, informational operations, paramilitaries, and special operation forces supported by the sophisticated Russian IT-RMA capabilities and by the military power of its allies, Moscow might minimize its visible presence—blurring, for domestic and international purposes, the line between its involvement and intervention. This does not mean, of course, that Russia will only take on operation design/management and air power responsibilities without sending operatives into the fray of ground warfare. Indeed, if the "polite people" of the Russian military, together with pro-Russian Chechen fighters and Donbass field commanders, start appearing on the Syrian battlefield, it should come as no surprise. Unlike in Donbass or Crimea, these fighters will have more issues with blending in. Given their experience and training, however, they can still act as a force multiplier. And if Russia deploys them while staying mindful of the reasonable sufficiency principle, it can hope to avoid a quagmire in Syria along the lines of the one in Donbass and achieve something closer to the effective campaign in Crimea.[60]

The Russian operation in Syria also corresponded to characteristics of cross-domain coercion, in terms of informational struggle and nuclear muscle-flexing.

Moscow operated the range of informational struggle capabilities for the purpose of a military-diplomatic antiaccess / area denial operation against adversarial activities. Establishing such an electromagnetic-cyber cordon sanitaire around the operational environment of the pro-Assad coalition can disrupt reconnaissance-strike unmanned aerial vehicles, PGMs, aerial operations, and political-diplomatic démarches. Also, dual-use platforms, both aerial and naval, appeared in the theater of operations and conducted limited conventional strikes. Although such conventional strikes produce limited battlefield effects, the actual operational outcome is less important. The main expected utility is an informational / public relations effect that enables Russian coercion signaling for regional and global purposes in the context of current or future tensions with the West. Such a standoff vis-à-vis the US and NATO is along the lines of the Russian cross-domain coercion that has been visible in European and Atlantic theaters during the last several years.

Because many actors follow Russian doctrine, the evolving Russian art of strategy may have second-order consequences for strategic stability. What lessons will China and Iran learn from recent Russian operations? Does Russia share its doctrinal knowledge or develop it in conjunction with China, Iran, or anyone else? On the Ukrainian battlefield, Russia fielded mid- and long-range ballistic and artillery capabilities, combined with high-end electronic warfare against the backdrop of a sophisticated digital-psychological informational struggle. It used high-power jamming to bring down unmanned aerial vehicles and to disrupt command-and-control communications and guided weapons systems. It also hampered NATO's training sessions in the Baltic Sea region. Capitalizing on this experience, Moscow can now offer to its clients and allies worldwide combat-proven, unique antiaccess / area denial capabilities and informational warfare lessons learned. Such products are likely to have high regional demand in the Middle East and in Asia. The Chinese People's Liberation Army is likely to learn lessons from emerging Russian military theory and practice on the subject. The first sales contract for advanced electronic warfare systems to the Middle East and North Africa was under negotiation in 2015. India recently expressed interest in Russian technical help in monitoring and struggling against the online and offline activities of the Islamic State of Iraq and Syria.[61] These are just minor indications that may suggest that Russian ideas and capabilities are likely to be diffused, as they resonate with central issues on the agendas of several strategic actors worldwide.

On a more theoretical and concluding note, this research concurs that "theories of victory," operational art, and coercion are social constructs and that their conceptualization is consequently not universal. Moreover, these concepts vary across strategic communities, have national characteristics, and may differ from Western strategic theory. As such, a one-size-fits-all, nontailored approach for examining operational art and the coercion styles of different actors may result in strategic blunders. Therefore, scholars should examine and measure the Russian modus operandi, especially in the fields of NGW and informational warfare, in a much more idiosyncratic manner. The ability to explore and understand the interplay between national security aspirations, strategic culture, and military tradition in the frame of the emerging version of Russian operational art is crucial for anyone seeking to engage Moscow on a host of geopolitical issues or seeking to enhance strategic stability, regionally and globally.

NOTES

1. The Russian notion of NGW is the closest equivalent of the Western concept of cross-domain deterrence. See Jon Lindsay and Erik Gartzke, "Cross-Domain Deterrence: Strategy in an Era of Complexity," paper presented at International Studies Association Annual Meeting, March 25, 2014, https://quote.ucsd.edu/deterrence/files/2014/12/EGLindsay_CDDOverview_20140715.pdf.

2. See, e.g., Janis Berzins, "Russian New Generation Warfare Is Not Hybrid Warfare," in *The War in Ukraine: Lessons for Europe*, ed. Artis Pabriks and Andis Kudors (Riga: University of Latvia Press, 2015), 43; and Roger McDermott, "Does Russian Hybrid Warfare Really Exist?" *Eurasia Daily Monitor* 12, no. 103 (June 3, 2015).

3. Berzins, "Russian New Generation Warfare," 40–52. See also McDermott, "Does Russian Hybrid Warfare Really Exist?"

4. See, e.g., Andrei Novikov, "Sovremennye transformatsii terrorisma," *Voennyi Diplomat* 1 (2007): 64–68; A. V. Serzhantov and A. P. Martofliak, "Analiz sovremennykh voennykh konfliktov," *Voennaya Mysl'* 5 (May 2011): 36–44; Igor' Popov, "Matritsa Voin Sovremennoi Epokhi," *Nezavisimoe Voennoe Obozrenie* 10 (March 22, 2013); Aleksandr Bartosh, "Gibridnye Voiny v Strategii SSha i NATO," *Nezavisimoe Voennoe Obozrenie* 36 (October 10, 2014); and Oleg Vladykin, "Voina Upravliaemogo Khaosa," *Nezavisimoe Voennoe Obozrenie* 38 (October 24, 2014).

5. Frank Hoffman and James Mattis, "Future War: The Rise of Hybrid Wars," *Proceedings* 13 (November 2005); Frank Hoffman, "Hybrid War and Its Challenges," *Joint Force Quarterly* 52 (January 2009); David Johnson, *Military Capabilities for Hybrid War: Insights from the Israeli Defense Forces in Lebanon and in Gaza* (Santa Monica, CA: RAND Corporation, 2010).

6. S. Chekinov and S. Bogdanov, "O Kharaktere i Soderzhanii Voiny Novogo Pokoleniia," *Voennaya Mysl'* 10 (2013): 15–16. See also V. Burenok, "Oblik Griadus-chikh i Novykh Sistem vooruzheniia operedelit' tol'ko nauka," *VPK* 10, no. 478 (March 2013).

7. Valerii Gerasimov, "'Tsennost' Nauki v Predvidinii," *VPK* 8, no. 476 (February 27, 2013). See also Nachialnik General'nogo Shtaba and Valerii Gerasimov, "O Sostoianii Vooruzhennykh Sil RF i Merakh po Povysheniiu ikh Boesposobnosti," *Konferentsiia Voennaia Bezopasnost' Rossii v 21 Veke*, December 5, 2013; Russian Military Doctrine, 2014; and Chekinov and Bogdanov, "O Kharaktere."

8. The choice of terminology, as well as direct reference at the end of the article, reflects an intellectual influence of Georgy Isserson's works.

9. Gerasimov, "'Tsennost' Nauki v Predvidinii."

10. In NGW, a special disinformation operation is a complex of interrelated moves conducted through diplomatic channels by the state and nonstate mass media, leaks from command-and-control organs, and deceiving statements by the senior political and military leadership.

11. Chekinov and Bogdanov, "O Kharaktere."

12. Ibid.

13. S. Chekinov and A. Bogdanov, "Assymetrichnye deistviia po obespecheniiu voennoi bezopasnosti Rossii," *Voennaya Mysl'* 3 (2010): 13–22.

14. G. Leer, *Metod voennykh nauk* (Moscow: SPB, 1894), 53–53; N. P. Michenic, *Strategiia* (Moscow: SPB, 1898), 203–4; V. Lobov, *Voennaia Khitrost'* (Moscow: Logos, 2001). See also I. Vorob'ev and V. Kiselev, "Strategiia nepriamykh desitvii v novom oblike," *Voennaya Mysl'* 9 (2006); and "Voennaia Khitrsot," in *Voenno-Entsiklope-dicheskii Slovar'* (Moscow: Voenizdat, 2007).

15. M. Gareev, "Voennaia nauka na sovremennom etape," *VPK* 13, no. 481 (April 2013).

16. S. K. Oznobishev, V. I. Potapov, and V. V. Skokov, *Kak Gotovilsia Asimetrichnyi Otvet na Strategicheskuiu Iadernuiu Initsiativu: Veikhov, Kokoshin i drugie* (Moscow: URSS, 2010); Andrei Kokoshin, "Asimetrichnyi Otvet," *SSha: Ekonomika, Politka Ideologiia* 2 (1987); Andrei Kokoshin, "Asimetrichnyi otvet na SOI kak primer strategich-eskogo planirovaniia v sfere natsional'noi bezopasnosti," *Mezhdunarodnaia Zhizn'* 2 (2007).

17. See Nathan Dubovitsky [Vladimir Surkov], "Bez Neba," *Russkii Pioner*, March 12, 2014.

18. For the most skillful synthesis and in-depth analysis of the force buildup and deployment principles in NGW, see Janis Berzins, *Russia's New Generation Warfare in Ukraine: Implications for Latvian Defense Policy* (Riga: Latvian Ministry of Defense, 2014); and Berzins, "Russian New Generation Warfare."

19. I. Gorbachev, "Kibervoina uzhe idet," *Nezavisimoe Voennoe Obozrenie* 13 (April 2013).

20. S. Modestov, "Strategicheskoe sderzhivanie na teatre informatsionnogo pro-tivoborstva," *Vestnik Akademii Voennykh Nauk* 1, no. 26 (2009).

21. V. Kariakin, "Khaosmiatezh—simvol nastupivshei epokhi," *Natsional'naia Oborona* 6 (2015); and Chekinov and Bogdanov, "O Kharaktere," 17–18.

22. For reflexive control, see M. D. Ionov, "O Refliksivnom Upravlenii Protivni-kom v Boiu," *Voennaya Mysl'* 1 (1995); Fedor Chausov, "Osnovy Refleksivnogo Upra-vleniia," *Morskoi Sbornik* 9 (1999); and N. I. Turko and S. A. Modestvov, "Refleksivnoe Upravelenie Razvitiem Strategicheskikh Sil Gosudarstva," in *Sistemnyi Analiz na Poroge 21 Veka* (Conference Proceedings, Moscow, 1996). See also S. Leonenko, "Refleksivnoe Upravlenie Protivnikom," *Armeiskii Sbornik* 8 (1995).

23. Chekinov and Bogdanov, "O Kharaktere."

24. See Vladimir Slipchenko, *Voiny Shestogo Pokoleniia* (Moscow: Olma Press, 2002); Vladimir Slipchenko, *Voiny Novogo Pokoleniia* (Moscow: Olma Press, 2004); I. N. Chibisov and V. A. Vodkin, "Informatsionno-udarnaia operatsiia," *Armeiskii sbornik* 3 (2011): 46–49; Vorob'ev and Kiselev, "Strategiia nepriamykh desitvii v novom oblike";

V. I. Kuznetsov, Y. Y. Donskov, and A. S. Korobeinikov, "O sootnoshenii kategorii 'radi-oelektronnaia borba' i 'informatsionnaia borba,'" *Voennaya Mysl'* 3 (2013): 14–20; V. A. Balybin, Y. Y. Donskov, and A. A. Boiko, "O terminologii v oblasti radioelektronnoi borby v usloviiakh sovremennogo informatsionnogo protivoborstvo," *Voennaya Mysl'* 9 (2013): 28–32; P. I. Antonovich, "O sushchnosti i soderzhanii kibervoiny," *Voennaya Mysl'* 7 (2011): 39–46; Y. I. Starodubtsev, V. V. Bukharin, and S. S. Semenov, "Tekhnos-fernaia voina," *Voennaya Mysl'* 7 (2012): 22–31; and Dima Adamsky, *The Culture of Military Innovation: The Impact of Cultural Factors on the Revolutions in Military Affairs in Russia, the US, and Israel* (Stanford, CA: Stanford University Press, 2010).

25. For the selected sources on this aspect of Russian operational art, see *Doktrina Informatsionnoi Bezopasnosti*; *Kontseptual'nue Vzgliady*; *Strategiia Natsionalnoi Bezopasnosti*; *Kontseptsiia Obshchestvennoi Bezopasnosti*; *Voennaia Doktrina*; Antonovich, "O sushchnosti i soderzhanii kibervoiny"; V. I. Kuznetsov, Y. Y. Donskov, and O. G. Nikitin, "K voprosu o roli i meste kiberprostranstva v sovremennykh boevykh deistviiakh," *Voennaya Mysl'* 3 (2014): 13–17; and S. G. Chekinov and S. A. Bogdanov, "Vliianie nepriamykh deistvii na kharakter sovremennoi voiny," *Voennaya Mysl'* 6 (2011): 3–13.

26. "Informatsionnoe protivobostvo," in *Voenno Entsiklopedicheskii Slovar'* (Mos-cow: Voenizdat, 2007); For doctrinal publications, see *Doktrina Informatsionnoi Bezo-pasnosti Rossiiskoi Federatsii* (2000), available at http://base.garant.ru/182535/; *Kontseptual'nue Vzgliady na Deiatel'nost' Rossiskikh VS v Informatsionnom Prostrans-tve* (2011); *Strategiia Natsionalnoi Bezopasnosti Rossiiskoi Federatsii do 2020 goda* (2009); *Kontseptsiia Obshchestvennoi Bezopasnosti Rossiiskoi Federatsii* (2013); and *Voennaia Doktrina Rossiskoi Federatsii* (2014). See also A. A. Strel'tsov, "Osnovnye zadachi gosudarstvennoi politiki v oblasti informatsionnogo protivoborstva," *Voennaya Mysl'* 5 (2011): 18–25; Kuznetsov, Donskov, and Korobeinikov, "O sootnoshenii kate-gorii"; V. A. Balybin, Y. Y. Donskov, and A. A. Boiko, "O terminologii v oblasti radioelek-tronnoi borby v usloviiakh sovremennogo informatsionnogo protivoborstvo," *Voennaya Mysl'* 9 (2013): 28–32; P. I. Antonovich, "O sushchnosti i soderzhanii kibervoiny"; and V. I. Kuznetsov, Y. Y. Donskov, and O. G. Nikitin, "K voprosu o roli i meste kiberpros-transtva v sovremennykh boevykh deistviiakh," *Voennaya Mysl'* 3 (2014): 13–17.

27. See K. I. Saifetdinov, "Informatsionnoe protivoborstvo v voennoi sfere," *Voennaya Mysl'* 7 (2014): 38–41; Chibisov and Vodkin, "Informatsionno-udarnaia operatsiia"; Strel'tsov, "Osnovnye zadachi gosudarstvennoi politiki"; "Sredstva Infor-matsionnoi bor'by (informatsionnoe oruzhie)," in *Voenno-Entsiklopedicheskii Slovar'* (Moscow: Voenizdat, 2007); I. N. Vorob'ev, "Informatsionno-udarnaia operatsiia," *Voennaya Mysl'* 6 (2007): 14–21; S. I. Bazylev, I. N. Dylevskii, S. A. Komov, and A. N. Petrunin, "Deiatelnost Vooruzhennykh Sil Rossiiskoi Federatsii v informatsionnom prostranstve: Printsipy, pravila, mery doveriia," *Voennaya Mysl'* 6 (2012): 25–28; Kuznetsov, Donskov, and Korobeinikov, "O sootnoshenii kategorii"; Antonovich, "O sushchnosti i soderzhanii kibervoiny"; Gerasimov, "'Tsennost' Nauki v Predvidinii"; V. I. Kuznetsov, Y. Y. Donskov, and O. G. Nikitin, "K voprosu o roli i meste kiberpros-transtva v sovremennykh boevykh deistviiakh," *Voennaya Mysl'*, no. 3 (2014): 13–17; Chekinov and Bogdanov, "Vliianie nepriamykh deistvii"; "Priroda i Soderzhanie voin novogo pokoleniia," *Voennaya Mysl'*, 2013; and A. A. Varfolomeev, "Kiberdiversiia i kiberterrorizm: Predely vozmozhnostei negosudarstvennykh subiektov na sovremen-nom etape," *Voennaya Mysl'*, no. 12 (2012): 3–11.

28. Itai Brun and Carmit Valensi, "The Other RMA," in *Contemporary Military Innovation*, ed. Dima Adamsky and Kjell Inge Bjerga (London: Routledge, 2012).

29. Dmitry "Dima" Adamsky, "Nuclear Incoherence: Deterrence Theory and Non-Strategic Nuclear Weapons in Russia," *Journal of Strategic Studies* 37, no. 1 (2014): 91–134.

30. V. M. Burenok and O. B. Achasov, "Neiadernoe sderzhivanie," *Voennaya Mysl'*, no. 12 (2007); V. V. Sukhorutchenko, A. B. Zelvin, and V. A. Sobolevskii, "Napravlenie issledovanii boevykh vozmozhnostei vysokotochnogo oruzhiia," *Voennaya Mysl'*, no. 8 (2009); R. G. Tagirov, Iu. A. Pecahtnov, and V. M. Burenok, "K voprosu ob opredelenii urovnei nepriemlimosti posledstvii," *Vestnik AVN*, no. 1 (2009); and A. G. Saveliev, *K Novoi Redaktsii Voennoi Doktriny* (Moscow: URSS, 2009), 182.

31. Viktor Litovkin, "Andrei Kokoshin," *Nezavisimoe Voennoe Obozrenie*, May 20, 2011; Viktor Litovkin, "Bomba spravliaet iubilei," *Nezavisimoe Voennoe Obozrenie*, November 26, 2010; Igor' Varfolomeev, "Iadernaia deviatka," *Krasnaia Zvezda*, May 25, 2011; and Viktor Ruchkin, "Balans interesov," *Krasnaia Zvezda*, December 28, 2010.

32. A. A. Kokoshin, *Obespechenie strategicheskoi stabilnosti* (Moscow: URSS, 2009), 183–86; and A. A. Kokoshin, *Iadernye konflikty v XXI veke* (Moscow: Media Press, 2003), 87–91.

33. V. V. Matvichiuk and A. L. Khriapin, "Sistema strategicheskogo sderzhivaniia," *Voennaya Mysl'*, no. 1 (2010); V. V. Matvichiuk and A. L. Khriapin, "Metodicheskii podkhod k otsenki effektinvosti," *Strategicheskaia Stabil'nsot'* 46, no. 1 (2009): 51–55; S. A. Bogdanov and V. N. Gorbunov, "O kharaktere vooruzhennoi bor'by," *Voennaya Mysl'*, no. 3 (2009); V. P. Grishin and S. V. Udaltsov, "Iadernoe sderzhivanie," *Vestnik AVN*, no. 1 (2008); V. V. Korobushin, "Nadezhnoe strategicheskoe iadernoe sderzhivanie," *Strategicheskaia Stabil'nost'* 46, no. 1 (2009): 14–18; A. A. Protasov and S. V. Kreidin, "Sistemy upravleniai voiskami," *Strategicheskaia Stabil'nost'* 46, no. 1 (2009): 23–26; Iu. D. Bukreev, "Puti povusheniia beospo-sobnosti sukhoputnykh voisk," *Strategicheskaia Stabil'nost'* 46, no. 1 (2009): 32–33; V. V. Korobushin, V. I. Kovalev, and G. N. Vinokurov, "Predelusokrascheniia SIaS Rossii," *Vestnik AVN* 28, no. 3 (2009); A. V. Muntianu and R. G. Tagirov, "Nekotorye problemnye voprosy v obespechenii voennoi bezopasnosti," *Strategicheskaia Stabil'nost'* 53, no. 4 (2010): 69; A. V. Muntianu and R. G. Tagirov, "O nekotorukh aspektakh vlianiia globalizatsii," *Strategicheskaia Stabil'nsot'* 54, no. 1 (2011): 25–28; Iu. A. Pechatnov, "Metod formirovaniia ratsionalnogo sostava grupirovki osnaschennoi vusokotochnum oruzhiem," *Strategicheskaia Stabil'nsot'* 53, no. 4 (2010): 58–64.

34. Russian Federation Military Doctrine, paragraphs 22 and 27, March 2010.

35. V. Matvichuk and A. Kriapin, "Sistema strategiccheskogo sderzhivaniia v novykh usloviiakh," *Voennaya Mysl'*, no. 1, 2010.

36. See, e.g., I. S. Ivanov, *Iadernoe Oruzhie I Strategicheskaia Stabil'nost'* (Moscow: RMSD, 2012).

37. This understanding also existed earlier. Generally, nuclear deterrence is defensive and can be employed only under a narrow range of scenarios (when the existence of Russia is under threat, according to the 2010 doctrine). I thank Nikolai Sokov for this comment.

38. Sergei Ermakov, "Iadernoe oruzhie vytesniat informatsionnye tekhnologii," *Pravda*, December 15, 2015.

39. "Strategicheskoe sderzhivanie" and "Demonstratsionnye deistviia," in *Voenno-Entsiklopedicheskii Slovar'* (Moscow: Voenizdat, 2007).

40. Leonid Ivashov, "Nado derzhat' Ameriku pod Pricelom," *Pravda Ru*, January 8, 2015.

41. Gerasimov, "'Tsennost' Nauki v Predvidinii."

42. Chekinov and Bogdanov, "Assymetrichnye deistviia," 20.

43. Ibid.

44. Ibid.

45. Ibid., 21.

46. Ibid., 22.

47. Ivashov, "Nado derzhat' Ameriku."

48. Chekinov and Bogdanov, "Assymetrichnye deistviia," 22.

49. Ibid., 3, 20.

50. A. Manoilo, "Upravlenie psikhologicheskoi voinoi v sisteme informacionnoi gosudarstvennoi politiki," *Politika i Obschestvo*, no. 2, 2004.

51. See, e.g., Pavel Sharikov, "V Boi Idut Kibervoiska," *Nezavisimoe Voennoe Obozrenie*, April 13, 2013; and "Informatsionnoe Sderzhivanie," *RSMD*, September 5, 2013.

52. Manoilo, "Upravlenie psikhologicheskoi voinoi."

53. A. Manoilo, "Kontseptsii politicheskogo regulirovaniia informatsionno-pshychologicheskoi voiny," *Mir i Politika*, May 12, 2012.

54. Chekinov and Bogdanov, "O Kharaktere," 19.

55. Modestov, "Strategicheskoe sderzhivanie."

56. M. Gareev, "Strategicheskoe sderzhivanie: Vazhneishee napravelnie natsional'noi bezopasnosti," *Stratgicheskaia Stabil'nost'*, no. 1, 2009.

57. Chekinov and Bogdanov, "Assymetrichnye deistviia," 23–24.

58. Dmitry Adamsky, "Putin's Damascus Steal: How Russia Got Ahead of the US in the Middle East," *Foreign Affairs*, September 2015.

59. Frederick Kagan and Kimberly Kagan, "Putin Ushers in a New Era of Global Geopolitics," *ISW Warning Intelligence Update*, September 27, 2015, 5.

60. Dmitry Adamsky, "Putin's Syria Strategy: Russian Airstrikes and What Comes Next," *Foreign Affairs*, October 2015.

61. Aman Shama, "India Wants Russia's Help to Corner Pakistan, ISIS Activity," *Economic Times*, September 14, 2015.

7

Conventional Challenges to Strategic Stability

Chinese Perceptions of Hypersonic Technology and the Security Dilemma

TONG ZHAO

TRADITIONALLY, within the Chinese strategic community, strategic stability constituted a comprehensive concept for describing the overall stability of a bilateral relationship that was affected by a wide range of factors—military, political, diplomatic, and economic.[1] In recent decades, the Western literature on nuclear weapons and deterrence issues has been introduced to and embraced by the Chinese strategic community. As a result, Chinese experts are increasingly using the term "strategic stability" to refer to a bilateral nuclear relationship of mutual vulnerability.[2] Maintaining such a mutually vulnerable relationship with other major nuclear powers, especially the United States, is of ultimate importance for Chinese decision makers. However, despite Beijing's efforts to enhance its nuclear retaliatory capability through modernization programs, it sees itself facing significant new challenges.

The emergence of advanced conventional weapons is widely recognized as one of the major challenges to strategic stability in the so-called second nuclear age. Such conventional weapons can travel at extremely high speeds and strike targets with extraordinary accuracy. Among all conventional military capabilities, hypersonic weapons present perhaps the greatest challenge. These types of weapons, which are currently under development in both the United States

174

and China, can potentially travel long distances at speeds of more than Mach 5, and they have a much greater capability to change flight trajectory than ballistic missiles. This emerging conventional military technology is potentially capable of disrupting mutually vulnerable relationships between nuclear powers by blurring the lines between conventional and nuclear warfare.[3]

The United States has the most advanced hypersonic technology development program, and it has expressed interest in deploying such weapons. According to the Obama administration's 2010 *Nuclear Posture Review Report*, for instance, conventional weapons are slated to play a more important role in the US deterrence posture.[4] Hence, the US investment in the development of hypersonic weapons is causing major Chinese concerns.

This chapter draws directly on the Chinese literature to answer these questions: What are China's specific concerns about hypersonic weapons? How do Chinese experts expect hypersonic technologies to alter future nuclear relationships and, therefore, affect traditional understandings of strategic stability? Also, what are the major mutual misunderstandings regarding each other's hypersonic technology development, and what are the implications for maintaining US-China strategic stability in the future?

THE CHINESE UNDERSTANDING OF THE DEFINITION AND SCOPE OF HYPERSONIC WEAPONS

The scholarly and policy communities in China have used different terms to refer to advanced conventional weapons similar to those being developed under the US Conventional Prompt Global Strike (CPGS) program. Such terms include, for instance, "hypersonic weapons" (高超音速武器), "global strike" weapons (全球打击武器), "prompt strike" weapons (快速打击武器), and "precision strike" or "precision-guided" weapons (精确打击武器/精确制导武器), among others. These terms are often used interchangeably by different experts without clear distinction. But a closer look reveals that different terms do sometimes tend to highlight different characteristics of weapons. For example, "hypersonic weapons" and "prompt strike" weapons highlight the high speed of such weapons; "global strike" weapons emphasize the capability of such weapons to strike long-range targets—usually in a very short time; and "precision strike" or "precision-guided" weapons underscore the high accuracy of such weapons.

This research compares the usage of these terms in documents contained in the China Knowledge Resource Integrated Database, the most inclusive collection of open source Chinese publications. It includes all major Chinese journals, newspapers, university theses and dissertations, conference papers, magazines, government reports, and more. When it comes to security studies, this database provides access to almost all openly published articles written by Chinese civilian scholars, military experts, and scientists in the defense industry. These articles provide a representative view of the Chinese strategic community on issues such as nuclear weapons, deterrence, CPGS, and missile defense.

Figure 7.1 provides a yearly breakdown of publications between 1975 and 2015, and table 7.1 lists the number of such publications during this period.[5] It appears that Chinese experts have used the term "precision strike" (or "precision-guided" and "precision guidance") much more frequently than other terms. However, a deeper look at these publications reveals that even though Chinese experts do sometimes use this term to refer to CPGS-type weapons, the term is more frequently used to refer to much less capable weapons that have been broadly defined as "precision" weapons. These include precision-guided artillery shells, subsonic cruise missiles, and guided gravity bombs—systems that bear no resemblance to the cutting-edge CPGS technology. Instead, "hypersonic weapon" (or "hypersonic technology") is the most frequently used term for CPGS-type weapons. This research, therefore, focuses on the "hypersonic weapon" (or "hypersonic technology") literature, and conducts an in-depth content analysis of such publications.

Figure 7.1 also reveals that the Chinese level of interest in hypersonic weapons corresponds largely with the United States' discussion of and investment in its CPGS program. The level of interest among Chinese authors picked up significantly after 2003, when the George W. Bush administration instructed the US Strategic Command to draft plans for carrying out "global prompt strike" operations.[6] The continued growth in the number of articles since that period underscores the fact that this issue is of increasing importance to the Chinese strategic community.

There is a consensus among Chinese experts that "hypersonic" means a speed at or higher than five times the speed of sound (Mach 5).[7] Some Chinese experts split hypersonic weapons into two categories: hypersonic vehicles and so-called high-speed kinetic-energy weapons.[8] Hypersonic vehicles include boost-glide weapons, hypersonic cruise missiles, and unmanned spacecraft like the X-37B. The term "high-speed kinetic-energy weapon" refers to systems such as the railgun, which can accelerate an armature to a muzzle speed of over Mach 5, and uses this high kinetic energy to destroy targets directly. Because hypersonic vehicles receive the most attention from Chinese experts, this research focuses the discussion solely on these systems.

Figure 7.1 Yearly Publication for Different Search Terms, 1975–2015

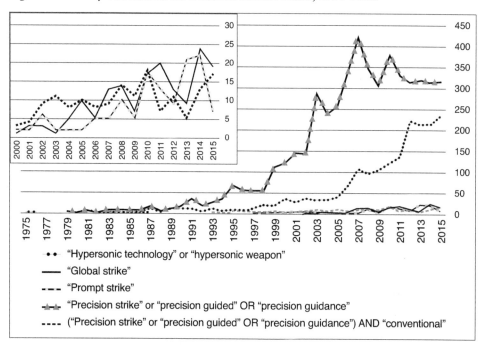

- •• "Hypersonic technology" or "hypersonic weapon"
- — "Global strike"
- --- "Prompt strike"
- ▲▲ "Precision strike" or "precision guided" OR "precision guidance"
- ---- ("Precision strike" or "precision guided" OR "precision guidance") AND "conventional"

Note: The 2015 figure is an estimation for the entire year based on data from the first seven months.
Source: "China Knowledge Resource Integrated Database," China Academic Journal (CD) Electronic Journals Publishing House, http://oversea.cnki.net/kns55/support/en/about_cnki .aspx.

Table 7.1 Number of Publications for Different Search Terms, 1949–2015

Search Term (search by keyword in title)	Number of Publications
"Hypersonic technology" or "hypersonic weapon" (高超音速武器 OR 高超音速技术)	1,805
"Global strike" (全球打击)	158
"Prompt strike" (快速打击)	137
"Precision strike" or "precision guided" or "precision guidance" (精确打击 or 精确制导)	4,977
("Precision strike" or "precision guided" or "precision guidance") and "conventional" ([精确打击 or 精确制导] and 常规)	192

Source: "China Knowledge Resource Integrated Database," China Academic Journal (CD) Electronic Journals Publishing House, http://oversea.cnki.net/kns55/support/en/about_cnki.aspx.

CHINESE UNDERSTANDING OF THE ADVANTAGES
OF HYPERSONIC WEAPONS

Why have hypersonic weapons received so much attention from the Chinese strategic community in recent years? This section explains that the discussions of Chinese experts have mostly focused on three key technical characteristics of such weapons.

Penetrating Capability

The ability to penetrate defensive systems is considered the most important feature of hypersonic weapons. The vast majority of Chinese experts maintain that hypersonic weapons cannot be defended against. This is based on several arguments. First, hypersonic weapons are difficult to track. Although some Chinese experts state that hypersonic weapons are very difficult to detect because of their high speed and capability to carry electronic countermeasure equipment, most argue that the detection of such weapons will not be a problem and recognize that hypersonic weapons are short on stealthiness.[9] Instead, it is the weapons' in-flight maneuverability that raises problems for tracking. For instance, one Chinese expert explains that all current missile and air defense systems, including those possessed by the United States and Russia, "would appear powerless when facing hypersonic weapons, because all these defensive systems are designed for targets that have predictable flight trajectories, whereas the advantage of a hypersonic weapon is its high speed, high altitude, and high maneuverability of flight trajectory."[10] Such difficulty with predicting the trajectory and landing point of a hypersonic weapon "means the inability to obtain accurate data (for interception)." As a result, hypersonic weapons would "have a very high rate of penetration against ballistic missile defense systems."[11]

The second argument is that it is difficult to respond quickly to a hypersonic weapon attack. Experts in the Chinese defense industry write that, as a country with limited early warning capability, China has only about 3 minutes' warning time before a hypersonic weapon traveling at Mach 10 and at an altitude of 20 kilometers would be able to strike a target in its territory. If the hypersonic weapon travels at Mach 6 and at an altitude of 100 kilometers, Chinese officials would still have only 11 minutes to act.[12] Such short warning times will not be sufficient for a defensive system to process relevant information and prepare an appropriate response upon receiving an interception order.[13]

Third, hypersonic weapons are difficult to intercept. The majority of Chinese scholars believe that hypersonic technology is capable of effectively penetrating "terminal phase missile defense systems."[14] The combination of the weapon's high speed and high maneuverability is perceived to give it a great advantage over terminal phase interceptors.[15] Chinese experts claim that even future missile defense technologies like laser interceptors will not be able to destroy hypersonic weapons. The outer casing of hypersonic weapons needs to endure the high temperature and high pressure as a result of its high traveling speed, and thus must be made very firm and strong. It therefore "won't be burned out even if it is shot at by a high-power laser beam."[16]

For these three reasons, the vast majority of Chinese experts conclude that hypersonic weapons "are the demolisher of antimissile systems."[17] However, some Chinese experts are not convinced that hypersonic weapons cannot be defended against. In their view, hypersonic weapons will be easy to detect and destroy for several reasons. For instance, in order to achieve high cruise speed and long travel range, hypersonic cruise missiles usually fly at higher altitudes than ordinary cruise missiles. Such high altitudes make them easier to detect through early warning radar and airborne early warning aircraft. According to Wang Jixin, of the People's Liberation Army Academy of Equipment Command and Technology, even a ground-based X-band radar installation could detect an X-51 type of hypersonic cruise missile flying at an altitude of 40 kilometers for a distance of 800 kilometers, which would allow enough time for land-based interceptors to respond.[18] In addition, hypersonic weapons will possess significant radar and infrared signal characteristics. The radar cross-section for weapons traveling at Mach 2–3 is more than ten times larger than that of subsonic weapons, and its infrared signal strength could be twenty to fifty times greater than subsonic weapons, in the wavelength range of 3–5 microns.[19] Together, these facts suggest to some Chinese experts that hypersonic weapons will be easily detectable and thus potentially vulnerable to existing defense systems (after upgrade).

Wang also doubts how maneuverable hypersonic weapons can be in reality. When an aircraft swerves, the turning radius is proportional to the square of its speed. Therefore, because hypersonic weapons travel at extremely high speeds, their normal acceleration overload would be very high as well. This high normal acceleration overload would not only increase aerodynamic drag but also require the weapon to have a particularly strong mechanical structure. It appears, then, that the weapon's defining feature—its high speed—could also undermine its maneuverability vis-à-vis interceptors.[20] Tang Zhicheng, a professor and senior colonel with the Second Artillery Command College, also claims that "the conclusion that hypersonic weapons cannot be intercepted is based on a set of specific assumptions."[21] In his view, the greatest significance of hypersonic weapons is that they can effectively penetrate terminal phase antimissile systems—and nothing more. They are almost equally vulnerable during the boost phase and midcourse of their flight.

These experts believe that weapons manufacturers can further develop existing ballistic missile defense systems capable of defending against hypersonic weapons. Here they use some existing US missile defense systems as examples. They point out that the speed of the interceptor, the lower limit of interception altitude, and the interception range can be reasonably extended for existing antimissile systems, such as the Terminal High Altitude Area Defense and SM-3 to make them capable of dealing with hypersonic weapons.[22]

Despite the fact that SM-3 is not a terminal phase missile defense system, many Chinese experts indicate that hypersonic weapons are less vulnerable to terminal phase missile defense systems than to other missile defense systems. This is different from the assessment of some experts in the United States, who point out that "point defense" rather than "area defense" is more likely to be achieved against CPGS weapons, where terminal phase missile defense is generally regarded as a "point defense" system.[23] It is necessary to note that the Chinese assessment is provided in very general terms and that the practical effectiveness of any defensive system is influenced very much by specific technical factors, such as the capability of the tracking radar, the relative maneuverability of the striking vehicle vis-à-vis the interceptor, and the speed of the striking vehicle during the terminal phase.[24] Chinese and Western analysts seem to have different assumptions about these technical factors, which may speak to the gap between respective Chinese and Western assessments.

Standoff Capability and Crisis Signaling

Chinese experts also consider hypersonic weapons' capability to launch strikes far away from the target country's territory as a critical defining feature. The Hypersonic Technology Vehicle 2 is planned to have a strike range of about 17,000 kilometers, which could reach China if launched from the continental United States.[25] Even shorter-range systems like the Advanced Hypersonic Weapon, which has a planned range of about 8,000 kilometers and a tested range of over 3,800 kilometers, can reach targets deep in China when launched from Guam.[26] These standoff capabilities have important implications for China because the United States would no longer need to use vulnerable military platforms such as bombers to put China's nuclear and strategic targets at risk. Several American scholars have noted that bombers could play an important role in conducting counterforce strikes against Chinese nuclear forces.[27] But they will no longer be needed after hypersonic weapons become operational.

According to Chinese experts, "The emergence of hypersonic weapons has completely removed the boundary between the frontline and the rear area."[28] Under these new conditions, "national leaders, strategic command-and-control centers, nuclear weapons bases, aerospace launch facilities, and critical economic infrastructures" will be on the target list of an enemy first strike by hypersonic weapons. The consequences of this will not only alter military balances but also have a psychological impact on decision makers during a crisis: "These targets will become extremely vulnerable," and this will "dramatically increase the psychological pressure of the national leadership, which will for sure affect decision making and will bring about significant change to the way war will be fought and won."[29] The long-range standoff capability of American hypersonic weapons will make the United States less dependent on forward deployment of shorter-range weapons. This will, as some Chinese experts argue, give the United States the "freedom of maneuver in the global commons" and "extricate the United States from its dependence on use of foreign military bases and foreign territorial land, air, and sea."[30]

In a crisis scenario, some characteristics of hypersonic weapons are seen as potentially useful for signaling purposes. Scholars at the Air Force Engineering University suggest that some hypersonic weapons have a significant part of their flight trajectories in near space, which is not part of any country's territory. As a result, during a crisis, a country could feasibly launch a test flight of such weapons that can travel above an enemy's territory without violating international laws. As they suggest, this can send a very strong signal and may cause maximum deterrence impact in the mind of the enemy.[31]

However, it might be necessary to note that this is not unique to hypersonic weapons. One can also use a ballistic missile to shoot over another country's territory. Most of the trajectory of a long-range ballistic missile would be in outer space, and therefore in theory it would not violate that country's sovereignty. But the psychological impact of such a signaling activity could be too strong to make consequence management possible. For example, the 1998 North Korean testing launch of its Taepodong missile, which flew over Japan and landed in the Pacific Ocean (which was not intended as a signal to Japan), has made Japan so concerned that it dramatically ramped up its missile defense capability and has been prepared to intercept subsequent North Korean missile tests that might again fly over or close to Japan.[32]

Furthermore, hypersonic weapons are fundamentally different from ballistic missiles because their trajectories can change during flight and therefore are much less predictable. This makes hypersonic weapons a very problematic instrument for signaling purposes. Because the enemy itself, by simply monitoring the flight, may not be able to discern whether it is the intended target of a hypersonic weapon, it may be inclined to act according to the worst-case scenario and assume that it is under attack. Therefore, an intended signaling activity could easily end up inadvertently provoking a military conflict. The danger would be even greater if the enemy possesses nuclear weapons and cannot distinguish a conventionally armed hypersonic weapon from a nuclear-armed one. A state may think that it is under nuclear attack and therefore decide to release its own nuclear weapons as retaliation. For such reasons, hypersonic weapons can cause crisis instability in ways that have not been carefully examined. The proposition that they may be used for crisis signaling purposes needs to be thoroughly examined and debated.

"Niche" Capability versus Massive Deployment

Some Chinese writers believe that hypersonic weapons are more cost-effective than other, alternative conventional strategic strike systems. For instance, conventional hypersonic weapons are seen as less expensive than conventional long-range ballistic missiles, which are too expensive to be built and used in large numbers. Short-range conventional tactical missiles are more affordable than long-range conventional ballistic missiles, but such weapons need forward bases to be deployed that raise their overall cost. In comparison, conventional hypersonic weapons are perceived to be as affordable as ordinary conventional cruise missiles but at the same time as swift and responsive as long-range ballistic missiles.[33] One technical reason these Chinese authors mention the relative low cost is that the scramjet engine used in a hypersonic cruise missile has a less complex structure than a traditional jet engine and thus costs less to manufacture.[34] In addition to boost-gliders and hypersonic cruise missiles, unmanned spacecraft like the X-37 are seen as a very cost-effective technology for conducting rapid-response military operations in space because the spacecraft can be used repeatedly.[35] Therefore, as the military analyst Gao Feng points out, the overall cost of hypersonic weapons is sufficiently low for them to "become the inevitable choice of military powers."[36]

This Chinese assessment—that hypersonic weapons are cost-effective—contradicts the mainstream US assessment. American experts believe that CPGS would be so expensive that it could be deployed only in very small numbers and become only a "niche capability."[37] As James Acton points out, the US assessment of hypersonic weapons has yet to include critical "enabling capabilities" that are necessary for the deployment of such weapons but may significantly increase their overall cost.[38] This appears to be true for Chinese assessments as well. Public discussions in China about hypersonic weapons have not looked extensively at necessary "enabling capabilities" for deploying hypersonic weapons. Their cost assessment does not seem to include such an expenditure either. That said, regardless of how inclusive the respective cost assessment may be in the two countries, the gap between current Chinese and US assessments about the relative cost of hypersonic weapons—which affects how many weapons can be procured and deployed—may undermine Chinese confidence in the often-heard US statement that as a "niche" capability, the American CPGS program will not be able to threaten China's small nuclear arsenal.

THE CHINESE UNDERSTANDING OF GENERAL IMPACT OF HYPERSONIC WEAPONS

Chinese experts seem to have a very pessimistic view of how hypersonic weapons will likely affect the existing strategic stability among major powers. In particular, they believe that such weapons will become a new type of strategic weapon, with the potential to break the existing nuclear/conventional boundary. They also generally agree that a new arms race over such weapons will soon begin.

Creating New Strategic Weapons and Breaking the Nuclear/ Conventional Boundary

Given the perceived advantages of hypersonic technology, many Chinese experts believe the implications of using such technology for military purposes would be far-reaching. A *PLA Daily* article points out that if hypersonic technology is applied to existing missiles and airplanes, the operational effectiveness of such weapons "will achieve a qualitative leap."[39] As a result, "a large number of new strategic weapons will emerge"; these weapons will not be matched by any existing weapon systems, because they "will keep the advantages of ballistic missiles in terms of range and responsiveness, but will also possess the strength of cruise missiles when it comes to high accuracy and low cost."[40] In this regard, Chinese analysts have taken particular note of reported Russian efforts to arm new liquid-fueled heavy intercontinental ballistic missiles with conventional warheads, which would thus render them a new type of "strategic conventional intercontinental ballistic missile."[41]

With these new strategic weapons, China worries that the United States might be tempted to use conventional hypersonic weapons to preemptively strike China's nuclear forces.[42] Even if the nuclear weapons and the delivery vehicles themselves can be protected from such a conventional strike, the command-and-control system might be vulnerable to a conventional strike.[43]

American scholars such as Fiona Cunningham and M. Taylor Fravel believe that China is deliberately making its no-first-use (NFU) policy a little ambiguous, especially when it comes to the issue of whether China will launch a nuclear retaliation after a conventional counterforce strike against its nuclear forces, in order to deter such a conventional strike. They argue that this ambiguity in NFU commitment could instead increase the chances of the nuclear/conventional firewall being broken inadvertently.[44] Senior Chinese military experts also point out that the increasing conventional threat to Chinese nuclear deterrence is driving debate in the national media (including social media) about the wisdom of unconditional NFU.[45]

In addition to the concern that the United States may use conventionally armed hypersonic weapons to strike China's nuclear weapons, some Chinese experts also worry that the line between nuclear and conventional wars may be crossed in other ways. For instance, Hu Wenlong, of the Academy of Military Sciences, writes that at the current level of technology development, the best way to defend against a conventional hypersonic strike "has to be using nuclear-armed air and missile defense systems," especially "the enormous shock wave generated by the air explosion of nuclear warhead to destroy the high-speed hypersonic vehicle."[46] He believes that this is the "only effective way to conduct interception." As a result, this will "for sure greatly increase the chances of nuclear weapons being used, will lower the nuclear threshold, and will further increase the interconnectivity between conventional and nuclear wars."[47]

Precipitating a New Arms Race

Chinese experts are concerned that the development of hypersonic weapons will have a direct impact on existing nuclear arms control arrangements. For instance, they worry that the United States' development of CPGS weapons may motivate Russia to develop its own conventional long-range strike capabilities and, therefore, abrogate the Intermediate-Range Nuclear Forces (INF) Treaty that imposes constraints on US and Russian conventional missile development.[48] After the abrogation of the Anti–Ballistic Missile Treaty and the stalling of the US-Russian bilateral nuclear disarmament process, the breakup of the INF Treaty will deal a major blow to the already weakened nuclear arms control regime.[49]

Another concern is that the nature of hypersonic weapons will render an arms race inevitable. Although nuclear weapons are instruments for deterrence rather than war fighting, hypersonic weapons—according to Chinese analysts—will mainly carry conventional warheads and will more likely become war-fighting weapons on the battlefield rather than weapons for deterrence.[50] Because hypersonic weapons are particularly useful for war fighting and "can effectively strike high-value targets, achieve 'decisive killing in one shot,' and are essential for determining the outcome of war," Chinese experts express a strong concern over the potential for unleashing a hypersonic weapons arms race.[51]

Thus far, no country has a clear advantage in their hypersonic weapons program. The United States remains the leader in technology development, but it has encountered major setbacks. Likewise, it has been far from smooth sailing for Russia and China.[52] Still, precisely because there is still considerable uncertainty surrounding the outcome of this competition, all major players will continue to do their best to gain an upper hand in the future. Everyone recognizes that "hypersonic weapons provide an important capability that is sufficient to change international strategic structure"; as a result, the existing uncertainty about the outcome of future competition over hypersonic technology leaves each state hoping that it can potentially tip the balance of power to its own favor by investing more in technology development. This, in turn, makes the incentive for participating in this competition even stronger.[53]

The fact that some hypersonic weapons will be deployed in outer space or travel through space or near space has also convinced some Chinese experts that the hypersonic competition will make a space arms race even more likely. According to these experts, because "the operational domains" of hypersonic weapons "are extended to the entire globe and the outer space," their advent may mean that "'Star Wars' will no longer be illusory."[54]

CHINESE PERCEPTIONS OF CHINA'S MOTIVATION IN DEVELOPING HYPERSONIC WEAPONS

Many Chinese experts call for China to invest major resources to develop its own hypersonic weapons. In doing so, they do not see China as initiating a new arms competition. Instead, they believe that hypersonic technologies represent a revolution in military affairs and that China must respond.

A New Revolution in Military Affairs

China's nuclear weapon technology development policies have historically been very much influenced by a desire to follow in the steps of other major military superpowers. China's decision to develop nuclear ballistic missile submarines, multiple independently targetable reentry vehicles, neutron bombs, and most recently an early warning system are all examples of a policy of "not falling behind" on major military technology development. The main purpose of this policy is to avoid a so-called technological surprise.[55] When it comes to the development of hypersonic technology, China's thinking seems to have been somewhat influenced by the same logic. One Chinese analyst stated that "the United States cannot monopolize the development of hypersonic vehicles; Europeans are also developing; so are the Russians and Japanese. Therefore, China has no reason not to do so too."[56]

That hypersonic technology is of great importance is now a consensus view among Chinese experts. Li Qingyuan and Shi Junhong of the China Academy of Launch Vehicle Technology state that "hypersonic technology is becoming the focus of aerospace and aeronautics research [in the world]."[57] Experts at the Third Academy of China Aerospace Science and Industry Corporation conclude that the hypersonic vehicle is going to change the patterns and concepts of future warfare.[58] Many Chinese experts, including technical and policy experts, have repeatedly referred to hypersonic technology as the "Third Technology Revolution" in aviation and aerospace history, stating that the weapon's high speed and long range are "bound to have a far-reaching impact on future warfare and [lead to a] military revolution."[59]

Believing that the United States seeks to broaden its military's technological gap with China, especially on strategic military technologies such as CPGS, a minority of Chinese experts openly call for an outright "military competition" with the United States in this field. They acknowledge that China should avoid an "arms race," but such experts see a "military competition" as a common practice between major powers—guided by a rational and sustainable strategy of resource consumption—and as much less harmful than an "arms race." These experts believe that China should not shy away from competing for military technology superiority (with the United States) if China's strategic security interests demand it.[60]

Addressing Imminent Security Challenges

The majority of Chinese experts, however, do not see winning a technology competition with the United States in the long run as the primary need for China to master hypersonic technology. Instead, most experts argue that the most important reason to prioritize hypersonic technology development is the necessity to counter specific security threats from increasingly sophisticated US military technologies, including CPGS.

This logic undergirds several different arguments that Chinese experts have presented in the literature. One such argument is that China needs to research and develop hypersonic technology simply to understand the technology and then find ways to counter US hypersonic weapons. Tang Huaiyu and Liu Jie of the People's Liberation Army Academy of Equipment Command and Technology cite the US Air Force's plan to build hypersonic strike weapons that can operate freely against the presence of enemy antiaccess / area denial (A2/AD) capabilities by 2030. They argue that China's A2/AD capability is "facing the threat from hypersonic weapons, so we have to master the same technology in order to develop necessary countermeasures."[61] Developing the same technology is the most direct way to regain the preexisting military balance: "The most critical issue is to break the US absolute superiority (on hypersonic weapons) and to protect one's own security through striving for a strategic balance."[62]

Other Chinese experts tie the need to develop hypersonic technology to specific US weapons programs. One very important argument is that hypersonic technology is a potential solution to address the threat of US ballistic missile defense on China's nuclear deterrence. The majority of Chinese experts believe that "hypersonic vehicles have a very high penetration probability against ballistic missile defense systems."[63] They argue that "if a country can develop a weapon that can effectively break the US ballistic missile defense systems, the difficult security problem will be nonexistent. This is the greatest value of hypersonic vehicles."[64] Some even claim that because hypersonic weapons can penetrate ballistic missile defense systems, "the shock it will bring to the world is going to be no less than that of nuclear weapons."

Specifically, some see hypersonic cruise missiles as the best way to improve China's nuclear deterrence against US missile defense capabilities. They argue that, unlike ballistic missiles, hypersonic cruise missiles do not need complex mission planning and can launch quickly after operators receive target information and a launch order. Furthermore, according to some Chinese experts, hypersonic cruise missiles fly at an altitude of approximately 25 kilometers, which is beyond the reach of most enemy air defense capabilities. The missiles' high maneuverability allows them to defeat most ballistic missile defense systems, such as PAC-3 and SM-3. Moreover, because current Chinese nuclear warhead delivery relies primarily on vulnerable ballistic missile systems, which are "facing serious threats" from antimissile technology, some Chinese experts assert that mounting nuclear warheads on hypersonic missiles would "greatly enhance our capability to deal with the enemy's missile defense threat."

Chinese experts are keen to note that China is not the only country interested in the potential of hypersonic weapons to counter rivals' antimissile systems. They believe that Russia's efforts to develop hypersonic weapons are also aimed at "breaking America's 'global antimissile system'" and that Russia is "striving to achieve a breakthrough of key (hypersonic) technology in order to complete the weaponization of such (hypersonic) technology."[65] Retired major general Xu Guangyu also points out that hypersonic weapons "make interception more difficult," which is why the United States, Russia, and India are all investing in their development.[66] For this reason, Chinese experts believe that their own development of hypersonic technology is necessary to correct the trend of a growing imbalance between the US and China, and therefore should contribute to a more stable bilateral nuclear relationship and international order.[67]

CHINESE PERCEPTIONS OF US MOTIVATIONS AND THE CAPABILITIES OF ITS HYPERSONIC WEAPONS PROGRAM

Some Chinese experts take note of the fact that the US investment in the CPGS program in recent decades was originally driven by a perceived need to strike high-value terrorist targets in a timely manner.[68] But unlike one well-known Western analysis, most Chinese experts tend not to see the US hypersonic development program as primarily technology-driven.[69] Rather, many Chinese experts make it very clear that they believe the United States has been motivated to obtain the capability to launch a preemptive conventional strike to destroy an enemy's strategic military assets.[70] Some believe that an enemy's nuclear forces are included in the intended targets of an American conventional hypersonic strike. One Chinese analyst articulates this view particularly clearly: "The US objective is, once it is in a conflict with an enemy country, it can use hypersonic weapons to wipe out the other's nuclear forces or chemical and biological weapons. Then the United States can send out airplanes to conduct preemptive air strikes. This strategy will ensure the United States' absolute strategic advantage."[71]

The literature suggests that this is a shared concern among Chinese experts. Said experts do diverge in their analyses of how far the United States will go for using its CPGS capabilities in counternuclear missions. For instance, some seem to believe that the United States' CPGS systems will play only a supplementary role to its existing nuclear strike capabilities, while others believe that American strategies are planning to create a new category of "conventional strategic weapons" that can gradually replace nuclear weapons because they can be used more easily and flexibly without causing tremendous civilian collateral damage. Li Qingyuan and Shi Junhong of the China Academy of Launch Vehicle Technology assert that "the reason why the United States had no difficulty in signing the New START (Strategic Arms Reduction Treaty) on April 8, 2010, is that the United States has established new types of conventional strategic strike capabilities in military domains where other countries have achieved no advantage, such as in outer space." "The United States," as they claim, "is in a transition from nuclear strategic strike capability to conventional strategic strike capability."[72]

There also are Chinese experts who see the United States' CPGS system as primarily aimed at striking nonnuclear strategic targets. The main US objective, they believe, is to address "the limits of existing nonnuclear strike capabilities" and to "effectively meet the needs of promptly striking time-sensitive high-value targets."[73] As a result, the United States can spare nuclear weapons from responding to some nonnuclear contingency scenarios.[74]

At the substrategic level, Chinese experts recognize that the United States' CPGS system will be used to counter China's so-called A2/AD capability. They point to US Department of Defense publications and US think tank reports that have explicitly pointed out that in potential conflicts and wars between the United States and regional powers, CPGS weapons are important instruments for countering A2/AD because of their high speed and high penetration capabilities.[75] Besides, Chinese experts perceive that the United States' planned CPGS system is a particular threat to China's A2/AD capability because CPGS weapons' long-range standoff capability makes them less dependent on forward deployment on overseas military bases for conducting strikes and thus renders them less vulnerable.[76]

At the Track II level bilateral dialogues, even though US officials and experts have tried to dismiss the Chinese claim that the United States seeks to obtain so-called absolute security, the US development of the CPGS program has only reinforced the Chinese conviction that the United States is often seeking its security at the expense of other countries' security.[77] Chinese analysts argue that hypersonic weapons make the United States capable of conducting accurate long-range standoff strikes, which minimizes the risk of US troops and pilots while also reducing the political and diplomatic cost of flying military aircraft over noninvolved countries en route to their intended target. In the final analysis, Chinese analysts maintain that the US military, despite its sizable technological advantage over potential adversaries, still strives to "further broaden the gap with other countries by seeking to establish strong technological superiority in hypersonic vehicles."[78] As argued by Chinese analysts, all this points to "the US pursuit of absolute superiority and absolute security."[79] As a result, they worry that "other countries which are put into insecurity as a result" will "for sure take measures to protect their own security. These countermeasures will certainly introduce new uncertainties into the international security situation."[80] The end result, as they imply, might be the intensification of a security dilemma that does not serve anyone's interests.

In summary, table 7.2 compares the United States' openly expressed motivations for developing hypersonic weapons and the Chinese perception of whether

Table 7.2 Chinese Perceptions of US Stated Motivations

US Perceptions of US Motivations	Chinese View of US Stated Motivations
Counterterrorism	Not an important motivation
Preemptive counternuclear	An important motivation
Retaliatory counternuclear	Little or no discussion
Preemptive counter-anti-satellite	Little or no discussion
Retaliatory counter-anti-satellite	Little or no discussion
Defense suppression	An important motivation

Source: James M. Acton, *Silver Bullet? Asking the Right Questions about Conventional Prompt Global Strike* (Washington, DC: Carnegie Endowment for International Peace, 2013).

these are real US motivations. Because the US government has yet to provide any authoritative statement about what military objectives it seeks to achieve through CPGS weapons, this table builds on James Acton's comprehensive summary of what US government officials have mentioned at various occasions about possible missions for CPGS weapons.[81]

As table 7.2 shows, Chinese experts agree that a preemptive counternuclear attack—a preemptive strike to disarm an adversary's nuclear forces—and defense suppression (counter-A2/AD) are very important motivations for the United States' CPGS program. They have seldom addressed the issue of retaliatory counternuclear attacks—military strikes to destroy an adversary's remaining nuclear forces after an attack by nuclear weapons. This seems to be the result of the general Chinese conviction that nuclear wars can be avoided but not managed; as long as a nuclear war breaks out, it basically means an all-out nuclear exchange, with little room for managing or controlling escalation.[82] As a result, Chinese experts have not been particularly interested in discussing specific escalation scenarios after the nuclear threshold is crossed.

It is also necessary to note that the United States has stated that the counternuclear mission for its CPGS weapons is aimed only at countering North Korean and Iranian (if Iran develops nuclear weapons) nuclear forces.[83] The *Nuclear Posture Review Report* issued by the Obama administration explicitly states that "any future US conventionally armed long-range ballistic missile systems are designed to address newly emerging regional threats, and are not intended to affect the strategic balance" with other nuclear weapons states.[84] However, such US statements do not seem to have alleviated Chinese concerns. Chinese analysts take seriously the assumption that the US conventional threat to Chinese nuclear deterrence is real and that China needs to address this threat.

As mentioned above, counterterrorism used to be a primary focus of the United States' CPGS development. The 2009 report of the Defense Science Board Task Force lists five scenarios for using CPGS weapons, and three of them are about striking various terrorist targets.[85] Although some Chinese experts acknowledge that counterterrorism was the original motivation for the United States to pursue hypersonic technology, many do not think this is an important motivation compared with other strategic benefits that the United States will obtain from mastering such technology. Still, they worry that CPGS will encourage the United States to engage in more activities that violate or interfere with others' national sovereignty. One analyst writes: "In three of the five scenarios when the United States might use conventional prompt global strike, the strike takes place in a neutral country. . . . This is a violation of this country's sovereignty."[86] Furthermore, Chinese experts see Beijing's development of so-called A2/AD capability as aimed at defending against US interference. Therefore, the expressed US intention to use CPGS against A2/AD systems has been interpreted by Chinese experts as indicative of a greater US willingness to conduct more aggressive military interference, which "will raise the intensity of regional conflicts, and become an important driving force for regional conflicts and escalation."[87]

Another interesting contrast is that a counter-ASAT (antisatellite) effort has been repeatedly discussed by US experts and officials as a possible mission for CPGS weapons.[88] And given the high-level attention in the United States about China's ASAT capability, China is apparently the main target of such counter-ASAT operations by CPGS weapons. But there has been little open discussion in China about this US motivation, in either a preemptive or retaliatory US counter-ASAT scenario against China.

POSSIBLE CHINESE RESPONSES TO US CAPABILITY

Most of the proposed countermeasures by Chinese experts are focused on how to maintain China's nuclear retaliation capability. Such proposals can be grouped into five main categories. First, the most straightforward solution is for the United States and China to agree not to use conventional weapons to strike each other's nuclear forces and nuclear facilities (or at least to agree to no first use of conventional weapons against each other's nuclear capabilities).[89] The optimistic side of this proposal is that it is not a totally unprecedented diplomatic arrangement. India and Pakistan, for instance, have implemented a mutual agreement since 1991, prohibiting them from attacking each other's facilities that contain radioactive materials. The pessimistic side is that for a long time the

United States has resisted reaching any agreement with China in which it agrees to NFU of even nuclear weapons. Accordingly, it will require tremendous diplomatic effort to convince Washington to accept an agreement for NFU of conventional weapons. Given that the United States is building hypersonic weapons precisely to give the president more options during a crisis, it seems unlikely that Washington would give up the option easily. Of course, even if an agreement to regulate the use of conventional weapons can be reached, the durability of such an agreement has not been thoroughly examined.

Second, if the threat from a US conventional first strike cannot be adequately addressed through diplomatic arrangements, Chinese experts have proposed unilateral steps to bolster its nuclear deterrence capabilities. For instance, a number of experts argue that China needs to enhance its so-called asymmetric nuclear strike posture. The thinking is that because the US hypersonic development program is significantly more advanced than that of China, it is likely that when the United States starts to deploy hypersonic weapons in the future, Chinese hypersonic weapons will still be under development. Because China will be under serious threat of a US hypersonic strike, it is argued that Beijing will need to launch nuclear retaliation against a conventional hypersonic strike. Similarly, in response to the perceived CPGS threat, some experts suggest that China should readjust its long-standing NFU policy from an unconditional NFU of nuclear weapons to a conditional NFU policy—that is, China should be able to launch a nuclear retaliation after its nuclear weapons are attacked by nonnuclear weapons.[90]

Some experts call for China to increase its number of submarine-launched ballistic missiles and its land-mobile intercontinental ballistic missiles to ensure the survivability of its nuclear deterrent.[91] Some even go as far as to argue that China should develop some type of nuclear war-fighting capability. This is a very rarely stated view, but several serious military professionals have expressed such opinions. For example, Yuwen Jingbo and Tang Liwen of the People's Liberation Army Academy of Equipment Command and Technology assert that "since the first day when China became a nuclear weapons state, China has promised not to use nuclear weapons first. However, the emergence of PGS [precision global strike] has posed new challenges to our nuclear strategy: The United States can use conventional weapons to strike our nuclear facilities. Therefore, we should, without changing the basic principles of nuclear strategy, change the utility of nuclear weapons from strategic deterrent to a combination of deterrent and war fighting."[92] A nuclear response to a conventional strike on nuclear forces could have negative implications for strategic stability because such policy would make it difficult for one to draw a clear redline for nuclear retaliation. A conventional strike on one's nuclear forces may cause limited but nonfatal damage; this would present one with a dilemma of whether a nuclear response would be justified or necessary. Without a clear and unequivocal redline, one's nuclear deterrence could be undermined rather than strengthened, and crisis stability could be adversely affected as well.

Third, some experts argue that China can maintain its mutual deterrent relationship with the United States by obtaining its own hypersonic weapons.[93] It is no secret that China has already been conducting research on hypersonic technology and has reportedly completed a few test flights during the past couple of years.[94] The question is, however, How would China achieve "mutual deterrence" with the United States by developing its own hypersonic capability? Given the fact that the Chinese nuclear arsenal is much smaller and much more vulnerable than that of the United States, it would be much easier, at least in theory, for the United States to conduct a conventional first strike against Chinese nuclear weapons than vice versa. But the Chinese experts have not elaborated on what this "mutual deterrence" might mean at the operational level. It is possible that China believes its capability to threaten a small number of US targets by using hypersonic weapons would be sufficient to deter the United States from using similar weapons against China. After all, China has maintained a small nuclear arsenal because of its belief that a very limited nuclear retaliation would be sufficient to deter even a nuclear superpower from launching a nuclear strike against China. If this is true, China might choose to focus on obtaining hypersonic technology rather than building up its hypersonic weapon stockpile in the future. This may help minimize the potentially adverse impact on existing strategic stability.

Fourth, probably because it is not easy for China's own hypersonic weapons to effectively neutralize or balance the US hypersonic weapons' advantage, some Chinese experts believe that China needs a defensive capability against hypersonic weapons. Some technical experts have conducted research about how this might be done, and have pointed out a few ways to work toward this goal. Active defense measures primarily entail two options: first, building both an integrated early warning and tracking system and new land-, air-, and space-based interception systems that respond quickly and travel fast enough to intercept hypersonic targets; and second, developing new concept weapons, such as the railgun.[95] Passive defense measures include further increasing the mobility of land-based missiles, enhancing the physical robustness of key military targets, and building backup facilities.[96] China has already taken some of these measures, like building robust underground facilities to shelter missiles and other key military targets. Although the construction of these facilities will increase the survivability of China's nuclear forces, it may also lead to a lesser degree of military transparency, given that military activities in underground facilities will be more difficult to monitor. The concept of strategic stability builds on the premise that countries have a relatively good understanding of each other's strategic military capabilities. Therefore, declining transparency will have a negative impact on strategic stability.

Fifth, because of the belief that the US development of CPGS, especially the unmanned spacecraft such as X-37, will inevitably lead to the further militarization of outer space, some Chinese experts argue that China must follow suit and enhance its own efforts to conduct "military aerospace technology research." This research will include space weapon launch and propulsion technology; surveillance, reconnaissance, and early warning technology; navigation and control technology; and reliable communication technology.[97] Such thinking reveals how a competition in hypersonic technology can carry the extra risk of spilling over and exacerbating arms competitions in other domains such as outer space. An intensified arms competition in outer space would further complicate efforts to maintain existing strategic stability.

One option that is missing from China's proposed responses are diplomatic arrangements to limit the size of hypersonic arsenals. Even though US officials often refer to the United States' CPGS program as a "niche capability" that is going to be very limited, no Chinese experts have proposed a negotiated agreement with the United States on capping or limiting hypersonic weapon deployment. This may be due to Chinese perceptions that it is premature to think about hypersonic arms control, given that the technology is still under development. But this also may reveal deeper thinking that, because the United States and Russia are the two leading actors in the hypersonic arms competition, the only likely solution is for these two countries to agree to negotiate first before others can get involved.[98] The second possible explanation is that Chinese experts do not think a negotiated arrangement on total numbers of hypersonic weapons is feasible. This pessimistic assessment may indicate a rather bleak future for hypersonic arms control.

CONCLUSION AND LESSONS TO BE LEARNED

Chinese experts have serious concerns that hypersonic weapons could undermine the credibility of China's nuclear deterrence. They worry particularly that the United States' CPGS weapons will be used against Chinese nuclear forces, together with US nuclear strike and missile defense capabilities. Against the combined forces of these US capabilities, China's nuclear retaliation capability might be vulnerable. Consequently, Chinese experts propose a wide range of countermeasures, some of which involve changing China's relatively restrained nuclear posture, calling for further expansion of its nuclear arsenal, and even building some kind of nuclear war-fighting capability to enable it to respond to CPGS strikes.

Even though Chinese experts are concerned about the possibility that hypersonic weapons could blur the line between nuclear and conventional weapons, and thus greatly increase the dangers of escalation, they have not elaborated on hypersonic weapons' specific pathways to possibly causing nuclear escalation. Looking at China's own nuclear development, it is clear that China has been introducing new dual-use missile systems (e.g., DF-21 and DF-26) that can accommodate both nuclear and conventional warheads and that do not seem to exhibit distinctive physical features between nuclear and conventional models. This contradictory practice may indicate that there is no consensus yet within the Chinese strategic community about the importance of segregating the nuclear and the conventional domains. There may also still be a serious lack of understanding about the practice of cross-domain deterrence and about managing escalations with intermingled conventional and nuclear capabilities.

That said, there seems to be a consensus among Chinese experts that it is imperative for China to develop its own hypersonic weapons. At the strategic level, this seems to be largely driven by the widely accepted perception that hypersonic weapons would be very effective in penetrating US missile defense systems. At the technical level, this is driven by the overwhelming consensus that hypersonic technology is going to bring about one of the most important military technology revolutions in the world's history, and therefore that China cannot fall behind. To many Chinese experts, an arms competition or even an arms race over hypersonic weapons is inevitable and is already happening. Because there is still great uncertainty about the future development of this technology, and about who may become the ultimate winner of this competition, Chinese experts think the competition will be extraordinarily intense. Consequently, they are not pinning their hopes for minimizing the destabilizing impact of hypersonic weapons on hypersonic arms control.

The emerging competition between China and the United States illustrates that fear and mismatched perceptions are contributing to biased understandings of each other's intentions, which in turn is exacerbating the existing security dilemma. From the perspective of those Western scholars who closely follow the development of the United States' CPGS program, this program has largely been driven by technology rather than by strategic planning. They see this as a major problem that needs to be addressed by engaging in more strategic thinking about the future development and deployment of such technologies.[99] The Chinese experts, conversely, see the United States' pursuit of hypersonic weapons without clearly expressed military purposes as evidence that the United States is simply trying to reinforce its military superiority and therefore is seeking "absolute superiority and absolute security."[100]

At the operational level, there is some debate among Chinese experts about whether the United States' CPGS program has a clear strategic objective and whether it has been well managed with an internally coherent logic. Some Chinese experts point out that the United States' CPGS program has suffered organizational problems and has lacked strategic objectives.[101] These are the same problems identified by Western experts.[102] But more Chinese experts believe that the US program is very coherent internally and is managed systematically by a top-down process. Such (mis)perceptions contribute to the Chinese belief that the United States has an overall strategic objective and a well-thought-out plan to develop CPGS capabilities.

The United States and China are already engaged in a negative action/reaction spiral with regard to the development of hypersonic weapons, which reflects an intense security dilemma between the two. China's motivation in developing its own hypersonic weapons may be multifold, including to penetrate the US missile defense systems and to understand the technology in order to develop countermeasures or to build a "technology reserve." From the Chinese perspective, these are primarily responses to threats posed by the United States' missile defense and CPGS programs. But as China responds to US programs, the United States has started to see the Chinese countermeasures as an original security threat in and of themselves. Such a negative action/reaction dynamic is bound to cause more frictions between the two countries down the road and is not likely to increase any party's security in the long term.

At a fundamental level, the reason hypersonic weapon development exacerbates the security dilemma between Washington and Beijing is that to some extent, the development programs in both countries are technology-driven rather than guided by clear military objectives. Both countries need time to study the full potential of this new technology before they can decide how to employ it to achieve a particular military purpose. Their inability to articulate clear military objectives for their own programs makes it very difficult for either state to reassure the other.

When it comes to the nuclear equation, the United States has expressed interest in using hypersonic weapons to strike small nuclear arsenals, such as that of North Korea. However, for Chinese analysts, the size of a US hypersonic weapon stockpile that can hold the North Korean nuclear arsenal at risk might not be easily distinguished from one that can threaten the Chinese nuclear arsenal. After all, China today has only about a dozen intercontinental ballistic missiles that can reach the continental United States. Furthermore, even if the

United States can draw a clear line between the two military missions and can effectively demonstrate that its hypersonic weapons stockpile can threaten only the North Korean nuclear arsenal (which continues to grow) without threatening the Chinese nuclear arsenal, the line might be easily crossed. This is because some Chinese experts, as mentioned above, believe that hypersonic weapons can be easily mass-manufactured at an affordable cost. Therefore, different US and Chinese understandings about some technical features—such as the cost—of future hypersonic weapons further exacerbate the security dilemma.

On the United States' side, its concern about China's hypersonic weapon development program is vague. Aside from China's development and deployment of an antiship ballistic missile, which is believed to be armed with a reentry vehicle that can glide to a target and which can threaten large US surface ships, Washington has not identified specific threats from China's program on hypersonic weapon development.[103] It is dangerous to allow such an abstract concern to drive arms competition. Bilateral dialogues at both the official and academic levels should be conducted to discuss divergent understandings about some of the technical and strategic factors surrounding hypersonic technology, given that this will substantially reduce misperceptions and reduce the intensity of the mounting security dilemma.

NOTES

1. Jin Wang and Wensheng Li, "The Controversies over the Two Plus Two: The Missile Defense and Strategic Weapons of the United States and Russia" ("2+2" 的"是非题" 美俄反导及战略武器), *Ordnance Knowledge 5* (2008); and Nengwu (徐能武) Xu, "The Threats and Challenges to Outer Space Security Posed by the Adjustment of the US Strategic Deterrent System" (美国战略威慑体系调整对外层空间安全的潜在威胁与挑战), *National Defense Science & Technology* 2 (2013).

2. Xiangli (孙向丽) Sun, "Theories and Practice in Arms Control" (军备控制的理论与实践), *Teaching and Research* (教学与研究) 6 (2001); and Jingping (李静平) Li, "A Preliminary Analysis on US-China Strategic Stability: Contructing US-China Strategic Stability beyond Strategic Weapons" (中美战略稳定初探——超越战略武器看中美战略稳定的构建), in *13th PIIC Beijing Seminar on International Security* (Beijing: Program for Science and National Security Studies, 2012).

3. Gregory D. Koblentz, *Strategic Stability in the Second Nuclear Age* (New York: Council on Foreign Relations, 2014); and Barry D. Watts, *Nuclear-Conventional Firebreaks and the Nuclear Taboo* (Washington, DC: Center for Strategic and Budgetary Assessments, 2013).

4. Office of the Secretary of Defense, *Nuclear Posture Review Report* (Washington, DC: US Department of Defense, 2010).

5. "China Knowledge Resource Integrated Database," China Academic Journal (CD) Electronic Journals Publishing House, http://oversea.cnki.net/kns55/support/en/about_cnki.aspx.

6. Zhixiong (张志雄) Zhang and Jiaomin (黄教民) Huang, "Status of Research and Impact of Long-Range Prompt Strike Weapons" (远程快速打击武器的研究现状和影响), *Defense Technology* (国防科技) 1 (2013).

7. Feng (高峰) Gao, "Hypersonic Weapons Open New Warfare Situations" (高超音速武器开启战争新态势), *Science 24 hours* (科学 24 小时) 5 (2015).

8. Ibid. Note that some hypersonic vehicles, such as boost-gliders, can also destroy targets just through their kinetic energy, and therefore they can also be called high-speed kinetic-energy weapons, technically speaking. The quoted Chinese expert is using the term "high-speed kinetic-energy weapon" to refer mostly to the railgun weapon.

9. For arguments that hypersonic weapons will be difficult to detect, see Jie (刘杰) Liu, Feng (何峰) He, and Jing (吴静) Wu, "Analysis of Developing Trend of Defending against Hypersonic Targets in Future Air Defense and Anti-Missile Operations" (未来防空反导作战中高超声速目标的发展趋势分析), *Cruise Missile* (飞航导弹) 1, no. 4 (2014). For arguments that detection will not pose a problem, see Wei (勇伟) Yong, Zemin (吴泽民) Wu, and Xiao (付晓) Fu, "High-Speed Killer Hidden in the Upper Air" (隐匿于高空中的极速杀手), *PLA Daily* (解放军报) September 13, 2014.

10. Zhuoqian (王卓谦) Wang, "Hypersonic Leading the New Trend in Aerospace Flight" (高超音速引领空天飞行新趋势), August 30, 2014.

11. Yong, Wu, and Fu, "High-Speed Killer."

12. Shuyan (李淑艳) Li, Lixia (任利霞) Ren, Qiugui (宋秋贵) Song, and Jinyu (王锦玉) Wang, "Near Space Hypersonic Weapon Defense Review" (临近空间高超音速武器防御综述), *Modern Radar* (现代雷达) 36, no. 6 (2014).

13. Gao, "Hypersonic Weapons Open New Warfare Situations"; and Shuyan et al., "Near Space Hypersonic Weapon Defense Review."

14. Li (贾利) Jia, "Russian Air and Space Forces Ready to Go" (俄罗斯空天军蓄势待发), April 28, 2015, *China National Defense News* (中国国防报).

15. Gao, "Hypersonic Weapons Open New Warfare Situations"; and Wenlong (胡文龙) Hu, "Air-Space Integrated Hypersonic Attack—the Upcoming New Round of Warfare Revolution" (空天化高超音速攻击——即将来临的新一轮战争变革), *Defense Technology* (国防科技) 36, no. 2 (2015).

16. Liang (张良) Zhang, "Hypersonic Weapons That Will Change the Rule of Future Warfare" (改变未来战争规则的高超音速武器), *Life and Disasters* (生命与灾害) 5 (2014).

17. Ruiliang (王瑞良) Wang, "Hypersonic Missiles for the Future" (为未来而来的高超音速导弹), *Science 24 hours* (科学 24 小时), no. 7 (2014).

18. Jixin (王继新) Wang, "Introducing Hypersonic Weapons" (高超音速武器漫谈), *Ordnance Knowledge* (兵器知识), no. 5 (2014).

19. Ibid.

20. Ibid.

21. Zhicheng (汤志成) Tang, "Hypersonic Weapon Cannot Be Intercepted Is Pseudo-Proposition" (高超音速武器无法被拦截是伪命题), *Ordnance Knowledge* (兵器知识), no. 2 (2015).

22. Wang, "Introducing Hypersonic Weapons."

23. James M. Acton, *Silver Bullet? Asking the Right Questions about Conventional Prompt Global Strike* (Washington, DC: Carnegie Endowment for International Peace, 2013).

24. Ibid.

25. Committe on Conventional Prompt Global Strike Capability, Naval Studies Board, Division on Engineering and Physical Sciences, *US Conventional Prompt Global Strike: Issues for 2008 and Beyond* (Washington, DC: National Research Council of the National Academies, 2008).

26. Ibid.; and Acton, *Silver Bullet?*

27. Keir A. Lieber and Daryl G. Press, "US Nuclear Primacy and the Future of the Chinese Deterrent," *China Security*, Winter 2007.

28. Hu, "Air-Space Integrated Hypersonic Attack."

29. Ibid.

30. Ibid.

31. Xu (刘旭) Liu, Weimin (李为民) Li, Zhipeng (姜志鹏) Jiang, and Wenjing (宋文静) Song, "Thoughts on Hypersonic Cruise Missile Combat Characteristics and Offense-Defense Model" (高超声速巡航导弹作战特点及攻防模式思考), *Cruise Missile* (飞航导弹) 9 (2014).

32. Nobuhiro Kubo, "Japan to Intercept Any North Korea Missile Deemed a Threat," Reuters, www.reuters.com/article/us-japan-korea-missiles-idUSBREA3404 I20140405.

33. Huaiyu (汤怀宇) Tang, "Military Significance of China's Hypersonic Weapons" (中国高超音速武器的军事意义), *Defense Times* (国防时报), April 16, 2014.

34. Gao, "Hypersonic Weapons Open New Warfare Situations"; Yazheng (杨亚政) Yang, Songnian (李松年) Li, and Jialing (杨嘉陵) Yang, "Hypersonic Vehicle and Its Key Technologies" (高超音速飞行器及其关键技术简论), *Advances in Mechanics* (力学进展) 37, no. 4 (2007).

35. Jingquan (王景泉) Wang, "Overview of US Military Spacecraft Development" (美国军用空间飞机发展概述), *Space International* (国际太空) 5 (2010).

36. Gao, "Hypersonic Weapons Open New Warfare Situations."

37. M. Elaine Bunn and Vincent A. Manzo, "Conventional Prompt Global Strike: Strategic Asset or Unusable Liability?" US Department of Defense, Defense Technical Information Center, 2011; and James M. Acton, *The Need for Speed? Debating Conventional Prompt Global Strike* (Washington, DC: Carnegie Endowment for International Peace, 2013).

38. Acton, *Silver Bullet?*

39. Xiaodong (柴晓东) Chai, Huasheng (王华胜) Wang, and Xinhong (周新红) Zhou, "Hypersonic Warfighting Platform Challenges Existing Joint Warfighting Operation System" (高超音速作战平台挑战现有联合作战体系), *PLA Daily* (解放军报), August 4, 2011.

40. Huaiyu (汤怀宇) Tang and Jie (刘婕) Liu, "Media Reports and China's Hypersonic Weapon" (从媒体报道看我国高超音速武器), *Ordnance Knowledge* (兵器知识) 5 (2014).

41. Shi (何适) He, "Russian Hypersonic Missiles Classified as 'Top Secrets' (俄高超音速导弹列入"绝密级"), January 23, 2013.

42. Xiangli (孙向丽) Sun, "New Challenges and New Agenda for China's Arms Control" (中国军控的新挑战与新议程), *Foreign Affairs Review* (外交评论) 3 (2010).

43. Fiona S. Cunningham and M. Taylor Fravel, "Assuring Assured Retaliation: China's Nuclear Posture and US-China Strategic Stability," *International Security* 40, no. 2 (2015).

44. Ibid.

45. Yunzhu Yao, "China Will Not Change Its Nuclear Policy," *China-US Focus*, April 22, 2013.

46. Hu, "Air-Space Integrated Hypersonic Attack."

47. Ibid.

48. "US Navy Explores Submarine Launched Hypersonic Missile" (美国海军探索潜射型高超音速导弹), *Ship Science and Technology* (舰船科学技术) 2 (2014).

49. Zhongping (宋忠平) Song, "Europe Will Get Caught in Arms Race If the US Breaks from INF Treaty" (一旦美废除中导条约 欧洲或陷入军备竞赛), China Social Science Network, 2015.

50. Zhongping (宋忠平) Song, "US Hypersonic Weapons Testing Will Lead to a New Military Imbalance" (美高超音速武器试验将引发新军力失衡), September 6, 2014.

51. Hu, "Air-Space Integrated Hypersonic Attack."

52. Tong (柯同) Ke, "Is Hypersonic Weapon Leading to a New Arms Race?" (高超音速武器引发新军备竞赛?), January 13, 2015.

53. Wenjie (单文杰) Shan and Cai Wenyi (蔡闻一), "Russia's 'Prompt Global Strike' to Target Whom?" (俄"全球快速打击"剑指何方?), September 27, 2014; Wang, "Hypersonic Leading the New Trend in Aerospace Flight"; and Ke, "Is Hypersonic Weapon Leading to New Arms Race?"

54. Chai, Wang, and Zhou, "Hypersonic Warfighting Platform."

55. Bin Li, Riqiang Wu, and Weidi Xu, "Why Is China Modernizing Its Nuclear Arsenal?" paper presented at Carnegie International Nuclear Policy Conference, Washington, DC, 2015; and Jonathan Ray, "Red China's 'Capitalist Bomb': Inside the Chinese Neutron Bomb Program," in *China Strategic Perspectives* 8 (Washington, DC: Center for the Study of Chinese Military Affairs, Institute for National Strategic Studies, National Defense University, 2015).

56. Yi (木易) Mu, "China and US Compete in Developing Hypersonic Missile; Global Anti-Missile Systems May Be Useless" (中美争研高超音速导弹 全球反导系统恐将作废), *Life and Disasters* (生命与灾害), no. 10 (2014).

57. Qingyuan (李清源) Li and Junhong (史俊红) Shi, "Hypersonic Technology Development Review" (高超音速技术发展概述), *Structure & Environment Engineering* (强度与环境) 39, no. 5 (2012).

58. Long (陈龙) Chen and Erqiang (王二强) Wang, "'Hypersonic': Weapon That Changes the Model of Future Warfare" ("高超": 改变未来战争模式的利器), August 21, 2012.

59. Chai, Wang, and Zhou, "Hypersonic Warfighting Platform"; Wang, "Hypersonic Missiles for the Future"; Wang, "Hypersonic Leading the New Trend in Aerospace Flight"; and Li et al., "Near Space Hypersonic Weapon Defense Review."

60. Hu, "Air-Space Integrated Hypersonic Attack."

61. Tang and Liu, "Media Reports."

62. Ke, "Is Hypersonic Weapon Leading to New Arms Race?"

63. Peng (崔鹏) Cui, "China's Hypersonic Aerocraft Test Receives International Attention" (我高超音速飞行器试验引关注), January 21, 2014.

64. Xuesong (张雪松) Zhang, "Why Are Hypersonic Flight Technologies Difficult?" (高超音速飞行技术难在哪里?), January 25, 2014.

65. Song, "US Hypersonic Weapons Testing."

66. Zhang, "Why Are Hypersonic Flight Technologies Difficult?"

67. Hu, "Air-Space Integrated Hypersonic Attack."

68. Hui (安慧) An, "Closely Watched Test of Advanced Hypersonic Weapon" (倍受关注的先进高超声速武器试验), *Space Exploration* (太空探索) 10 (2014); Liping (夏立平) Xia, "US Conventional Prompt Global Strike Plan from the 'High Frontier' Theory Perspective" (高边疆" 理论视阈下美国全球快速常规打击计划), *International Observer* (国际观察) 5 (2014); and Ke, "Is Hypersonic Weapon Leading to New Arms Race?"

69. Acton, *Silver Bullet?*

70. Hong (黎弘) Li, "Complex and Diverse Global Nuclear Security Environment" (复杂多元化的全球核安全环境), *Peace and Development* (和平与发展) 3 (2010); and Yong (方勇) Fang, "US Pushes Forward with Prompt Global Strike Program" (美国推进快速全球打击计划), *New Age Defense* (新时代国防), no. 8 (2010).

71. Ke, "Is Hypersonic Weapon Leading to New Arms Race?"

72. Li and Shi, "Hypersonic Technology Development Review."

73. Youpei (方有培) Fang, Liping (汪立萍) Wang, Yamei (蔡亚梅) Cai, and Liling (陈利玲) Chen, "US 'Global Strike' System Technology Defect Analysis" (美军 "全球快速打击" 系统技术缺陷分析), *Aerospace Electronic Warfare* (航天电子对抗) 29, no. 3 (2013).

74. Zhang and Huang, "Status of Research."

75. Fang et al., "US 'Global Strike' System Technology Defect Analysis."

76. Aiguo (党爱国) Dang, Xiaojun (李晓军) Li, and Bao (徐宝) Xu, "Foreign Military Rapid Global Strike Capability Developments" (外军快速全球打击能力发展动态), *Cruise Missile* (飞航导弹) 7 (2012); and Hu, "Air-Space Integrated Hypersonic Attack."

77. Brad Glosserman, David Santoro, and Ralph A. Cossa, "US-China Strategic Nuclear Relations: Time to Move to Track-1 Dialogue," *Issues and Insights* 15, no. 7 (2015).

78. Wang, "Hypersonic Leading the New Trend in Aerospace Flight."

79. Zhongyan (胡仲衍) Hu, Changfu (郭昌福) Guo, and Xiaodong (耿晓东) Geng, "US Hijacks the World with Hypersonic Missiles" (美用高超音速导弹 "挟持全球"), *Global Military* (环球军事) 5 (2009).

80. Kelin (全克林) Quan, "On the US 'Prompt Global Strike' Plan" (略论美国的 "快速全球打击" 计划), *Contemporary International Relations* (现代国际关系) 11 (2007).

81. Acton, *Silver Bullet?*

82. Jiadong (张家栋) Zhang and Xin (金新) Jin, "Sino-US New Type of Major Power Relationship: History, Theory, and Reality" (中美新型大国关系: 历史, 理论与现实), *International Observer* (国际观察) 5 (2013).

83. "The Status of United States Strategic Forces," US House of Representatives Armed Services Committee, Strategic Forces Subcommittee, March 2, 2011; and Ronald Kerber and Robert Stein, "Report of the Defense Science Board Task Force on Time-Critical Conventional Strike from Strategic Standoff," Office of the Under Secretary of Defense for Acquisition, Technology, and Logistics, Washington, DC, 2009.

84. Office of the Secretary of Defense, *Nuclear Posture Review Report.*

85. Kerber and Stein, "Report of the Defense Science Board Task Force."

86. Xia, "US Conventional Prompt Global Strike Plan."

87. Ibid.; An, "Closely Watched Test"; and Fang, "US Pushes Forward."

88. Acton, *Silver Bullet?*

89. Xia, "US Conventional Prompt Global Strike Plan."

90. Ibid.

91. Ibid.

92. Jingbo (宇文静波) Yuwen and Liwen (唐立文) Tang, "Discussion and Implications of the American 'Prompt Global Strike' Program" (美国 "快速全球打击" 计划探讨与启示), *Journal of the People's Liberation Army Academy of Equipment Command & Technology* (装备指挥技术学院学报) 22, no. 3 (2011).

93. Xia, "US Conventional Prompt Global Strike Plan."

94. Richard D. Fisher Jr., "US Officials Confirm Sixth Chinese Hypersonic Manoeuvring Strike Vehicle Test," *IHS Jane's Defence Weekly*, November 26, 2015.

95. Liu, He, and Wu, "Analysis of Developing Trend"; Jianbin (李剑斌) Li, Xiansi (谭贤四) Tan, Zhihuai (李志淮) Li, and Cong (吴聪) Wu, "Near Space Hypersonic Targets Ascent Phase Interception Requirements Analysis" (临近空间高超声速目标上升段拦截需求分析), *Modern Defense Technology* (现代防御技术) 42, no. 5 (2014); Hailin (张海林) Zhang, Lin (周林) Zhou, Lin (张琳) Zhang, and Guobao (刘国宝) Liu, "Characteristics of Near Space Hypersonic Missile Targets" (临近空间高超声速导弹目标特性研究), *Cruise Missile* (飞航导弹) 2 (2015); and Jing (张晶) Zhang, Zhenghong (贺正洪) He, and Bo (王博) Wang, "Near Space Hypersonic Vehicle Development and Defense Strategies" (临近空间高超声速飞行器发展及防御策略研究), *Cruise Missile* (飞航导弹) 2 (2015): 4.

96. Liu et al., "Thoughts on Hypersonic Cruise Missile Combat Characteristics."

97. Yuwen and Tang, "Discussion and Implications of the American 'Prompt Global Strike' Program."

98. Niu et al., "Development Review."

99. Acton, "Need for Speed?"

100. Hu, Guo, and Geng, "US Hijacks the World with Hypersonic Missiles"; "Experts: US X-37b Aerospace Plane More Dangerous Than Nuclear Weapons" (专家: 美国x-37b空天战机比核武器更危险), *Global Times*, April 8, 2010.

101. Zilin (魏子淋) Wei, Zhide (刘治德) Liu, and Xiangdong (徐向东) Xu, "US Near Space Prompt Global Strike Weapons Status and Development" (美军临近空间快速全球打击武器现状与发展), *Cruise Missile* (飞航导弹) 2 (2012).

102. See, e.g., James M. Acton, "Prompt Global Strike: American and Foreign Developments," Testimony, US House of Representatives, Armed Services Subcommittee on Strategic Forces, December 8, 2015.

103. Mark Stokes, *China's Evolving Conventional Strategic Strike Capability: The Anti-Ship Ballistic Missile Challenge to US Maritime Operations in the Western Pacific and Beyond* (Washington, DC: 2049 Project Institute, 2009).

8

The India-Pakistan Nuclear Dyad

Strategic Stability and
Cross-Domain Deterrence

HAPPYMON JACOB

Do the second-generation nuclear-armed states and dyads have unique and distinct understandings of strategic stability? Are notions of strategic stability in their regional settings informed by regional specificities and characteristics? If so, what constitutes different understandings of stability, and what implications do they have for the nuclear postures and strategies of those states and regions and, more important, for international security?

This chapter addresses these questions by examining Indian and Pakistani notions of strategic stability.[1] The argument advanced here is that a state's notion of strategic stability contributes to how cross-domain deterrence operates on the ground, but the existence of such cross-domain deterrence simultaneously has an impact on its notion of strategic stability—the two are mutually constituted. Accordingly, Indian and Pakistani notions of strategic stability have an impact on how their dyadic relationship is shaped, and their dyadic relationship has had an impact on their individual notions of strategic stability, albeit in distinct ways.

The chapter is divided into four sections. The first one explains the classical understandings of strategic stability and deterrence stability. An attempt is made throughout the chapter to compare and contrast the classical understandings of deterrence with those of the Indian and Pakistani notions. The second section operationalizes the notion of strategic stability in the South Asian context in order to contrast the Indian and Pakistani perspectives. The third section explores cross-domain deterrence issues in the Indo-Pak nuclear dyad in light of these strategic similarities and differences. It focuses on four levels of cross-domain deterrence—use of subconventional actors, waging conventional war, use of tactical nuclear weapons (TNWs), and the development of ballistic missile defense (BMD)—and how each side differs on whether each of these elements is offensive or defensive. The conclusion examines the policy implications of their differing notions of strategic stability and the resultant strategic behavior.

THE CLASSICAL UNDERSTANDING OF STRATEGIC STABILITY

In the Cold War setting, the foremost concern of the stability theorists was resolving the challenge of a surprise attack by the adversary. This theoretical preoccupation led to the formation of the concept of strategic stability.[2] In responding to this problem, Cold War thinkers, such as Bernard Brodie and William Borden, focused on the invulnerability of nuclear forces to a surprise attack by the adversary and the assured ability to retaliate in kind.[3] According to Elbridge Colby, this line of thinking meant that "a situation would be stable when both parties would see that massively launching first—whether to avoid being neutered or to try to disarm one's opponent—would be either unnecessary or foolish."[4] In a stable situation, a "major war would only come about because one party truly sought it, not because of miscalculation."[5] Andrei Kokoshin, a senior Russian analyst and policy maker, has a similar definition: "Generally speaking, strategic stability is based on the inability of each of the sides to deliver a preemptive or a fixed-time strike capable of disabling the major part (if not all) of the nuclear forces that other side could use in the delivery of a retaliation strike."[6] In other words, the concepts of mutually assured destruction (MAD) and a balance of terror (BoT) were key to maintaining strategic stability between the Cold War rivals, as conceived of and stipulated by the stability theorists.[7]

Deterrence stability and strategic stability are defined similarly in the deterrence literature. For instance, the definition of deterrence stability provided by Thomas Schelling and Morton Halperin is not different from the above definitions of strategic stability: A "balance of deterrence" is a situation in which the incentives on both sides to initiate war are outweighed by the disincentives.[8] Colin Gray also goes on to assert that "stable deterrence theory will refer to the proposition that stability in arms competition and in time of crisis is maximized when each side is unambiguously vulnerable at home, and also confident that a large number of its strategic offensive weapons are invulnerable prior to launch and during mission execution."[9] Accordingly, key preconditions for deterrence stability are the absence of a nuclear arms race, the presence of mature arsenals and declared doctrines, and the credibility and the willingness to discourage nuclear exchanges.

INDIAN AND PAKISTANI NOTIONS OF STRATEGIC STABILITY

How does one make sense of the unique notions of strategic stability in non-classical contexts? Because there are no objective criteria to assess national understandings of strategic stability in regional settings, this chapter uses these aspects of the Indo-Pakistani deterrence engagement to illuminate the Indian and Pakistani notions of strategic stability: the role of nuclear weapons in the strategic imagination of a state; the operational level of deterrence; the attitude toward limited war under nuclear overhang; the focus on building stability; the extent of deterrence engagements; the emphasis on invulnerable arsenal; the belief in MAD; and the pursuit of balance versus parity.

Contrasting Views on the Role of Nuclear Weapons

In August 2015, during heightened tensions between India and Pakistan, the adviser to Pakistan's prime minister on foreign affairs and (then) national security, Sartaj Aziz, said that "Modi's India acts as if they are a regional superpower, [but] we are a nuclear-armed country and we know how to defend ourselves."[10] The Indian response to this rather uncalled-for remark was muted, and the leadership chose not to issue any counternuclear threats. Union Minister Rajiv Pratap Rudy quipped, "It is an irresponsible statement. If people at that level make such utterances, then there are hardly any words to indicate the country's mind-set."[11]

This statement from one of Pakistan's highest-ranking security officials is not a rare occurrence and is indeed illustrative of Pakistan's thinking about nuclear weapons, which it considers central to its strategic stability. In the Pakistani military strategy, a nuclear weapon is not a weapon of last resort but something that forms the very basis of the nation's survival. Pakistan intends to use its nuclear weapons not for existential purposes but to ward off any conventional aggression by India.

Nuclear weapons are frequently mentioned in the country's national security discourse, in political articulations, in defense planning and posturing, and when signaling the adversary. Indeed, there are also concerns about the heightened readiness state of Pakistan's weapons and the potential predelegation of the launch authority of its TNWs. Pakistan regularly refers to the military and deterrent value of its nuclear arsenal and its potential targets. After the Nasr short-range ballistic missile was tested in 2011, Lt. Gen. (Retired) Khalid Ahmed Kidwai, the director-general of the Strategic Plans Division, unveiled the fact that Nasr formed an important milestone in Pakistan's "full-spectrum" nuclear doctrine.[12]

For Pakistan, nuclear weapons have a specific purpose—to militarily defend against potential Indian aggression—not as a political weapon to be used toward other ends, such as prestige, international standing, and grander balance-of-power purposes. If anything, Pakistan's nuclear ambitions and activities have only damaged its reputation and standing in the international system. And there is no sign of Pakistan's integration into the international nuclear order, in contrast to how the international community has viewed India.[13] As noted by Dalton and Krepon, for most practical purposes, India has been accommodated into the international nuclear order, while Pakistan's global stature has either been opposed or supported only with strict conditions.[14]

Pakistan's thinking about the role of nuclear weapons in its military strategy is very close to the Cold War understanding of the role of strategic/deterrence stability. Although analysts have argued that Pakistan's nuclear posture resembles that of NATO during the Cold War, it also partly resembles the US-Soviet strategies.[15] During the Cold War, nuclear weapons played a pivotal role in the defense preparations of both superpower rivals. Moreover, the superpowers not only kept their weapons on high alert but also communicated to the other side what they intended to do with their nuclear weapons in case of a conflict. Today, Pakistan follows a similar strategy, in which nuclear weapons play a pivotal role, something that Pakistan repeatedly conveys to the international community and to India.

For India, conversely, nuclear weapons are seen as last resort weapons that are not to be kept ready to fire (on hair-trigger alerts), and are not mainstreamed into the nation's national security discourse, military planning, political articulations, or signaling of the adversary. Nuclear strategy planning and conventional military planning in India progress in parallel trajectories, without any linkages between them. For India, nuclear weapons are political weapons, for a variety of reasons. First, with its explicit no-first-use (NFU) policy, nuclear weapons have nothing but political value.[16] Given its NFU doctrine, India views nuclear weapons as political weapons and derives political values such as prestige and status from them. As Elizabeth Whitfield argues, "India values its international reputation surrounding nuclear weapons—it has reaped dividends from being perceived internationally as a responsible nuclear power."[17] Second, nuclear weapons do not figure in the Indian state's security articulations—or, moreover, in its periodic defense planning or preparedness. Indeed, since India's 2003 articulation of its official one-page nuclear doctrine, it has not made any official pronouncements on its nuclear strategy or arsenal. Finally, the slow growth of India's nuclear arsenal, despite the fact that it has sufficient amounts of fissile material at its disposal, also shows the underemphasized nature of its nuclear weapons program, which is not oriented toward specific military outcomes.

India's foreign policy articulations—official statements and speeches by the leadership in various international forums, policy documents, and the like— rarely refer to nuclear weapons or their military utility. Both in its own under- standing and in the eyes of others, India deemphasizes the military nature of its nuclear arsenal, however contradictory this might sound.[18] Such a "nonmili- tary" emphasis on nuclear weapons could also indicate that India does not view its nuclear arsenal as fundamental to strategic stability in the region, unlike Pakistan. India hardly ever uses its nuclear arsenal to signal to Pakistan or even China, with which India has an uneasy relationship, perhaps because it does not feel greatly vulnerable in a region that it physically dominates.

India's nuclear behavior also suggests that its nuclear arsenal is useful in extending its political influence. The first-generation nuclear powers—especially the two superpowers—had an unambiguous military logic to their nuclear weapons. They considered nuclear weapons as weapons that would give them military utility; political influence was the secondary purpose of their nuclear weapons. India seems to utilize its nuclear weapon capability as a means to nonmilitary ends: political influence, alliance building, and fulfillment of other ideational, nonmaterial objectives such as achieving international recognition and acceptance.[19] The essential difference in political utility versus military util- ity is a philosophical approach to nuclear weapons.

The political value of India's nuclear weapons is self-evident. India does not pitch its survival as a state on nuclear weapons (unlike Pakistan, and even the superpowers during the Cold War) but on a variety of other factors. As Adm. Arun Prakash points out: "Post-1998, India's leadership has unambiguously enunciated its belief that nuclear weapons are political instruments rather than military tools. This belief is underpinned by the logic that the sole purpose of nuclear weapons is to deter war."[20] Adm. Verghese Koithara, writing about India's nuclear forces in 2012, argued:

> From the very beginning, political factors—international prestige and enhancement of domestic confidence—have played major roles in shap- ing India's nuclear discourse. India's steadfast and ultimately successful resistance to the NPT [Nuclear Non-Proliferation Treaty] regime, which

had excluded it from its privileged tier, is widely seen as a unique political achievement that only a country with true great power potential could have pulled off. This line of thinking has led to the country's nuclear capability being seen as a prop for its great power status, and only secondarily as something that enhances security.[21]

Koithara also argued that "during its long and unfocused nuclear weapons quest, India came to develop a highly self-absorbed approach. This was because India's dominant objective was political and technological prestige, while for every other nuclear weapon state it was deterrence."[22]

How does Pakistan view India's political arsenal? The evidence seems to suggest that Pakistan does not accept such "benign" explanations about the Indian nuclear arsenal or posture, as Pakistan is indeed seeking to develop countermeasures. However, if Pakistan does actually think that Indian weapons are political, the former might be inclined to test the latter's resolve further, given its conviction that India might not use nuclear weapons in situations short of existential ones. In a sense, then, India's Massive Retaliation policy, as enshrined in its 2003 doctrine, might pose a problem for its deterrence credibility. In any case, this mismatch between the thinking on both sides could have destabilizing implications for crisis management and conflict escalation.

Deterrence in Operation

For Pakistan, nuclear deterrence is very much in operation, as nuclear weapons are intended to ensure deterrence against an immediate, specific adversary—India. Indeed, Pakistan's 1999 decision to take its chances in occupying the Kargil Heights, a territory that was under India's control, was seen by some analysts as being influenced by its belief that India would be deterred against striking against the intruders for fear of Pakistani nuclear weapons and early use signals. There also were reports that Pakistan was readying its nuclear arsenal during the Kargil War.[23] It is this deterrent value of nuclear weapons to which former Pakistani foreign secretary Shamshad Ahmad refers when he writes: "For India, it is global status, and for Pakistan it is its security and survival. While India's tests destabilized the security environment in South Asia, Pakistan's tests restored the nuclear and strategic balance, and also averted the risk of a disastrous conflict that could have resulted from any misadventure by India."[24]

Moreover, Pakistan's development of tactical nuclear weapons also indicates that it intends to use them in case there is conventional aggression from India. That is, if India decides to operationalize its "Cold Start" doctrine or a similar doctrine, Pakistan could potentially counter it with its tactical weapons, thereby lowering its nuclear threshold.[25]

By contrast, India does not intend to deter Pakistani aggression with nuclear weapons for two reasons. First, India has conventional superiority, so it does not need to use nuclear weapons to deter subconventional or conventional aggression from Pakistan. Second, although the threat to escalate any potential crisis to a TNW level might give Pakistan some psychological advantage before the actual TNW use, Pakistan would not be in a position to gain escalation dominance after the first TNW shot was fired. It therefore makes military sense for India not to rely on its nuclear arsenal to deter Pakistan.

In summary, whereas for Pakistan deterrence is clearly in operation, this is not the case for India. For India, then, reacting to a nuclear strike is unlikely to be along a predetermined path.

The Possibility of Limited Wars under the Nuclear Overhang

Because India's military posture and planning proceed without any emphasis on the military utility of its nuclear weapons, as pointed out above, Indian decision makers also fancy the possibility of limited conventional wars under the nuclear overhang. That is, given its deemphasis of nuclear weapons, New Delhi seems to be under the impression that its stance that nuclear weapons will not play a role in a conflict with Pakistan and these limited wars are a viable method of responding to Pakistan's Kargil-like aggression and use of nonstate actors against India.[26] That said, it is important to clarify that, from an official Indian standpoint, there is no Cold Start doctrine in existence. Moreover, a 2010 diplomatic cable from the US ambassador in India, leaked by WikiLeaks, states that the Cold Start Doctrine "is a mixture of myth and reality."[27]

However, the danger lies in Pakistan's avowal to use tactical nuclear weapons to counter India's limited conventional aggression, thereby fusing the conventional and strategic levels. Although this is certainly not new to the South Asian context—a similar situation prevailed between the NATO forces and the USSR in the European theater—what is new about the South Asian situation is the subconventional variable in it, which was absent in the Cold War context. This new variable, the role of nonstate actors, can and has put the two countries on an escalation ladder. In any case, the classical deterrence logic is not in sync with the possibility of a conventional war under nuclear conditions.

Thus, Pakistan wants to puncture any Indian myth about the space that India has for conventional maneuvers between the subconventional and nuclear domains. If India hopes to counter Pakistan's subconventional aggression with conventional superiority, Pakistan intends to counter India's conventional aggression with nuclear weapons. In other words, Pakistan does not believe in short conventional wars, even as it seems to be confident about keeping a nuclear conflict short.

The Desire for Stability

How do India and Pakistan view the desirability of stability? Does the goal of achieving stable deterrence rank high on their list of priorities? Stability is here understood as a systemic/subsystemic condition, wherein the possibility of major war is ruled out. Security, conversely, is understood as pertaining to lower- and immediate-level concerns that may or may not have implications for stability. Before proceeding, it is important to note that the respective desire for stability needs to be seen in the context of the overall strategic postures adopted by India and Pakistan. Whereas India is a status quo power, seeking to preserve the existing order, Pakistan is a revisionist power, seeking to undo the "stable" regional order. This has implications for the region's strategic (nuclear) stability as well.

In the Indian context, security takes precedence over anxieties about stability. Stability is desirable, but it represents a big picture concern in the Indian mind. Security, conversely, is of utmost importance and is linked to the everyday life of the Indian state. In other words, what is of great immediate importance to the country are worries about terrorist attacks, infiltration by nonstate elements from Pakistan, and constant tension and firing along the border with Pakistan, rather than the larger issues of strategic stability at the crux of nuclear crisis behavior. Nuclear weapons have no role to play in addressing the country's immediate and pressing security concerns.

One reason for this focus on security is a fear about the possibility of accidents and unintended escalation to higher levels. The problem of accidents leading to escalation and conflict was largely, if not entirely, a second-order concern in the Cold War context, but it could play a major role in the South Asian context in the future.[28] Accidents, at sea or along the border if tactical nuclear weapons are deployed with predelegation, can be destabilizing, and recurrent worries about accidents can shift the focus from security to stability, even while intensifying concerns about both.

For Pakistan, regional stability, especially in its relationship with India, is a major concern, which explains its desire to seek matching warhead capability with India. But more important, and unlike India, Pakistan does not make a distinction between security and stability considerations. Lower-order conventional conflicts, typically issues belonging to the security basket, are viewed by Pakistan as stability issues and therefore require redress with nuclear weapons.

For Pakistan, security is stability. Faced with a superior adversary in its neighborhood that aims to use a conventional military against it, Pakistan, from its point of view, does not have the luxury to be concerned about the implications of its TNWs for the region's stability. This is precisely what makes Pakistan seek to include conventional arms in strategic stability discussions, which for India covers only confidence building regarding its nuclear arsenal and these weapons' management.[29]

In other words, the desire for stability manifests differently in Indian and Pakistani thinking. For India, security is what is important vis-à-vis Pakistan, not issues of stability. For Pakistan, security also matters, but it falls within the stability basket. As a result, there is no mutual understanding of strategic stability that the two countries could attempt to bring about.

As mentioned above, these differing approaches to stability and security by India and Pakistan need to be understood in the larger context of the rivalry between them. India is a power oriented toward the status quo; Pakistan is a regional revisionist power. Hence, even as India seems to prioritize security over stability, it seeks to preserve the region's order and stability. Conversely, Pakistan equates security and stability, and its general posture is revisionist in essence. As a result, even though Pakistan's focus is on regional stability issues, it ends up undermining this stability through its revisionism.

Deterrence Engagements

Deterrence theory assumes a certain amount of trust and the presence of "deterrence engagements" between nuclear adversaries, which are seen as essential for the maintenance of deterrence stability.[30] Deterrence requires a "cooperative relationship" between adversaries, despite their mutual animosity, without which there will be no stable deterrence, only an unstable and crude form of restraint. Such a crude form of deterrence is understood here as possession of nuclear weapons and delivery mechanisms by adversaries, but without any nuclear confidence-building measures to enable stability.

In order to establish a substantive deterrence relationship between the adversaries of a nuclear dyad, the two sides should have mutual desires to avoid conflict, maintain crisis stability, minimize nuclear escalation, engage each other on nuclear confidence-building measures, and establish doctrinal clarity as well as conceptual harmony as much as possible. In other words, despite their rivalry, the nuclear adversaries can constructively engage one another to avoid disaster. As Michael Krepon argues, "Western experience suggests that constructive engagement between nuclear adversaries can follow chastening experiences of flirting with disaster."[31]

Indeed, such measures were present in abundance during the Cold War, especially after the late 1960s. By way of arriving at nuclear confidence-building measures, attempts were made by the two superpowers to engage in a deterrence communication with the other side. However, despite confronting a number of potentially disastrous escalatory situations, the South Asian neighbors have not yet decided to enter into a deterrence relationship.

There have been sporadic efforts at institutionalizing a deterrence relationship between India and Pakistan, but they have at best been half-measures and have achieved very little. India and Pakistan committed to have biannual "Expert-Level Talks on Nuclear Confidence-Building Measures." However, these meetings have been far from satisfactory, judging by their output since the inception of this dialogue process. Moreover, the two countries' negotiators have left the substantive aspects of the India-Pakistan nuclear dimension consistently untouched. Finally, the group has not held a meeting in the past two years.

The challenge of "deterrence engagements" should also be explored in the context of whether the two states have common notions about strategic stability, deterrence stability, escalation management, arms control, and so on. The absence of formal, officially structured deterrence engagements reduces the possibility of exploring whether there are common understandings of such concepts. Indeed, one of the reasons why the Indo-Pakistani strategic dialogue has not been fruitful is because, according to Indian officials, Pakistan insists on simultaneous negotiations on nuclear confidence-building measures and conventional force reduction, something the Indian side is unwilling to accept. As discussed above, this demand by Pakistan is reflective of its understanding of strategic deterrence stability, which is inseparably interconnected with a conventional balance with India.

The absence of substantive deterrence engagements is a key feature of the nuclear dynamics between India and Pakistan. This is symbolic of the state of relations between the two sides and also of how they think very differently about deterrence and stability issues. This lack of engagement has, in turn, negative implications for stability in the region.

An Invulnerable Arsenal

Classic deterrence theory posits that the vulnerability of countervalue targets and the invulnerability of nuclear forces—that is, mutual vulnerability—contributes to stability between nuclear adversaries. How does this precondition operate in the minds of the decision makers in South Asia? Interestingly, the invulnerability of its strategic arsenal does not seem to figure prominently in Indian thinking. As a result, there is a relaxed, slow-phased approach to building an assured retaliation capability. In other words, New Delhi has neither demonstrated any urgency in building an invulnerable nuclear arsenal nor unequivocally communicated to its adversaries that it possesses an invulnerable arsenal. Rather, India's retaliatory policy in the nuclear domain continues to be ambiguous, inspiring only a vague belief that it would be in a position to respond upon sustaining a first strike. It may indeed have a robust, invulnerable arsenal in its own estimation, but it has not bothered to communicate this strength.

Notwithstanding Islamabad's views to the contrary, from New Delhi's perspective, India's BMD is intended to cater to potential deterrence failures that might occur during a military standoff. Although a limited BMD does, at least theoretically, provide an element of countervalue "invulnerability" to India, that is not the strategic intent behind the program.[32] At the same time, even though there is no search for invulnerability in India's thinking, this does not mean that it favors a situation of MAD (as was the case during the Cold War years).

Also, regardless of the fact that India does not yet have a triad in place, even though sixteen years have passed since it overtly developed nuclear weapons (close to a quarter century since it first embarked on the weaponization process), there does not seem to be any desire to acquire thermonuclear capability.[33] This is the case despite the credible doubts about India's claims of having successfully conducted a thermonuclear test in 1998.[34] New Delhi also continues to stand by its pledge to maintain nothing more than a minimum deterrent capability, quite unlike the behavior of the Cold War rivals who built tens of thousands of weapons in search of ensuring a survivable arsenal. There has never been any thinking in India to acquire such nuclear capability so as to carry out a bolt-from-the-blue decapitation strike against Pakistan.[35] Indeed, none of the three nuclear-capable states in the region has first-strike advantage against the others—and they are not planning to have it any time soon.

Neither Pakistan's population nor its nuclear arsenal is invulnerable to Indian strikes; but unlike India, Pakistan's management of its nuclear arsenal is robust and shows a certain level of urgency. Pakistan has been increasing the size of its nuclear arsenal and fissile material stockpile, and it is slated to have the world's third-biggest arsenal in the next decade or so.[36] Also, its Strategic Plans Division is a highly professional organization that not only oversees the country's nuclear arsenal but also engages in nuclear doctrinal and strategic thinking.

On Mutually Assured Destruction

India's political and official articulations about nuclear weapons do not refer to mutually assured destruction or the balance of terror. It refrains from using these or related phrases in its declarations and statements, and it does not even indirectly refer to such intentions. The thinking within the Indian strategic community on nuclear weapons mirrors the official thinking. Given the minimum deterrent that it aims to develop and maintain, MAD or BoT strategies have not dominated Indian thinking on strategic stability. Although nuclear weapons do contribute to the sense of India's existential security as a weapon of last resort, they do not play a fundamental role in India's defense strategies vis-à-vis Pakistan. Nor does India have a sense of shared nuclear fate with Pakistan.

Instead, there is a widespread feeling across the Indian strategic community that nuclear weapons are an insurance policy but do not form the crux of the country's national security strategy. As noted above, there is hardly any discussion within the strategic community about what kind of destruction will be delivered, the number of casualties that might occur, the desirability of bolt-from-the-blue strikes, the preparations for nuclear war fighting, and so on. It is likely that India will attempt to resolve conflicts at lower levels without invoking nuclear threats, as it has in the past. In fact, as discussed below, this is the very logic behind the so-called Cold Start doctrine. Accordingly, even if New Delhi were convinced that it would get away with limited damage if it were to carry out a first strike against Pakistan using nuclear weapons, it would be highly unlikely to succumb to such a temptation. Moreover, even if there were a militarized conflict between India and Pakistan, nuclear weapons would be unlikely to play a role in the resolution of that conflict, at least from the Indian point of view. Even though India claims that it will use nuclear weapons against Pakistan in retaliation for an attack with weapons of mass destruction, in keeping with its 2003 doctrine, there is a certain belief that Pakistan will not be able to carry out a first strike that could result in the complete destruction of India.[37] Hence, India's NFU policy.

Although Pakistan also does not rest its deterrence logic purely on MAD or BoT, its posture is significantly different from that of India. And though New Delhi professes its disinclination to use its nuclear weapons first through its NFU declaration, Pakistan does not rule out a first use of its weapons in case of an existential "non-nuclear" situation. It is not confident that it could thwart a conventional attack with conventional weapons, hence the Pakistani argument that it may escalate to the nuclear level to defend itself. It would be an illusion to imagine that Pakistan would be able to survive as a viable state after a nuclear exchange with India. Such an exchange would bring destruction to both, but more so to Pakistan, because the postexchange situation would not be one of "mutually" assured destruction.

This also means that Pakistan is seemingly prepared to live in a MAD/BoT world; but India, or for that matter China, is unprepared to do so. As a result, the Pakistani nuclear arsenal is believed to be more launch-ready than the Indian one. And yet the launch-readiness of both the Indian and Pakistani nuclear arsenals is way below those of the American and Soviet arsenals during the Cold War years, when the weapons were kept on hair-trigger alert.[38] In short, Pakistan's nuclear posture is closer to MAD than India's.

Balance versus Parity

Questions regarding parity and balance should also be considered when examining how India and Pakistan think about MAD and BoT. There seems to be no push in India to look for numerical parity in strategic systems with either China or Pakistan; nor is there any appetite in New Delhi to match Islamabad's tactical nuclear weapon capability. Indeed, both China and Pakistan have more nuclear weapons than India, collectively and individually. And yet there seems to be no insecurity about this in New Delhi, as is evident from the fact that there are no worried statements from officials or feverish attempts to build more weapons.[39]

Despite being sandwiched between two nuclear-armed adversaries that collectively have at least 450 weapons and missiles that can reach anywhere in India, New Delhi does not seem to have the desire to revisit the country's minimum deterrence postures. Trilemma concerns do influence Indian deterrence thinking, but these have not led India to fundamentally alter its doctrine or the pace of weapons development.[40] That said, adhering to minimum deterrence in the longer run will depend on increases in Pakistani and Chinese arsenals, given that the Indian decision makers have referred to the "minimum" as being dynamic. Therefore, what India is looking for is balance as opposed to parity, which roughly translates into

- An emphasis on denying overwhelming quantitative and qualitative superiority of strategic arsenal to the adversary. This explains the Indian articulation of minimum deterrence as dynamic.
- Maintaining a regional balance of power and building strategic alliances with the major powers in the international system.
- Achieving (sub)conventional stability.
- Enhancing the deterrent effects of its nuclear arsenal as well as strengthening deterrence by denial, by way of investing in a limited BMD program.
- Achieving proficiency with advanced technology, thereby improving command, control, communication, intelligence, surveillance, and reconnaissance capabilities and investing in antisatellite technology.
- Enhancing second-strike capability by investing in triad and long-range systems.

- Having a willingness to live with asymmetric balance vis-à-vis China—that is, maintaining lower numbers while focusing on existential deterrence.[41]

Pakistan has a very different understanding of balance and parity. Although maintaining parity (or superiority) of nuclear weapons with India seems to be important for Pakistan, it is seeking not only strategic parity with India but also parity in comprehensive military power. Put differently, strategic parity for Pakistan is not exclusive of conventional parity, and so Pakistan is looking for a broad-based balance to deter India. To use Pakistan's retired Air Vice Marshal Shahzad Chaudhry's phrase, for Pakistan strategic balance is the "national capacity to deter war"—"within the military connotation of this concept of balance versus parity, the nuclear fills in where the conventional lags, and the conventional should fill in where the nuclear may consider itself suspect. Full disclosure of the other may never be realized. In this sense, Pakistan's entire force structure is built around a composite defensive capability of both the nuclear and the conventional mix."[42] This understanding of balance seems to be different from the way it is used in the context of Cold War deterrence literature.

If so, the operationalization of Pakistan's official policy of full-spectrum deterrence needs to be seen as linked to its concept of strategic balance.[43] This would imply that Pakistan is likely to look for superiority in its strategic arsenal to balance India's conventional superiority, even as the search for a conventional balance will continue as far as possible. On the positive side, this could imply a willingness to engage in arms control negotiations—Pakistan would be open to discussing arms control with India for parity, at the strategic and conventional levels, to cater to its need for overall balance. This suits Pakistan's interest in bringing India to the negotiating table to talk about nuclear and conventional arms control, provided they are discussed as part of a single basket of issues. Any unchecked Indian military growth runs counter to Pakistan's strategic interests.

OFFENSE/DEFENSE DILEMMAS AND CROSS-DOMAIN DETERRENCE

In the India-Pakistan context, there are four operative levels of cross-domain deterrence—use of subconventional actors, the Cold Start doctrine, introduction of TNWs, and the development of BMD—and there are contrasting views from each country on the offensive or defensive nature of these levels. These offense/defense dilemmas are, to a great extent, born out of each country's unique notions of strategic stability.

As described above, Indian and Pakistani notions of strategic/deterrence stability tend to differ fundamentally, leading to a major conceptual dissonance between them. To the Indian mind, Pakistan's stated aim of lowering the nuclear threshold, along with its use of subconventional actors, is a recipe for disaster vis-à-vis the region's stability. To Pakistan, India's threat to use conventional forces against the conventionally inferior Pakistan is the mother of all problems—it is the reason why Islamabad needs to lower the nuclear threshold in the first place. Using conventional forces to settle scores in a nuclear theater is irresponsible, the Pakistani argument goes, especially in response to acts committed by a third party over which Pakistan has no control.[44]

Let us now consider the sequence of a potential escalation ladder in the India-Pakistan context to see how deterrence works in a cross-domain fashion, wherein both India and Pakistan "seek to counter threats/inferiority in one sphere by using capabilities in a different arena where the deterring actor may have an advantage."[45] A typical example in the Indo-Pakistani context would be India's threat to use conventional forces against Pakistan in the event of a subconventional provocation by Pakistan. This interplay of cross-domain deterrence is not merely a result of making up for one's deficiencies in one domain with its edge in another, but is essentially due to fundamentally different views about strategic/deterrence stability.

Subconventional Aggression

India views Pakistan as a revisionist state with a deeply entrenched unease about the balance of power and status quo in the region. Pakistan's rivalry with India stems from its quest to wrest Kashmir from India and also from the hurt and humiliation it suffered when India helped in the creation of Bangladesh, carving out Pakistan's eastern part. This has prompted Islamabad to adopt ways and means to disrupt the region's status quo and decline to accept the regional order, which it thinks is dictated by New Delhi. This has led to the use of nonstate, subconventional actors against India, especially in the state of Jammu and Kashmir. At the lowest rung on the ladder, then, is the use of subconventional (terrorist) actors by the Pakistani state to destabilize India. When confronted with nonstate actors such as the Islamist terrorist group Lashkar-e-Taiba, India is befuddled and is at a loss for how to respond. For Pakistan, sponsoring terrorism, which it calls the freedom struggle, is a cheap strategy that allows plausible deniability to compel India to make concessions on Kashmir.[46]

New Delhi is unable to respond to Islamabad in the same domain because it does not feel comfortable in doing so; nor does it think such a strategy would be useful. Despite the Pakistani argument about India's fomenting terrorism on Pakistani soil, there is little evidence to suggest that India has been directly or indirectly committing terrorism in Pakistan.[47] This dilemma—resulting from India's unwillingness, on one hand, to respond to Pakistan's use of terrorism with nonstate actors and, on the other hand, India's setting a bad precedent by not responding to such Pakistani attacks for fear of nuclear escalation[48]—has been a source of distress for New Delhi, and the leadership considers it to be costly both domestically and internationally. On at least two occasions, New Delhi has actively considered conventional retaliation to terrorist attacks by Pakistan-based (and allegedly Pakistani-supported) terrorist groups: the December 2001 attack on the Indian Parliament and the November 2008 Mumbai attacks. Yet, ultimately, India demonstrated restraint. India's reluctance probably comes from its fear of potential early Pakistani nuclear use. If so, Pakistan has succeeded in deterring conventional Indian aggression using nuclear threats, even though Pakistan cannot be sure of such an Indian response each and every time. And yet there has been considerable thinking within India on how to carry out a limited conventional strike against Pakistan to retaliate against terrorist attacks, which would constitute a shift to a higher domain.

Enter "Cold Start"

This thinking has led to the new, but unofficial, "Cold Start" doctrine of the Indian army (the phrase that is more in circulation today is "proactive operations"). Using the potential of the conventional Cold Start strategy, New Delhi hopes to counter provocation in the subconventional domain. Cold Start imagines enabling the Indian military to carry out quick, offensive operations against Pakistan without crossing the latter's nuclear redlines in order to dismantle the terrorist infrastructure on the Pakistani side as well as to carve out some territory for negotiating purposes.[49]

Conversely, India's Cold Start strategy is designed to be below the nuclear threshold, and therefore need not be ruinous for strategic stability, even though Pakistan considers it to be a serious threat to strategic stability. Although, for New Delhi, Cold Start is merely making the covert conflict overt and official, it crosses a major threshold for Islamabad. Indian strategists reason that Pakistan would not be able to defeat India at the conventional level because of the latter's conventional superiority, and may not even use nuclear weapons against it, because this would break a very strong normative barrier. And though, for India, Cold Start is a way of defending against subconventional aggression, for Pakistan it is an offensive strategy.

Cold Start is also referred to as limited war under the nuclear umbrella. A former army chief who led the Indian army during the Kargil conflict with Pakistan has gone on record to argue that limited wars under the nuclear umbrella are indeed a viable method of responding to Pakistan's Kargil-like aggression and use of nonstate actors against India.

However, there is also a lot of skepticism about India's Cold Start strategy. Critics have argued that the doctrine is nothing but "hot air," given that it does not have New Delhi's political backing and is not considered a serious war-fighting strategy by the Indian army.[50] Although such skepticism may or may not be well founded, the fact is that some Pakistani war planners believe that India is somewhat serious about Cold Start. As a result, Pakistan has responded by lowering its nuclear threshold and potentially forward-deploying its nuclear weapons as a counterstrategy.[51]

For India, its failure to respond to Pakistan's subconventional strategy is also a matter of its deterrence reputation consistently failing to do anything to deter Islamabad's harmful impact on New Delhi's deterrence reputation, both domestically and internationally. Cold Start, then, is a logical response to this dilemma.[52] For New Delhi, Cold Start does not damage strategic stability in the region but indeed enables its maintenance. For Pakistan, Cold Start crosses a major redline and is a declaration of war by India. Nevertheless, Pakistan finds itself unable to respond in the same domain. For Pakistan, then, the answer to India's Cold Start lies in a higher domain—greater reliance on tactical nuclear weapons.

Tactical Nuclear Weapons Lower the Threshold

From the Pakistani strategic perspective, TNWs are an effective means for dealing with conventional Indian aggression. Pakistan simply has no choice but to escalate the conflict if it must defend itself. There is no way it can deal with India in the same conventional domain, so it must reach a higher-domain capability to cater to its defense needs. The development of short-range, nuclear-capable ballistic missiles, the 60-kilometer range Hatf IX, or Nasr missile, first tested in 2011, is seen as very much in keeping with this thinking. Indeed, the press release issued at the time of the testing of Nasr by Inter-Services Public Relations was unambiguous: "The missile has been developed to add deterrence value to Pakistan's Strategic Weapons Development program at shorter ranges. Nasr, with a range of 60 kilometers, carries nuclear warheads of appropriate yield with high accuracy, shoot, and scoot attributes. This quick response system addresses the need to deter evolving threats."[53]

What impact do TNWs have on strategic stability from Pakistan's perspective? First, Islamabad hopes to dissuade New Delhi with a nuclear deterrent threat so that the latter does not open conventional hostilities with the former. That is, Pakistan's argument is that the ball is in India's court because the decision to provoke Pakistani nuclear use lies with India. Second, by adopting such a strategy, Pakistan would also think that a tactical nuclear use would not lead to an all-out nuclear war between the two countries. From this perspective, the introduction of TNWs to counter India's conventional offensive does not damage strategic stability; it only enables Pakistan's survival, given that the Indian conventional offensive has the capability to seriously compromise Pakistan's war-fighting capacity. For Pakistan, TNWs are defensive armaments that will help it offset India's conventional superiority. It is indeed this offense/defense dilemma that made Khalid Kidwai argue that TNWs are weapons of peace in South Asia.[54]

For New Delhi, however, TNWs undermine stability in the region, given the fact that nuclear weapons are not central to its understanding of strategic stability and therefore do not form the core of New Delhi's strategy for conflict management in South Asia. Although India has not explicitly ruled out the development of TNWs, it has unambiguously said that nuclear weapons are for strategic, not tactical, use. In any case, it views Pakistan's TNWs as deeply destabilizing.

The Indian BMD Program

Pakistan's introduction of TNWs into its war planning against India has forced New Delhi to consider the development of BMD.[55] The Pakistani decision to introduce TNWs does precede India's decision to strengthen its BMD program. Moreover, BMD is seen by Indian strategists as a useful tool for responding to Pakistan's lowering of the nuclear threshold. That is, Islamabad's potential use of nuclear weapons has New Delhi worried and looking for countermeasures not just to oppose TNWs on the battlefield but also to defeat the potential first use of Pakistani nuclear weapons.

In this context, a limited BMD system could potentially increase deterrence through denial. The deterrence effect of BMD is applicable not only between rational state actors but also when nonstate (rational or irrational) actors target state actors. For instance, as pointed out in the previous section, if a Pakistani-based nonstate actor or rogue elements from the Pakistani armed forces target India with nuclear weapons, New Delhi will be able to properly comprehend and analyze the situation before contemplating an appropriate response.[56] This is possible only if the political decision-making organs and nuclear command and control in New Delhi are unaffected by such an attack.

Rajesh Basrur, in this context, argues that missile defense has certain values: "It can limit damage to oneself in the event deterrence fails. There are three ways in which deterrence might not work: if there is an accidental launch, if there is an unauthorized 'renegade' launch, and if an undeterrable adversary engages in a suicidal launch."[57] Accordingly, to New Delhi, development of BMD is a logical step, given that stability in the region can be maintained only by proactive strategies when Islamabad insists on lowering the nuclear threshold, thereby damaging deterrence stability. For New Delhi, then, BMD helps strengthen deterrence rather than damaging it.

Pakistan not only considers Indian BMD to be deeply damaging to stability in the region; it is also actively exploring ways to defeat it. The Pakistani scholar Mansoor Ahmed explains potential Pakistani countermeasures against Indian BMD:

> Countermeasures could range from maneuverable reentry vehicles (MRVs) to maneuverable warheads deployed on single warhead systems such as the road-mobile Shaheen I & II. These missiles can be launched on relatively short notice and are capable of striking targets deep inside India. Pakistan may already have developed MRVs for its Shaheen series of missiles, which would make it difficult for Indian BMDs to shoot them down. However, the development and deployment of multiple independently targetable reentry vehicles (MIRVs) seems to be the logical next step for Pakistan as a response to India's BMD. But MIRVs require mastery in developing miniaturized, efficient, lightweight, powerful warheads whose yield may vary from kilotons to megatons. If the official claim of having built a nuclear-capable tactical / battlefield Nasr ballistic missile is credible, then Pakistan appears to have succeeded in acquiring the capability to miniaturize nuclear warheads, to the extent that these can be launched from tactical missiles, MIRVs, and cruise missiles.
>
> With MIRV and miniaturized warhead capability in place, Pakistan is likely to proceed with the deployment of compact and sophisticated plutonium-based, boosted-fission, and/or thermonuclear warheads on a variety of launch platforms, such as aircraft, land-based mobile or silo-launched ballistic missile sites, and most importantly submarines.[58]

Strategic Implications

Indian and Pakistani notions of and approaches toward strategic stability and deterrence stability differ in many fundamental ways from the classic Cold War understanding, especially in the case of India. Such differences do have important policy implications, given that a state's sense of strategic and deterrence stability has an impact on its force structures, postures, and doctrines, and also on the linkages between conventional and strategic domains. What is remarkable is that such differences continue despite the great amount of nuclear learning that has happened in India, not only from its own past crises with Pakistan under the nuclear shadow but also from external sources and intellectual inspirations.[59] Indian and Pakistani unique thinking on strategic stability in the South Asian region has a number of implications for policy and theory.

First, India does not see strategic or conventional arms control mechanisms or dialogues as critical, because its thinking about nuclear strategy and strategic/deterrence stability is not governed by the logic of MAD or BoT. Consequently, chances of accidents, miscalculations, and crisis escalation may indeed rise, given that India does not feel the urgency to engage in nuclear/strategic confidence-building measures (CBMs) with Pakistan. In general, then, as Rajagopalan argues, "Just as it is cautious in advancing its nuclear weapons arsenal, it will also be cautious in advancing on the nuclear arms control and disarmament agenda. India is unlikely to sign either the CTBT [Comprehensive Nuclear-Test-Ban Treaty] or the FMCT [Fissile Material Cutoff Treaty], should they be presented to New Delhi in the next couple of years."[60] Moreover, because nuclear weapons are not mainstreamed into its military/defense thinking, New Delhi is less likely to worry about the problems of a hair-trigger alert, which could put considerably less pressure on its decision makers to engage in CBM talks and conclude them.

We should expect the opposite behavior in Pakistan's case, given that it has mainstreamed its nuclear weapons into its national strategy. As a matter of fact, Pakistan has evidently been more willing than India to talk about nuclear CBMs, even though it often attempts to couple talks about conventional and nuclear CBMs. In other words, a state's understanding about the likelihood of a nuclear confrontation influences its desire for CBMs.

Second, the lack of thinking about a doomsday scenario could encourage risk-taking tendencies, thereby having a negative impact on stability. This is especially true in the Indian case. Because New Delhi believes that deterrence holds at the strategic level, it rules out low-level nuclear use, which could encourage risk-taking at the conventional level. It could also have negative implications for the state's defense preparedness. Pakistan, for instance, thinks that its use (or at least India's uncertainty about its use) of nonstate proxies has no impact on the strategic stability with India, while India, in turn, thinks that its use of conventional means (Cold Start) to respond to Pakistan's subconventional aggression would not disturb strategic stability. Both these beliefs are detrimental to the region's stability. India, while being concerned about Cold Start inducing nuclear escalation or Pakistan's threatening to do so, would hope that it can still call Pakistan's nuclear bluff, and hence would conclude that its own actions would not affect stability in the region beyond a point.[61] Pakistan, conversely, believes its low nuclear threshold would dissuade India from carrying out its Cold Start strategy, and thus its own use of terrorism would not have any impact on regional stability. These beliefs could enable risk-taking tendencies in the respective countries.

Third, as discussed above, India also apparently has a relaxed attitude toward improving its deterrence capabilities. This is seen in India's willingness to live with less than absolute deterrence (without thermonuclear and tactical nuclear capabilities, and with not much focus on specificities). This may have a positive effect on overall stability in the region, because it could potentially dissuade India's adversaries from developing larger arsenals. However, this relaxed approach to deterrence and stability also has negative implications for stable deterrence in the long run. For instance, it could lead to less political oversight of the evolution of the country's nuclear capability, thereby leading to a situation in which the military could potentially become the key nuclear decision maker.

Pakistan, conversely, has a far clearer sense of the role of nuclear weapons in its defense planning and posture. It also keeps its nuclear weapons more launch-ready than India does. Yet this readiness could also have negative implications for strategic stability in the region. For instance, the short warning time between the two countries, and the country's first-strike doctrine and potential forward deployment of nuclear assets, in combination, could inherently increase the likelihood of nuclear use by Pakistan.

Finally, India's and Pakistan's differing perceptions of strategic/deterrence stability and the role of nuclear weapons would also have implications for bargaining strategies and crisis de-escalation mechanisms that they would adopt, along with the dynamics of escalation dominance in a potential conflict. For instance, if Pakistan believes that the use of nonstate actors, with plausible deniability, has nothing to do with larger issues of strategic stability, it is unlikely to back down when the Indian side reacts to it. Moreover, if the nonstate actor has engaged in an attack without official Pakistani sanction, Pakistan might respond disproportionately to India's reaction. In other words, if India thinks that nonstate actors' attacks damage its notion of security and stability, India's "legitimate" reaction to this could be seen as an "overreaction" by Pakistan, leading the latter to respond likewise.

CONCLUSION

The burden of this chapter has been to make the argument that a state's notion of strategic stability contributes to how cross-domain deterrence operates on the ground, even as the nature and dynamics of such cross-domain deterrence simultaneously have an impact on its notion of strategic stability—the two are mutually constituted. This chapter has shown that India's and Pakistan's notions of strategic stability have had an impact on how their dyadic relationship is shaped, and their dyadic relationship has had an impact on their individual notions of strategic stability, albeit in distinct ways.

The chapter has also argued that India and Pakistan maintain drastically different conceptions of strategic stability—rooted in their strategic postures—as, respectively, a status quo power or a revisionist power. These differing conceptions, the chapter has argued, have implications for regional stability.

In light of the chapter's discussion, it becomes clear that three key measures should be given priority by the Indian and Pakistani governments in order to strengthen stability in the region. First of all, the two governments need to address issues related to instability at the lower levels of the conflict, because it is not major war efforts that will drive the two states into a fight but escalation from the lower levels. Second, the two states need to institute joint mechanisms to arrest the escalation process at the lower levels, where it is easier to control the dynamics. Such joint mechanisms could include the establishment of a bilateral Nuclear Risk Reduction Center as well as predetermined, regular lines of communication between the commanders of various forces and theater commanders to make sure that they address escalation at the lower rungs before it reaches the nuclear levels.

Third, the two governments need to recognize the utility of talks on nuclear CBMs, strategic concepts, and military doctrines. At the moment, however, the two sides are not engaged in a dialogue on either conventional or strategic CBMs. The intermittent bilateral dialogue process, which often gets ruptured, has not been able to address some of the biggest challenges between the two sides.

NOTES

1. It is pertinent to point out here that what is described in this chapter is merely the view of the author. There are, indeed, several views in India on the issue of strategic stability in the India-Pakistan context.

2. Michael S. Gerson, "The Origins of Strategic Stability: The United States and the Threat of Surprise Attack," in *Strategic Stability: Contending Interpretations*, ed. Elbridge A. Colby and Michael S. Gerson (Carlisle, PA: Strategic Studies Institute of US Army War College, 2013), 5.

3. Bernard Brodie, ed., *The Absolute Weapon: Atomic Power and World Order* (New York: Harcourt, Brace, 1946); William Liscum Borden, *There Will Be No Time: The Revolution in Strategy* (New York: Macmillan, 1946); and Gerson, "Origins."

4. Elbridge Colby, "Defining Strategic Stability: Reconciling Stability and Deterrence," in *Strategic Stability*, ed. Colby and Gerson, 48.

5. Ibid., 57.

6. Andrei Kokoshin, "Ensuring Strategic Stability in the Past and Present: Theoretical and Applied Questions," Belfer Center for Science and International Affairs, Harvard Kennedy School.

7. John D. Steinbruner, "National Security and the Concept of Strategic Stability," *Journal of Conflict Resolution* 22, no. 3 (1978).

8. Cited by Robert Ayson, *Thomas Schelling and the Nuclear Age: Strategy as Social Science* (London: Frank Cass, 2004), 56.

9. Colin S. Gray, "Strategic Stability Reconsidered," *Daedalus* 109, no. 4 (1980).

10. "We are a nuclear power, and know how to defend ourselves: Sartaj Aziz," *Dawn*, August 24, 2015, www.dawn.com/news/1202323.

11. Mohammed Uzair Shaikh, "Pakistan's Nuclear Threat: BJP Calls Islamabad Irresponsible; Assures to Raise Issue Internationally," India.com, August 24, 2015, www.india.com/news/india/pakistans-nuclear-threat-bjp-calls-islamabad-irresponsible -assures-to-raise-issue-internationally-517451/.

12. Inter-Services Public Relations, "PR-94/2011-ISPR," press release, April 19, 2011, www.ispr.gov.pk/front/main.asp?o=t-press_release&id=1721.

13. There has been a great deal of concern within the international community with regard to Pakistan's nuclear nonproliferation record. See "WikiLeaks Cables Highlight Pakistani Nuclear Terror Threat," *The Guardian*, December 1, 2010, www.theguardian .com/world/2010/dec/01/wikileaks-cables-pakistan-nuclear-threat; and Gabriel Domínguez and Shamil Shams, "Why Pakistan's Nuclear Obsession Is Reason for Concern," DW, August 28, 2015, www.dw.com/en/why-pakistans-nuclear-obsession-is-reason-for -concern/a-18679176.

14. See Toby Dalton and Michael Krepon, *A Normal Nuclear Pakistan* (Washington, DC: Henry L. Stimson Center and Carnegie Endowment for International Peace, 2015).

15. Vipin Narang, *Nuclear Strategy in the Modern Era: Regional Powers and International Conflict* (Princeton, NJ: Princeton University Press, 2014), 92–93.

16. Analysts have pointed out, as does the Indian nuclear doctrine, that India does not have an "absolute" no-first-use policy, given that the doctrine envisions the usage of nuclear weapons in retaliation to biological and chemical weapons. See Vipin Narang, "Five Myths about India's Nuclear Posture," *Washington Quarterly* 36, no. 3 (2013). However, even though the doctrine includes chemical and biological weapons use by the adversary as a potential trigger for nuclear use by India, that does not make it any less as political weapon. More important, the larger point here, that India has underplayed its nuclear weapons in its security articulations, is not negated by the argument about India's conditional no-first-use policy.

17. Elizabeth Whitfield, "Fuzzy Math on Indian Nuclear Weapons," Carnegie Endowment for International Peace, April 19, 2016, http://carnegieendowment.org /2016/04/19/fuzzy-math-on-indian-nuclear-weapons/ixas; and Sushant Singh, "Nukes Are Not for War," *Indian Express*, December 25, 2015, http://indianexpress.com/article /opinion/columns/india-shouldnt-abandon-its-nuclear-doctrine-because-of-pakistans -tactical-nukes/.

18. Key players in the international system refer to India's nuclear program as a responsible one, which means that India is not a proliferator and that it has a responsible nuclear posture. See "India a Responsible Nuclear State," Rediff.com, May 16, 2005,

www.rediff.com/news/2005/may/16inter1.htm; 154 *Congressional Record* H22125, daily ed., September 26, 2008, Testimony of Congressman Frank Pallone; and 154 *Congressional Record* H22127, daily ed., September 26, 2008, Testimony of Congressman Gary Akerman.

19. D. Bala Venkatesh Varma, "India's Views on Contemporary Disarmament Issues," lecture, Jawaharlal Nehru University, New Delhi, February 11, 2015. Varma is ambassador and permanent representative of India to the UN Conference on Disarmament, Geneva, and he emphasized the Indian belief that nuclear weapons are a major source of influence in contemporary world politics.

20. Arun Prakash, *India's Nuclear Deterrent: The More Things Change . . .* (Singapore: S. Rajaratnam School of International Studies, 2014).

21. Verghese Koithara, *Managing India's Nuclear Forces* (Washington, DC: Brookings Institution Press, 2012), 3.

22. Ibid., 7.

23. Agha Shahi, Zulfiqar Ali Khan, and Abdul Sattar, "Securing Nuclear Peace," *The News*, October 5, 1999.

24. Shamshad Ahmad, "A South Asian Reality," *The News*, May 28, 2012, www .cssforum.com.pk/general/news-articles/61669-south-asia-important-articles.html.

25. Walter C. Ladwig III, "A Cold Start for Hot Wars: The Indian Army's New Limited War Doctrine," *International Security* 32, no. 3 (2007–8).

26. V. P. Malik, "Limited War and Escalation Control I," Institute of Peace and Conflict Studies, November 30, 2004, www.ipcs.org/article/nuclear/limited-war-and -escalation-control-i-1570.html.

27. "US Embassy Cables: India 'Unlikely' to Deploy Cold Start against Pakistan," *The Guardian*, February 16, 2010, www.theguardian.com/world/us-embassy-cables -documents/248971.

28. Ward Wilson and Scott Sagan have written about this; see Ward Wilson, *Five Myths about Nuclear Weapons* (New York: Houghton Mifflin Harcourt, 2013); and and Scott Sagan, *Limits of Safety: Organizations, Accidents, and Nuclear Weapons* (Princeton, NJ: Princeton University Press, 1993). They observe how there were many near accidents, even among the technologically more sophisticated first-generation nuclear weapon states.

29. Discussion with senior official in the Indian Ministry of External Affairs, July 23, 2014.

30. Patrick M. Morgan, *Deterrence Now* (Cambridge: Cambridge University Press, 1993), 22.

31. Michael Krepon, "The Stability-Instability Paradox, Misperception, and Escalation Control in South Asia," in *Escalation Control and the Nuclear Option in South Asia*, ed. Michael Krepon, Rodney W. Jones, and Ziad Haider (Washington, DC: Henry L. Stimson Center, 2004), www.stimson.org/sites/default/files/file-attach ments/stability-instability-paradox-south-asia.pdf.

32. By all accounts, India's BMD program is a limited one geared to protect two cities—Mumbai and Delhi. See "Interceptor Missile Tested 7 Times, DRDO's Rajini-kanth Moment Still Far," *Indian Express*, May 4, 2015, http://indianexpress.com/article /explained/interceptor-missile-tested-7-times-drdos-rajinikanth-moment-still-far /#sthash.yMq7iuvB.dpuf.

33. Shyam Saran, "Is India's Nuclear Deterrent Credible?" *Arms Control Wonk*, April 24, 2013, http://krepon.armscontrolwonk.com/files/2013/05/Final-Is-Indias -Nuclear-Deterrent-Credible-rev1-2-1-3.pdf.

34. Rama Lakshmi, "Key Indian Figures Call for New Nuclear Tests Despite Deal with US," *Washington Post*, October 5, 2009, www.washingtonpost.com/wp-dyn/content /article/2009/10/04/AR2009100402865.html.

35. The Indian nuclear doctrine refers to only a second strike. Moreover, retired Indian officials have even advocated for a "no-first-use agreement with Pakistan." Shyam Saran, for instance, has argued that "an agreement on no first use of nuclear weapons would be a notable measure following up on the commitment already made by the two countries to maintain a moratorium on nuclear testing." See "India's Nuclear Deterrent Credible?" lecture, India Habitat Centre, New Delhi, April 24, 2013, www.armscontrol wonk.com/files/2013/05/Final-Is-Indias-Nuclear-Deterrent-Credible-rev1-2-1-3.pdf.

36. Tim Craig, "Report: Pakistan's Nuclear Arsenal Could Become the World's Third-Biggest," *Washington Post*, August 27, 2015, www.washingtonpost.com/world /asia_pacific/report-pakistans-nuclear-arsenal-could-become-the-worlds-third -biggest/2015/08/26/6098478a-4c0c-11e5-80c2-106ea7fb80d4_story.html.

37. Ashley J. Tellis, *India's Emerging Nuclear Posture: Between Recessed Deterrent and Ready Arsenal* (Santa Monica, CA: RAND Corporation, 2001); and Ali Ahmed, "Reviewing India's Nuclear Doctrine," Institute of Defense Studies and Analyses, April 24, 2009, www.idsa.in/policybrief/reviewingindiasnucleardoctrine_aahmed_240409.

38. Narang, "Five Myths." While Narang argues that India's arsenal is more ready than usually assumed, it is important to note that even though some of its weapons are "likely pre-/mated to the delivery vehicle and kept hermetically sealed for storage and transport," it does not mean that the weapons are kept ready for "launch on warning" or will be launched automatically after a Pakistani strike. More so, while some of its weapons may be pre-mated, most are not. Finally, the doctrine, unlike in the Cold War case, rules out a first strike.

39. See, e.g., Ashley J. Tellis, "China, India, and Pakistan Growing Nuclear Capa-bilities with No End in Sight," Carnegie Endowment for International Peace, February 25, 2015, http://carnegieendowment.org/2015/02/25/china-india-and-pakistan-growing -nuclear-capabilities-with-no-end-in-sight.

40. Linton Brooks and Mira Rapp-Hooper use the term "security trilemma"; see Linton Brooks and Mira Rapp-Hooper, "Extended Deterrence, Assurance, and Reassur-ance in the Pacific during the Second Nuclear Age," in *Strategic Asia 2013–14: Asia in the Second Nuclear Age*, ed. Ashley J. Tellis, Abraham M. Denmark, and Travis Tanner (Washington, DC: National Bureau of Asian Research, 2013). Gregory D. Koblentz explains it as "actions taken by one state to defend against another state have the effect of making a third state feel insecure." Gregory D. Koblentz, *Strategic Stability in the Second Nuclear Age* (New York: Council on Foreign Relations, 2014), 20, i.cfr.org /content/publications/.../Second%20Nuclear%20Age_CSR71.pdf.

41. Tellis, "China, India, and Pakistan."

42. A. V. M. Shahzad Chaudhry, "Seeking a Way out of a Nuclear Arms Race," unpublished paper shared with the author, 2015.

43. Inter-Services Public Relations, "PR-133/2013-ISPR," press release, Septem-ber 5, 2013, www.ispr.gov.pk/front/t-press_release.asp?id=2361&print=1.

44. "Pak Charges India with Pursuing 'Dangerous, Provocative and Irresponsible Doctrines,'" United News of India, October 30, 2015, www.uniindia.com/pak-charges -india-with-pursuing-dangerous-provocative-and-irresponsible-doctrines/world/news /254200.html.

45. Erik Gartzke and Jon Lindsay, "Cross-Domain Deterrence: Strategy in an Era of Complexity," conference paper, International Studies Association Annual Meeting, Toronto, March 25, 2014, https://quote.ucsd.edu/deterrence/files/2014/12/EGLindsay _CDDOverview_20140715.pdf.

46. See "'Freedom Fighters' Fighting in Kashmir, Not Terrorists, Says Musharraf," *Dawn*, December 9, 2015, www.dawn.com/news/1225049; and "Every Claim of India about 26/11 Backed by Man Who Headed Pak Probe," NDTV.com, August 4, 2015, www.ndtv.com/india-news/mumbai-attacks-launched-from-pakistan-soil-says -former-pak-investigator-in-article-1203702.

47. Pakistan has often argued that India has been interfering in its Balochistan province (and supporting the anti-Pakistan activities there) through Afghanistan, but it has never presented any evidence to back up this allegation. See "US Snubs Pakistan's Bogus Complaint about Indian Interference in Balochistan," *Times of India*, October 22, 2015, http://timesofindia.indiatimes.com/india/US-snubs-Pakistans-bogus-complaint -about-Indian-interference-in-Balochistan/articleshow/49489193.cms.

48. For more on this, see Toby Dalton and George Perkovich, "India's Nuclear Options and Escalation Dominance," Carnegie Endowment for International Peace, May 19, 2016. http://carnegieendowment.org/2016/05/19/india-s-nuclear-options-and -escalation-dominance/iydh.

49. For an assessment of the Cold Start strategy, see Walter C. Ladwig III, "A Cold Start for Hot Wars? The Indian Army's New Limited War Doctrine," *International Security* 32, no. 3 (2007–8): 158–90. On the efficacy of the doctrine, see Shashank Joshi, "India's Military Instrument: A Doctrine Stillborn," *Journal of Strategic Studies* 36, no. 4 (2013).

50. Shashank Joshi, "India's Military Instrument: A Doctrine Stillborn," *Journal of Strategic Studies* 36, no. 4 (2013).

51. Varghese K. George, "Battlefield Nuke Deployment by Pakistan Raises Risk: US," *The Hindu*, March 30, 2016; and Jaganath Sankaran, "The Enduring Power of Bad Ideas: 'Cold Start' and Battlefield Nuclear Weapons in South Asia," *Arms Control Wonk*, November 4, 2014, www.armscontrol.org/ACT/201_11/Features/Cold-Start -and-Battlefield-Nuclear-Weapons-in-South-Asia.

52. Deterrer's Dilemma is a situation of "damned if you do, damned if you don't" faced by the defender while responding to the challenger in the context of the former's deterrence commitments. On this, see Emanuel Adler, "Complex Deterrence in the Asymmetric-Warfare Era" in *Complex Deterrence: Strategy in the Global Age*, ed. T.V. Paul, Patrick M. Morgan, and James J. Wirtz (Chicago: University of Chicago Press, 2009).

53. Inter-Services Public Relations, "PR-94/2011-ISPR," press release, April 19, 2011, www.ispr.gov.pk/front/main.asp?o=t-press_release&id=1721.

54. Khalid Kidwai, *Nuclear Risks in South Asia*, YouTube video, 23:03, from the keynote address given at the Pugwash Annual Conference on November 2, 2015, https:// pugwash.org/2015/11/02/video-gen-kidwai-on-nuclear-risks-in-south-asia-nagasaki -conference/.

55. Although the Indian BMD has been in development since the mid-1990s, the project assumed importance in the Indian strategic thinking only in the mid-2000s. India first tested its Prithvi Air Defence (PAD) capability in 2006 and the Advanced Air Defence (AAD) capability in December 2007, and there have since been a number of repeat tests. The two systems, which were in their trial phase until 2011, were declared by the Defence Research and Development Organisation (DRDO) as fully developed and ready to be inducted in 2012. V. K. Saraswat, the then chief of DRDO, argued in 2012 that "the ballistic missile defence shield is now mature. . . . We are ready to put phase I in place, and it can be put in very short time," meaning that the system, which currently has a 2,000-kilometer range, will be upgraded to 5,000 kilometers by 2016. "Missile Defence Shield Ready: DRDO Chief," *The Hindu*, May 6, 2012, www.the hindu.com/news/national/missile-defence-shield-ready-drdo-chief/article3390404.ece.

56. Amit Gupta, "Special Commentary: India's Missile Defence," Institute of Peace and Conflict Studies, April 12, 2013, www.ipcs.org/article/nuclear/special-commentary -indias-missile-defence-3880.html; Ali Ahmed, "Implications of Indian BMD Development," Institute of Peace and Conflict Studies, March 8, 2011, www.ipcs.org/article /india/implications-of-indian-bmd-developments-3341.html; and Bruno Tertrais, "Pakistan's Nuclear and WMD Programmes: Status, Evolution and Risks," *Non-Proliferation Papers*, no. 19, July 2012, www.nonproliferation.eu/documents/nonproliferationpapers /brunotertrais5010305e17790.pdf.

57. Rajesh M. Basrur, "Missile Defense: An Indian Perspective," in *The Impact of Missile Defenses on Southern Asia*, ed. Chris Gagne and Michael Krepon (Washington, DC: Henry L. Stimson Center, 2001), www.stimson.org/images/uploads/research -pdfs/SABMDBasrur.pdf. See also Ashley J. Tellis, "The Evolution of US-Indian Ties: Missile Defense in an Emerging Strategic Relationship," *International Security* 30, no. 4: 142–43.

58. Mansoor Ahmed, "Security Doctrines, Technologies and Escalation Ladders: A Pakistani Perspective," in *US-Pakistan Strategic Partnership, A Track II Dialogue, Sixth Iteration, Phuket, Thailand*, ed. Feroz H. Khan and Nick M. Masellis (Monterey, CA: Center for Contemporary Conflict, US Naval Postgraduate School, 2012).

59. Happymon Jacob, "Conceptualizing Nuclear Learning: A Study of the Indian Experience," in *Nuclear Learning: The Next Decade in South Asia*, ed. Feroz Hassan Khan, Ryan Jacobs, and Emily Burke (Monterey, CA: US Naval Postgraduate School, 2014), https://my.nps.edu/documents/104111744/106151936/Nuclear+Learning+in +South+Asia_June2014.pdf/db169d3c-6c10-4289-b65d-a348ffc9480f.

60. Rajesh Rajagopalan, "India's Nuclear Policy," in *Major Powers' Nuclear Policies and International Order in the 21st Century*, conference proceedings, 12th NIDS International Symposium on Security Affairs (Tokyo: National Institute for Defense Studies, 2010), www.nids.go.jp/english/event/symposium/pdf/2009/e_06.pdf.

61. Sandeep Unnithan, "Why India Didn't Strike Pakistan after 26/11," *India Today*, October 14, 2015, http://indiatoday.intoday.in/story/why-india-didnt-strike-pakistan -after-26-11/1/498952.html.

9

The Road Not Taken

Defining Israel's Approach to Strategic Stability

ILAI Z. SALTZMAN

IN MID-2016, the fifth Dolphin-class nuclear-capable submarine had concluded its journey to the Israeli navy base in Haifa from the shipyard in Kiel, Germany. Israeli prime minister Benjamin Netanyahu declared upon its arrival, "Our submarine fleet will act as a deterrent to our enemies who want to destroy us." Israeli defense minister Moshe Ya'alon added that beyond the protection of its coastline, Israel's submarine fleet is also equipped with "offensive capabilities that enable us to strike in any place we choose, along Israel's coasts and far from them."[1] According to the conventional wisdom in deterrence theory, second-strike capabilities, such as this latest addition to Israel's submarine fleet, are instrumental for the creation and maintenance of strategic stability because they make preemptive or first strikes intolerably costly and therefore improbable.[2] Yet the term "strategic stability" was not used by Netanyahu, or by any other official for that matter. In fact, the unprecedented public release of the Israeli Defense Forces' strategy by Chief of Staff Gadi Eisenkot in August 2015 contained no reference to strategic stability either.[3]

Does this suggest that Israeli decision makers and strategic planners are oblivious to this concept or its relevance for their national security, even though, in part, they follow its overarching logic? My answer is that they have a different understanding of the term that partly overlaps and partly diverges from the traditional usage, and that this reflects a particular set of strategic circumstances that do not follow the original meaning or the application of the term in the US-Soviet context.

Originally, the term "strategic stability" emerged during the early decades of the Cold War, when the United States and the Soviet Union sought to structure their global nuclear relations in the shadow of East/West rivalry.[4] Although the term was an extremely common concept in the broader jargon associated with the nuclear revolution, there is, as discussed in the introduction to this volume, no clear consensus with regard to its actual meaning. This ambiguity results, first and foremost, from the fact that the term's origins and applicability were both time- and actor-specific, and its underpinnings were idiosyncratic with regard to the desired means and ends.[5]

In a recent study, Elbridge Colby argued that an appropriate and updated definition of strategic stability is "a situation in which no party has an incentive to use nuclear weapons save for vindication of its vital interests in extreme circumstances."[6] Still, scholars and practitioners alike have thus far failed to produce a satisfactory definition of the term. Frank Rose, deputy assistant secretary of the Bureau of Arms Control, Verification, and Compliance, has recently commented that "strategic stability is a term we use a lot, but one that is difficult to define. . . . In today's world, strategic stability encompasses much more than just nuclear relations."[7]

Various scholars and analysts have turned to reevaluate the relevance of the term "strategic stability" in order to account for the dynamics among nuclear powers in the post–Cold War era, or what some of them call the "second nuclear age."[8] Israel, however, is a rather sui generis nuclear power. Its nuclear posture, although created during the "first nuclear age," was molded in an untraditional fashion that has largely remained consistent since, and is not expected to change in the foreseeable future. Israel has never admitted that it had a military nuclear program; nor has it joined the Non-Proliferation Treaty, although it has become an open secret that it has about eighty nuclear warheads with multiple delivery systems, such as ballistic missiles and submarines.[9] Moreover, as Gregory Koblentz acknowledged in his study of present-day challenges to the maintenance of strategic stability, "Israel is not in a deterrent relationship with any of the existing nuclear weapon states, limiting its influence on, and exposure to, variations in strategic stability among these states."[10]

Over the years, however, Israeli policymakers have translated their distinctive notion of strategic stability into an elaborate policy designed to achieve three key goals. The first is to prevent an all-out conventional war resulting from direct state-to-state hostility. The second goal is to prevent regional escalation potentially generated by irregular warfare (terror and guerrilla) across Israel's borders. And the third goal is to stop the proliferation of nuclear weapons. Israel went to great lengths to convince its neighbors in words and deeds (with mixed results) that it would not accept any violation of these principles and that all options are on the table. Israeli governments authorized attacks against state and nonstate actors across the Middle East, and these adversaries were led to understand the dangers associated with any attempts to undermine the country's strategic stability as its leaders perceived and defined it. But beyond the varying nature of the targets, in order to preserve its strategic stability, Israel has used a multitude of measures, such as preemptive and preventive war, disproportionate force, proxy wars, and, most recently, cyberwarfare.

This chapter advocates a broader conceptualization of strategic stability that goes beyond merely describing the relationship between nuclear powers. As the case of Israel's approach to strategic stability suggests, a more multifaceted, analytical approach that addresses different target audiences (state and nonstate actors) and utilizes a variety of military means (kinetic and nonkinetic, conventional and asymmetric) is very much needed. Redefining the term to address the cross-domain aspects of "strategic stability" will undoubtedly increase its conceptual relevance and applicability to the post–Cold War era and contribute to the understanding of the interaction between nuclear and nonnuclear powers alike.

DENUCLEARIZING ISRAEL'S APPROACH TO STRATEGIC STABILITY

Although the state of Israel was born into the nuclear age, its major security concern was not of a nuclear nature but rather the fear of a combined Arab conventional attack that would benefit from the Arabs' commanding quantitative advantage. Thus, Israeli deterrence was overwhelmingly conventional in nature because, as Jonathan Shimshoni rightly notes, the strategic environment was "essentially conventional."[11] Of a lesser degree was the threat of irregular warfare through infiltration across Israel's porous borders, which was also sponsored by Arab regimes, and beyond its demoralizing features had the potential of escalating into an all-out war.[12] The following discussion describes how Israeli policymakers and strategic thinkers reconciled the possession of nuclear weapons with the geostrategic realities they faced.

Beyond the Nuclear Logic of Strategic Stability

The question of whether to integrate nuclear weapons into Israel's broader security strategy, and especially into its regional deterrence system designed to maintain strategic stability, divided Israeli leadership in the early 1960s—after the original civilian nuclear program had also produced a military option. During critical internal debates throughout 1962, one group, headed by Moshe Dayan and Shimon Peres, argued that if Israel were equipped with nuclear weapons as part of an overt deterrence system, it would be able to compensate for its quantitative inferiority and discourage the Arabs from pursuing military actions, and achieve security at a lower cost.

Others, such as ministers Yigal Allon and Israeli Galili, believed that a militarized nuclear program would be both unwarranted and disastrous. It would be unwarranted because conventional superiority was not waning and there was no possibility of crafting mutual nuclear deterrence in the absence of nuclear counterparts. It would be disastrous because it would trigger a regional nuclear arms race that the Arabs would probably win, given their abundant resources.[13] Moreover, the Kennedy administration's continuous pressure for greater transparency with regard to the nuclear facility in Dimona suggested that the existing nuclear powers would not tolerate any Israeli attempt to establish overt nuclear deterrence, and that the United States would not provide the same political and technological support that the Soviets would most probably give to the Arabs.[14] Consequently, after a fierce internal debate among the proponents and the opponents of the nuclear option, prime minister and minister of defense David Ben-Gurion categorically decided that nuclear weapons would not be integrated into the preexisting strategic and doctrinal architecture of the Israeli Defense Forces, and that the military nuclear option would be clandestinely developed alongside, rather than as part of or instead of, Israel's conventional security posture.[15]

Thus, the Israeli leadership flatly rejected the basic premise of strategic stability that calls for conspicuous and credible nuclear deterrence, and de facto entrenched the notion that regional deterrence was to be founded on conventional capabilities alone.[16] In fact, Israel repeatedly avoided any reference to a nuclear option, and Prime Minister Levi Eshkol set the general tone of the country's ambiguity policy when he noted in a speech to the Knesset in May 1966 that "Israel will not be the first to introduce nuclear weapons in the Middle East."[17] The ineffectiveness of Israel's nuclear capability—bounded by ambiguity and the exclusion of the nuclear option from its overall military posture—as a generator of strategic stability may be illustrated by the fact that it did not deter Arab belligerence before the Six-Day War in June 1967, and it was irrelevant to the Israeli-Egyptian War of Attrition (1969–70).

Israel's nuclear arsenal did not prevent the all-out Arab surprise attack against Israel in October 1973 or Iraq's missile attacks during the 1991 Gulf War.[18] Furthermore, recent reports suggest that Israel's nuclear option was discussed by Defense Minister Dayan and Prime Minister Golda Meir during the second day of the 1973 war, but only *after* it appeared that Israel was on the verge of defeat—and even then, Meir told Dayan "forget it," and Galili angrily added, "Drop it. We'd fight conventionally."[19] According to other accounts, the nuclear option was debated *after* the initial failure of the Israeli counteroffensive and solely in order to energize the Nixon administration to approve the desperately needed airlift. Thus, nuclear weapons had no preventive contribution in their own right, only a diplomatic role as a cry for help in order to ensure Israel's survivability after the war took a turn for the worse, given Meir's unwillingness to use them as a last resort.[20]

The Israeli Version of Strategic Stability

Traditionally, the conceptualization and pursuit of strategic stability predominantly revolve around the need to reduce the prospects of a nuclear first strike and the proliferation of nuclear weapons by developing and maintaining robust nuclear deterrence.[21] But if, as the case of Israel suggests, there is no overt nuclear deterrence that is based on a mutually assured destruction (MAD) logic, because the mere possession of nuclear weapons is neither denied nor confirmed, and the entire security architecture has not been modified to integrate a nuclear posture, what is the role of strategic stability for Israeli strategic planners and policymakers? Moreover, how is this Israeli conceptualization different from the more traditional one used during the Cold War and, to a large extent, still employed to this very day? The answer is that successive Israeli governments have historically held different definitions of what the terms "strategic" and "stability" actually entail, definitions that are different from the nuclear-oriented understanding of both practitioners and scholars in a number of key ways.

First, from a geostrategic and geopolitical perspective, Israel and the Cold War–era great powers had different strategic boundaries. For the great powers, there were no peripheral areas, and the entire international system was the strategic domain in which their multifaceted interaction took place. Israel is a power, but a regional one. Consequently, though Israel was attentive to global developments, and especially its relationship with the United States, its geostrategic and geopolitical focus was primarily the Middle East, with some extension to the Persian Gulf. It was a regionally focused approach that was especially shaped by the relatively limited territorial scope of the Israeli-Arab conflict.[22]

Second, for the Soviets and the Americans, "strategic" was mostly a function of nuclear capabilities that, based on the logic of first strike and MAD, were designed to prevent nuclear war. For Israeli policymakers, however, "strategic" was, by and large, a function of the distribution of conventional military capabilities, both in quality and quantity, across the region. Although Israeli governments were extremely protective of their military nuclear program, even vis-à-vis their American benefactors, they did not integrate it into their regional security posture. Instead, the pursuit and maintenance of conventional military superiority was the key provider of security in general and of regional deterrence-based stability in particular.[23] According to Yigal Allon, who was among the leading opponents of nuclearizing Israel's security posture, "The polarized asymmetry between the size and intentions of the Arab states and those of Israel, and the extreme contrast in the anticipated fate of each side in the event of military defeat, obliges Israel to maintain constantly that measure of strength enabling it to defend itself in every regional conflict and against any regional combination of strength confronting it, without the help of any foreign army."[24]

Third, for the Americans and the Soviets, "stability" predominantly suggested a condition in which the use of nuclear weapons is both futile and undesirable; and therefore, nuclear war—in itself, or as a result of a conventional conflict spiraling out of control—is highly improbable. For Israeli policymakers, there were no regional nuclear "interlocutors" with which such an arrangement could be created. In fact, as opposed to the Soviets or the Americans, who highlighted the nonusability of their nuclear capabilities as part of their pursuit of strategic stability, the Israelis were much more inclined to use conventional military force in order to achieve and maintain regional stability.[25] Moreover, "stability," from the Israeli vantage point, primarily revolved around three key indicators: (1) minimizing and delaying the possibility of armed conflict with its Arab neighbors; (2) suppressing the threat of various belligerent nonstate actors, especially the Palestinian Liberation Organization (PLO) and Hezbollah; and (3) preserving Israel's regional nuclear monopoly, or, put differently, preventing nuclear proliferation. To sum up, the Israeli approach to strategic stability was regional, conventional, and, to a large extent, state-centric.

Even when it targeted nonstate actors dubbed by many Israeli policymakers as propagators of regional instability and potential triggers of a major war, considerable efforts were also invested in deterring their sponsors and making national governments more accountable for any violent activities facilitated through their support. For example, after Hezbollah had abducted three soldiers near the Israeli-Lebanese border in the summer of 2006, the Israeli government issued an official statement that it "holds the sovereign government of Lebanon as responsible for the action which emanated from its territory and for the safe return of the abducted soldiers." Israeli prime minister Ehud Olmert later declared in a press conference that "this morning's events were not a terrorist attack, but the action of a sovereign state that attacked Israel for no reason and without provocation. The Lebanese government, of which Hezbollah is a member, is trying to undermine regional stability. Lebanon is responsible, and Lebanon will bear the consequences of its actions."[26]

OPERATIONALIZING THE ISRAELI PURSUIT OF STRATEGIC STABILITY

Considering that Israeli governments held to an entirely different conceptualization of strategic stability, it should come as no surprise that its implementation manifested itself in a rather unorthodox fashion. The reliance on nonnuclear deterrence has shifted the center of gravity toward the pursuit of strategic stability through conventional and political means, as the following discussion suggests.

The Obsolescence of the "All-Out War" Scenario

First and foremost, Israeli strategic stability entailed avoiding an all-out conventional war against a coalition of Arab countries; and to achieve this overarching objective, it pursued a two-pronged approach. On one hand, Israeli governments sought to achieve and maintain conventional military superiority. At first, it was the British and the French who throughout the 1950s supplied Israel with invaluable arms, and Paris was also the patron of the Israeli nuclear program.[27] The relationships between Jerusalem and Paris and London waned, and the flow of arms to Israel had virtually stopped by the late 1950s. The United States gradually assumed the role of the military benefactor of Israel as part of the emergence of the "special relationship" between both countries. The special relations started with the Kennedy administration's decision to approve the sales of Hawk antiaircraft missiles in 1962, and were strengthened as a result of the Johnson administration's decision to sell fighter jets to Israel in December 1968.[28]

Although Israel also developed its own military industry in order to maintain some self-sufficiency and hedge against the risk of losing all access to external arms, its close association with the United States provided Israel with unprecedented access to superior military technology.[29] This relationship created the conditions for what American administrations have referred to as Israel's Qualitative Military Edge. Indeed, it became obvious that though the Arab countries clearly had the quantitative advantage, Israel could achieve and maintain its qualitative military superiority to deter and defeat its adversaries in the Middle East. According to one congressional report, since 1948 the United States has provided Israel with $127.4 billion in assistance, predominantly military aid.[30]

On the other hand, Israeli governments have continuously attempted to drive a wedge between the Arab countries to weaken their political cooperation and military effectiveness in a form of "divide and rule." After the 1973 war, for example, Egypt became the major target for such attempts due to its pivotal political role in the Arab world and its principal part in forming and leading previous Arab military coalitions in battle against Israel.[31] This logic and its policy implications were evident in the Meir government's decision to sign the Separation of Forces Agreement (Sinai I) in January 1974 and in the Rabin government's decision to sign the Sinai Interim Agreement (Sinai II) in September 1975 with the Egyptian regime. Israel also offered similar interim agreements to Jordan and Syria, but less favorable domestic circumstances thereof, the eruption of the Lebanese civil war, and the looming presidential elections in the United States disrupted any such initiative.[32]

Although the first Israeli-Egyptian agreement was more technical in nature, and was primarily designed to address the operational redeployment of Egyptian and Israeli forces on the Sinai Peninsula, the second agreement went further, to announce that the conflict between Egypt and Israel "shall not be resolved by military force but by peaceful means."[33] Indeed, as Yitzhak Rabin noted in his memoirs, "The [Interim] agreement gave further impetus to developments already in train, moving Sadat further away from the Soviet Union, depriving the Egyptian army of further supplies of Soviet arms, and widening the rift between Egypt and Syria. In this manner we hoped to leave Sadat with only one choice: a political solution."[34]

Throughout the arduous negotiations that ensued after the election of Menachem Begin in 1977, and under the direction of Foreign Minister Dayan, the members of the Egyptian side repeatedly complained about their mounting isolation from their Arab counterparts, most notably Iraq and Syria, who chastised Egypt for its betrayal of Arab unity. After Egyptian president Anwar El Sadat visited Jerusalem in November and delivered a speech in the Israeli Parliament, several Arab countries—including Syria, Libya, Algeria, and Yemen—met in December in Tripoli and decided to break all diplomatic relations with Egypt, impose economic sanctions on Egyptian companies, and even form an anti-Egyptian "front for resistance and confrontation" under Syrian leadership.

Moreover, Saudi Arabia had slashed its financial aid to Egypt, which was critical for the procurement of advanced F-15 warplanes, to Egypt.[35] After Israel and Egypt signed the Camp David Peace Accords in March 1979, Egypt was suspended from the Arab League, whose headquarters was relocated from Cairo. Moreover, Egypt was expelled from the Organization of the Islamic Conference and was banished from a number of economic institutions, such as the Federation of Arab Banks and the Organization of Arab Petroleum Exporting Countries.[36]

From a strategic perspective, beyond the recognition and legitimization that the peace agreement bestowed on Israel, the accord was also a major step toward strategic stability, in that the ostracizing of Egypt made an all-out war—such as the ones fought in 1948, 1967, and 1973—virtually impossible.[37] As the final details of the Israeli-Egyptian peace accords were further negotiated by late 1978, Egyptian prime minister Mustafa Khalil acknowledged this premise when he told Dayan in Brussels that "no Arab state could embark on a war against Israel without Egypt." Dayan, on his part, concurred, and stated that "Egypt could not be part of the common front of our adversaries, and at the same time maintain peaceful relations with us [Israel]."[38]

Deterring the Undeterrable?

Israel's approach to strategic stability, which transcended nuclear realities, was also evident in its policies toward belligerent nonstate actors, a key national security challenge because of these organizations' potential to generate and propagate instability and also drag their backers into conflict. On the face of it, there seems to be a fundamental disconnect between the attempts to establish interstate nuclear deterrence and deterring terrorists as part of a state's pursuit of strategic stability. However, a closer look may reveal that the principle is the same—dissuading an adversary from using violence in order to achieve certain political goals.[39] The discussion here is not intended to provide an exhaustive review of the Israeli counterterrorism or counterinsurgency experience but rather to highlight two key features that exemplify the attempt to deter such actors that are supposedly beyond conventional deterrence, the primary military technique used by Israel to achieve strategic stability.[40]

First, Israel has invested considerable resources to decimate the leaders of organizations perceived to pose a national security threat, under the assumption that such measures would elicit greater restraint and caution. This policy has been applied since the early 1970s, with the rise of Palestinian global terrorism, especially aircraft hijackings and attacks against Israeli or Jewish targets abroad, albeit with exceedingly mixed results.[41] After the 1972 Munich

Olympics terrorist attack, which resulted in the killing of eleven Israelis, Prime Minister Golda Meir authorized a concerted effort by the Mossad to locate and assassinate the terrorists who participated in the attack. As Aaron Klein has noted, "The hope was that a withering series of assassinations would deter terrorists, those assisting them and those contemplating joining their ranks."[42] Similarly, Hezbollah's general secretary, Sheikh Abbas Musawi, was assassinated in mid-February 1992 in response to a growing number of attacks on Israeli and South Lebanon army bases and the killing of three Israeli soldiers by the PLO. The logic behind the decapitation of Hezbollah, articulated by Israeli defense minister Moshe Arens, was, "Whoever opens an account with us will have the account closed by us. . . . This is true for all the bands, all the terrorist organizations, all the leaders."[43]

Second, Israel has repeatedly threatened or used extensive military force against terrorist groups' host countries whenever the Israeli leadership believed that preexisting deterrence had weakened. For example, after largely avoiding attacking government targets during the Second Lebanon War to encourage the Lebanese government to curb Hezbollah's attacks, senior Israeli defense officials publicly stated that in the next round of violence, the Lebanese government would be held accountable, even going so far as threatening Lebanon's critical infrastructure, a form of extended deterrence: "It was a mistake not to attack Lebanese government targets during the [Second Lebanon] War in 2006. . . . We will not be able to hold back from doing so in a future war, . . . particularly now that Hezbollah and the government are effectively one and the same."[44]

Preempting MAD

Because Israel's clandestine military nuclear program was designed to serve as a latent measure of last resort, Israel vigorously and openly sought to prevent other regional adversaries from developing nuclear weapons. The first concrete implementation of this interpretation of strategic stability as proactive counterproliferation revolved around Saddam Hussein's pursuit of a nuclear program in the late 1970s and early 1980s.[45] After Iraqi nuclear scientists began exploring ways to independently produce plutonium and Baghdad signed an agreement with France for the provision of two nuclear reactors and a radioactive waste treatment station in mid-November 1975, Israeli intelligence began showing considerable interest in the possibility that the Iraqi government would develop nuclear weapons.[46]

The Israeli government, in cooperation with the American administration, unsuccessfully attempted to diplomatically dissuade the French from continuing their support for the Iraqi nuclear program. Consequently, the Israeli Mossad sabotaged some of the cooling systems manufactured in France before they were shipped to Iraq, but to no avail.[47] Therefore, in 1979 the Israeli chief of staff ordered the Israeli Defense Forces to begin exploring various options for the destruction of the nuclear reactor before it became operational. Despite fierce disagreement among the Israeli leadership—including opposition from the deputy prime minister, Yigal Yadin; the defense minister, Ezer Weizman; and the heads of Military Intelligence and the Mossad—Prime Minister Menachem Begin was adamant about the need to destroy the nuclear facility before it became operational and able to produce sufficient enriched uranium for a nuclear bomb.[48]

After an Iranian attempt to destroy the nuclear reactor in September 1980 failed, and given intelligence reports suggesting that the reactors would become active in either early July or September 1981, Begin realized that time was running out. After several delays resulting from internal leaks, an attack was conducted by the Israeli air force on June 7, 1981, which resulted in the complete destruction of the reactor. After the operation, the Israeli government issued a statement noting that "the atomic bombs that this reactor would have been capable of producing, with enriched uranium or plutonium, were of the type dropped on Hiroshima. In this way, a danger to Israel's existence was being produced. . . . We were therefore forced to defend ourselves against the construction of an atomic bomb in Iraq, which itself would not have hesitated to use it against Israel and its population centers."[49]

What has become known as the Begin Doctrine, or the Israeli determination not to allow any adversary to acquire nuclear technology that can be used to develop a nuclear bomb by any means possible, was also applied on at least two other occasions. The first case involved the bombing of a nuclear facility built by North Korea near Deir el-Zor in Syria in September 2007. Information about the construction of the nuclear facility surfaced by late 2006 and was detected by the Israeli and American intelligence services. Corroborating information was obtained by Mossad agents, who accessed the personal computer of the head of the Syrian Atomic Energy Commission while he was attending a meeting of the International Atomic Energy Agency (IAEA) in Geneva. According to the collected evidence, which included photos from within the facility, it was clear that this was a plutonium nuclear reactor.[50]

After various discussions between the Israeli prime minister and his key advisers, the leaders decided to seek physical evidence for the nature of the suspected Syrian nuclear facility. Thus, in March 2007 Israeli Special Forces flew across the Syrian border in order to collect soil samples from the areas surrounding the site. The findings allegedly confirmed the original suspicion that this was a plutonium reactor in the making.[51] By mid-May, the Israeli head of the Mossad, Meir Dagan, met with senior officials in the White House and shared with them the newly acquired information. According to Elliott Abrams, Dagan made it clear that from the Israeli perspective, "the reactor had to go away."[52]

After Dagan's visit, Israeli prime minister Ehud Olmert called US president George W. Bush and asked that the Americans take the initiative and bomb the Syrian reactor. Bush asked for some time to consult his advisers, and after several months of internal deliberation, the president decided to pursue the diplomatic option. The United States would go to the IAEA and to the UN Security Council, but it would also threaten to use military force in case the Syrian regime did not cooperate. Bush called Olmert in mid-July to convey this decision. According to Bush's recollections, Olmert disappointedly replied that "this is something that hits at the very serious nerves of his country," and that Syria's pursuit of a nuclear program poses an "existential" threat for Israel.[53] Abrams's recollection suggested that Olmert's response was significantly more alarmed: "We told you from the first day, when Dagan came to Washington, and I've told you since then whenever we discussed it, that the reactor had to go away. Israel cannot live with a Syrian nuclear reactor; we will not accept it. It would change the entire region and our national security cannot accept it. You are telling me you will not act; so, we will act. The timing is another matter, and we will not do anything precipitous."[54]

The facility was attacked nearly two months later, in September, only after all the military and technological preparations were completed. Israel never took responsibility for destroying the nuclear site, in order to avoid forcing Syrian president Bashar al-Assad to respond. Although the attack clearly had an immediate objective, to preemptively eliminate the prospects of a Syrian nuclear program, it was also clearly intended, according to one senior Israeli official, to "re-establish the credibility of our deterrent power."[55]

The other manifestation of the Begin Doctrine involves Israel's continuous attempts to curtail Iran's nuclear program. Iran's nuclear ambitions began during the time of the shah, who benefited from President Eisenhower's Atoms for Peace initiative. However, Iran's efforts were primarily focused on nuclear energy rather a military program, as exemplified by the shah's decision to join the Non-Proliferation Treaty in July 1968. This, along with the fact that the Iranian regime and Israel were close allies with one another, as well as client states of the United States, alleviated all Israeli concerns.[56]

After the 1979 Iranian Revolution that ousted the shah and led to the rise of Ayatollah Khomeini as the country's supreme religious leader, Tehran announced that it would terminate its nuclear and chemical weapons program because weapons of mass destruction were prohibited by Islam.[57] However, fear of defeat during the Iran-Iraq War, along with reports that Saddam Hussein was developing nuclear weapons, pushed Tehran to begin exploring the possibility of renewing its military nuclear program. The major turn occurred by the late 1980s, when the founder of Pakistan's nuclear program, Abdul Qadeer Khan, provided Iran with the technological know-how necessary to manufacture a nuclear bomb.[58]

By 2002 it became clear to American intelligence agencies that the Iranians had constructed two facilities designed to produce nuclear weapons: a uranium enrichment plant at Natanz and a heavy water plant at Arak, both constructed with Russian assistance.[59] The Iranian nuclear program continued to grow dramatically until 2003, when the United States invaded Iraq, leading Tehran to freeze its nuclear program and publicly declare that it would stop enriching uranium in its nuclear facilities and allow for more intrusive IAEA inspections after initial inspections found traces of highly enriched uranium in several locations.[60] From the Israeli perspective, as Prime Minister Ariel Sharon explained in an interview in early 2005, there was "no doubt that they [the Iranians] are working now in order to possess a nuclear weapon, which we regard to be a great danger, not only for Israel, but for Europe and the United States."[61]

After Mahmoud Ahmadinejad was elected president of Iran in August 2005, he declared that Iran would resume the conversion of uranium, and he began making increasingly frequent references to the regime's wish to destroy Israel.[62] Rather than bomb the Iranian nuclear facilities, due to limited operational feasibility, the Israeli government had devised an elaborate strategy designed to prevent Iran from acquiring a nuclear bomb that included international diplomatic pressure, assassination of leading figures associated with the Iranian nuclear program, and sabotage of the uranium enrichment process through cyberwarfare.[63]

From the diplomatic perspective, Israeli leaders have continuously and effectively solicited the international community to impose crippling sanctions against Iran that not only would signal that Tehran's pursuit of nuclear weapons was unacceptable but also would have a tangible effect on its capacity to make progress therein.[64] After the IAEA found Iran in breach of its previous commitments, especially with regard to enriching uranium, in late 2006 the UN Security Council imposed sanctions on Tehran with the support of China and Russia.[65] In a meeting with Russian president Vladimir Putin the following year, Olmert noted that "effective sanctions by all the international community would have the potential to stop Iran pursuing the nuclear path."[66]

But by mid-2008, it appeared that the sanctions were ineffective, as the Iranian regime remained committed to maintaining its nuclear program, albeit arguing that it was of a civilian nature. Consequently, Israeli leaders renewed their calls to militarily attack Iran's nuclear sites, and former chief of staff and minister of defense Shaul Mofaz, for example, warned that "if Iran continues with its program for developing nuclear weapons, we will attack it. The sanctions are ineffective."[67] When Bush visited Israel in May 2008, Olmert reportedly asked that the United States consent to an Israeli unilateral attack against Iran's nuclear facilities, but the president refused.[68]

The intensity of the sanctions regime increased by 2010, after unilateral American financial sanctions were supplemented by a set of sanctions imposed by the UN Security Council, essentially isolating Iran economically and preventing it from importing and exporting dual-use goods that could support its nuclear program. After the fourth round of UN sanctions was announced, the Israeli ambassador to the United States, Michael Oren, remarked that the decision "can serve as a viable platform for launching very far-reaching sanctions by the United States or like-minded nations against Iran."[69] Indeed, the US Congress, energized by the Israeli government and pro-Israeli lobby groups such as the American Israel Public Affairs Committee, in June passed the Comprehensive Iran Sanctions, Accountability, and Divestment Act of 2010, which was signed into law by President Obama a month later.[70]

Because the military option was still impracticable from an operational standpoint, and considering the United States' political aversion to such action, the Israelis joined the American administration in developing and deploying a cyberwarfare option. Although the technical preparations for this secret campaign started in 2006, it was broadened and intensified after Obama took office. The results of these efforts became evident by the summer of 2010, when a computer worm later known as Stuxnet attacked the nuclear facility in Natanz. Specifically, Stuxnet repeatedly targeted the computer system that controlled the centrifuges that purified the uranium and disrupted their normal activity, to the extent that about 1,000 centrifuges had to be discarded.[71] Though not taking full responsibility for the attack, or crediting the Israelis, one senior Obama administration official commented, "I'm glad to hear they are having troubles with their centrifuge machines, and the US and its allies are doing everything we can to make it more complicated."[72]

On a different front, between 2007 and 2011 the Israeli Mossad supposedly began targeting key Iranian scientists whose contribution to Iran's nuclear program was defined as critical, with some having specific roles in the military dimensions of the program. Alongside these assassinations, in December 2011 the Mossad was able to plant a bomb in a missile-testing base near Tehran, and the explosion killed dozens, including a senior Revolutionary Guard Corps general who was entrusted with the development of long-range missiles.[73]

The agreement with Iran signed in July 2015 may suggest that Israel failed to prevent a nuclear Iran, because it formally allowed Tehran to enrich low-grade uranium. However, it seems that this is not a complete failure, for three main reasons. First, Israel did not forfeit its right to unilaterally attack the Iranian nuclear sites if it determined that Tehran was violating its international commitments. Second, after the American administration signed the agreement, it offered a rather generous compensation package to Israel that included increased military aid, including advanced F-35 fighter jets and antimissile defense systems.[74] And third, by emphasizing the limitations of the agreement and continuing his pressure on the American administration and the international community, Netanyahu believed he would be in a better position to enforce a stricter implementation of the agreement. Although he criticized the agreement at the UN General Assembly in October 2015, he nonetheless added that "as this deal with Iran moves ahead, I hope you'll enforce it. . . . How can I put this? With a little more rigor: . . . Make sure that the inspectors actually inspect. Make sure that the snapback sanctions actually snap back. And make sure that Iran's violations aren't swept under the Persian rug."[75]

CONCLUSIONS

From an Israeli perspective, the common use of the term "strategic stability" is ill suited and, to a large extent, distorts consecutive Israeli governments' desired aims and practical policies. When Israeli leaders and planners think about strategic stability, they mostly focus on *regional* stability and the *conventional* ways to achieve it. There is no overwhelming reliance on the nuclear origins of deterrence, as the Soviet-American experience during the Cold War warranted, nor is the fear of a nuclear war omnipresent.

Although nuclear weapons are part of Israel's military arsenal, they have not been integrated into its security posture or strategy and, in fact, proved to be irrelevant in the Israeli-Arab conflict. Nor have they been the main point of reference when Israeli policymakers evaluate their strategic environment or its stability. When the Israeli government discussed its nuclear posture in the early 1960s, Ben-Gurion made a strategic decision to go for an opaque and deniable weaponized military program that would not be an integral part of Israel's overarching security posture. Consequently, the policy of nuclear ambiguity was introduced, and it has been pursued ever since. Even when the possibility of using nuclear weapons was considered during the 1973 Yom Kippur War, it was primarily designed to signal to the United States that Israel desperately needed military aid that the Nixon administration had previously refused to send.

Indeed, for the most part, Israeli governments have been more concerned by the possibility of an all-out war against an Arab coalition. Capitalizing on major regional developments after the Yom Kippur War, the Rabin and Begin governments wanted to eliminate the possibility of such a scenario by removing Egypt from the historically unwavering anti-Israeli coalition. After the signing of the Camp David Accords in 1979, without Egyptian leadership, the Arab coalition became unfeasible.

But state-to-state deterrence was coupled with the destabilizing effect of terrorism, mainly from the PLO and Hezbollah. With regard to both organizations, Israel employed a multitude of countermeasures designed to establish and maintain strategic stability. In addition to assassinations of key leaders as a way to discourage future attacks, the Israeli government also approached the challenge by creating extended deterrence vis-à-vis the host countries' national governments.

One particular notion of strategic stability that Israeli governments have historically held to, that is largely reminiscent of the original conceptualization of the term as part of the Cold War's nuclear discourse, revolved around preventing adversaries from developing a nuclear program, civilian or military. For this reason, Israel foiled the Egyptian attempts to develop nuclear and long-range missile programs in the early 1960s, and it attacked and destroyed an Iraqi nuclear reactor in 1981 as well as a Syrian nuclear site in 2007. Furthermore, Israel's desire to prevent Iran from developing a nuclear bomb resulted in an ongoing campaign to cripple its nuclear program that included advocating economic sanctions, targeted assassinations, sabotage, and cyberwarfare.

As for Iran, since the signing of the nuclear agreement in July 2015 and even after Donald Trump, who was critical of the accords with the Iranians, took office, it appears that the Israeli government has ostensibly accepted the possibility that strategic stability would be outsourced to the Americans through the ensuing diplomatic and technical arrangements designed to prevent Iran from pursuing a militarized nuclear program. In fact, in a public event, Chief of Staff Eisenkot stated that the nuclear agreement signed with Iran "is a significant change of course for Iran. There are many risks but also opportunities." Moreover, he declared that as the prospects of a nuclear Iran have diminished considerably, given the robust monitoring and verification procedures, the center of gravity in Israel's strategic environment has shifted to "Hezbollah, which today represents the most serious threat to Israel" because of its approximately 150,000 rockets.[76] Hence, strategic stability, from Eisenkot's vantage point, is currently more threatened by a nonstate actor's possessing conventional weapons and acting as a major proxy of a non-nuclear-weapons state, an observation that illustrates the intricacy and fluidity of Israel's cross-domain approach to strategic stability. This observation was recently reaffirmed amid the growing presence of Iranian forces in Syria that have been actively supplying arms to Hezbollah in Lebanon. According to Israeli prime minister Benjamin Netanyahu, as the Islamic State is decimated in Syria, "Iran moves in, but they want to bring their air force there, right next to Israel; they want to bring Shi'ite and Iranian divisions right next to Israel, they want to bring submarines and military vessels into the Mediterranean, right next to Israel. So we will not let that happen; we will resist it."[77]

Because it was introduced during the Cold War, and considering that it is overwhelmingly attributed to nuclear deterrence, the term "strategic stability" proves inadequate to explain the major trends in Israel's strategic posture. This is not to say that the term is entirely irrelevant but rather to suggest that the meaning and operationalization of strategic stability are largely a function of the nature of the strategic environment and the security objectives and needs of the country in question. In other words, countries develop and maintain a different understanding of strategic stability, making it significantly more actor-specific than previously thought.

NOTES

1. Herb Keinon and Yaakov Lappin, "Netanyahu, IDF High Command Tout New German-Made Submarine," *Jerusalem Post*, January 12, 2016.
2. David P. Barash and Charles P. Webel, *Peace and Conflict Studies* (Los Angeles: Sage, 2014), 109.
3. Chief of Staff, *IDF Strategy* (in Hebrew) (Tel Aviv: Chief of Staff, 2015).
4. John D. Steinbruner, "National Security and the Concept of Strategic Stability," *Journal of Conflict Resolution* 22, no. 3 (September 1978): 411–28.
5. On the connections between perception and deterrence, see Robert Jervis, Richard Ned Lebow, and Janice Gross Stein, eds., *Psychology and Deterrence* (Baltimore: Johns Hopkins University Press, 1989).
6. Elbridge Colby, "Defining Strategic Stability: Reconciling Stability and Deterrence," in *Strategic Stability: Contending Interpretations*, ed. Elbridge A. Colby and Michael S. Gerson (Carlisle, PA: Strategic Studies Institute of US Army War College, 2013), 55.
7. Frank A. Rose, "Ballistic Missile Defense and Strategic Stability in East Asia," February 20, 2015. For the full text of the speech, see https://2009–2017.state.gov/t/avc/rls/2015/237746.htm.
8. See, e.g., Paul Bracken, *The Second Nuclear Age: Strategy, Danger, and the New Power Politics* (New York: Times Books, 2012); and Toshi Yoshihara and James R. Holmes, eds., *Strategy in the Second Nuclear Age: Power, Ambition, and the Ultimate Weapon* (Washington, DC: Georgetown University Press, 2012).
9. Hans M. Kristensen and Robert S. Norris, "Israeli Nuclear Weapons, 2014," *Bulletin of the Atomic Scientists* 70, no. 6 (2014): 102.
10. Gregory D. Koblentz, *Strategic Stability in the Second Nuclear Age*, Special Report 71 (New York: Council on Foreign Relations, 2014), 7.
11. Jonathan Shimshoni, *Israel and Conventional Deterrence: Border Warfare from 1953 to 1970* (Ithaca, NY: Cornell University Press, 1988), 30. See also John J. Mearsheimer, *Conventional Deterrence* (Ithaca, NY: Cornell University Press, 1983), chap. 5.

12. Benny Morris, *Israel's Border Wars, 1949–1956* (Oxford: Oxford University Press, 1993).

13. Shlomo Aronson, *David Ben-Gurion and the Jewish Renaissance* (Cambridge: Cambridge University, 1999), 305–6; and Edwin S. Cochran, "Israel's Nuclear History," in *Israel: The First Hundred Years*, ed. Ephraim Karsh (London: Frank Cass, 2000), 2:137.

14. Avner Cohen, *The Worst-Kept Secret: Israel's Bargain with the Bomb* (New York: Columbia University Press, 2010), 64–65.

15. Avner Cohen, *Israel and the Bomb* (New York: Columbia University Press, 1998), chap. 8; and Yair Evron, *Israel's Nuclear Dilemma* (London: Routledge, 1994), chap. 2.

16. Uri Bar-Joseph, "Variations on a Theme: The Conceptualization of Deterrence in Israeli Strategic Thinking," *Security Studies* 7, no. 3 (Spring 1998): 146.

17. Quoted by Ofer Israeli, "Israel's Nuclear *Amimut* Policy and Its Consequences," *Israel Affairs* 21, no. 4 (2014): 545.

18. Zeev Maoz, "The Mixed Blessing of Israel's Nuclear Policy," *International Security* 28, no. 2 (Fall 2003): 44–77.

19. Amir Oren, "In 1973, Dayan Suggested Israel Prepare Nukes for Action, but Golda Meir Refused," *Haaretz*, October 3, 2013.

20. Seymour M. Hersh, *The Samson Option: Israel's Nuclear Arsenal and American Foreign Policy* (New York: Random House, 1991), chap. 17.

21. Steven Pifer, "Bilateral and Multilateral Nuclear Arms Reductions," in *Routledge Handbook of Nuclear Proliferation and Policy*, ed. Joseph F. Pilat and Nathan E. Busch (New York: Routledge, 2015), 290. See also Colby, "Defining Strategic Stability," 48–49.

22. See, e.g., Zeev Maoz, ed., *Regional Security in the Middle East: Past, Present, and Future* (London: Frank Cass, 1997).

23. Zeev Maoz, *Defending the Holy Land: A Critical Analysis of Israel's Security and Foreign Policy* (Ann Arbor: University of Michigan Press, 2009), 12.

24. Yigal Allon, "Israel: The Case for Defensible Borders," *Foreign Affairs* 55, no. 1 (October 1976): 40.

25. I am grateful to Adam Stulberg for raising this point.

26. Gideon Alon, Amos Harel, and Aluf Benn, "Hezbollah Attack: Gov't Okays Massive Strikes on Lebanon; Israel Readies for Rocket Attacks in North," *Haaretz*, July 13, 2006.

27. Zach Levy, *Israel and the Western Powers, 1952–1960* (Chapel Hill: University of North Carolina Press, 1997), 58–59.

28. Abraham Ben-Zvi, "Influence and Arms: John F. Kennedy, Lyndon B. Johnson and the Politics of Arms Sales to Israel, 1962–1966," *Israel Affairs* 10, nos. 1–2 (2004): 29–59.

29. Sharon Sadeh, "Israel's Beleaguered Defense Industry," *Middle East Review of International Affairs Journal* 5, no. 1 (March 2001): 64–77.

30. Jeremy M. Sharp, *US Foreign Aid to Israel* (Washington, DC: Congressional Research Service, 2016).

31. See Avi Kober, *Coalition Defection: The Dissolution of Arab Anti-Israeli Coalitions in War and Peace* (Westport, CT: Praeger, 2002).

32. Ronald Ranta, *Political Decision Making and Non-Decisions: The Case of Israel and the Occupied Territories* (New York: Palgrave Macmillan, 2015), 157–58.

33. Quoted by Yoram Meital, *Egypt's Struggle for Peace: Continuity and Change, 1967–1977* (Gainesville: University Press of Florida, 1997), 149.

34. Yizhak Rabin, *The Rabin Memoirs* (Berkeley: University of California Press, 1996), 274.

35. Marvine Howe, "Hard-Line Arab Bloc Is Formed at Tripoli," *New York Times*, December 6, 1977.

36. Glenn E. Perry, *The History of Egypt*, 2nd ed. (Santa Barbara, CA: ABC-CLIO, 2016), 140.

37. Kober, *Coalition Defection*, 111.

38. Moshe Dayan, *Breakthrough: A Personal Account of the Egypt-Israel Peace Negotiations* (New York: Alfred A. Knopf, 1981), 254.

39. See, e.g., Andreas Wenger and Alex Wilner, eds., *Deterring Terrorism: Theory and Practice* (Stanford, CA: Stanford University Press, 2012).

40. Boaz Atzili and Wendy Pearlman, "Triadic Deterrence: Coercing Strength, Beaten by Weakness," *Security Studies* 21, no. 2 (June 2012): 305–35.

41. Ariel Merari, "Israel Facing Terrorism," *Israel Affairs* 11, no. 1 (January 2005): 232–33.

42. Aaron J. Klein, *Striking Back: The 1972 Munich Olympics Massacre and Israel's Deadly Response* (New York: Random House, 2007), 102.

43. Caryle Murphy, "Israeli Raid Kills Hezbollah Leader," *Washington Post*, February 17, 1992.

44. Yaakov Katz, "Lebanese Targets Fair Game in War with Hezbollah," *Jerusalem Post*, April 11, 2012.

45. An Egyptian attempt to develop an embryonic nuclear program in the early 1960s failed from the start and did not attract any attention from the Israeli government. See Yair Evron, "The Arab Position in the Nuclear Field: A Study of Policies up to 1967," *Cooperation and Conflict* 8, no. 1 (March 1973): 19–31; and Shai Feldman, *Nuclear Weapons and Arms Control in the Middle East* (Cambridge, MA: MIT Press, 1997), 59.

46. Matthew Fuhrmann, *Atomic Assistance: How "Atoms for Peace" Programs Cause Nuclear Insecurity* (Ithaca, NY: Cornell University Press, 2012), 117.

47. Uri Bar-Joseph, Michael Handel, and Amos Perlmutter, *Two Minutes over Baghdad* (London: Frank Cass, 2003), 49.

48. Shlomo Nakdimon, *First Strike: The Exclusive Story of How Israel Foiled Iraq's Attempt to Get the Bomb* (New York: Summit Books, 1987), 95.

49. David K. Shipler, "Israeli Jets Destroy Iraqi Atomic Reactor," *New York Times*, June 9, 1981.

50. David Makovsky, "The Silent Strike: How Israel Bombed a Syrian Nuclear Installation and Kept It Secret," *The New Yorker*, September 17, 2012.

51. Erich Follath and Holger Stark, "The Story of 'Operation Orchard': How Israel Destroyed Syria's Al Kibar Nuclear Reactor," *Der Spiegel*, November 2, 2009.

52. Elliot Abrams, *Tested by Zion: The Bush Administration and the Israeli-Palestinian Conflict* (Cambridge: Cambridge University Press, 2013), 227.

53. George W. Bush, *Decision Points* (New York: Crown, 2010), 421.

54. Abrams, *Tested by Zion*, 246–47.

55. David E. Sanger and Mark Mazzetti, "Israel Struck Syrian Nuclear Project, Analysts Say," *New York Times*, October 14, 2007.

56. Sasan Fayazmanesh, *The United States and Iran: Sanctions, Wars and the Policy of Dual Containment* (London: Routledge, 2008), 6.

57. Gareth Porter, "When the Ayatollah Said No to Nukes," *Foreign Policy*, October 16, 2014.

58. Kenneth Pollack, *Unthinkable: Iran, the Bomb, and American Strategy* (New York: Simon & Schuster, 2014), 36.

59. Nazila Fathi, "Iran and Russia Sign Accord to Speed Nuclear Power Project," *New York Times*, December 26, 2002.

60. Felicity Barringer, "Inspectors in Iran Find Highly Enriched Uranium at an Electrical Plant," *New York Times*, September 26, 2003.

61. Tyler Marshall, "Sharon Denies Any Plan to Bomb Iranian Nuclear Plants," *Los Angeles Times*, April 14, 2005.

62. See, e.g., Ewen MacAskill and Chris McGreal, "Israel Should Be Wiped Off Map, Says Iran's President," *The Guardian*, October 26, 2005.

63. Ronen Bergman, *The Secret War with Iran: The 30-Year Clandestine Struggle against the World's Most Dangerous Terrorist Power*, trans. Ronnie Hope (New York: Free Press, 2007), 342–43.

64. On the concerted sanctions campaign, see Michael Jacobson, "Sanctions against Iran: A Promising Struggle," *Washington Quarterly* 31, no. 3 (Summer 2008): 69–88.

65. Elissa Gootman, "Security Council Approves Sanctions against Iran over Nuclear Program," *New York Times*, December 24, 2006.

66. Mansur Mirovalev, "Olmert Tells Putin of Iran Concerns," *Washington Post*, October 18, 2007.

67. Dan Williams, "Israel to Attack Iran Unless Enrichment Stops," Reuters, June 6, 2008.

68. Jonathan Steele, "Israel Asked US for Green Light to Bomb Nuclear Sites in Iran," *The Guardian*, September 25, 2008.

69. Barak Ravid, "Netanyahu: Iran Nuclear Sanctions a 'Positive' Step," *Haaretz*, June 9, 2010.

70. Peter Baker, "Obama Signs into Law Tighter Sanctions on Iran," *New York Times*, July 1, 2010.

71. David E. Sanger, *Confront and Conceal: Obama's Secret Wars and Surprising Use of American Power* (New York: Broadway, 2012), chap. 8.

72. William J. Broad, John Markoff, and David E. Sanger, "Israel Tests on Worm Called Crucial in Iran Nuclear Delay," *New York Times*, January 15, 2011.

73. Dan Raviv and Yossi Melman, *Spies against Armageddon: Inside Israel's Secret Wars* (Sea Cliff, NY: Levant Books, 2014), 11.

74. Barak Ravid, "Away from Spotlight, Israel and US Begin Post-Iran Deal Security Talks," *Haaretz*, September 13, 2015.

75. For the full text of the speech, see http://mfa.gov.il/MFA/PressRoom/2015 /Pages/PM-Netanyahu-addresses-the-UN-General-Assembly-1-Oct-2015.aspx.

76. Yoav Zitun and Itay Blumenthal, "Iran Deal Is an Opportunity," *Ynetnews*, January 18, 2016.

77. Amos Harel, "Netanyahu: Iran Seeks to Send Its Submarines to Syria's Mediterranean Ports," *Haaretz*, November 5, 2017.

10

Maintaining Sovereignty and Preserving the Regime

How Saudi Arabia Views Strategic Stability

ALA' ALRABABA'H

ON JULY 14, 2015, the five permanent members of the UN Security Council and Germany signed the Joint Comprehensive Plan of Action (JCPOA), which guarantees the peaceful nature of Iran's nuclear program. Saudi Arabia cautiously welcomed this deal, claiming that it limits Iran's potential to develop nuclear weapons. But it warned that if Iran spends its sanctions relief funds on acts that destabilize the region, then these acts "will be strictly faced by the region's countries."[1]

Saudi commentators were more candid in their opposition to the deal. Jamal Khashoggi, a prominent journalist with ties to members of the royal family, asserted that "Iran under sanctions was a pain in the neck for the Saudis, and it will be more of a pain in the neck without sanctions."[2] Abdulrahman al-Rashed, another prominent Saudi commentator, described Iran as a monster that was previously tied to a tree, but the nuclear deal set the monster loose.[3] He later wrote an op-ed article titled "Is the Gulf Relationship with Washington a Historical Mistake?" After explaining the history of cooperation between the United States and Saudi Arabia, al-Rashed describes the ongoing dispute between the United States and the Gulf countries over the Iran nuclear deal as "the worst disagreement in the history of both sides," though he concludes that the alliance between the two will remain intact.[4]

The United States has been trying to reassure its Gulf allies. Before reaching a deal, President Barack Obama met with representatives from the Gulf countries at Camp David to reassure them of continuing US security guarantees, such as massive arms sales and defense support against foreign threats.[5] After the signing of the JCPOA, the United States pledged to expedite arms sales to the Gulf countries.[6] But to understand how the Gulf countries, and especially Saudi Arabia, will react to the Iran nuclear deal over the longer term, it is important to examine their military strategy.

Saudi Arabia does not have any military strategy in the Western sense. Several Arab and American diplomats interviewed for this chapter described the Saudi strategy as unpredictable and personality-based. A Saudi major general, Muhammed bin Yahya Al-Jaday'i, wrote a paper that was published on the Royal Saudi Air Defense Forces website, describing the absence of a Saudi military strategy.[7] Without directly saying that Saudi Arabia lacks a military strategy, he described his reasons why the country should develop one, which included Iran's increasing military threat to the region and the wide array of ideological threats facing the kingdom. He also described the difficulties of preparing a Saudi strategy, such as the absence of a written Saudi military policy, the lack of transparency and clarity from government organizations, and the deficiency in resources.

Despite these limitations, the contours of a Saudi strategic vision do exist. These contours are not based on a Saudi view of regional or strategic stability, but on two goals: maintaining sovereignty and regime stability.[8] Maintaining sovereignty entails preventing a foreign invasion or domination of the Saudi regime. Regime stability entails securing the rule of the Al Saud family inside the kingdom. The two goals are intertwined. The Saudi regime needs an independent state to rule. For the members of Al Saud (House of Saud), the ruling royal family, to maintain their domestic legitimacy, they not only need to provide public goods but also need to be seen as the guardians of Islam's holiest sites. This means not being dominated by another regional power, especially one with a different ideology. At the same time, it also involves maintaining sovereignty and not being seen as clients of a Western power.

This chapter discusses Saudi Arabia's view on strategic stability in its neighborhood. I begin by discussing how Saudi Arabia views threats to its regime. First, the kingdom feels threatened by an unstable regional system, in which one power comes to dominate or when a strong ideological movement undermines the legitimacy of the royal family. After explaining how Saudi Arabia views threats, I discuss how it attempts to combat them. To maintain a relative balance of power in the Gulf region and the wider Middle East, and to overcome any ideological threat to the regime, the kingdom has resorted to three tools: allying with the United States, internal balancing through strengthening Saudi Arabia's military power, and using Saudi Arabia's position in the Islamic world to establish ideological deterrence—though, as the analysis shows, these tools have sometimes undercut one another.

STABILITY

The Saudi leadership places the sovereignty of the state and the stability of its regime above all else. State sovereignty implies preventing a foreign invasion and controlling foreign and domestic policy to fend off coercive action against the Saudi leadership. Meanwhile, regime stability requires the survival of the Al Saud family as the leaders of the kingdom. However, the pursuit of regime stability can undermine the security of the kingdom. For example, Saudi Arabia has often allowed its religious establishment to maintain a hard-line rhetoric, even when this may have radicalized people who then turned against the kingdom. This leads to a complicated relationship between regional and domestic stability. For the Saudis, regional stability demands maintaining Saudi hegemony over the Arabian Peninsula and a stable balance of power in the Persian Gulf and the Arab world. As a result, Riyadh may sometimes view regional conflict as stabilizing. One could argue that the 1967 war against Israel, which the Arabs lost, increased Saudi Arabia's regime stability by weakening Egypt's dominance of Arab politics and leading to the withdrawal of Egyptian troops from Yemen. Likewise, the recent nuclear deal with Iran, though it may have prevented the turmoil of another war in the region, is perceived as a destabilizing development by the Saudi regime because it may shift the balance of power in favor of Iran. Iran may use its increased funding to strengthen its influence over Iraq, Syria, and Lebanon, thus weakening the Saudis' position in the region.

On the Arabian Peninsula, Saudi Arabia aims to maintain its hegemony. Saudi territory covers the vast majority of the peninsula, and other countries are relatively weak or small. This has shaped Saudi policy toward the peninsula—it has long believed that any foreign interference on the peninsula can compromise its sovereignty and must be countered. Saddam Hussein's invasion of Kuwait was thus deeply destabilizing, regardless of whether he planned to advance on Saudi Arabia. Likewise, Egypt's intervention in Yemen in the 1960s and allegations about Iran's interfering in Bahrain and Yemen have been very disconcerting for the Saudis.

Beyond the peninsula, Saudi Arabia cannot hope to be the dominant power. In the Gulf region, Iran has a much larger population than Saudi Arabia or Iraq—a fact of which the kingdom has always been painfully aware.[9] Given this limitation, Saudi Arabia has aimed to maintain a balance of power, rather than hegemony, over the Gulf region. Similarly, in the larger Middle East, countries like Egypt, Turkey, and Israel have often been more powerful, so Riyadh has often tried to maintain a balance of power at the regional level as well.

THREATS TO THE ARABIAN PENINSULA

Since the establishment of the modern Saudi state in 1932, three major incidents by Middle Eastern powers have threatened Saudi dominance over the Arabian Peninsula or had the potential to upend the regional balance of power. Those are Egypt's intervention in Yemen in the 1960s; Iraq's occupation of Kuwait in 1990; and, most recently, Iran's increasing influence over the region.

An early threat to the regional balance of power occurred with Egypt's activist foreign policy starting in the early 1960s. In September 1962, free Yemeni officers, inspired by the republican regimes in Egypt and Iraq, staged a coup in which they toppled Yemen's monarchical regime of Imam Muhammed al-Badr. This coup led to a civil war in Yemen that lasted for eight years. Egypt intervened militarily on behalf of the republicans, while Saudi Arabia supported the monarchists.

According to Riyadh, the change in Yemen constituted an existential threat to Saudi Arabia for several reasons. For one, the Saudi military was underprepared. The weakness of the Saudi military at the time may be best demonstrated by an Al Saud family story. Once the Egyptian force intervened to support the new republic in North Yemen, Crown Prince Faisal of Saudi Arabia appointed his brother, Sultan, as defense minister. Sultan assured Faisal that he would immediately head to the operations room and attend to Saudi defenses. Faisal smiled but did not respond. When Sultan went to his office, he asked for the operations room. His staff looked confused as they responded, "What operations room?" The Ministry of Defense also did not have a General Staff, and it had not devised any plans to counter the Egyptians. Sultan then ordered the Saudi air force to engage the Egyptians, but this proved impossible because none of the Saudi planes could fly.[10]

Yemen's proximity to Saudi Arabia was a particular cause of concern. Although Saudi policies toward Yemen may seem "opaque, ad hoc, and sometimes contradictory," the kingdom has often tried to ensure that problems in Yemen are contained and do not spill over to Saudi Arabia.[11] But when Yemeni military officers felt inspired by republican regimes to topple their monarchy, the Saudis feared that this could threaten Saudi hegemony by bringing a republican, pro-Nasser regime to the peninsula. The Saudis also feared that this wave of military coups could even spill into the kingdom—Yemen was just the latest in a sequence of military coups that had overthrown monarchs in Egypt, Iraq, and Syria over the past decade.[12] This was particularly disturbing for the Saudi monarchy.

Riyadh feared that the Yemenis would actively attack Saudi Arabia, leading to instability in the kingdom. In October 1962, shortly after the coup, Yemen's new president, Abdullah al-Sallal, made clear his intention to extend a "republican form of government" across the Arabian Peninsula.[13] In October, Yemen's deputy prime minister warned that he would take the battle to Saudi territory "and to Riyadh itself."[14] The Yemeni leadership also claimed that several Saudi provinces on the Yemeni border in fact belonged to Yemen. In 1963 and 1964, North Yemenis launched several incursions into Saudi Arabia.[15] This provided the Saudis with ample reason to worry.

In addition, Saudi Arabia feared that regime change in Yemen provided Gamal Abdel Nasser, Egypt's president and dictator, with a foothold onto the Arabian Peninsula. Nasser had already been trying to undermine Al Saud—for example, in October 1962, Cairo Radio threatened the Saudi regime, saying that "the sons of all the Arabian Peninsula lie in wait for you and your family. . . . Faisal, nothing but death awaits you."[16] After Egyptian troops poured into Yemen, Egyptian jets carried out several attacks on Saudi towns.[17] One such attack, on Abha in March 1963, killed thirty-six patients at a hospital. Additionally, Egyptian planes dropped weapons on Saudi territory in November 1962, in an attempt to bolster the Saudi opposition, although the latter was quite weak and Saudi security forces ultimately captured the weapons.[18] Nonetheless, the Saudis realized that North Yemen provided the Egyptians with a staging ground to maintain their foothold on the peninsula and even attack Saudi Arabia.

The Iraqi invasion of Kuwait in 1990 was arguably even more threatening than Egypt's intervention in Yemen. Saudi Arabia feared that by maintaining control over Iraq and Kuwait, Saddam Hussein would not only continue to have a large army but also come to possess vast resources through Iraqi and Kuwaiti oil that would allow him to dominate the Gulf. Even if Hussein never attacked Saudi Arabia, the kingdom would still need to "bend to [Hussein's] will" because of his dominance over the region.[19] As long as Hussein maintained control over Kuwait, Saudi Arabia would cease to be independent, particularly when it came to foreign and oil policies.

The Iraqi threat was exacerbated by the possibility of a direct attack on Saudi Arabia. For the first time in its modern history, the kingdom was under danger of invasion by a "brotherly" Arab country, according to a Saudi prince.[20] Hussein was able to threaten the oil fields in the kingdom's Eastern Province that are close to the Kuwaiti border. Although the kingdom had spent excessively on its military before 1990 (about 20 percent of gross domestic product through the 1980s), it was still underprepared to defend against Saddam Hussein's large army.[21] As Prince Khalid bin Sultan, who commanded the Saudi forces during the Gulf War, described the situation:

> My troops? A terrible shock awaited me. The northern border of the Kingdom was very lightly defended. When, before the crisis, we had evaluated the potential threats to our Eastern Province, we had discounted the early possibility of being exposed to a land threat from our northern Arab neighbors. We had, of course, considered the real possibility of air, naval, missile and terrorist threats from across the gulf and we were well prepared to face these dangers—but not a land threat, not tanks and troops pouring across our borders in a land war. For this reason, we maintained only small land forces in northeastern Arabia.[22]

The Saudi military lacked the ability to stop Hussein if he had decided to invade the Eastern Province. Because he continued to reinforce his troops in Kuwait, the Saudis were seriously concerned that he could continue to attack the kingdom.[23] This posed an existential threat to the kingdom—an invasion of the Eastern Province would have cost Saudi Arabia many of the oil fields on which it relies for income. The Saudi leadership wondered whether the Iraqi leader wanted to "topple all six GCC [Gulf Cooperation Council] states" or to "redraw the whole map of Arabia."[24]

In addition, the threat was urgent. Although the United States was interested in defending Saudi Arabia, the Saudi leadership could not completely rely on the United States if Hussein proceeded to attack. As Khalid bin Sultan explains: "Once Saddam seized control of more than 40 percent of world oil reserves, the West might think twice before challenging him. It might have to deal with him—and that could have been his ultimate intention."[25]

More recently, Iran has significantly increased its involvement in the region, bringing an end to the stable balance of power that the Saudis desired to keep. Though hostile relations between Iran and Saudi Arabia intensified after the 1979 Islamic Revolution, relations between the two countries have been particularly tense since 2015. Before 2003, Iraq managed to balance against Iran, which provided for a relative balance of power. And after the invasion of Iraq, the US military presence helped to maintain the balance. But since the withdrawal of US forces, the Saudis have viewed the regional balance of power as largely skewed toward Iran.

The problem began with the collapse of Saddam Hussein's regime in Iraq. Saudi Arabia viewed the US invasion of Iraq as handing the country to Iran on a silver platter. Speaking to the Council on Foreign Relations in 2005, the late Saudi foreign minister, Saud al-Faisal, said: "We fought a war together to keep Iran from occupying Iraq after Iraq was driven out of Kuwait. Now we are handing the whole country over to Iran without reason."[26] In another speech, he added: "With the quiet and the peace that has been established in the south, the Iranians have moved into all these governments with money, with people, and even with religious scholars and are settling themselves in these governments, mind you, under the protection of the military forces of the United States and Britain."[27]

The threat of Iran significantly increased following two major events in the region. In December 2011, the United States completed the withdrawal of its forces from Iraq.[28] This provided Iran with ever-increasing influence over the Iraqi government.[29] Although Iran had influenced Iraqi politics since the collapse of Saddam Hussein's regime, the US occupation authorities went to great lengths to limit Iran's involvement.[30] Following their withdrawal, Iran had a free hand to influence Iraqi politics and aimed at creating a "stable but reliant ally, not a regional competitor" in Iraq.[31] From the Saudi point of view, this strategy was successful, given that "any effort to form an Iraqi government must be negotiated in Tehran, rather than Baghdad."[32] The decline of Iraq from a leading force in the Arab world that "once waged a horribly bloody war against Iran" to a country that is "completely beholden to Iran" has horrified the Saudi monarchy.[33]

Additionally, as Iranian influence has increased since 2011, Saudi influence in the region has decreased since the 2011 uprisings. When the uprisings occurred, the regimes of traditional Saudi allies such as Egypt were toppled, while Bahrain was threatened by wide protests. Meanwhile, the uprising against Iran's regional ally—Syria, whose regime is ruled by Bashar al-Assad—failed to topple Assad, and Houthi advances in Yemen in late 2014 and early 2015 undermined Saudi security and provided Iran with a foothold on the peninsula. Prominent Saudi thinkers viewed the Houthis as a group similar to Hezbollah—a group trained and armed by Iran that has the hope of dominating the country.[34] This led to the view that Iran was encircling Saudi Arabia, controlling Iraq, Syria, and Lebanon in the north and Yemen in the south.[35]

Iran lacks the capability to conquer any major regional powers, but its conventional weapons still pose a serious threat to Saudi Arabia. For one, Iran might use its missile capability to threaten Saudi oil fields or desalination plants.[36] Iran could also attempt to close the Strait of Hormuz or attempt to conquer strategic territory.[37] Further, Iran could use money from its overseas assets that have been unfrozen as a result of the nuclear deal to invest in conventional capabilities, increasing the threat perceived by regional countries.

Along with Iran's activist foreign policy in the region, the Saudis have been concerned about Iran's nuclear program. Among the major Saudi concerns is that an Iranian nuclear weapon could lead to further proliferation and an arms race in the Middle East.[38] Saudi Arabia also is likely to fear that a nuclear Iran could pursue an emboldened foreign policy because it would not fear regime change from abroad. At the same time, Saudi Arabia fears that the nuclear deal with Iran could provide Iran with the economic resources to spend on its activities in the region, while at the same time providing it with the nuclear capability to develop a bomb once the deal ends.[39]

IDEOLOGICAL THREATS

Because the ultimate aim of Saudi policy is to maintain the kingdom's sovereignty and regime stability, ideological threats can be particularly dangerous. Ideological threats could undermine the kingdom's domestic political stability by disputing the regime's legitimacy, which could lead to social unrest.[40] In the Middle East, ideological threats can lead to what is referred to as an "ideational security dilemma."[41] This occurs when the region's countries use ideational power for purely domestic reasons, such as building up the regime's legitimacy. This use of ideational power is often uncertain, and it could be perceived as an ideational attack by adversaries in foreign countries. Thus, one regime's attempt to secure itself leads to insecurity among unfriendly regimes.[42]

Ideational threats to regime stability are important for understanding Gulf politics. Both states and nonstate actors in the Middle East often utilize ideological issues to undermine the domestic stability of adversaries. Some scholars even argue that threats to domestic stability emanating from abroad (many of them ideological) tend to alarm Gulf leaders more than changes in power distribution.[43] In the Saudi view, there have been three major ideological threats to the regime in the past several decades: pan-Arab nationalism, revolutionary Shi'ism, and political Islam. Political Islam, for the Saudis, includes both violent extremist groups like al-Qaeda and the Islamic State of Iraq and Syria and moderate groups like the Muslim Brotherhood.

The first major ideational threat that Al Saud faced was secular pan-Arabism. Arab nationalism in the region was born and developed as a response to Western colonialism and the emergence of Israel. Pan-Arabism was a serious threat to the Saudi regime because it appealed both to the Saudi public at large, which allowed the opposition to utilize it, and also to members of the royal family. The ideas of pan-Arabism limited the extent to which Saudi Arabia could collaborate with the United States. To ensure its continuing legitimacy, Saudi Arabia could not be seen as dependent on the United States, and thus it occasionally acted to minimize its cooperation with the United States in order to reduce criticism.

Arab nationalism had wide appeal in the Arab world throughout the 1950s and 1960s, not least among the Saudi princes. Prince Khalid bin Sultan described Nasser's appeal in the 1950s by saying: "He had been our hero. All the young princes loved him. We used to fight over who loved him most. We were all Nasserites, in fact all the Arabs were."[44] But the popularity of Gamal Abdel Nasser and his version of pan-Arabism proved dangerous to the kingdom. In 1960, a group of Saudi princes, led by the minister of finance, Prince Talal bin Abdulaziz, called for constitutional reform in the kingdom that would lead to a constitutional monarchy.[45] The Free Princes, as they came to be known, were inspired by Nasser and by the replacement of several monarchies with republican regimes across the Arab world, including in Egypt and Iraq. Although other senior princes in Saudi Arabia, such as the Crown Prince Faisal, categorically rejected their demands, the example of the Free Princes shows how ideological threats from abroad could threaten the Saudi regime.

Foreign adversaries of Saudi Arabia used the appeal of pan-Arabism inside the kingdom to influence Saudi politics. During the Yemen crisis, Nasser capitalized on the pan-Arab sentiment by declaring that in order to "liberate all Jerusalem, the Arab peoples must first liberate Riyadh."[46] Furthermore, during the war, the Egyptians recruited King Saud, who was in exile in Cairo (while Crown Prince Faisal ruled over the country) to oppose the Saudi regime. They also supported several "liberation movements" inside Saudi Arabia.[47] These efforts limited the extent to which the monarchy could collaborate with the West without being seen as a puppet.

The spread and influence of Arab nationalism quickly dwindled after the Arab countries lost to Israel in the 1967 war. However, by the late 1970s, the ideological threat of pan-Arabism was replaced by the threat of revolutionary Shi'ism. Although, before 1979, many Shia in the Eastern Province and across the Gulf sympathized with the more inclusive pan-Arab ideals, the Iranian Revolution and the desire to export it across the Gulf made the Arab monarchies wary. Shortly after the collapse of the shah's regime in 1979, a wave of Shia unrest in support of the revolution spread among several Arab countries, including Iraq, Bahrain, and Saudi Arabia. The same year, Shia in Saudi Arabia, defying a government ban, publicly observed 'ashura, a commemoration of the martyrdom of Imam Hussein.[48] Shia protests in the Eastern Province were so widespread that about twenty thousand Saudi soldiers were required to pacify the region.[49]

The Saudis were particularly fearful because Iran had both inspired and supported the Shia protests. Even before the Iranian Revolution, Ayatollah

Khomeini sent emissaries in 1978 to the monarchies and appointed Friday prayer leaders, who later mobilized the Shia community against the Saudi state.[50] Khomeini also declared monarchical and hereditary regimes, like the Gulf monarchies, to be an "evil system of government," and he announced that "they have no place in Islam."[51] Following the 1979 Revolution, Iran started an Arabic radio broadcast aimed at inspiring Shia to protest, and openly called for the overthrow of the Saudi regime.[52] Throughout the 1980s, Khomeini called on Iranian pilgrims to Mecca to demonstrate against the Saudis. Many heeded this call over the years, culminating in clashes between pilgrims and Saudi forces in 1987 that killed four hundred people.[53]

In addition to protests, the Saudi regime was threatened by militarized Shia groups, many of which received Iranian support. In 1981, the Islamic Revolutionary Guard Corps established several revolutionary movements abroad. Those included the Movement for Vanguards Missionaries, which set up local branches for revolutionary groups in Saudi Arabia, such as the Organization of the Islamic Revolution and Hezbollah al-Hejaz, a terrorist group that operated in Saudi Arabia, Bahrain, and Kuwait.[54] Hezbollah al-Hejaz advocated the overthrow of the Saudi regime through violence, and it conducted attacks on petroleum and chemical facilities in the late 1980s.[55] In 1996, after the Khobar Towers attack, in which nineteen US soldiers working at Dhahran Airbase were killed and hundreds were injured, Saudi and American investigators concluded that Hezbollah al-Hejaz had been involved.[56] Since 1979, Iranian-inspired groups have occasionally conducted attacks and have attempted to instigate a revolution against the Saudi regime.

Following Khomeini's death in 1989, tensions decreased between Iran and Saudi Arabia—especially because Iran largely abandoned the goal of exporting the revolution.[57] Yet these tensions resurfaced with the Arab uprisings. The Saudis blamed the 2011 protests in the Eastern Province and Bahrain on "foreign parties," referring to Iran.[58] An op-ed published in the Saudi-owned *Al-Hayat* in October 2011 called for repressing Saudi Shia after accusing them, without real evidence, of having trained groups to fight in Iran, Syria, and Lebanon.[59]

Although the changing balance of power is significant, the conflict between Saudi Arabia and Iran is rooted in perceptions. Saudi Arabia views Iran as a sectarian power that is trying to dominate the Gulf and Levant regions. The Saudi leadership views its assertive policy in Yemen and Syria as a response to Iran's increasing influence. The Saudi regime thinks that Iran sees the Saudi monarchy as un-Islamic and therefore as illegitimate. In this view, Saudi Arabia does not believe in the possibility of reconciling relations with Iran as long as the revolutionary Shia regime remains in Iran. Because of this ideological conflict, even the emergence of new threats such as that of the Islamic State has not pushed the Saudis to fix relations with Iran. This ideational conflict is likely to remain for the foreseeable future.

Political Sunni Islam has also threatened Saudi interests. The Saudi regime finds political Islamists worrying, regardless of whether they are peaceful, such as the Muslim Brotherhood, or violent, such as al-Qaeda and the Islamic State. Political Islam is threatening because it challenges the dominant version of Islam in Saudi Arabia, which is often referred to as Wahhabism. Two important fundamentals of Wahhabism are not mixing religion and politics (though still calling for Islam to govern society) and avoiding chaos, which entails support-ing existing rulers almost unconditionally.[60] Political Islamists often reject both principles. Although this has led to tensions between the Saudi leadership and political Islamists, the relationship has in fact been more complicated. The Saudi regime has often felt threatened by political Islamists, but at the same time they have used them to counter other ideological threats.

Early on, Saudi Arabia tried to use the Muslim Brotherhood to counter the influence of pan-Arabism. However, when terrorist groups, primarily al-Qaeda, attacked Western targets, Saudi Arabia tried to blame their terrorist methods purely on the Muslim Brotherhood and not on Saudi Wahhabism. For example, in a 2004 speech at the Council on Foreign Relations, the late Saudi foreign minister, Saud al-Faisal, claimed: "Though [Osama bin Laden is] a Saudi by birth, he developed his ideology and methodology in Afghanistan, under the tutelage of a radicalized cult of the Muslim Brotherhood."[61] Yet Al-Faisal did not address what inspired Bin Laden to even go to Afghanistan in the first place. In reality, organizations like al-Qaeda were influenced by both the political activism of the Muslim Brotherhood and the radical teachings of Wahhabism.

The Muslim Brotherhood's threat to the Saudi regime peaked during the Arab uprisings. After the uprisings, parties associated with the Brotherhood won elections in Egypt and Tunisia and gained a strong foothold in countries such as Yemen and Syria. The Brotherhood's ideology and success undermined Wahhabism and challenged the legitimacy of the Saudi regime. The Brother-hood has advanced an alternative view of Sunni Islam that is more moderate than that in Saudi Arabia and that has proven popular across several Arab countries. Additionally, the Brotherhood has shown through electoral victories that Islam and democracy are not incompatible. This runs counter to what many Wahhabis have claimed.[62]

Violent Islamic movements have constituted another kind of ideological threat to the stability of the Saudi regime. Al Saud has often used violent move-ments to its own advantage, but when these groups have challenged Saudi policies, the Saudis have frequently found themselves repressing the same groups they previously supported. One such group was the Ikhwan (literally meaning "brotherhood" but unrelated to the Muslim Brotherhood). The Ikhwan were tribesmen who received a puritanical education on Islam. They were also fierce fighters who helped the Saudis conquer much of Arabia in the 1910s and 1920s, before the declaration of the kingdom. However, they were agitated by the Saudis' collaboration with the British and by Saudi orders (through the British) to not expand beyond the kingdom's borders into neighboring countries such as Iraq and Jordan. In the late 1920s, King Abdulaziz was faced with either endangering relations with the British or repressing the Ikhwan, and he chose the latter. This led to several battles with the Ikhwan, after which the king successfully repressed them.

A similar story occurred vis-à-vis al-Qaeda. Saudi Arabia supported Osama bin Laden and other fighters who went to Afghanistan to fight against the Soviets throughout the 1980s, and when bin Laden returned to the kingdom in 1989 he was welcomed as a hero.[63] The Saudis also supported local Afghan fighters. In fact, when Saudi Arabia wanted to liberate Kuwait in 1991, the Saudi commander, Prince Khaled bin Sultan, boasted that between a few dozen and three hundred Afghan mujahideen came to fight with the Saudis.[64] Yet bin Laden's time in Afghanistan had led him to espouse a global version of jihad that combined elements from both Wahhabism and the activism of the radical elements of the Muslim Brotherhood.[65]

The threat of bin Laden and al-Qaeda increased over time. In 1996, dissatisfied with the presence of American forces in Saudi Arabia, bin Laden declared jihad against them. This was particularly worrying because bin Laden used the same religious legitimacy that Al Saud had used to condemn the royal family's policies. The presence of American troops in Saudi Arabia proved controversial and led to the Islamic Awakening movement, in which clerics declared that the kingdom was resorting to "an evil greater than Saddam, that is the USA" to liberate Kuwait.[66] Thus, when bin Laden declared jihad against the American troops in Saudi Arabia in 1996, there was already dissatisfaction among many clerics with the Americans. The threat from al-Qaeda significantly increased again in 2003, when it launched a terrorist campaign in Saudi Arabia that lasted until 2006.[67] Since 2014, the Islamic State has developed a similar threat; it launched several attacks against Shia in Saudi Arabia in 2015.[68] Because the Saudi state itself repressed its Shia citizens, it was initially difficult for the Saudi regime to effectively fight against the Islamic State on its own soil.[69]

DETERRENCE

Saudi Arabia has attempted to deter its enemies by threatening punishment against an attack on the regime's interests. To ensure deterrence, Saudi Arabia has relied on three main tools. First, the kingdom uses its alliance with the

United States to ensure that foreign adversaries do not threaten its stability, while still realizing that the great power will not always defend Saudi interests. Second, the kingdom has acquired sophisticated weapons to ensure that it can deter its enemies and act alone when it must. And third, ideologically, the Saudi regime has often employed its position in the Islamic world to support Islamic groups and compete with rival ideologies.

Alliance with the United States

When King Abdulaziz fought to unite Saudi Arabia in the early years of the twentieth century, he depended on support from the British, who provided him with funding and weapons. Yet he did not always trust the British, because they were also the backers of his main rivals, the Hashemites, who controlled Western Arabia and then Jordan and Iraq.[70] In the early 1930s, he started giving oil concessions to American companies.[71] Relations between the United States and Saudi Arabia developed when oil was discovered in the kingdom in the late 1930s. In 1943, President Franklin Roosevelt declared that "the defense of Saudi Arabia is vital to the defense of the United States," and that the kingdom was therefore eligible for military assistance.[72] President Roosevelt and King Abdulaziz then met on board the USS *Quincy* in 1945. Although the meeting was largely about the future of Palestine, the two countries date their special relationship to that meeting.[73] Saudi oil, which has been important for the US and the global economy, has continued to be the main reason behind this special relationship.

The Saudi royal family has always seen its alliance with the United States as an integral part of its attempt to deter its enemies and defend the kingdom. Prince Khaled bin Sultan explains that there has been a consensus among the leading members of Al Saud "that if our security and the integrity of our territory were threatened, and if our own forces were in danger of being overwhelmed, then we would not hesitate to request assistance from any friendly nations with which we had common interests—including the United States."[74] Although Saudi policies may change with the change in leadership, reliance on the United States to ensure deterrence has been a constant for decades.

The Saudi leadership has benefited immensely from its alliance with the United States. During the conflict in Yemen in the 1960s, as Egyptians bombed Saudi cities, the superpower came to Saudi Arabia's rescue. President John Kennedy had previously promised the Saudis of "full US support for the maintenance of Saudi Arabian integrity."[75] Thus, the United States then flew American jets over Riyadh and Jeddah in solidarity, and the British placed a dozen combat aircraft in the south of the country.[76] Two decades later, during the Iran-Iraq War, the Saudis feared that the war could spill over into the kingdom, especially as they were not impartial and had shown support for Iraq. The Saudis then asked the Americans for a demonstration of support to deter Iran. The Reagan administration responded by dispatching the Airborne Warning and Control System (known as AWACS) before pushing Congress to allow the sale of this system to the kingdom. Reagan even offered to establish a formal American military presence in Saudi Arabia, but the Saudis refused.[77]

Saudi Arabia's alliance with the United States perhaps proved most important when Saddam Hussein attacked Kuwait in 1990. The Saudis feared that he would go on to attack the kingdom—the oil fields in eastern Saudi Arabia were only a few days' march away from the Iraqi army. Immediately after the invasion of Kuwait, the United States sent two aircraft carrier groups to the Gulf as well as some aircraft to Saudi Arabia in order to prevent an Iraqi advance into the kingdom.[78] Then Saudi Arabia and the United States worked on not only liberating Kuwait but also destroying Iraq's war-making capability to prevent future aggression.[79]

Since the Iran nuclear deal in 2015, the Saudis have claimed that the United States has abandoned them in favor of improving relations with Iran. Despite these claims, the Saudi alliance with the United States remains vital to securing Saudi interests. For example, though they are worried about Iran's increasing influence in the region, the Saudis are not worried about a direct attack from Iran. This is partly because the United States has pledged that it would defend Saudi Arabia and the Gulf countries, using military force if necessary.[80]

Nuclear Weapons and Extended Deterrence

Although Saudi Arabia opposes the spread of nuclear weapons in the Middle East, it has not adopted a military doctrine that addresses how to deter a nuclear attack. Given Saudi-Israeli relations, it makes sense that Saudi Arabia has not felt particularly threatened by Israeli nuclear weapons. As exemplified by its minimal involvement in the Arab-Israeli wars, Saudi Arabia has largely opposed Israel diplomatically but not militarily.[81] Relatedly, Saudi Arabia has repeatedly called for a weapons of mass destruction–free zone in the Middle East, but it has not attempted to take any additional steps, such as trying to acquire nuclear weapons of its own.[82] Additionally, Saudi Arabia may fear that nuclear weapons development could risk Israeli retaliation or compromise its relations with the United States. This would undermine both Saudi Arabia's sovereignty and the regime's stability, encouraging both foreign and domestic enemies to take advantage.[83]

The Iran nuclear deal presents an unusual challenge to the Saudis vis-à-vis deterrence. The deal allows Iran to enrich uranium up to 3.67 percent. Even though this is not enough for Iran to acquire nuclear weapons, it recognizes Iran's right to enrich uranium and to be a "nuclear threshold" country, implying its ability to break out to making a nuclear bomb in a relatively short time.[84] Saudi officials have repeatedly said that they would match Iran's nuclear capability and that they deserve the same concessions that have been given to Iran. For example, Saudi prince Turki al-Faisal claimed that "whatever the Iranians have, we will have, too."[85] The United States has promised the Gulf countries increased security guarantees, but it has not yet delivered on these promises.[86]

Some Saudi officials have hinted that the Iran deal marks the end of the historic alliance between the United States and Saudi Arabia, at least in its current form. Speaking in Seoul, Prince Turki al-Faisal used the past tense when he said, "We were America's best friend in the Arab world for fifty years."[87] Yet the Saudis realize that they need American support to confront a more assertive Iran. During Operation Decisive Storm, which Saudi Arabia launched in March 2015 to counter the Houthis in Yemen, the kingdom depended heavily on equipment and intelligence from the United States.[88] So far, the only superpower that can project its influence across the Gulf is the United States, and Saudi leaders realize this.

There are two streams of Saudi thinking about the Iran deal. It is possible that Saudi Arabia would maintain diplomatic pressure and use hard power to counter Iran's rising influence in the region. Alternatively, the Gulf Cooperation Council may open up relations with Iran economically and hope that this will slowly stabilize the region.[89] So far, the first scenario seems to dominate Saudi thinking. But in the medium to long terms, there could be an opportunity to create a security zone in the Gulf that encompasses both the monarchies and Iran.[90]

If the Iran deal fails, Saudi Arabia may react differently than it did to Israel's nuclear weapons development. The Saudi reaction will largely depend on how much of a threat Iran poses at the time. In fact, in a recent book on Saudi Arabia and nuclear weapons, Norman Cigar identified Iran as the key variable to understanding Saudi thinking on nuclear weapons. Cigar asserts that "had Iran acquired nuclear weapons at any point, Saudi Arabia would also have done so. . . . And as long as Iran adheres to the agreement concluded in July 2015, . . . and does not acquire nuclear weapons for the next 15 years, very likely neither will Saudi Arabia."[91]

Iran's commitment to nuclear weapons is the most important factor in Saudi decision making about nuclear weapons, but this has only been a recent phenomenon. In 2006 the Saudi foreign minister claimed that the kingdom would not acquire nuclear weapons even if Iran developed them.[92] Only more recently did Saudi Arabia vow that it would match Iran's nuclear capability. Although the change in the Saudi position may have been partially aimed at pressuring Washington not to reach a nuclear agreement with Tehran, Iran's threat to Saudi Arabia has significantly increased since 2011, which may have changed the Saudi calculation.

In response to Iran's pursuit of nuclear capability, some have suggested that Saudi Arabia may want to acquire nuclear weapons from its long-standing ally, Pakistan. Relations between the two countries have long been close—in fact, the former head of Saudi intelligence, Prince Turki al-Faisal, once described the relations between them by saying: "It's probably one of the closest relationships in the world between any two countries without any official treaty."[93] Saudi Arabia also provided financial assistance to Pakistan that enabled the country to build its nuclear weapons program when it was under sanctions.[94] This has led some to suggest that there is a secret deal between Saudi Arabia and Pakistan, under which the kingdom can buy weapons from Pakistan whenever they are needed. But this is unlikely to be true. According to Feroz Khan, a former brigadier in the Pakistani army who has written one of the best books about Pakistan's nuclear program, there is no nuclear deal between Saudi Arabia and Pakistan, and there are no plans to provide extended deterrence or sell nuclear technology to the kingdom.[95] Furthermore, Pakistan's unwillingness to deploy troops to fight in Yemen at the request of Saudi Arabia provides additional reasons to doubt that Pakistan would provide Saudi Arabia with nuclear weapons.[96]

Although nuclear weapons play little role in current Saudi strategy, nuclear energy is poised to have an important role in the future. The kingdom's rising electricity demands and its need to diversify the economy have pushed it to begin investing in nuclear energy programs.[97] However, Saudi Arabia is unlikely to want to sign a so-called 123 Agreement with the United States, under which it would give up its right to enrich uranium and reprocess spent fuel. Though the United States has reached such an agreement with the United Arab Emirates, other countries in the region, such as Jordan, have refused similar agreements. This may worry American officials and nuclear nonproliferation experts, who fear that a Saudi refusal to sign such an agreement (which could lower the cost of pursuing nuclear energy) could be driven by some willingness to proliferate. This fear is likely unwarranted. It assumes that because the Saudis are unwilling to go for the cheaper option (which would be giving up the right to enrich), then the leadership might have hidden motives to pursue enrichment, such as building nuclear weapons. However, when it comes to making decisions about nuclear energy, many countries tend to emphasize sovereignty and matching the technological capabilities of their neighbors.[98] The Saudis would like to develop an indigenous capability to enrich uranium for the purposes of maintaining sovereignty and keeping up with Iran's capabilities.

Despite the nuclear deal with Iran, there is still a role for extended deterrence in the Gulf region. The Iran deal is not a permanent one—many of its constraints will expire in about a decade. These may be renewed later, but the United States may want to use this time to begin building the infrastructure required to provide extended deterrence for its allies in the Gulf. In this case, the Saudi alliance with the United States would play an important role. To be sure, because the Saudis do not fully trust the Americans with their security, they may prefer to have their own nuclear weapons. However, if the United States were to prevent Saudi Arabia from developing nuclear weapons, the kingdom's preferred option would be to have US nuclear forces under joint control between the two countries, as it has done with other NATO members.[99] The United States is unlikely to accept this outcome, because it would require relinquishing some control to the Saudis. A more realistic scenario might be maintaining nuclear deterrence with the US Fifth Fleet in the Gulf region. Some transparency about the number and types of nuclear weapons might be useful for both reassuring Gulf allies and deterring a nuclear-armed Iran.

As discussed above, Iran poses a serious conventional threat to Saudi Arabia and other countries in the region. Extended deterrence by the United States has played an important role in countering this threat. Iran knows that if it attempts to close the Strait of Hormuz, the United States would use overwhelming force to reopen it. Thus, Saudi Arabia is likely to continue relying on American troops in the region to provide extended deterrence against Iran. In fact, Saudi Arabia and the other Gulf countries could use even more American help to counter Iran, including the development of a joint missile defense system. At the same time, the Gulf countries need to overcome their own resistance to information sharing and the development of the missile defense system.

Internal Balancing

The Saudi leadership realizes that there is nothing inevitable about US support for the kingdom. Prince Khaled bin Sultan cites Somalia and Bosnia as examples of American reluctance to send troops to resolve a conflict.[100] The Saudi regime also remembers how the United States abandoned the shah of Iran after the 1979 Revolution and Hosni Mubarak during the 2011 protests. As Prince Khaled bin Sultan explains: "If vital Western interests in our region are threatened, then we believe we can confidently count on Western help. If such interests are not threatened, then we might have to make do on our own."[101]

Although Saudi Arabia and the United States have worked together for decades, there have been many instances of tension in their alliance. During the War of the Cities between Iran and Iraq, when the two countries used ballistic missiles to terrorize the enemy's population, Saudi Arabia wanted to acquire ballistic missiles to deter such attacks. The Americans refused to sell ballistic missiles to the Saudis, and even attempted to block other countries from doing so.[102] Additionally, the United States has often been an inconvenient ally due to its negative image in the Arab world. Saudi Arabia came under much domestic and regional criticism for allowing American troops into the kingdom after the Iraqi invasion of Kuwait. After the war, when the Gulf monarchies entered into formal defense agreements with the United States, the Saudis refused to do so.[103] Because the Saudis are short on human capital, they often require foreign troops to protect their key installations. Rather than resorting to the Americans, they have traditionally asked Muslim Pakistani troops to fill this role.[104]

For these reasons, Saudi Arabia tried to develop its own military forces so it would not remain dependent on US protection. In doing so, the kingdom has often emphasized acquiring technologically advanced weapons rather than maintaining a large standing army. Saudi Arabia is a large yet thinly populated country, making a land invasion difficult for any adversary. This has allowed the country to focus on developing its air defenses, especially around its strategic oil installments and cities. It also developed its air force by acquiring a fleet of the latest aircraft.[105]

Showing the Saudi emphasis on internal balancing would require data on military spending and perceptions of threats, which the Saudis' lack of transparency makes impossible to obtain accurately from the kingdom's public or unclassified records.[106] Instead, a brief discussion of the Saudis' purchase of Chinese ballistic missiles can show how the kingdom attempts to maintain parity with its adversaries rather than completely rely on the United States. Even before the 1980s, Israel's military prowess, nuclear weapons, and long-range missiles have long threatened Saudi Arabia.[107] Yet this threat escalated during the War of the Cities between Iran and Iraq.[108] During this war, Iran also attacked Saudi and Kuwaiti oil tankers, and an Iranian F-4 flew over Saudi territorial waters (before being intercepted by a Saudi F-15).[109] These developments led the Saudi regime to consider purchasing ballistic missiles.

When the United States did not agree to provide the kingdom with ballistic missiles, the Saudi government secretly approached China to purchase DF-3A (CSS-2) ballistic missiles. After intense negotiations in 1986, the Saudis purchased the missile purely as a deterrent weapon. Prince Khaled bin Sultan, who negotiated the deal on behalf of the Saudis, explains the logic of purchasing the weapons for deterrence:

The effectiveness of a deterrent capability depends on a potential enemy knowing of its existence. . . . I wrote an analysis for the high command suggesting that, if our acquisition of Chinese missiles were not detected by November 1988, this would be an advantage; if not by February 1989, this would be greatly in our favor; if, however, it was not detected by June 1989, we should consider leaking the news ourselves as the object of acquiring the weapon would not have been achieved.[110]

Unfortunately, in 1991 the DF-3A did not prevent Saddam Hussein from using Scud missiles to target Saudi cities. And Saudi Arabia's subsequent hesitation to use DF-3A missiles in retaliation against the Iraqi population may have further weakened its credibility. Saudi hesitation was largely driven by the inaccuracy of DF-3A missiles, which would have likely caused many civilian casualties at a time when Saudi Arabia was claiming that it was fighting against the Hussein regime and not the Iraqi people. According to Prince Khalid bin Sultan, King Fahd refrained from using the missiles, fearing that they would "cause casualties among innocent Iraqis."[111] To increase this credibility, there are indications that Saudi Arabia may have purchased DF-21 (CSS-5) missiles from China (though this has not yet been confirmed), which are more accurate.[112] If this is true, DF-21 missiles can increase the credibility of Saudi Arabia's deterrence because they would allow the country to attack military targets in a future conflict rather than population centers. Thus, Saudi Arabia would not need to hesitate again, as it did in the 1991 war against Iraq, for fear of civilian casualties. This episode shows that the Saudi regime has tried to maintain the credibility of the country's deterrence not only through reliance on the United States but also by strengthening its own arsenal.

IDEOLOGICAL DETERRENCE

Because of the ideological threats to the stability of the Saudi regime, Saudi Arabia has often resorted to its status in the Islamic world to deter and counter ideological threats. In this sense, ideological power represents soft power. Countries can respond to ideological threats in two ways: with counterframing, which involves rebutting, undermining, or neutralizing an opponent's ideological framing, and with resource mobilization, to support efforts that "mitigate the spread of subversive ideas and enhance the spread of favorable ideas."[113] Saudi Arabia has used both methods for ideological deterrence. The kingdom hosts the two holiest mosques for Muslims, in Mecca and Medina, and the Saudi leadership has allied with the descendants of Mohammed bin Abdul Wahhab and Saudi Salafists, who espouse a very austere Islam. These factors have led Saudi Arabia to increase its influence and respond to threats by emphasizing its status as a leader in the Islamic world.

Early on, the Saudi regime tried to defend itself from the attacks of pan-Arabism and to spread its version of Islam in order to increase its legitimacy. When the threat of Arab nationalism was heightened, in 1962 the Saudi leadership established the Muslim World League, whose announced goals at its founding were to defend the Islamic Ummah from threats emanating from "communism" and from the "irreligious" Egyptian president Gamal Abdel Nasser.[114] The league was based in Mecca, and it was initially headed by the grand mufti of Saudi Arabia, Mohammed bin Ibrahim al-Shaykh, a descendent of Mohammed bin Abdul Wahhab. In its early days, the organization was able to subject other competing Islamic organizations in the Arab world to its control, and it was used to undermine secular pan-Arabism as well as enhance the spreading of the Saudi version of Islam. After Nasser's death, it continued to counter other pan-Arab secular regimes, such as the Baathists in Iraq and Syria.[115] During the next few decades, Saudi Arabia reportedly continued to use the Muslim World League to support nonstate actors, such as al-Qaeda, Gamaat Islamiya, the Islamic Jihad in Egypt, and Abu Sayyaf in the Philippines.[116]

After the Iranian Revolution, the Saudi regime began to work on balancing the influence of revolutionary Shi'ism in Saudi Arabia and the wider region. As was explained above, Khomeini had condemned the Saudi monarchy as un-Islamic and claimed to be a leader in the Islamic world. The Soviet invasion of Afghanistan provided Saudi Arabia with an opportunity to increase the kingdom's legitimacy within the region, hence deterring Iran's idea of revolutionary Shi'ism. Saudi Arabia supported the Sunni mujahideen in Afghanistan, raising the kingdom's Islamic credentials. And the Saudis have also allowed charities to support Islamic fighters in a wide range of areas—such as Bosnia, Kosovo, Somalia, Syria, and Yemen—to raise the regime's Islamic credentials and maintain clerics' support for the regime.[117] The Saudi royalty also controls several major Arabic media outlets, and the Saudi Foreign Ministry has been buying media outlets in several Arab countries, such as Syria, Jordan, Kuwait, the United Arab Emirates, Lebanon, and Mauritania.[118] Saudi Arabia uses these tools to subvert the ideological appeal of its opponents, such as Iran and its supporters in the region.

However, this strategy is sometimes undermined by Saudi Arabia's alliance with the West. Very often, Islamic groups supported by Saudi Arabia turn against the kingdom for its alliance with Western countries. The Ikhwan revolted against King Abdulaziz in the late 1920s because of his relations with Britain, while al-Qaeda's campaign against the kingdom came after King Fahd allowed US troops to be stationed there. In both cases, Saudi Arabia understood the importance of its alliance with Western countries for deterring other regional powers, and it thus suppressed both the Ikhwan's and al-Qaeda's campaigns against it. Nevertheless, Saudi Arabia has been limited in its alliance with the West because of the ongoing battle of ideologies. After the liberation of Kuwait, Saudi Arabia was the only Gulf monarchy not to have a formal security agreement with the United States.[119]

Another prominent example of how ideological deterrence is at odds with Saudi Arabia's alliance with the West is King Faisal's 1973 decision to place an oil embargo against the United States. In April 1973, months before Egypt and Syria attacked Israel, Egyptian president Anwar El Sadat informed King Faisal of his decision to go to war. King Faisal, in turn, informed the US Central Intelligence Agency, and he added that unless the United States prevented the war, the kingdom would be under pressure to use the "oil weapon" against the West.[120] Although the kingdom had used ideological battles to counter secular Arab nationalism, it could not help but stand with Egypt and Syria against Israel, which Saudi Arabia perceived as a more significant enemy than both the pan-Arabist and Islamist movements. Additionally, Egypt under Sadat and Syria under Assad had both improved relations with Saudi Arabia—and the kingdom could not be seen to be working against both pan-Arabist and Islamist feelings.[121] As such, the kingdom felt pressured to use the oil embargo against supporters of Israel. Saudi Arabia insisted that the United States commit itself to Syrian-Israeli mediation before it could lift the oil embargo.[122]

CONCLUSION

Since King Salman came to power in January 2015, Saudi Arabia has changed its policies in significant ways. Most important, the Saudis have escalated their confrontation against the Iranians and their affiliates in the Middle East, starting a military operation in Yemen to counter the Houthis' advance, declaring Hezbollah to be a terrorist group, and furthering cooperation with Turkey against Iran's ally, Assad.[123] This was largely due to the influence of Crown Prince Mohammed bin Salman, the son of the Saudi king, indicating the importance of personalities in transforming Saudi policy.

Nevertheless, the contours of Saudi Arabia's strategy are still similar. The Saudi leadership continues to emphasize sovereignty and regime stability. The new leadership simply identified Iran as the biggest threat to its interest. As perceived by the Saudis, Iranian power in the Levant and Yemen could undermine the sovereignty of the kingdom because Iran could use its proxies or the Shia within Saudi Arabia to launch attacks against the kingdom or simply to encircle Saudi Arabia with areas of Iranian influence. At the same time, the increased Iranian influence in the region, along with Iran's competing ideology, could also undermine regime stability in Saudi Arabia. In either case, the new leadership has become more active in the region in order to counter these threats and restore the regional balance.

This chapter has important implications for US policy. Reduced US involvement in the region since President Obama's pivot to Asia may have signaled to the Saudi rulers that protecting the interests of the state and preserving the Saudi regime require further regional intervention by the Saudi military. However, it is unclear whether this perception will last for long. Saudi Arabia's long war in Yemen, and its lack of success in toppling the Syrian regime, may show the Saudi leadership the limits of adopting an aggressive foreign policy. If these campaigns fail to achieve their goals, the Saudi leadership will be likely to return to a more defensive posture. This would be especially likely if the United States keeps an aircraft carrier in the Gulf and continues to assure Saudi Arabia of its willingness to defend the kingdom from any direct attacks by foreign powers, even as the United States reduces its regional role.

Another important implication of this chapter is that if Iran ever develops nuclear weapons, the United States is likely to be able to stop Saudi Arabia from proliferating—and even perhaps from enriching uranium at all. To be sure, the kingdom wants to enrich uranium to maintain its sovereignty. However, it continues to rely on the United States as a major pillar for its protection, and there is no alternative great power ally to replace the US. Thus, the United States continues to possess significant leverage over the kingdom, and it can prevent Saudi Arabia from enriching uranium or developing nuclear weapons even if the Saudi leadership wanted to do so. Though Saudi Arabia does not always act in ways that satisfy the United States, their alliance is a major component of Saudi strategy, and the kingdom is unlikely to risk this alliance. Using a combination of security assurances and pressure, the United States can ensure that Saudi Arabia will not enrich uranium or develop nuclear weapons in the future.

NOTES

1. "Official Source on Nuclear Deal between Iran and P5+1 Group," Saudi Press Agency, July 14, 2015, www.spa.gov.sa/English/details.php?id=1380735.

2. Ben Hubbard, "Arab World Split over Iran Nuclear Deal," *New York Times*, July 14, 2015, www.nytimes.com/2015/07/15/world/middleeast/iran-nuclear-deal-pro vokes-sharp-reactions-across-the-arab-world.html.

3. Abdulrahman al-Rashed, "Iran's Nuclear Deal and Us," Al Arabiya, July 16, 2015, https://english.alarabiya.net/en/views/news/middle-east/2015/07/16/Iran-s-nuclear -deal-and-us.html.

4. Abdulrahman al-Rashed, "Is the Gulf Relationship with Washington a Historical Mistake?" Al Arabiya, July 27, 2015, https://english.alarabiya.net/en/views/news/middle-east/2015/07/27/Is-the-relationship-with-Washington-a-historical-mistake-.html.

5. Julie Hirschfeld Davis and David Sanger, "Obama Pledges More Military Aid to Reassure Persian Gulf Allies on Iran Deal," New York Times, May 14, 2015, www.nytimes.com/2015/05/15/world/middleeast/obama-saudi-arabia-iran-persian-gulf-security.html.

6. "US to 'Expedite' Arms Sales to Gulf Countries," Al Arabiya, August 3, 2015, http://english.alarabiya.net/en/News/middle-east/2015/08/03/Gulf-ministers-Kerry-to-discuss-Iran-deal-in-Doha-.html.

7. Mohammed bin Yahya Al-Jaday'i, "Preparing Military Strategy: Challenges and Difficulties," Royal Saudi Air Defense Forces, www.rsadf.gov.sa/Articles.aspx?id=6.

8. F. Gregory Gause III, "The Foreign Policy of Saudi Arabia," in The Foreign Policies of Middle East States, ed. Raymond A. Hinnebusch and Anoushiravan Ehteshami (Boulder, CO: Lynne Rienner, 2002).

9. Faisal bin Salman al-Saud, Iran, Saudi Arabia and the Gulf: Power Politics in Transition, 1968–1971 (London: I. B. Tauris, 2003), viii.

10. Khaled bin Sultan and Patrick Seale, Desert Warrior: A Personal View of the Gulf War by the Joint Forces Commander (London: HarperCollins, 1995), 78.

11. Sarah Phillips, Yemen and the Politics of Permanent Crisis (London: Routledge, 2011), 76.

12. Saeed Badeeb, The Saudi-Egyptian Conflict over North Yemen, 1962–1970 (Boulder, CO: Westview Press, 1986), 50.

13. Ibid., 52.

14. Ibid., 53.

15. Ibid., 50.

16. Ibid., 52.

17. Ibid., 51.

18. Ibid., 52.

19. Bin Sultan and Seale, Desert Warrior, 19.

20. Ibid., 8–9. To be sure, there were incursions from Yemen in the 1960s, but the Iraqi invasion risked toppling the Saudi monarchy and not simply attacking some towns.

21. Anthony Cordesman, Saudi Arabia: Guarding the Desert Kingdom (Boulder, CO: Westview Press, 1997), cited by Madawi al-Rasheed, A History of Saudi Arabia (Cambridge: Cambridge University Press, 2002), 163; and Michael O'Hanlon, "Defense Budgets and American Power," Foreign Policy Paper 24, Brookings, 2010, 2, www.brookings.edu/~/media/research/files/papers/2010/12/defense-budget-ohanlon/12_defense_budget_ohanlon.pdf.

22. Bin Sultan and Seale, Desert Warrior, 8.

23. Ibid., 11.

24. Ibid., 12.

25. Ibid.

26. Saud al-Faisal, "The Fight against Extremism and the Search for Peace HRH Prince Saud Al Faisal, September 20, 2005," Ministry of Foreign Affairs, January 15,

2012, www.mofa.gov.sa/sites/mofaen/ServicesAndInformation/ImportantIssues/Pages/NewsArticleID39983.aspx.

27. Saud al-Faisal, "Saudi Arabia and the International Oil Market," James A. Baker III Institute for Public Policy, September 21, 2005, 10, http://bakerinstitute.org/files/2421/.

28. "US Flag Ceremony Marks Formal End of Iraq War Role," BBC, December 15, 2011, www.bbc.com/news/world-us-canada-16192105.

29. See, e.g., Ned Parker, "Ten Years after Iraq War Began, Iran Reaps the Gains," *Los Angeles Times*, March 28, 2013, http://articles.latimes.com/2013/mar/28/world/la-fg-iraq-iran-influence-20130329.

30. Anthony Cordesman and Sam Khazai, "Iraq after US Withdrawal: US Policy and the Iraqi Search for Security and Stability," Center for Strategic and Security Studies, July 2, 2012, ii, http://csis.org/publication/iraq-after-us-withdrawal.

31. Ibid., vii.

32. Mansour Almarzoqi, "Saudi Arabia: Don't Blame It All on the Islamic State," Al Jazeera, July 9, 2014, www.aljazeera.com/indepth/opinion/2014/07/saudi-view-iraq-don-blame-it-al-201477122146606416.html.

33. Al-Faisal, "Saudia Arabia," 39.

34. Abdulrahman al-Rashed, "Defending the Saudi Kingdom from the Houthi Threat," Al Arabiya, April 23, 2015, http://english.alarabiya.net/en/views/news/middle-east/2015/04/23/Defending-the-Saudi-kingdom-from-the-Houthi-threat-.html.

35. Abdulrahman al-Rashed, "Iran at Saudi Arabia's Frontiers," March 2, 2015, http://english.alarabiya.net/en/views/news/middle-east/2015/03/02/Iran-is-on-Saudi-fronts.html.

36. Steven Pifer, Richard C. Bush, Vanda Felbab-Brown, Martin S. Indyk, Michael O'Hanlon, and Kenneth M. Pollack, "US Nuclear and Extended Deterrence: Considerations and Challenges," Brookings Arms Control Series, May 2010, 38, www.brookings.edu/~/media/research/files/papers/2010/6/nuclear-deterrence/06_nuclear_deterrence.pdf.

37. See, e.g., Caitlin Talmadge, "Closing Time: Assessing the Iranian Threat to the Strait of Hormuz," *International Security* 33, no. 1 (Summer 2008).

38. Al-Faisal, "Saudia Arabia," 38.

39. "Why Saudi Arabia and Israel Oppose Iran Nuclear Deal," Al Jazeera, April 14, 2015, www.aljazeera.com/news/2015/04/saudi-arabia-israel-oppose-iran-nuclear-deal-150401061906177.html.

40. Lawrence Rubin, *Islam in the Balance: Ideational Threats in Arab Politics* (Stanford, CA: Stanford University Press, 2014), 21.

41. Ibid., 24.

42. Ibid.

43. F. Gregory Gause III, *The International Relations of the Persian Gulf* (Cambridge: Cambridge University Press, 2010), 9.

44. Bin Sultan and Seale, *Desert Warrior*, 58.

45. Richard Dekmejian, "The Liberal Impulse in Saudi Arabia," *Middle East Journal* 57, no. 3 (Summer 2003): 402.

46. Robert Lacey, *The Kingdom* (New York: Harcourt Brace Jovanovich, 1981).

47. Nadav Safran, *Saudi Arabia: The Ceaseless Quest for Security* (Ithaca, NY: Cornell University Press, 1985), 121.

48. Gause, *International Relations*, 47.

49. "Saudi Opposition Group Lists Insurgents' Demands," *MERIP Reports*, no. 85 (February 1980), 16.

50. Frederic Wehrey, *Sectarian Politics in the Gulf: From the Iraq War to the Arab Uprisings* (New York: Columbia University Press, 2014), 26.

51. Ruhollah Khomeini, *Islam and Revolution: Writings and Declarations of Imam Khomeini*, trans. Hamid Algar (London: KPI, 1985), 31.

52. Gause, *International Relations*, 48.

53. Ibid., 77.

54. Wehrey, *Sectarian Politics*, 26.

55. Toby Matthiesen, "Hizbullah al-Hijaz: A History of the Most Radical Saudi Shi'a Opposition Group," *Middle East Journal*, Spring 2010, 185–87.

56. Ibid., 191–94.

57. F. Gregory Gause III, "Balancing What? Threat Perception and Alliance Choice in the Gulf," *Security Studies*, Winter 2003, 289; and Gause, *International Relations*, 135.

58. Wehrey, *Sectarian Politics*, 143.

59. Hani al-Dhahiri, "'Darajat al-Basij' fi al-'Awamiya!" ("Basij Motorcycles" in al-'Awamiya!), *al-Hayat*, October 11, 2011, cited by Wehrey, *Sectarian Politics*, 137.

60. Robert Leiken and Steven Brooke, "The Moderate Muslim Brotherhood," *Foreign Affairs*, March–April 2007, www.foreignaffairs.com/articles/2007-03-01/moderate-muslim-brotherhood.

61. Saud al-Faisal, "The United States and Saudi Arabia: A Relationship Threatened by Misconceptions," Council on Foreign Relations, April 27, 2004, http://web.archive.org/web/20110622094432/http://www.cfr.org/saudi-arabia/united-states-saudi-arabia-relationship-threatened-misconceptions/p6982.

62. Madawi al-Rasheed, "Saudi Arabia Pleased with Morsi's Fall," *Al-Monitor*, July 4, 2013, www.al-monitor.com/pulse/originals/2013/07/saudi-arabia-glad-to-see-morsi-go.html.

63. Gause, *International Relations*, 138.

64. Bin Sultan and Seale, *Desert Warrior*, 248, 302.

65. Gause, *International Relations*, 138.

66. Al-Rasheed, *History*, 166.

67. Thomas Hegghammer, "The Failure of Jihad in Saudi Arabia," Combating Terrorism Center, February 25, 2010, 18, www.ctc.usma.edu/v2/wp-content/uploads/2010/10/CTC_OP_Hegghammer_Final.pdf.

68. Fahad Nazer, "ISIS Will Fail in Saudi Arabia," Middle East Institute, June 15, 2015, www.mei.edu/content/article/isis-will-fail-saudi-arabia.

69. Frederic Wehrey, "Saudi Arabia Has a Shiite Problem," *Foreign Policy*, December 3, 2014, http://foreignpolicy.com/2014/12/03/saudi-arabia-has-a-shiite-problem-royal-family-saud/.

70. David B. Ottaway, *The King's Messenger: Prince Bandar bin Sultan and America's Tangled Relationship with Saudi Arabia* (New York: Walker, 2008), 13.

71. David Ottaway, "The US and Saudi Arabia since the 1930s," Foreign Policy Research Institute, August 2009, www.fpri.org/article/2009/08/the-u-s-and-saudi-arabia-since-the-1930s/.

72. Ottaway, *King's Messenger*, 11.

73. Ottaway, "US and Saudi Arabia."

74. Bin Sultan and Seale, *Desert Warrior*, 24.

75. Lacey, *Kingdom*, 347.

76. Ibid., 347; and Bin Sultan and Seale, *Desert Warrior*, 78.

77. Gause, *International Relations*, 69.

78. Bin Sultan and Seale, *Desert Warrior*, 12.

79. Ibid., 315.

80. Kevin Liptak and Elise Labott, "Obama: US Would Use Military Force to Defend Gulf Allies," CNN, May 15, 2015, http://edition.cnn.com/2015/05/13/politics/obama-saudi-gcc/.

81. Gawdat Bahgat, *The Proliferation of Nuclear Weapons in the Middle East* (Gainesville: University Press of Florida, 2007).

82. See, e.g., Turki al-Faisal, "A Political Plan for a Weapons of Mass Destruction–Free Zone (WMDFZ) in the Middle East," Belfer Center for Science and International Affairs, July 9, 2013, http://belfercenter.ksg.harvard.edu/publication/23220/political_plan_for_a_weapons_of_mass_destructionfree_zone_wmdfz_in_the_middle_east.html; and "Statement for BBC2 Newsnight from the Royal Embassy of Saudi Arabia, London," Embassy of the Kingdom of Saudi Arabia in the United Kingdom, November 6, 2013, http://embassies.mofa.gov.sa/sites/uk/EN/AboutDiplomaticMission/MissionNews/Pages/ennews08112013001.aspx.

83. Anthony Cordesman and Nawaf Obaid, *National Security in Saudi Arabia: Threats, Responses, and Challenges* (Westport, CT: Praeger Security International, 2005), 254–55.

84. Yoel Guzansky and Udi Dekel, "Recognizing Iran as a Nuclear Threshold State: Implications for Israel and the Middle East," Institute for National Security Studies, March 25, 2015, www.inss.org.il/index.aspx?id=4538&articleid=9004.

85. David Sanger, "Saudi Arabia Promises to Match Iran in Nuclear Capability," *New York Times*, May 13, 2015, www.nytimes.com/2015/05/14/world/middleeast/saudi-arabia-promises-to-match-iran-in-nuclear-capability.html.

86. "Gulf Allies 'Back Iran Nuclear Deal' after US Security Guarantees," BBC, August 3, 2015, www.bbc.com/news/world-middle-east-33758939.

87. David Sanger, "Saudi Arabia Promises to Match Iran in Nuclear Capability," *New York Times*, May 13, 2015, www.nytimes.com/2015/05/14/world/middleeast/saudi-arabia-promises-to-match-iran-in-nuclear-capability.html.

88. "US to Accelerate Support for Operation Decisive Storm," *Middle East Monitor*, April 8, 2015, www.middleeastmonitor.com/news/americas/17924-us-to-accelerate-support-for-operation-decisive-storm.

89. Interview with Yahya al-Zahrani, a professor at Naif Arab University for security sciences in Riyadh.

90. For details about what this could look like, see Frederic Wehrey and Richard Sokolsky, "Bridging the Gulf in the Gulf," *Foreign Affairs*, July 14, 2015, www.foreignaffairs.com/articles/persian-gulf/2015–07–14/bridging-gulf-gulf.

91. Norman Cigar, *Saudi Arabia and Nuclear Weapons: How Do Countries Think about the Bomb?* (Oxford: Routledge, 2016).

92. Bahgat, *Proliferation*.

93. Farhan Bokhari, Stephen Fidler, and Roula Khalaf, "Saudi Oil Money Joins Forces with Nuclear Pakistan," *Financial Times*, August 5, 2004, www.ft.com/content/33019f30-e67c-11d8-9bd8-00000e2511c8.

94. Feroz Hassan Khan, *Eating Grass: The Making of the Pakistani Bomb* (Stanford, CA: Stanford University Press, 2012).

95. Ibid.

96. "Yemen Conflict: Pakistan Rebuffs Saudi Coalition Call," BBC, April 10, 2015, www.bbc.com/news/world-asia-32246547.

97. Mark Hibbs, "Saudi Arabia's Nuclear Ambitions," Carnegie Endowment for International Peace, July 20, 2010, http://carnegieendowment.org/2010/07/20/saudi -arabia-s-nuclear-ambitions-pub-41243.

98. Jeffrey Lewis, "It's Not as Easy as 1–2-3," *Foreign Policy*, August 1, 2012, http://foreignpolicy.com/2012/08/01/its-not-as-easy-as-1–2-3/.

99. Mark Doyle, "A Nuclear-Armed Iran and US Extended Deterrence in the Gulf," *Strategic Assessment* 16, no. 3 (October 2013).

100. Ibid., 462–63.

101. Ibid.

102. Wyn Q. Bowen, *The Politics of Ballistic Missile Nonproliferation* (New York: St. Martin's Press, 2000), 47.

103. Gause, *International Relations*, 128.

104. Ihsaan Tharoor, "Pakistan's Long History of Fighting Saudi Arabia's Wars," *Washington Post*, March 27, 2015, www.washingtonpost.com/news/worldviews/wp /2015/03/27/pakistans-long-history-of-fighting-saudi-arabias-wars/.

105. Bin Sultan and Seale, *Desert Warrior*, 79, 314, 472.

106. Cordesman and Obaid, *National Security*, 170.

107. Ibid., 143.

108. Ibid., 144.

109. Ibid.

110. Ibid., 150.

111. Bin Sultan and Seale, *Desert Warrior*, 350.

112. Ala Alrababah and Jeffrey Lewis, "Saudi Rattles Its Saber," Nuclear Threat Initiative, December 15, 2014, www.nti.org/analysis/articles/saudi-rattles-its-saber/.

113. Rubin, *Islam in the Balance*, 37–38.

114. John L. Esposito, ed., *The Oxford Encyclopedia of the Islamic World* (Oxford: Oxford University Press, 2009).

115. Ibid.

116. Anthony Cordesman, *Saudi Arabia Enters the 21st Century: IV, Opposition and Islamic Extremism*, December 31, 2002, 7, http://csis.org/files/media/csis/pubs/s21 _04.pdf.

117. Ibid., 6–7, 66; and Robert Worth, "Saudis Back Syrian Rebels Despite Risks," *New York Times*, January 7, 2014, www.nytimes.com/2014/01/08/world/middleeast /saudis-back-syria-rebels-despite-a-lack-of-control.html.

118. "Leaks from Saudi Ministry Appear to Show Extent of Influence over Regional Media," *Middle East Eye*, June 20, 2015, www.middleeasteye.net/news/leaks-saudi -foreign-ministry-appear-show-extent-influence-over-regional-media-1007963853.

119. Gause, *International Relations*, 128.

120. Ibid., 30n28.

121. Ibid., 30.

122. Ibid., 31.

123. Jared Malsin, "Yemen Is the Latest Victim of the Increase in Iran-Saudi Arabia Tension," *Time*, January 11, 2016, http://time.com/4174837/yemen-analysis/; "GCC Declares Lebanon's Hezbollah a 'Terrorist' Group," Al Jazeera, March 2, 2016, www.aljazeera.com/news/2016/03/gcc-declares-lebanon-hezbollah-terrorist-group-160302090712744.html; and Sinem Cengiz, "A Turkish-Saudi Push against Bashar al-Assad?" Al Arabiya, May 10, 2015, http://english.alarabiya.net/en/views/news/middle-east/2015/05/10/A-Turkish-Saudi-push-against-Bashar-al-Assad-.html.

Conclusion to Part II

Regional Variations on Deterrence and Stability

JEFFREY W. KNOPF

MANY OF THE CONCEPTS employed by strategic analysts had their origins in a specific context: the US-Soviet nuclear relationship during the Cold War. The notion of "strategic stability" is a prime example. This term, developed mainly by Western analysts concerned about the danger of nuclear war, is generally taken to refer to a situation involving nuclear-armed rivals in which neither side would have any incentive to launch nuclear weapons first during a time of heightened tensions. Awareness of the historical origins of this term raises obvious questions: Does a concept that emerged in the context of a particular relationship during a particular period still apply to different relationships or different periods? Does it apply to strategic interactions other than those involving nuclear weapons?

After the Soviet Union collapsed, leaving the United States as the world's only superpower, US concerns shifted. For US officials, maintaining stability with Russia, which inherited the Soviet nuclear arsenal, no longer seemed to be a pressing concern. Instead, US policy moved to focus on so-called asymmetric threats—dangers that weaker actors would use weapons of mass destruction, cyberattacks, or terrorist violence as a way to work around the vast US superiority in conventional armaments. In this context, US defense planners coined a new term: "cross-domain deterrence." This refers to the idea that a state could employ means in one domain to deter threats that would utilize means from a different domain. In the most controversial formulation, some analysts have suggested that the United States consider threatening nuclear retaliation as a way to deter large-scale cyber assaults.[1]

The preceding chapters in part II have examined how actors other than the United States think about strategic stability and cross-domain deterrence in contemporary contexts. Two chapters deal with two of the most important great powers, Russia and China. In chapter 6 Dima Adamsky focuses on how Russia perceives the role of information operations in contemporary conflict—an issue that has become especially salient in the wake of allegations that Russia sought to interfere in the 2016 US presidential election. And in chapter 7 Tong Zhao surveys Chinese perceptions of US hypersonic weapons programs in the context of US interest in conventional prompt global strike capabilities. The remaining chapters in part II address two critical regional contexts: South Asia and the Middle East. In chapter 8 Happymon Jacob compares Indian and Pakistani thinking about nuclear weapons. And with respect to the Middle East, in chapter 9 Ilai Saltzman describes Israeli strategic priorities, while in chapter 10 Ala' Alrababa'h examines how Saudi Arabia approaches strategic issues.

The preceding chapters all grapple to some extent with three basic questions about the states they examine. First, do analysts and policymakers in these states even use terms like "strategic stability" and "cross-domain deterrence," or are such notions not significant parts of their conceptual vocabulary? Second, to the extent that they take it into account, what priority do these countries assign to goals like strategic stability? And third, do they use these terms in the same way as the United States does, or do they conceive of them in different ways? These questions are descriptive in nature. In answering them, the authors of the preceding chapters have described how the strategic environment is viewed inside the countries they studied. These authors have not, however, limited themselves solely to describing strategic thinking. In each chapter, a final question is evaluative. Based on how the various countries in question think about strategy, deterrence, and stability, what are the likely consequences? In particular, are their national approaches conducive to strategic stability, or do they create risks of inadvertent escalation and unwanted conflict?

If one theme emerges from the chapters in part II, it is the lack of uniformity in how states think about deterrence and stability. Saltzman ends his chapter with a call to make the concept of strategic stability "significantly more actor-specific." Adamsky similarly suggests moving away from a one-size-fits-all approach to a greater appreciation for distinct "national characteristics" in strategic thinking.

Indeed, the countries studied in this part of the book have not exactly embraced either the Cold War era or the current US discourse on strategy. In none of the states in question do elites tend to use the term "cross-domain deterrence." References to strategic stability are also rare, and they do not usually reflect the meaning of that term developed by Western arms control theorists during the Cold War. Instead, the preceding chapters show that strategic discourse in each of the countries in question has a more traditional cast. Discussions of deterrence, without the "cross-domain" modifier, are common. And comments about stability almost always refer to the stability of the state's deterrence efforts. In short, every country has concerns about the effectiveness of its own deterrent posture.

Of course, the United States has always been concerned about maintaining effective deterrence as well. And deterrence stability can be considered a logical component of strategic stability. But the two terms are not interchangeable. Strategic stability inherently implies an element of mutuality. In the Cold War context, it involved acceptance, however reluctantly, of a condition of mutual deterrence. The US-Soviet relationship remained competitive, and the leaders on the two sides mistrusted each other—but they also perceived a common danger of stumbling into a nuclear war that neither side desired. Each side recognized that the other side perceived this danger, creating a sense of a shared fate.[2] Deterrence is usually thought of as a one-way street: Side A deters side B. Strategic stability implies a two-way street: Side A and side B, while still having elements of conflict in their relationship, also work together to maintain stability so as to avoid losing control over events and thereby finding themselves in an escalatory process that results in mutual catastrophe. This strong concern with autonomous risks of inadvertent escalation, leading to a sense of shared fate and a perception of security as mutual, is strikingly absent in the strategic thinking described in the case studies in part II.

Each country examined in the preceding chapters puts security first. Strategic stability does not rank as high in national priorities as do traditional efforts to achieve robust defense and deterrence capabilities. Each country perceives potential vulnerabilities, and it directs its efforts to addressing them. In practice, this is leading many of the states studied here to what are de facto cross-domain approaches, even though they do not label them as such.

For Israel, Saltzman notes, the goal is to maintain conventional superiority. But to do this, Israelis believe, requires holding on to their nuclear monopoly in the Middle East. Hence, Israel is willing to take action, ranging from covert operations to preventive military strikes, to keep other regional powers from acquiring nuclear weapons. Israel has no interest in accepting a situation of mutual deterrence, and it will apply means from many different domains to prevent this.

Alrababa'h points out that for Saudi Arabia, security means first and foremost regime security. A focus on regime survival makes internal, ideological threats a potential concern. But this has also opened the door to an intuitively cross-domain approach. The Saudis use the ideological appeal of their unique status in the Muslim world as a means to deter regional challengers.

On the Indian subcontinent, Jacob finds that there is a fundamental difference between the Indian and Pakistani notions of strategic stability. He astutely observes that this has led both sides to adopt what are de facto cross-domain approaches to deterrence. India has responded to Pakistani willingness to sponsor terrorism at the subconventional level with conventional military threats. Pakistan has responded to its vulnerability at the conventional level by developing tactical nuclear weapons. India, in turn, has responded with threats of strategic nuclear retaliation and by pursuing ballistic missile defenses. Like many analysts, Jacob sees this situation as one that creates significant dangers of instability. In South Asia, strategic stability does not appear to be a priority policy objective for either side, a fact that makes the situation all the more dangerous.

Chinese analysts believe that the US pursuit of hypersonic capabilities creates a terrifying vulnerability for their country. As Tong Zhao shows, many Chinese see this as part of a deliberate US strategy to develop the means to preempt the Chinese nuclear arsenal. Chinese analysts have contemplated both a response in kind, which could lead to an arms race in hypersonic weapons, and an asymmetric response that could involve an increase in the size of the Chinese nuclear arsenal or even a willingness to launch nuclear weapons first. Zhao argues that the United States and China are caught in a security dilemma, leading them to become "engaged in a negative action/reaction spiral" that could seriously undermine strategic stability.

Adamsky demonstrates similarly that Russian strategic thinkers see themselves as responding to what they perceive as threats from the West, ranging from NATO's expansion to support for the so-called Color Revolutions. The Russian response, in Adamsky's apt phrase, has been a move toward "cross-domain coercion," which blurs the distinction between deterrence and compellence. In an inherently cross-domain move, Russia's strategic thought places information operations at the center of its efforts to blunt Western conventional military advantages. Its strategy involves not just cyberoperations to knock out hardware but also more broadly informational campaigns designed to deceive and confuse the other side, thereby disrupting its ability to respond militarily.

Although the Russians hope their use of information operations will reduce the chances of military conflict, Adamsky notes that this approach could lead the Russians to miscalculate how far they can push before they provoke a military response. In this case, as in the others, the trends are not necessarily favorable for strategic stability.

The case study chapters in part II show that the Cold War level of concern about strategic stability was unusual, even fragile.[3] More subtly, the chapters also help make it clear that stability is not just a structural condition. The arms control theorists of the Cold War era emphasized the importance of military force postures and the need to avoid doctrines and capabilities that could raise doubts about the other side's ability to maintain a secure second-strike capability. But in addition to the relationship of the two sides' military forces and doctrines, strategic stability involves a cognitive element. Both sides need to recognize that if they are not careful, they will face a mutual risk of inadvertent escalation. Moreover, they need to place a value on avoiding scenarios that could lead to such escalation, and both sides must believe that the other side shares this concern. Even as they pursue a rivalry, they need to develop some sense of a shared fate and a belief in following certain rules of the road to avoid mutual disaster.

This sense of shared risk and the accompanying need to develop norms that encourage mutual restraint do not loom large in the analyses of the countries examined in the preceding chapters. However, despite the concerns that may follow from this observation, it is not necessary to end this summary of part II's case study chapters on an entirely pessimistic note. Because the chapter authors offer such incisive analyses of how current trends create risks of instability, they also provide a foundation for potential reassessments of policy that could enable key states to pursue their national security interests while reducing the chances of unnecessary conflicts.

NOTES

1. Elbridge Colby, "Cyberwar and the Nuclear Option," *The National Interest*, June 24, 2013, http://nationalinterest.org/commentary/cyberwar-the-nuclear-option -8638.

2. I have emphasized the importance of a shared understanding of nuclear dangers in "The Concept of Nuclear Learning," *Nonproliferation Review* 19, no. 1 (March 2012).

3. Even at the time, US officials did not give strategic stability priority over all other objectives, and they regularly harbored doubts about whether Soviet leaders truly embraced it as a concern.

PART III

Findings and Implications

11

Foreign Views of Strategic Stability and US Nuclear Posture

The Need for Tailored Strategies

MATTHEW KROENIG

IN THE 2010 *Nuclear Posture Review* of the United States of America, then–defense secretary Robert Gates declared that "reinforcing strategic stability" was a foremost goal of US nuclear policy.[1] Although there are many possible definitions of this term, the most common interpretation holds that strategic stability is being maintained when no nuclear power has an incentive to intentionally launch a nuclear first strike. It is understandable why US officials believe that reducing the risk of a nuclear exchange should be a leading objective of US nuclear policy. As Bernard Brodie once argued about politics in the nuclear age, "Thus far the chief purpose of our military establishment has been to win wars. From now on its chief purpose must be to avert them."[2]

The studies in this volume suggest, however, that a common understanding of strategic stability is not universally held, at least not beyond the major nuclear powers of China, Russia, and the United States. Moreover, the chapters in this volume demonstrate that the maintenance of strategic stability may not be the predominant foreign policy objective for any of the states reviewed here. Instead, and understandably, stability generally takes a backseat to the pursuit of other, more pressing national security objectives. Washington must, therefore, take these realities into account as it seeks to provide for its security and the security of its allies. Given the diversity of views across countries and global regions, Washington will need to tailor its approach accordingly.

Turning first to Russia, chapter 2, by Andrei Pavlov and Anastasia Malygina, demonstrates that conceptions of strategic stability in Moscow largely match those in Washington. This is not surprising, given that these two nations have shared decades of exchanges, dialogues, and arms control negotiations, and have successfully completed accords on these issues. A shared definition does not, of course, necessarily translate into shared interests. As this chapter shows, and as becomes even more evident in chapter 6, by Dima Adamsky, Russia's current defense policy is not aimed at reinforcing stability but rather at achieving an asymmetric advantage over possible competitors through the employment of its New Generation Warfare strategy.

Moreover, as Adamsky himself argues, this strategy has the potential to be highly destabilizing. He states that by linking together and orchestrating all forms of coercion—nuclear, conventional, and informational—inadvertent escalation and crisis instability can result, making escalation to kinetic forms of warfare more likely. Furthermore, in the event of conflict with NATO, Adamsky and Pavlov and Malygina write that Moscow may engage in "prenuclear deterrence," conducting long-range conventional strikes against the enemy's critical infrastructure targets. In addition, Russia also plans for possible "de-escalatory" nuclear strikes to force NATO to sue for peace on terms favorable to Moscow.[3] Although this "holistic coercion" strategy and associated military capabilities may have first evolved from a defensive position, the crises in Ukraine and Syria demonstrate that it can also be repurposed toward aggression and opportunism.

Russia's strategy poses a clear threat to strategic stability and US interests, and it is currently a subject of grave bipartisan concern in Washington. The United States and NATO must develop a strategy to counter Russian New Generation Warfare, and this begins by closing the gaps in NATO capabilities that Moscow attempts to exploit. The best way to prevent nuclear conflict is to deter the onset of lower-level conflicts. The United States must, therefore, develop a more serious and effective counter-information warfare capability and deploy a larger contingent of conventional forces in NATO's easternmost states. Furthermore, Washington must also make it clear to Moscow that it has sorely miscalculated if it believes that it can stand to gain from a nuclear strike against NATO. The United States and NATO must strengthen its nuclear deterrence posture and ensure that it possesses a credible response to a limited Russian nuclear "de-escalation" strike.

China poses a different set of challenges. Due to its long-standing belief in a "lean and effective" arsenal and its no-first-use policy, early Chinese escalation to nuclear use is of less immediate concern. This does not mean, however, that the Sino-US strategic relationship is problem free. In chapter 7 Tong Zhao writes that the continuing US interest in developing conventional prompt global strike (PGS) capabilities, including hypersonic glide vehicles, threatens to undermine strategic stability between the United States and China.

Zhao will find common ground with some in Washington who have voiced similar concerns, and one of the most obvious ways to rein in an arms race in this domain would be through cooperative confidence-building measures.[4] As Zhao himself acknowledges, however, attaining agreement on this issue— which, to be effective, would require bringing in Russia and also perhaps other states—will be a tall order. The most likely outcome, therefore, is that great powers will continue to develop and deploy PGS capabilities. It would be prudent, therefore, for Washington to continue to position itself to compete in this new domain, even as it pursues the possibility of cooperative measures, a subject to which I return below.

Indeed, though Beijing is understandably concerned about the United States enhancing its strategic capabilities, it is not clear that US pursuit of PGS undermines stability with China, as Zhao claims. China has undertaken intensive efforts to ensure its maintenance of an assured retaliation capability—including tunneling, mobile missiles, and its move to sea—and the survivability that these moves give will not be easily undone by PGS. Moreover, the existing Asian security architecture has for decades rested on overwhelming US strategic superiority. Washington's efforts to maintain an edge as Beijing increases its military capabilities may be, therefore, a necessary ingredient for continued stability in Asia. The alternative—standing still, as Chinese military expansion upsets the balance of power in the region and calls into question America's extensive alliance commitments—would potentially be much more destabilizing than a United States that continues to modernize its military capabilities. The only future stable equilibrium, therefore, may be one in which China maintains a secure second-strike capability, but Washington retains an unquestionable strategic advantage.[5] This should be the objective of US strategic policy in the region, and it can also provide a formula for new, more creative arms control agreements. The United States could offer to place reasonable limits on technologies that China fears will undermine its assured retaliatory posture, including PGS, in exchange for Beijing's recognizing a quantitative US strategic superiority.

As we turn our attention to South Asia, it is clear that Washington has less of a direct interest in this region, given that neither New Delhi nor Islamabad is a close ally nor a sworn rival. Still, the United States has objectives in the region, which include preserving stability on the subcontinent and preventing these two states from devastating each other in a catastrophic nuclear exchange.

Unfortunately, as chapters 1, 3, and 8—by, respectively, Evan Montgomery, Sadia Tasleem, and Happymon Jacob—make clear, there is an all-too-plausible pathway to nuclear war between these nuclear rivals. Emboldened by the protection afforded by a nuclear overhang, Pakistan has sponsored a series of cross-border raids and terror attacks in recent years. Since the two most recent attacks, India has been seriously considering a conventional military response to cross the border and dismantle Pakistan's terror networks, consistent with its Cold Start, or proactive operations, doctrine. Colleagues in New Delhi report that its patience may be wearing thin. If India were to move across the Pakistani border, Islamabad could use tactical nuclear weapons to stop the advance of Indian forces on Pakistani territory. Indeed, Pakistan's change to a nuclear war-fighting doctrine and rapid nuclear buildup in recent years were geared for just such a contingency.[6] As Jacob points out, India's response to suffering a tactical nuclear attack is uncertain, but it could very well result in a larger nuclear exchange.

Perhaps the part of Jacob's chapter that is of most concern, however, is the claim that India has not shown any evidence of thinking about nuclear exchange scenarios. Unfortunately, this unwillingness to think the unthinkable is not limited to India but is also common in the United States and many other states living with real, if remote, nuclear threats. Working through scenarios familiarizes senior leaders with the stakes involved and generally contributes to better policy. To counteract this problem, the United States could sponsor Track II dialogues, tabletop exercises, and other mechanisms to force officials and thought leaders in South Asia to grapple with these scenarios, with the ultimate goal of arriving at a more stable nuclear deterrence relationship. In addition, such meetings could be used to explore common ground for possible agreement on negotiated restraints on strategic capabilities.

In the Middle East, strategic stability defined as a relationship of mutually assured destruction between nuclear powers does not exist, because of Israel's regional nuclear monopoly. The authors of these chapters, therefore, had a more difficult task than the others; but most defined strategic stability from their country's point of view, as more or less synonymous with the national interest. Perhaps the most striking theme to emerge from these chapters is the clear zero-sum game between Israel and Saudi Arabia, on one hand, and Iran, on the other hand. According to Annie Tracy Samuel in chapter 5, Iran's foreign policy objectives are characterized as promoting itself as a leader in regional and global affairs and resisting Western hegemony. Moreover, Iran views Israel as an enemy and considers the United States to be the primary threat to regional stability. Finally, its foreign policy tools include the development of a nuclear weapons capability and "indirect regional deterrence"—that is, supporting violent nonstate groups. Many of these goals are understandable when viewed from an Iranian perspective, and Tracy Samuel articulates them well, but they conflict directly with the interests of the United States and its partners in the region. As Ilai Saltzman and Ala' Alrababa'h maintain, respectively, in chapters 9 and 10, Saudi Arabia and Israel both seek to combat violent nonstate actors and to prevent the rise of a dominant and competing regional power. Moreover, as Emily Landau explains in chapter 4, Iran's nuclear program has prompted feelings of insecurity in the region that, for a variety of reasons, Israel's arsenal simply never did.

Balancing these competing sets of objectives is a difficult task, and the United States will inevitably face strong incentives to choose sides. Although some hoped that the Iran nuclear deal would lead to a broader rapprochement between Washington and Tehran, it is clear that Iran's foreign policy, even with this deal in place, continues to threaten US allies and interests in the region and that the best available option for Washington is to strengthen its relationship with its traditional partners and balance against Iran.

In practice, this means that the United States must do more to reassure its nervous allies and to push back against Iran's malign influence throughout the region. As Alrababa'h makes clear, Saudi Arabia does not foresee a direct Iranian attack, but it is concerned about Iran's recent interventions in Iraq, Yemen, Syria, and elsewhere. To comfort Riyadh, Washington must, therefore, increase its efforts to counter Tehran's destabilizing regional activities. This could be accomplished in part by bolstering the US presence on the ground in Iraq, increasing international pressure on the Russia–Iran–Hezbollah–Assad alliance in Syria, and stepping up the interdiction of Iranian arms shipments to Yemen.

According to Salzman and Landau, however, Israel's major preoccupation is the more significant, and indeed possibly existential, threat posed by a nuclear-armed Iran. To address this concern, Washington must maintain its policy of preventing Tehran from acquiring nuclear weapons. One hopes that this goal will be accomplished by the Iran nuclear deal; but if the deal fails for any reason, Washington must be prepared to snap back international sanctions and, if necessary, use military force to keep Tehran from building a bomb. After all, as then–president Barack Obama said many times, nothing would do more to upset stability in the Middle East than a nuclear-armed Iran and the regional nuclear arms race that this might trigger.[7]

Perhaps the greatest challenges for the future of strategic stability, however, are those that are only beginning to emerge. In chapter 1 Montgomery identifies three trends that may undermine stability from a US perspective: the lowering of the nuclear threshold, especially in Russia and Pakistan; nuclear multipolarity in Eurasia; and the possibility that other nuclear nations could attempt to extend a nuclear umbrella to friends and allies, thus ending America's current monopoly on this practice. His broad recommendations to counter these trends—maintaining US global leadership, supporting allies, and retaining a robust nuclear posture—are accurate and mirror many of the recommendations I propose in this chapter.

In conclusion, it is commonly argued that to effectively deter a particular adversary, one must first understand that adversary. After all, at the end of the day, deterrence is a psychological relationship, and one cannot hope to influence the calculations of an opponent without first knowing its mind. The chapters in this volume reveal much about how other nations, both allies and potential competitors, think about their national security interests. This information will contribute to Washington's understanding of the international security environment as it seeks to formulate an effective nuclear deterrence policy in pursuit of the continued maintenance of US leadership and global strategic stability.

NOTES

1. Office of the Secretary of Defense, *Nuclear Posture Review Report* (Washington, DC: US Department of Defense, 2010), www.defense.gov/Portals/1/features/defenseReviews/NPR/2010_Nuclear_Posture_Review_Report.pdf.

2. Bernard Brodie, ed., *The Absolute Weapon: Atomic Power and World Order*, 1st ed. (New York: Harcourt, Brace, 1946).

3. Matthew Kroenig, "Facing Reality: Getting NATO Ready for a New Cold War," *Survival* (February–March 2015): 49–70.

4. James Acton, "Silver Bullet? Asking the Right Questions about Conventional Prompt Global Strike," Carnegie Endowment for International Peace, 2013, http://carnegieendowment.org/2013/09/03/silver-bullet-asking-right-questions-about-conventional-prompt-global-strike.

5. For a similar argument, see James Steinberg and Michael E. O'Hanlon, *Strategic Reassurance and Resolve: US-China Relations in the 21st Century* (Princeton, NJ: Princeton University Press, 2014).

6. On Pakistan's nuclear posture, see Vipin Narang, *Nuclear Strategy in the Modern Era: Regional Powers and International Conflict* (Princeton, NJ: Princeton University Press, 2014).

7. Jeffrey Goldberg, "Obama to Iran and Israel: 'As President of the United States, I Don't Bluff,'" *The Atlantic*, March 2, 2012, www.theatlantic.com/international/archive/2012/03/obama-to-iran-and-israel-as-president-of-the-united-states-i-dont-bluff/253875/.

12

Implications for US Policy

Defending a Stable International System

ADAM MOUNT

AT A TIME when strategic stability is coming under increasing pressure, the prevailing theory in Washington is that US policy is forced into a reactive position to maintain stability in the face of threats from external actors. However, as the chapters in this volume demonstrate, this understates the strain that some US policies are placing on strategic stability and understates the extent to which US officials have options that may moderate these pressures. The debate over these options—including acceptance of mutual vulnerability with China, the requirements of extended deterrence, and the shape of US nuclear modernization—will turn on how Washington thinks about strategic stability.

The chapters in parts I and II of this volume point to an important ambiguity about the concept of strategic stability. The term "stability" strongly implies that it is an objective property of the international system—or, at least, of a group of states. Yet with remarkable consistency, the authors report that states tend to think about strategic stability as a subjective interest of the state that is threatened by an adversary's actions. States tend to be less concerned with how their own actions could deleteriously affect strategic stability and more concerned with finding ways to strengthen their hands. In short, many states seem to interpret strategic stability as something more like "national defense" than a calculated "balance of power."[1] As Matthew Kroenig writes in chapter 11 above, "Stability generally takes a backseat to the pursuit of other, more pressing national security objectives"—but for some countries, the concepts may in practice be indistinguishable.

For Iran, strategic stability comprises both "regional stability" and "the termination of outside influence." Where the former term might be thought of as a systemic property, Tracy Samuel writes in chapter 5 that "the goal of both deterrence and regional stability is the prevention of an armed conflict in the Middle East, particularly a conflict that would directly threaten Iran's security and territory." Furthermore, strategic stability requires not only the maintenance of conventional deterrence to prevent military aggression but also preventing the intrusion of US cultural influence that could undermine the national identity of the Iranian state.[2]

In chapter 2 above, on Russia, there is little discussion of threats to strategic stability beyond threats to the Russian state. Not surprisingly, threats of this type are met by military strength: "The first and most obvious option is to build up strategic nuclear forces." Yet, though armaments can under some circumstances promote crisis stability, they are also the primary determinant in precipitating an arms race, which in itself is a major indicator of strategic instability.

American strategic discourse also contains an ambiguity between strategic stability as a systemic and a subjective property. On one side of this division are those who primarily think of strategic stability as a lens for assessing threats to the United States. In this sense, strategic stability exists to the extent that the national interest is secure. Actions that revise a military balance that had been favorable to US interests constitute a threat to strategic stability. Russian and Chinese nuclear modernization programs alter the dyadic balance of strategic forces between these countries and the United States, and therefore they constitute a threat to strategic stability. For this group, the necessary response to actions that revise regional and strategic balances is to exert military power to redress the imbalance. Strategic stability requires ensuring that the US nuclear modernization program maintains a margin of superiority over potential adversaries. Regional stability requires that the United States employ military coercion—through joint exercises, prepositioning, and assertive posturing such as freedom-of-navigation operations—to deter further threats to US allies.

Understanding strategic stability as equivalent to US interests leaves little room for the possibility that US policies or capabilities could be destabilizing. There has long been deep discomfort in American strategic circles about the idea of mutual vulnerability, which has caused the United States at various times to threaten the survivability of an adversary's strategic forces. For example, during the Cold War, US attack submarines routinely tracked Soviet nuclear-powered, ballistic-missile-carrying submarines, and naval officials publicly boasted about their ability to do so.[3] Today, the United States refuses to publicly acknowledge mutual vulnerability with China, a condition that Tong Zhao argues in chapter 7 above is "of ultimate importance for Chinese decision makers." Prominent US operational concepts plan to overwhelm the defensive systems of a capable adversary, and even to establish and defend a lodgment on enemy territory.[4] This line of thinking is dismissive of foreign warnings that they face threats from US capabilities. It accepts the official claim that US missile defense systems, nuclear modernization, forward basing of conventional forces, and joint military exercises with allies pose no threat to potential adversaries like Russia and China.

The alternative is to see strategic stability as an objective property of a dyadic relationship between states, a regional order, or the international system as a whole. According to this view, strategic stability exists to the extent that no country faces a threat of sufficient gravity that it could force them to discard deterrent threats and employ a nuclear weapon. Seen in an objective way, as most academics would, strategic stability results from a balance of capabilities, interests, and intentions of all states. This objective interpretation is present in US strategic discourse, but it tends to be passed over in favor of subjective considerations in practical policy matters. As a conceptual matter, strategic stability is analytically useless if it is not an objective property at the systemic level; as a practical matter, policymakers cannot afford to devote their attention and effort solely to the maintenance of any systemic property.

Policymakers who hold the objective interpretation of strategic stability are more likely to understand the potential for their country's actions to be destabilizing. In practice, however, the need to defend the United States makes it difficult to weigh in against specific capabilities or policies that could attenuate pressing threats. As a result, the US policy process tends to be more concerned with expanding capabilities to overcome threats than with exploring whether restraint can attenuate them. There has been relatively little study or discussion about whether new US capabilities could provoke arms races or a preemptive war. Some observers will justify this position by arguing that American values and a history of stabilizing behavior will assure the world that American primacy is not threatening to their interests; however, the decades since the end of the Cold War have made this a doubtful proposition.[5]

This volume suggests that any discussion of "strategic stability" in the policy community needs to begin not from an objective definition of this term but from the subjective concepts of strategic stability that guide the behavior of the relevant countries.[6] How is the United States to behave in a world that does not share a consensus about the definition of and the conditions required for strategic stability?

The United States, like all countries, must pursue a military policy that is sufficient to meet its deterrence and defense requirements while minimizing the destabilizing effects of its behavior. Given that the United States retains a wide margin of military primacy twenty-five years since the end of the Cold War, it likely has the most latitude to accept vulnerability for the sake of maintaining strategic stability and the most to gain from doing so. Consider three ongoing debates: whether to accept strategic stability with China, the conduct of extended deterrence, and modernization of US strategic forces.

As China's strategic forces continue to develop gradually, the United States is faced with the question of whether to accept mutual nuclear vulnerability with China—to concede that Chinese strategic forces are capable of executing a second strike against US territory. Though the 2010 *Nuclear Posture Review* makes frequent reference to the need to preserve strategic stability with China and with Russia, the United States does not today acknowledge that China's nuclear force has a second-strike capability. This was a key question for the 2018 *Nuclear Posture Review*. If China believed such a declaration, it could help ameliorate pressures on the Chinese leadership to launch its nuclear weapons early in a crisis for fear of losing them to US conventional and nuclear strike capabilities. Conversely, many US officials worry that the declaration could cause concern in Seoul and Tokyo and lead to behavior that is itself destabilizing.

This leads to the second issue, the role of nuclear weapons in US extended deterrence commitments. Though there is no consensus on these issues and official dialogue remains complementary, certain groups in both Washington and foreign capitals disapprove of the role of nuclear weapons in US extended deterrent postures. In Seoul and Tokyo, there are calls for Washington to raise the profile of the nuclear umbrella or to deploy new capabilities to demonstrate the US security commitment. One consequence of these efforts has been to disparage the efficacy of conventional deterrence, which is required to deter both the onset of a conflict as well as a gray zone or subconventional provocations. Whether and how the United States can resolve these marginal tensions will be critical to strategic stability. A unanimous finding of the earlier chapters in this book is that potential adversaries will consider new deployments of nuclear systems—whether US assets or those of its allies—to be highly destabilizing and likely to provoke a response.

Decisions on these issues—acceptance of mutual vulnerability, and the role of nuclear weapons in extended deterrence—will drive US requirements for the modernization of the nuclear triad, which will in turn have deep implications for the military requirements of both allies and adversaries. As China and Russia continue to modernize their armed forces, their acquisition of advanced air defense and precision strike capabilities has led Pentagon officials to worry that the margin of US military advantage is narrowing.[7] Even as the United States undertakes major new programs to modernize its fighter fleets, expand its naval surface fleet, procure new attack submarines and aircraft carriers, and modernize its nuclear arsenal, the Pentagon leadership is making investments to identify emerging technologies capable of overcoming adversaries' antiaccess / area denial strategies. At the end of 2015, officials inched away from their insistence that modernization is necessary for safety and surety, and they have begun to describe it as a reaction to Russian capabilities.[8] According to former secretary of defense Bill Perry, these efforts run the risk of fueling a new arms race, forcing China and Russia to take countervailing steps to deny access to their territory and ensure the survivability of their nuclear forces.[9]

As this volume shows, both China and Russia perceive US capabilities as major threats to strategic stability. The acceleration of US nuclear modernization and its development of prospective technologies—including hypersonics, offensive cyber capabilities, and developments in space—could place strategic stability under considerable strain. US officials will need to calibrate these programs to achieve deterrence and defense requirements while minimizing their destabilizing effects. Strategic stability in the twenty-first century depends substantially on the extent to which the United States is willing to assume the risk of restraint or is able to reach negotiated agreements to regulate competition. The ongoing debate about the extent to which a new nuclear-capable cruise missile, the Long-Range Standoff Option, could be destabilizing in a crisis is one subset of a larger conversation.[10]

The fate of arms control is uncertain in a world where there is little consensus on the meaning of strategic stability. While US and Soviet negotiators jockeyed for minor advantages during the Cold War, they shared an overriding conviction that subjective national defense required an objective measure of strategic stability. With some important exceptions, each side proved willing to relinquish powerful weapons systems that threatened to destabilize the strategic balance. Today, the prospects for major arms control arrangements have narrowed considerably because the United States refuses to negotiate limits on missile defense and its conventional force posture; Russia declines to enter arms control negotiations and stands in defiance of existing commitments under the Intermediate-Range Nuclear Forces Treaty; and China insists that its capabilities are too far below parity to require control.[11] Although all three countries understand that cyber capabilities and hypersonic capabilities will have major effects on strategic stability, the possibility of an arms control agreement in these domains is even more remote.

In conclusion, though the United States is now forced to respond to the actions of potential adversaries that threaten strategic stability, it still possesses considerable latitude to take the initiative in maintaining strategic stability. One of the lessons of this volume—that other states largely do not adhere to an objective concept of strategic stability—suggests that the United States cannot necessarily rely on others to help maintain the strategic balance.[12] The outcomes of the three questions explored above—mutual vulnerability, extended deterrence, and military modernization—will have a significant effect on strategic stability. All three depend on the extent to which US strategic culture thinks of strategic stability as a subjective property that requires supremacy or as an objective property that requires restraint. Certainly, it will be difficult to socialize other countries into an objective interpretation of strategic stability while US policymakers themselves remain ambivalent about its meaning.

NOTES

1. As a corollary, there is relatively little discussion about how disputes and actions between third parties can damage strategic stability at the regional or systemic level. For the strategic stability implications of third parties, see Gregory D. Koblentz, *Strategic Stability in the Second Nuclear Age*, Special Report 71 (New York: Council on Foreign Relations, 2014), https://www.cfr.org/report/strategic-stability-second-nuclear -age ; and Linton Brooks and Mira Rapp-Hooper, "Extended Deterrence, Assurance, and Reassurance in the Pacific during the Second Nuclear Age," in *Strategic Asia 2013–14: Asia in the Second Nuclear Age*, ed. Ashley J. Tellis, Abraham M. Denmark, and Travis Tanner (Seattle: National Bureau of Asian Research, October 2013).

2. On a state's need to defend a national identity, see Jennifer Mitzen, "Ontological Security in World Politics: State Identify and the Security Dilemma," *European Journal of International Relations* 12, no. 3 (2006).

3. Austin Long and Brandan Rittenhouse Green, "Stalking the Secure Second Strike: Intelligence, Counterforce, and Nuclear Strategy," *Journal of Strategic Studies* 38, nos. 1–2 (2015).

4. US Department of Defense, "Joint Concept for Entry Operations," April 2014, www.dtic.mil/doctrine/concepts/joint_concepts/jceo.pdf.

5. Stephen Walt, *Taming American Power* (New York: W. W. Norton, 2006).

6. This problem may be the latest installment in an important body of deterrence theory that began with concerns over mirror imaging and most recently took the form of debates over how to tailor deterrence to a specific adversary. See M. Elaine Bunn, "Can Deterrence Be Tailored?" *Strategic Forum* 225 (January 2007); and Michael Johnson and Terrence K. Kelly, "Tailored Deterrence: Strategic Context to Guide Joint Force 2020," *Joint Force Quarterly* 74 (July 2014), http://ndupress.ndu.edu/Media/News /News-Article-View/Article/577524/jfq-74-tailored-deterrence-strategic-context -to-guide-joint-force-2020/.

7. Robert Work, "The Third US Offset Strategy and Its Implications for Partners and Allies," US Department of Defense, January 28, 2015, www.defense.gov/News /Speeches/Article/606641; Chuck Hagel, "Reagan National Defense Forum Keynote," Simi Valley, CA, November 15, 2014, www.defense.gov/News/Speeches/Speech-View /Article/606635.

8. Hans M. Kristensen, "Pentagon Portrays Nuclear Modernization as Response to Russia," Federation of American Scientists, February 11, 2016, https://fas.org/blogs /security/2016/02/russiajustification.

9. William J. Perry, *My Journey at the Nuclear Brink* (Stanford, CA: Stanford University Press, 2015).

10. William J. Perry and Andy Weber, "Mr. President, Kill the New Cruise Missile," *Washington Post*, October 15, 2015, www.washingtonpost.com/opinions/mr-president -kill-the-new-cruise-missile/2015/10/15/e3e2807c-6ecd-11e5–9bfe-e59f5e244f92 _story.html; and Aaron Mehta, "Senators Urge Obama to Cancel Nuclear Cruise Missile," *Defense News*, July 21, 2016, www.defensenews.com/story/defense/policy -budget/congress/2016/07/21/senators-obama-nuclear-missile-lrso/87384128/.

11. Alexei Arbatov, "An Unnoticed Crisis: The End of History for Nuclear Arms Control?" Carnegie Endowment for International Peace, 2015, http://carnegieendow ment.org/files/CP_Arbatov2015_n_web_Eng.pdf; and Adam Mount, "Anticipatory Arms Control," Deep Cuts Commission working paper, June 2016, www.deepcuts.org /images/DeepCuts_WP6_Mount.pdf dime.

12. However, it should be noted that most of the essays in this volume cover US adversaries. More work is needed to learn whether US allies hold a different conception of strategic stability.

Conclusion to the Book

LAWRENCE RUBIN AND ADAM N. STULBERG

WHAT WILL the international system look like in the future? Will strategic stability and deterrence continue to serve as the assumed anchors for international peace and security? What will these concepts mean for nuclear powers, latent nuclear states, and aspirant nuclear states? These questions constitute some of the most pressing international security issues that policymakers will face in the coming years, and we can no longer rely on deterrence models and understandings of strategic stability from the Cold War era. The international system, the nature of the threats, and the sources of threats are different. Shifts in the balance of power highlight the growing regionalization of security. Yet such changes are not rooted solely in new distributions of capabilities, nuclear or otherwise. There are regional, national, and local factors that shape calculations of threat and risk, along with the ways states signal to each other, especially during crises. These second-order effects may, in turn, influence the manner in which regional adversaries choose to respond. Meanwhile, nonstate actors and ascendant states may pose asymmetric threats and utilize emerging technologies to challenge the international order. Taken together, these new forces have revolutionized how nuclear and latent nuclear states think about strategic stability and deterrence in a post–Cold War world.

This comment concludes the volume by identifying core analytical threads that connect the different sections and that warrant further study. Specifically, three major themes stand out to illuminate future challenges and opportunities for assessing the strategic impact of regional nuclear weapons diffusion and latency: the contested meaning of strategic stability, the role of nonstate actors, and dual effects of transparency.

THE CONTESTED NATURE OF STRATEGIC STABILITY

The first and major takeaway is that there is no consensus about how states understand strategic stability, deterrence, and cross-domain deterrence. This is quite striking, given that mutual understanding of strategic stability and deterrence was assumed to be the linchpin of the global order during both the Cold War and immediate post–Cold War periods. When discussing strategic stability, US policymakers often assume there is a shared understanding of strategic stability and deterrence. But states—particularly regional adversaries and global competitors such as the United States, Russia, and China—may not have always interpreted the terms in the same way, and certainly do not understand them the same way today. The evolution of the US-Soviet relationship, the foundation on which much of the field of security studies is based, exemplifies this point.

Strategic stability, in fact, appears to be much more subjective than objective (Mount, chapter 12). Not only are states more concerned with their own security than they are to adhere to a common notion of strategic stability (Mount), a state's pursuit of its national security simply trumps stability concerns (Kroenig, chapter 11). The manifestation of this self-interested behavior varies across states. For some states, stability rests with ensuring superiority; and for the United States, this may mean nuclear superiority or escalation dominance. For other states, such as nuclear-armed Israel, conventional superiority is a necessary condition to achieve strategic stability in its region. Conversely, for states such as China, rival states' pursuit of superiority constitutes the very source of nuclear instability; strategic stability ultimately derives from qualitative nuclear parity (Zhao, chapter 7).

Strikingly, there is also a considerable gap between how regional actors themselves understand these concepts and how the United States thinks regional actors understand them. For example, India and Pakistan's respective understandings of strategic stability and deterrence may differ from one another, but each has a better grasp of how the other understands these concepts than does the United States, particularly during a crisis. Accordingly, a region's adversaries may have a greater appreciation for each other's expected behaviors and respective nuclear taboos, as well as escalation triggers, than do third-party global actors such as the United States. These differences can carry policy implications. Specifically, local actors may use incomplete understandings to get the United States to intervene in regional crises. India and Pakistan, to continue the example, may be well poised to exploit an asymmetry between mutual normative aversions to nuclear war and American fears of inadvertent use. Knowing that the United States fears a short path toward nuclear escalation, one actor could intentionally act recklessly to provoke intervention on its behalf so that a crisis could be managed or resolved on favorable terms or so that it could save face without granting any concessions.

Strategic stability and deterrence may still dominate our discourse, but these concepts have lost the salience they once had (Basrur, concluding comment on part I). As the contributors to this volume relate, sociocultural and even linguistic differences prevent common understandings of these terms and may distort signaling to extraregional actors, such as the United States. In fact, Tasleem (chapter 3) claims that certainty, stability, and crisis prevention are simply not priorities for India and Pakistan. Although the effects of these differences are no less relevant today, the reason these terms need to be reexamined is that the structure of the international system has changed. Put simply, mutually assured destruction no longer undergirds a bipolar structure of the international system. Perhaps the more interesting question is why it has taken so long to come to this realization, and why other terms and concepts have not emerged to replace them.

How change in the structural environment has affected understandings of strategic stability and deterrence is worth further elaboration. Since the end of the Cold War, the multiple sources and types of effective nonkinetic power have made the international system—both global and regional—a different place. The collapse of the bipolar world that came with the fall of the Soviet Union created opportunities for both regional and nonstate actors. Even though there is now greater interdependence between global and regional states (Basrur), the security competition between rising regional actors and global actors is generating new dynamics that are increasingly relevant for international order. China, for example, has long played a role in both regional and global security. Thus, China's rise has implications for regional strategic stability on the Korean Peninsula, in the South China Sea region, and on the South Asian subcontinent—as well as on the global level vis-à-vis Russia and the United States. Strategic stability may indeed have multiple meanings, depending on the context of the strategic interaction.

HOW NONSTATE ACTORS MATTER

In this new structural environment, nonstate actors play an even greater role than in the past, by complicating established models of international politics. These nonstate actors fall into two categories. The first comprises those groups that act independently of states but occupy parts of previously sovereign territory, such as al-Qaeda and its affiliates, and the Islamic State of Iraq and Syria. The second category of nonstate actors comprises those that have an ambiguous relationship with states. At times, these groups can pursue interests that converge with those of a host state, appearing as a proxy of that state to bolster the credibility of threats against a regional rival. This relationship affords the host state plausible deniability. But as interests diverge with a host state, the same nonstate actors can become a liability if their independent actions are difficult to restrain, whereby escalation between rival states may spiral out of control.

As this book's chapters elucidate, this second category of nonstate actors has a direct impact on strategic stability and deterrence between asymmetric nuclear rivals. The implications for states, such as Pakistan and India, are especially illuminating. Pakistan, for example, may indeed have an incentive to sponsor militant proxies to gain bargaining leverage over India, given the latter's superiority at the conventional level. If Pakistan wields control over the nontraditional actor, it has an interest to sow uncertainty by publicly denying such control for tactical reasons. Yet the proxy may lose its incentive for restraint and perpetuate attacks on the stronger state. As the violence escalates, the costs and risks accumulate for Pakistan, both vis-à-vis India's retaliation and the threat of internal subversion perpetrated by increasingly violent and independent militant actors that may be beyond Islamabad's capacity to repress. Whereas the former scenario risks uncontrolled escalation of hostilities with India, the latter may prevent Pakistan from extending credible commitments or reaching a desired settlement. The extent to which India perceives these militant groups to be outside Pakistan's control affects India's incentive structure. India would have little incentive to demonstrate restraint or extend concessions if it perceives Pakistan as lacking the ability to credibly commit.

The nonstate actor dynamic underscores the idea that nuclear security is only one part of the foreign policy decision-making calculus. Pakistan's security posture includes asymmetric warfare using nonstate actors against conventionally superior India, which has adopted the Cold Start doctrine in response. Islamabad's lowering of the nuclear threshold through its introduction of theater nuclear weapons has prompted New Delhi to develop ballistic missile defense (Jacob, chapter 8). However, the action/reaction dynamic is not limited to this dyad. This evolving security dilemma is really a "trilemma," because India's moves affect China's security posture as well (Jacob). These cross-regional effects make strategic stability that much more challenging. To bring the point full circle, nonstate actors can affect more than just the dyad in which they act; they can also have second-order effects on other relationships through the described mechanism.

In a different context, Iran has used asymmetric warfare through its non-state proxies to challenge Israel and Saudi Arabia. Iran's view of strategic stability includes maintaining regional stability and preventing outside influence, and it uses nonstate actors to pursue these aims. Although Israel maintains an undeclared nuclear monopoly for now, it vociferously opposes Iran's acquisition of nuclear weapons, and it has engaged in clandestine activities to thwart the program. Nonetheless, Israel's military and strategic attention is focused on Iran's asymmetric capabilities, such as its support for nonstate actors, particularly Hamas and Hezbollah. Israel's strategic stability is pursued by maintaining deterrence through dominance rather than through balance (Saltzman, chapter 9). For nuclear-armed Israel, Iran's acquisition of nuclear weapons may affect how Israel would view these Iranian-backed nonstate groups. By comparison, although Saudi Arabia has not developed clear conceptions of strategic stability and deterrence, aside from relying on the United States for its security, the kingdom sees the ideological and military challenges posed by Iranian-backed nonstate actors as politically destabilizing (Alrababa'h, chapter 10). It has thus embraced alliance relationships, ideational balancing and ideological deterrence (Alrababa'h).[1]

To summarize, the nuclear balance matters less than it did in the past for maintaining regional order because the structure of the international system has changed. As a result, conventional and subconventional capabilities play a greater role in international politics today. In this regard, nonstate actors have had a much bigger impact on the international system and political stability than their actual conventional military power conveys. Specifically, nonstate actors, particularly in the India-Pakistan and Israel-Iran dyads, can play important and diverse roles regarding crisis initiation, peace, and security. Interestingly, both these dyads have used cross-domain deterrence and asymmetric warfare as part of their postures. These findings challenge the belief that decision making is driven by the prevailing nuclear balance.

WHEN TRANSPARENCY MATTERS

A third important theme that cuts across many of the cases is the extent to which transparency matters for strategic stability and deterrence. The assumption has been that transparency is a requirement for strategic stability because one state's uncertainty about another state's intentions and capabilities may cause inadvertent escalation and conflict. In the nuclear realm, the risks are that much greater, and this reasoning captures the basic logic that underlines crisis bargaining and arms control negotiations. Thus, information, and in some cases information asymmetries, drives the outcomes of these processes.

This volume has shown that transparency can be a source of both stability and instability. In some cases, regional adversaries assess the risk of nuclear escalation to be much lower than actors outside the conflict that have no direct national security interest at stake. As Tasleem relates, India and Pakistan may be more comfortable with opacity than is appreciated by outsiders such as the United States. In the Middle East, similarly, Landau (chapter 4) suggests that Israel's policy of nuclear opacity may have directly contributed to stability. Israel's neighbors likely preferred this policy because they did not need to face many domestic pressures resulting from a declared program possessed by their regional rival. Landau argues that Iran's lack of transparency has been destabilizing because its leadership has not provided the necessary assurances about the intentions of its program. In this case, the opacity surrounding Tehran's nuclear ambitions has only fueled collective anxieties and confirmed pervasive pessimism among all of Iran's regional neighbors. Although Tracy Samuel (chapter 5) recounts that Iran sees its own policies as defensive, Israel and Saudi Arabia perceive Iran's regional activities as indicators of its malign intentions. Iran's asymmetric activities reinforce its neighbors' fears concerning the aggressive intentions behind its nuclear program (Landau; Alrababa'h). Even though the Joint Comprehensive Plan of Action is being implemented, providing greater transparency for Tehran's nuclear program, the process itself has not eliminated suspicions.

Finally, too much transparency, as in the case of US congressional debates over hypersonic weapons or nuclear modernization, may exacerbate the threat perceptions of China and Russia, respectively (Zhao). In this domain, the airing of a broad spectrum of views may provide fodder for selective interpretation by hard-liners within Russia and China, and it may have the adverse effect of drowning out the more limited intentions and signals surrounding the actual deployments. These domestic-international and intraregional dynamics indicate that greater specificity is needed regarding the conditions under which transparency is stabilizing versus destabilizing.

STRATEGIC STABILITY: A CONCEPT HANGING IN THE BALANCE

The absence of a shared understanding of strategic stability certainly limits the global community's ability to discuss important matters of global peace and security. But not having a shared understanding of stability is not necessarily a cause of instability. States and leaders have ways of communicating their intentions and capabilities. What is crucial, however, is that the interested parties realize that there are differences and make an effort to communicate them.

This volume has shown that strategic stability and deterrence are contested but persistent concepts, and that there is little consensus on their meaning and components. Examining deterrence in more than one system underscores this point. In a number of cases, cross-domain activities can induce instability (Zhao; Adamsky, chapter 6) by providing components that allow states to find equilibrium under the rules of the game (Saltzman; Jacob; Tasleem). The case of Saudi Arabia suggests that the definition of cross-domain deterrence may need to be expanded to include ideological activities. This could make the playing field more dangerous, both domestically (Alrababa'h) and internationally, in direct and indirect conflicts (Adamsky). But activities across domains also allow for competition in risk-taking to occur outside one's own borders, avoiding direct military escalation and thus adding rungs to the escalation ladder.

The ideas presented in this volume call for a research agenda to expand the intellectual horizons for understanding stability. New actors and new technologies complicate old models, stabilizing some relationships while destabilizing others. As confusing as it may be, recognizing that there is no consensus about the meaning of fundamental concepts that undergird security studies across countries and conflicts is an important first step in achieving global peace and security.

NOTE

1. Lawrence Rubin, *Islam in the Balance: Ideational Threats in Arab Politics* (Stanford, CA: Stanford University Press, 2014).

CONTRIBUTORS

Dmitry "Dima" Adamsky is associate professor in the Lauder School of Government, Diplomacy, and Strategy at the Interdisciplinary Center, Herzliya. His research interests include international security, strategic studies, and US, Russian, and Israeli national security policy. He has published on these topics widely in leading academic journals. His books—*Operation Kavkaz* (2006) and *The Culture of Military Innovation* (Stanford University Press, 2010)— earned the annual prizes for the best works on Israeli security.

Ala' Alrababa'h is a PhD candidate in political science at Stanford University, where he focuses on political violence in the Middle East. He graduated magna cum laude from Dartmouth College and received high honors in government. In 2014 and 2015, he worked as a junior fellow at the Carnegie Endowment for International Peace. His writing has appeared in *Foreign Affairs* and *Al-Monitor*, and on the Nuclear Threat Initiative's website.

Rajesh Basrur is a professor of international relations at the S. Rajaratnam School of International Studies of Nanyang Technological University in Singapore. He received his MA and MPhil in history (Delhi) and his MA and PhD in political science (Bombay). Previously, he taught history and politics at the University of Mumbai (1978–2000), and he has held visiting appointments at, among others, the University of Oxford, Stanford University, the Brookings Institution, and the University of Illinois at Urbana-Champaign. He has written five books, including (with Kate Sullivan De Estrada) *Rising India: Status and Power* (Routledge, 2017) and *India's Nuclear Security* (Stanford University Press, 2006). He has also edited nine books and published more than ninety papers in various journals and edited volumes.

Happymon Jacob is an associate professor of diplomacy and disarmament studies at Jawaharlal Nehru University in New Delhi. He is a regular op-ed contributor to *The Hindu*, India's leading English-language daily newspaper.

He has organized or participated in influential India-Pakistan track-two dialogues, including the Chaophraya Dialogue, the Pugwash India-Pakistan Dialogue, and the Ottawa India-Pakistan Dialogue. He has written extensively on India's foreign policy, India-Pakistan relations, and security issues.

Jeffrey W. Knopf is a professor at the Middlebury Institute of International Studies in Monterey, California. At the institute, he serves as both chair of the MA program in nonproliferation and terrorism studies and also as a senior research associate at the Center for Nonproliferation Studies. His most recent book is an edited volume, *International Cooperation on WMD Nonproliferation* (University of Georgia Press, 2016).

Matthew Kroenig is an associate professor in the Department of Government and the Edmund A. Walsh School of Foreign Service at Georgetown University, and a senior fellow at the Brent Scowcroft Center on International Security of the Atlantic Council. He is the author or editor of six books, including *The Logic of American Nuclear Strategy* (Oxford University Press, 2018). His articles have appeared in many publications, including the *American Political Science Review*, *Foreign Affairs*, *Foreign Policy*, *International Organization*, the *Wall Street Journal*, and the *Washington Post*. He has served in several positions at the US Department of Defense and the Central Intelligence Agency, and he regularly consults with US government entities.

Emily B. Landau is a senior research fellow at the Institute for National Security Studies in Tel Aviv and the head of the Arms Control and Regional Security Program. Her books and monographs include *Israel's Nuclear Image: Arab Perceptions of Israel's Nuclear Posture* (coauthor; Institute for National Security Studies, 1994) and *Arms Control in the Middle East: Cooperative Security Dialogue and Regional Constraints* (Sussex Academic Press, 2006). Her comments and interviews have been featured in the *New York Times*, the *Washington Post*, the *Wall Street Journal*, *Time Magazine*, *The National Interest*, the *Financial Times*, *The Guardian*, Reuters, Bloomberg, and *USA Today*, among others, and in *The Times of Israel*, the *Jerusalem Post*, *Haaretz*, *Maariv*, and the *Jerusalem Report*. She received a PhD from the Hebrew University of Jerusalem.

Anastasia Malygina received her PhD in political science. She is an associate professor at Saint Petersburg State University, where she teaches courses on arms control, multilateral nonproliferation regimes, and military innovations for students in the Strategic and Arms Control Studies Master's Program.

Evan Braden Montgomery is a senior fellow at the Center for Strategic and Budgetary Assessments, where he focuses on long-term competitions, trends in future warfare, East Asia security issues, and US nuclear policy. He is the author or coauthor of numerous center reports as well as articles in *Foreign Affairs*, *International Security*, *Security Studies*, and the *Journal of Strategic Studies*. His recent book is *In the Hegemon's Shadow: Leading States and the Rise of Regional Powers* (Cornell University Press, 2016).

Adam Mount, PhD is a senior fellow and director of the Defense Posture Project at the Federation of American Scientists. Previously, he was a senior fellow at the Center for American Progress, a Stanton Nuclear Security Fellow at the Council on Foreign Relations, and directed the CFR Independent Task Force on US Policy Toward North Korea. Dr. Mount's other writing has been published by *Foreign Affairs, The Atlantic, Survival, Democracy*, and other outlets, and he is a columnist at the *Bulletin of the Atomic Scientists*. His analysis has been cited in *The New York Times, The Wall Street Journal, The Washington Post, Politico,* AFP, AP, and Reuters, and he has appeared on CNN, CBS, BBC, MSNBC, and CNBC programs. He has testified before the House Armed Services subcommittee on strategic forces. He holds a PhD and MA from the Department of Government at Georgetown University, and a BA from Reed College.

Andrey Pavlov received a PhD in history. He is a professor at Saint Petersburg State University and the chair of the Strategic and Arms Control Studies Master's Program. His research interests include strategic studies, nuclear strategy, World War I military strategy, and Russian national security policy.

Lawrence Rubin is an associate professor in the Sam Nunn School of International Affairs at the Georgia Institute of Technology. He is the author of *Islam in the Balance: Ideational Threats in Arab Politics* (Stanford University Press, 2014) and a coeditor of *Terrorist Rehabilitation and Counterradicalisation* (Routledge, 2011). In addition to academic publications, his articles have appeared in the *Washington Post, The National Interest*, and the *Washington Quarterly*. He has held positions at the Harvard Kennedy School's Belfer Center for Science and International Affairs, the RAND Corporation, and the US Department of Defense. During 2017 and 2018, he was an International Affairs Fellow in Nuclear Security of the Council on Foreign Relations, funded by the Stanton Foundation.

Ilai Z. Saltzman is the associate director for academic programs at the Israel Institute in Washington. He is the author of *Securitizing Balance of Power*

Theory: A Polymorphic Reconceptualization (Lexington Books, 2012). He has published scholarly articles in *Foreign Policy Analysis, Orbis, Contemporary Security Policy, Israel Affairs, International Politics, Israel Studies,* and the *International Studies Review,* and he writes op-eds for *Haaretz,* the *Jerusalem Post,* and the *Los Angeles Times.* He received a PhD in political science from the University of Haifa.

Adam N. Stulberg is Neal Family Professor, associate chair–research, and codirector of the Center for International Strategy, Technology, and Policy in the Sam Nunn School of International Affairs at the Georgia Institute of Technology. He was codirector of the Program on Strategic Stability Evaluation from 2009 to 2016, and he has written extensively on global nuclear security, US-Russian strategic relations, and emerging technologies and international security. He is coeditor of *The Nuclear Renaissance and International Security* (Stanford University Press, 2013). His current research interests include Russia's approach to cross-domain statecraft, nuclear networks and stability, and asymmetric power and grand strategy.

Sadia Tasleem teaches in Quaid-i-Azam University's Department of Defense and Strategic Studies in Islamabad. As a core member of the Program on Strategic Stability Evaluation, she has done extensive research on various aspects of strategic stability, arms control, nuclear learning, and the implications of knowledge diffusion. Previously, she worked as a senior research scholar at the Institute for Strategic Studies, Research, and Analysis of the National Defense University; as a research associate at the International Islamic University; and as a lecturer in the Department of International Relations of the National University of Modern Languages in Islamabad.

Annie Tracy Samuel is an assistant professor of history at the University of Tennessee at Chattanooga. She has held fellowships at the Belfer Center for Science and International Affairs at Harvard University and at the Truman Research Institute for the Advancement of Peace. Her writing on Iran and the Middle East has appeared in *International Security* and *Diplomatic History,* among other publications. Her current research focuses on Iran's Islamic Revolutionary Guards Corps and the Iran-Iraq War of 1980–88.

Tong Zhao is a fellow in the Nuclear Policy Program of the Carnegie Endowment for International Peace, based at the Carnegie-Tsinghua Center for Global Policy in Beijing. His research focuses on strategic security issues, including nuclear weapons policy, arms control, nonproliferation, missile defense, space security, and China's security and foreign policy. He was previously a Stanton Nuclear Security Fellow at the Belfer Center for Science and International Affairs at Harvard University. He received a PhD in science, technology, and international affairs from the Georgia Institute of Technology and a BS in physics and an MA in international relations from Tsinghua University. He is an associate editor of the journal *Science and Global Security* and a member of the Asia-Pacific Leadership Network for Nuclear Non-Proliferation and Disarmament.

INDEX

Figures, notes, and tables are indicated by f, n, and t following the page number.

deterrence *(continued)*
  minimum, 69, 77, 213, 215; mutual, 13, 62,
  128, 193, 280, 281; of nonstate actors,
  238–239; in Saudi thinking, 261–263; in
  South Asia, 76–77, 208–209; versus strategic stability, 5, 114, 204–205; theory of, 211

Egypt: relations with Israel, 95–98, 103–104,
  237–238, 245; relations with Arab neighbors, 97–100, 104, 109n21, 237–238,
  252–254, 262, 269–270
escalation: asymmetric, 28, 67, 76, 192; dominance, 25–28, 34, 209, 223, 299;
  inadvertent, 4, 15, 165, 210, 280, 282, 286,
  301, 303; nuclear, 10, 33, 38n12,195, 211,
  218, 222, 300; in South Asia, 67, 77, 208–
  210, 217–218, 223–224
existential threat: to Israel, 90, 94–95, 98, 105,
  241, 289; to Pakistan, 214; to Saudi Arabia,
  253–255

firebreak, 25. *See also* nuclear threshold
first strike. *See* no-first-use (NFU) policy
Fissile Material Cutoff Treaty, 69, 222

Gerasimov Doctrine, 153. *See also* New Generation War
Gorbachev, Mikhail, 42–44

hair-trigger alert: during the Cold War, 215;
  and Indian nuclear weapons, 69, 206, 222,
  227n38; and Pakistani nuclear weapons, 69,
  215, 223. *See also* high alert
high alert, 142, 206
Hussein, Saddam: pursuit of nuclear weapons,
  239; war with Iran, 117; Saudi Arabia's fear
  of, 252, 254–255, 263, 268
hybrid warfare (HW), 151–152, 156, 159
hypersonic weapons, 174–175; advantages of,
  178–179, 180, 182; China's reasons for
  developing, 185–188; in Chinese scholarship,
  175–177; in crisis signaling, 181; disadvantages of, 179–180; and the security dilemma,
  196; US reasons for developing, 188–191

ideological (ideational) threats, 257
informational struggle, 156–159
Intermediate-Range Nuclear Forces (INF)
  Treaty, 2, 26, 184, 295
Iran: 2015 nuclear agreement (*see* Joint Comprehensive Plan of Action [JCPOA]);
  challenges of post-revolutionary transition,

119, 125; isolation of, 119–120; nuclear
  program of, 102, 241–243; regional aspirations of, 102; regional perceptions of, 100,
  119
Iran-Iraq War, 117–120, 124–125, 263, 267
Iraq: invasion of Kuwait, 93, 252, 254–255,
  261, 263, 267; nuclear ambitions of, 101,
  239; reasons for starting Iran-Iraq War, 117
Islamic State of Iraq and Syria (ISIS), 123, 168,
  257, 260, 261, 301

Joint Comprehensive Plan of Action (JCPOA),
  91–92, 114; Iranian perspective of, 14, 122,
  131–133; regional perspectives of, 122, 245,
  250–251, 264, 303

Kargil Crisis, 70, 74, 208
Khan, Abdul Qadeer, 74, 242
Khomeini, Ayatollah Ruhollah, 117, 241, 259
Kvashnin, Anatoly, 46–47

bin Laden, Osama, 260–261
Lahore Declaration, 70

Mattis, James A., 1
multipolar nuclear competitions: complica-
  tions of, 28–29, 116; in East Asia, 30, 142;
  in the Middle East, 29–30; Russia-US-
  China, 56; in South Asia, 29. *See also*
  trilemma
Muslim Brotherhood, 260–261
mutually assured destruction (MAD), 43, 204,
  213–215, 234, 288, 300
mutual vulnerability, 212; Chinese understanding of, 15, 174; in the Cold War context, 6,
  9, 143; in US thinking, 291–294

Nasser, Gamal Abdel, 96, 254, 258
Netanyahu, Benjamin, 230, 244, 245
New Generation War (NGW), 149, 152–156;
  differences from hybrid warfare, 152, 159;
  informational struggle in, 156–159
New Start (Strategic Arms Reduction Treaty),
  49–50, 57, 188
no-first-use (NFU) policy: Chinese policy on,
  184, 192, 286; Indian policy on, 206,
  225n16, 227n35; Israeli policy on, 94; Pakistani policy on, 79, 88n61, 214; Russian
  policy on, 25, 38n12; US policy on, 25
nonstate actors: in South Asian escalation
  dynamics, 209, 217–218, 220, 222, 223; as
  a threat to Israel, 235, 238–239, 245, 289;

and Saudi Arabia, 260–261, 289. *See also* strategic stability, nonstate actors and

nonstrategic nuclear arsenal, 144; of Russia, 26–27, 53, 56, 59; of the United States, 25–26, 35, 37n10. *See also* tactical nuclear weapons

North Atlantic Treaty Organization (NATO): eastward expansion of, 42, 46; nuclear sharing arrangements of, 34; and relations with Russia, 17, 27, 45, 56, 168, 286

North Korea, 30, 39n27, 142, 181, 196–197, 240

nuclear ambiguity, 14, 90, 93–95, 233, 244

nuclear arsenal: of China, 193, 195; of India, 207, 212–213; of Israel, 231; of North Korea, 30, 196–197; of Pakistan, 66–67, 78, 213, 215–216; of Russia, 46–47, 57–59, 62; of the United States, 35

nuclear doctrine: of India, 206–207, 214, 227n35, 227n38; of Israel, 94–95; of Pakistan, 67, 87n55, 87n61, 205–206, 214, 288; of Russia, 60; of the United States (*see* Nuclear Posture Review). *See also* no-first-use (NFU) policy

Nuclear Non-Proliferation Treaty (NPT): and India, 207–208; and Iran, 92, 102, 241; and Israel, 95–96, 231

Nuclear Posture Review (NPR): of 1994, 26; of 2010, 25, 26, 175, 190, 285, 294; of 2018, 1, 294

nuclear sharing: by NATO, 34; between Pakistan and Saudi Arabia, 265

nuclear threshold: hypersonic weapons and, 184; Pakistan's lowering of, 77, 209, 217–223, 289, 301. *See also* firebreak

nuclear triad: of India, 29, 213; of Russia, 46; of the United States, 2, 5, 26, 47, 294

nuclear umbrella. *See* extended deterrence

Obama, Barack, 29, 40n35, 49, 243, 251, 289

passive defense, 128–129

perestroika, 42–43

post–Cold War era: differences from Cold War era, 6–8, 23, 36, 72, 141–142, 174; general trends of, 3; strategic stability during, 23, 231, 299; US and Russian force structure during, 26–27. *See also* second nuclear age

precision-guided munitions (PGMs): in Chinese publications, 176–177; in Russian New Generation Warfare, 153, 160; in US-Russia relations, 52–53, 57

proliferation: cascade (*see* arms race); Israel's efforts to prevent, 239–24; and Saudi Arabia, 265, 271; US worries of, 68–69

Putin, Vladimir, 2, 47, 49, 59, 242

al-Qaeda, 257, 260–261, 269

Qualitative Military Edge, 237

redline: and advanced conventional weapons, 192–193; for Israel, 94; in South Asia, 218–219

regime stability, 251–252, 270–271

regional stability: in Iranian thinking, 114, 117, 121, 123, 127, 288, 292, 302; in Israeli thinking, 235, 244; in Pakistani thinking, 210, 223; in Saudi thinking, 252; in US thinking, 9, 292

restraint, strategic (nuclear), 143, 211; between India and Pakistan, 8, 14, 66, 69, 72, 81; in US policy, 293, 295. *See also* minimum deterrence

revisionist power: as a challenge for strategic stability; 13, 16, 24; Iran as, 144; Pakistan as, 28, 210–211, 217; Russia as, 27

Saudi Arabia: military strategy of, 251; relations with Yemen, 253–254

second nuclear age, 4–7, 24, 32, 141, 174, 231. *See also* post–Cold War era

second Strategic Arms Reduction Treaty (START II), 44, 49

security dilemma, 16, 128, 195–197, 257, 281, 302

Sergeev, Igor, 46–47

signaling: with advanced conventional weapons, 159, 180–182; with nuclear weapons, 2, 79, 164, 205, 206

space-based weapons, 54–55

stability/instability paradox, 10, 28, 70

State Armament Program 2020, 58–59

Strategic Arms Reduction Treaty (START), 43

strategic balance, 67; during the Cold War, 67, 295; and hypersonic technology, 187, 190; in Indian thinking, 215; in Pakistani thinking, 81, 208, 216; in Russian thinking, 43, 45, 50, 56, 62; in US thinking, 35, 296

strategic partnership, 44–46, 56, 73–74

strategic stability: academic definitions of, 4–5, 23, 204, 230–231, 278, 285, 293; ambiguity and contestation of, 4–6, 43, 231, 279–280, 291–293, 299, 303–304; in American thinking, 23, 285, 289–290, 291–293, 296;